Wild Diplomacy

SUNY series in Environmental Philosophy and Ethics
———————
J. Baird Callicott and John van Buren, editors

Wolves Tracking along a Snowy Road. Credit: Éditions Wild Project. © S. Bence

Wild Diplomacy
Cohabiting with Wolves on a New Ontological Map

BAPTISTE MORIZOT

translated by
Catherine Porter

Cover illustration: George Catlin, *Buffalo Hunt under the Wolf-skin Mask* (1832–1833). Gift of Mrs. Joseph Harrison, Jr., 1985.66.414, Smithsonian American Art Museum

Published by State University of New York Press, Albany

© 2022 State University of New York

This book was originally published in France © Editions Wildproject, 2016.

All rights reserved

Printed in the United States of America

No part of this book may be used or reproduced in any manner whatsoever without written permission. No part of this book may be stored in a retrieval system or transmitted in any form or by any means including electronic, electrostatic, magnetic tape, mechanical, photocopying, recording, or otherwise without the prior permission in writing of the publisher.

For information, contact State University of New York Press, Albany, NY
www.sunypress.edu

Library of Congress Cataloging-in-Publication Data

Names: Morizot, Baptiste, author. | Porter, Catherine, translator.
Title: Wild diplomacy : cohabiting with wolves on a new ontological map / Baptiste Morizot, translated by Catherine Porter.
Description: Albany : State University of New York Press, [2022] | Series: SUNY series in Environmental Philosophy and Ethics | Includes bibliographical references.
Identifiers: ISBN 9781438488394 (hardcover : alk. paper) | ISBN 9781438488417 (ebook)
Further information is available at the Library of Congress.

10 9 8 7 6 5 4 3 2 1

Diplomatic climaxes are rarely dramatic.

—Henry Kissinger, *Years of Renewal*

Contents

Gallery of Diplomats   ix

Acknowledgments   xi

Part One
The Diplomatic Crisis: Cohabiting with Large Predators

Introduction   3

1. The Diplomatic Model   15
2. Seeking King Solomon's Ring   27
3. Understanding and Influencing Behavior   51
4. Animal Political Philosophy   83

Part Two
Diplomatic Intelligence: For a Wolf Science

5. Orienting Wolf Pack Cultures   107
6. Toward the Social Sciences of Wolves: Interiority, Variability, Sociality   113

7. A Laboratory Called Yellowstone — 119

8. On Intentionality: Toward an Animist Epistemology — 139

9. A Differently Rational Shamanism — 149

10. On Tracking — 173

Part Three
The Diplomatic Project: An Ethics of Relations

11. The Power That Is Diplomacy — 195

12. We Have Invented the Wolf — 201

13. Constitutive Relations — 215

14. What Mutualisms in Our Relations with Wolves? — 243

Notes — 261

Bibliography — 305

Gallery of Diplomats

The Lion Man of the Hohlenstein-Stadel: A Mythic Precursor of Zoocephalic Diplomats	20
St. Francis: The Impossible Diplomat	28
Charles Darwin: The Zoomorphic Diplomat of Common Lineages	32
Konrad Lorenz: The Diplomat on His Way	34
Thomas Henry Huxley: The Diplomat of Taxonomic Cohabitation	38
Two Amerindian Hunters of the Plains: Intertwined Diplomats	45
Three Woodsmen: The Were-tigers of the Brahmaputra Region	69
Georges Leroy: The Diplomat of the Animal Enlightenment	72
Jean-Marc Landry: The Diplomat Specializing in Subtle Stimuli	79
Dave Ausband: The Cartographic Diplomat	95
Rick McIntyre: The Historiographer Diplomat	127
Temple Grandin: The Diplomat of Animal Genius	197
Ernest Thompson Seton: A Diplomat Torn	229
Lucy King: The Perspectivist Diplomat	235
Aldo Leopold: The Mountain Diplomat	238

Acknowledgments

Among all those who helped make this book possible, I want to express my warmest gratitude to the following:

Florence Burgat, whose interest in the first version of these ideas led me to expand them into a book; Thibaut Rioufreyt and Sophie Bouchet, for their very careful reading and their help in pulling together a sprawling manuscript; Pierre Charbonnier, for his intuitions and constructive criticisms, and for inviting me to his seminar, where I was able to test some of the founding intuitions of this book; Donato Bergandi, for his benevolence and for welcoming me to his seminar, where I was able to develop some of the theses in this book more fully; Antoine Nochy, for having put me on the track of the wolf question, and for sharing his knowledge during a few brief days in the Cévennes; Jeff Mauffrey, for his insightful reading of part 1, which he enriched with his ecological erudition, and for our long discussions, which nourished the environmentalist aspects of this study; Marie Cazaban-Mazerolles, for her enlightened opinions; Raphaël Larrère, whose reading of the initial manuscript was crucial for the improvement and equilibration of the book project; Aurélien Gros, for collaborating with me in writing the chapter on environmental history blended with ontology, a chapter I could not have written alone, and for his rereadings and his synthetic grasp of the book as a whole, which greatly contributed to its strengths; Baptiste Lanaspeze, for his editorial work, his ability to deal with everything through dialogue, and our endless conversations on what the book should be, culminating in something like a consensus; Estelle Zhong Mengual, whose lively intelligence, subtle vision, and inexhaustible energy contributed to every aspect of this book, as well as to every stage in its conception.

PART ONE

THE DIPLOMATIC CRISIS

COHABITING WITH LARGE PREDATORS

Introduction

This book addresses a problem that is above all one of land usage. How are we to react to the spontaneous return of predators to a region from which they had vanished? Taking the return of wolves to France as our case study, we shall consider the implications of their dispersal throughout a mountainous landscape so depopulated that it has almost reverted to its pre-Roman past. This return developed into a problem without much fanfare. In 1992, a pair of Italian wolves went off exploring. They established their kingdom in the little valley of Mollières, north of Nice in the Southern Alps; they preyed in part on the relatively unprotected flocks of sheep in the Maritime Alps. Conflicts with livestock farmers arose. The wolves scattered and founded new kingdoms. They traveled by night, passed over highways, swam across rivers; they were invisible because they were inconceivable. One day, a wolf was spotted in the Vosges. He had come from the Mercantour. Another day, someone saw him in the Madre mountains, deep in the Pyrenees. He was in Canjuers, in the Bargème valley. He was in the Jura, in the Massif Central. In the Meuse region. One day he was somewhere else, then he was close at hand. "The wolf is here," foresters and hermits exclaimed from the safety of cafes. The wolf was there. The murmured cry spread and echoed from one hunting blind to the next, from bell tower to bell tower, until it reached the outskirts of big cities. The two wolves present in 1992 had become more than three hundred spread throughout the French countryside in 2015, according to official counts. The populations are hard to localize, hard to quantify, hard to tell apart. For wolves have the peculiar ability to be present and invisible—except to those whose flocks are subjected to repeated attacks. When once-silent shepherds and farmers engage the media, what were once private problems become a political problem.

The Impossibility of Stewardship

The political solution seemed initially to lie in a straightforward zootechnical approach: drawing on ecological knowledge to manage the age-old phenomenon of wild predators, dangerous pests.

And yet a problem has emerged: the two traditional models for ecological stewardship of wildlife have proved inadequate in the face of the wolves' return. The first and oldest model, population control by hunting, is the zootechnical side of a "biopower" that has not deviated from the life-and-death prerogatives claimed by "sovereign power," to use Michel Foucault's language. This approach can lead ultimately to extermination, in the case of predators: this was the fate of wolves in France until the twentieth century. But in legal, moral, and practical terms, the hunting model is now obsolete. Legally, wolves are protected by the 1979 Bern convention, which went into effect in 1982 and was adopted in France in 1990; they are also protected by the European Community's 1992 Habitats directive (wolves were officially classified as a protected species in 1993). Morally, the rise in biocentric, pathocentric, and ecocentric ethics has challenged the traditional anthropocentric reflexes. Given the moral sensibilities of the twenty-first century, it is not easy to see how one could justify the speciocide of an admired and respected form of wildlife. In practical terms, finally, it is no longer clear how to hunt wolves, protected as they are by the loss of cynegetic knowledge (knowledge related to hunting behavior: how to train dogs to hunt wolves, what tactics to deploy) that has resulted from the eradication of wolf populations and the emptying out of the countryside.

The second model of ecological stewardship, the creation of wilderness sanctuaries, is defended by a number of associations advocating the protection of natural resources; it consists first of all in instituting nature preserves, regulated by strict rules of conduct, in which the wild world, intact and protected, can in principle live in spaces that have been more or less restored to their "natural" state. (In practical terms, in France, these spaces are identified with the natural and historical patrimony as preserved in national parks.) While this undertaking is necessary from the standpoint of conservation biology, it comes with its own problems: it entails zoning, losing the economic use of the land involved, isolating gene pools too limited to ensure perpetuation of the species, assigning the status of patrimony or museum to natural wilderness areas. The sanctuary model is obsolete in any case for the management of wolves, who categorically refuse to remain within preserves or natural parks. Biologically, they are governed by a law of dispersal that ensures their future evolution by limiting the chances of extinction; this law consists in centrifugal diffusion through extensive colonization of new territories that are explored and conquered by young wolves known as "dispersers."[1] Moreover, the principle of keeping the animals at a distance is often connected with sacralization of wildlife.[2] The sanctuary model cannot hold up in the face of frequent attacks carried out on herds by wolves who, for their part, do not deem us "sacred" enough to refuse all contact. To live up to the sanctuary ideal, we would have to allow these predators to settle in and live among us, without directly interfering in their behavior, concentrating all our efforts instead on the practical need to modify the way pastures are protected. Such reforms are legitimate and necessary, but it is not clear that they would be sufficient. In this paradigm, any approach to stewardship that seeks to change the animals' behavior is condemned as intrusive, in the name of the purity of wildness.[3]

Two models, then, both unsuccessful.

It has been suggested that thinking begins where instinct and habit fail.[4] We have to start thinking when the familiar old techniques for managing reality run up against an obstacle—when they no longer work. When the old ontological maps—the maps that mark out for us the nature of the beings with which our experience brings us into contact and show us how we are to interact with them—lead us astray in practice, leave us in distress. In such cases, it seems necessary to change our survival tactics and our mental maps. If we are to do this, we need to begin with an archaeology of the ontological maps of our relationships with wild animals, maps that have been developed throughout history and naturalized by habit.

Ontological Maps and Paths of Action

The connections between representations (by way of words or concepts) and action, between theory and practice, are generally underrated; and yet every human action is organically articulated with a representation, to such an extent that one can even deduce from a representation the types of action that it implies. For example, if we develop a collective representation of wolves as "harmful,"[5] or "invasive,"[6] the resulting action, spontaneously and necessarily, will take the form of regulation and/or extermination. The causal relation can of course be inverted; it is the correlation that matters. The issue is not which comes first, for the relation is one of interdependence. If a collective cartography of the wolf as a sacred wild animal is developed, if wolves are seen as vestiges of intact, original nature, then the inevitable spontaneous reaction will be to confine them to sanctuaries and museums. Words do not represent things, they change them. They configure our relations toward things, our modes of acting on things.

Each everyday gesture of language that is intended to define something confronts the irreducible responsibility of transforming it and determining a limited field of action with regard to it. Mastering this Adamic gesture (naming a thing, configuring it, orienting action toward it) amounts to defending and practicing a considered use of words that brings about their transmutation into concepts, that is, into rigorous mental models defined precisely in terms of their philosophical foundations and their remote cartographic repercussions. For concepts operate above all as ontological maps[7]—in other words, as transcendental models of experience that build bridges where the old maps indicated breaks. These new maps bring distant features closer, recast the ontological structure of classes of phenomena, and thus "open up paths of action."[8]

The challenge, then, is to diagnose the toxic effects of the maps in use today, to confirm the inadequacy of the "paths of action" they impose and draw up new maps for the *Canis lupus* phenomenon, maps designed to open up other paths for viable, healthy, and efficient interactions, with the aim of enhancing the political, technical, and ecological management of the wolves' return.

Taking the long view, we can see that addressing the problem of cohabiting with wolves is a step toward addressing the civilizational problem of the return of wildness. Wildness is coming back into play as an economic reality induced by population decline in rural areas; the extent to which its symbolism is being reevaluated points up a growing tendency to reject the ideology of a civilization that separates the human from the natural.[9]

The Impotence of the Old Maps

The problems raised by cohabitation with wild nature are laden with political stakes: they spontaneously corrode the ideologies defending the transcendent sovereignty of the human order. The wolves' return highlights the deep *metaphysical* and generally invisible infrastructures of our relation to nature. The wolves' return brings metaphysical concerns to the attention of even a former motorcycle racing champion such as Christian Estrosi, the mayor of Nice and a conservative member of the French Parliament: in the context of a 2003 investigation, Estrosi urged the government to apply "the absolute principle of the priority of humans, their activities and their traditions."[10] Wild animals prod us to reveal our underlying conceptions regarding the relations between humans and nature; one of the extreme polarities of that spectrum consists in a sovereign anthropocentrism.

A similar anthropocentrism is also apparent in various critiques of political laxity with respect to wolves; under the cover of sociopolitical analysis, these critiques spontaneously revert to the lexicon of a certain Judeo-Christian anthropology: "What are the consequences for democracy if . . . NGOs condition the relations between humans and nature to such an extent that humans abandon their preeminence on earth, their power and their sovereignty, to the benefit of the predators?"[11] The return of the hated predator is scripted as a civilizational syndrome: our very preeminence on Earth and our total priority over the other species appear to be at stake. This rhetoric goes back to the theme of war against wild nature, a war that we thought we had won through pitched battles in the past, thanks to technological and civilizational progress, but that once again threatens to overtake us with the return of these carnivores.

But what if the very formulation of the problem is askew? The wolves' return is a philosophical problem, to the extent that it enables us to question our cohabitation with other species—species symbolically encumbered with the ideology of the war against nature. Might it be time to abandon the model of human sovereignty over the other species, not *to the benefit* of the predators (we can hear the traumatic historical echoes of such rhetoric), but in favor of a different paradigm for our relation to life forms, to the biota as a whole, and more specifically, in this instance, to wolves?

This is where policies and procedures take on their full political and philosophical scope, for the current approaches are failing to manage the crisis effectively. Livestock farmers are suffering significantly from the wolves' predatory behavior, and they are rightfully demanding solutions. Yet we know that eradicating wolves is impossible in France: it is indefensible, and it is illegal. Wolves have been protected since 1993 by the European Union's Habitats directive. There is solid proof that their return to France was spontaneous; no one reintroduced them. More than three hundred genetic tests have shown that French wolves are indeed descendants of wolves from the Abruzzi region, dispersed into France via the Apennines and then the Alps, according to a logic of territorial exploration that is characteristic of the species and that is not found among reintroduced captive wolves.

In a standoff with livestock farmers, as we have seen, certain ecologists are calling for policies that would preserve wolves in sanctuary spaces. These ecologists often dismiss the challenging situation facing farmers and herders, while at the same time they misunderstand the eco-ethological phenomenon of the wolves' return: humans cannot opt to coexist by occupying separate spaces and maintaining wolves in natural sanctuaries (an approach tried in the United States that has met with failure), for wolves disperse spontaneously to conquer new territories. The population decline in rural France offers them millions of acres of forested and uncultivated lands and an increasing abundance of game.

The only solution, then, is a middle way, consisting in genuine cohabitation. Rather than confining predators to separate zones, this approach calls for sharing the uses of one and the same territory. The zoning approach is based on outdated beliefs about the habitat required by wolves, for these animals are reinventing the way they define their territory. No longer limiting themselves to intact natural spaces, they are moving closer to humans, weaving themselves into the interstices of our carefully mapped-out spaces.

To achieve this middle way today, we shall have to think about wildlife in new ways and update our knowledge of predators. We know very little about wolves. We exterminated them before the development of reliable animal sciences, before population ecology and ethology existed as fields of study. Ethology in particular requires real-time observation of animals in their habitats, an activity that wolves make very difficult owing to their "invisibility." Yet we need to learn to know wolves in order to familiarize ourselves with their ways of being, just as we need to know storms, soils, and rivers if we are to make the natural world inhabitable. The wolves' return raises a problem that is indeed civilizational in scope. But the problem is not how we can best protect our supremacy; the problem is how we can learn to coexist with even the most stigmatized forms of the biodiversity that grounds our own existence. It is the problem of our ability to cohabit with our wild animals.

Our urgent philosophical task is thus to draw an ontological map designed to replace the firmly entrenched old models, both the one that treats wolves as harmful pests and the one that deems them worthy of protection in sanctuaries. These contentious opposites are in fact based, as we shall see, on the same ontological infrastructure, the one in which humans have been extracted from nature. But this extraction can be assigned different values. For some, it is conceived as transcendence; for others, as a curse.

The Failure of Earlier Models: Diplomatic Misunderstandings

As a way of launching this inquiry into political ethology, it will be useful to consider the historical genesis of our relation to wild wolves. Ever since Charlemagne's legal definition of the wolf as a harmful pest, a ruling that has been maintained in mental space-time by Christian pastoral imagery, in which each parishioner is symbolically a sheep to be protected from the "rampaging wolf" (that is, the devil), our relation has been conceived as a war in which an invisible enemy is fantasized and ideologically endowed with all sorts of perversions. This attitude toward wolves was a spur to extermination. Anthropologists have thoroughly analyzed the various phantasmagoric constructions of the figure of the enemy and the way he wages war. American manuals of military psychology produced in the context of the Iraq wars devote whole chapters to the way an individual enemy can be depersonalized and characterized as despicable, thus setting up a psychological disposition that facilitates professional exploits—an outlook that makes it easier, in other words, for soldiers to kill.[12] In the case of wolves, this process works through tales and legends ("Little Red Riding Hood," for instance, or "Peter and the Wolf") and through Christian pastoral metaphors as well as through the abhorrent figure of the werewolf.

This specific interaction (demonization-extermination) can be analyzed on the basis of parameters associated with the ethological nature of wolves, in two ways: the wolf can be understood both as an *invisible* potential predator and as an ecological competitor. The first approach stems from wolves' characteristic mode of appearing. In this respect they are an object of *phanerology*, the science of animals' modes of appearing: this rare discipline at the crossroads between biology and phenomenology has been developed by Adolf Portmann.[13] In a phanerological framework, wolves are an intriguing phenomenon whose way of appearing is a key to understanding the political problems they raise: a wolf appears as *an invisible presence*. This quite particular mode of presence implies manifest effects without any perceptible access to their *cause*.[14] Wolves are cryptic animals: under natural conditions, they are extraordinarily difficult to observe for any length of time. Their flight distance—the minimal zone of approach beyond which they will flee and vanish—is hard to measure, but it far exceeds the human ability to spot them. A wolf can sense and recognize its prey from a distance of up to two kilometers away; its hearing is so acute that any attempt to approach it is seriously compromised. Moving toward a wolf on foot in the forest entails dispersing around oneself an expanse of odors and sounds over a diameter of several hundred meters, an expanse whose reach will trigger the animal's flight at the first step taken in its direction.[15] In France, one indication of this state of affairs is the impersonal character of certain grammatical structures that have evolved in rural areas to note the animal's presence: not "There's the wolf" or "a wolf" or "wolves," but "There's wolf."

This phanerological dimension has had three consequences. First, as wolves returned and recolonized particular local areas, French society was slow to react and to come up with appropriate solutions. The proliferation of stories about wolves in the media today, largely focused on attacks, makes it clear that the problem has taken on emotional and ideological proportions that interfere with cool-headed reflection.

A second consequence has deepened the conflict over how to deal with the wolf problem: since wolves are not visible, only a human who has been subjected to their effects is confronted with the reality of their presence—in other words, the livestock farmer or herder, whose solitude in confronting the problem must not be underestimated. These are often the only people who have actually seen a wolf, the only ones to pay the price and to bear the weight of that presence, and these factors intensify their latent conflict with an urban population for which a wolf is only an abstract image with a positive valence, known either through iconography (the handsome alpha male) or through symbolism (the return of wildlife as breathing new life into a state of society that has gone astray in its domination of life forms). These abstract representations are not false, but they can heighten the conflict with the rural world, which bears the burden of wolves all by itself.

Finally, this phanerological modality of invisible presence implies a problematic relation to wolves in the field of representation: an animal that produces effects without being seen, without being trackable, necessarily generates phantasmatic extrapolations and anthropomorphic projections. An absence of perceptual representations (what is a wolf, exactly?) gives way to imaginary content that may well be inaccurate. An age-old mental mechanism for capturing the unknown by way of the known produces the phantasm of a wolf.

From a potential predator whose attacks on herds are rare,[16] the wolf is transformed into a deadly, omnipresent threat and a symbol of evil. In such a situation, the only good wolf is a dead wolf . . . And like the American Indians, who remained invisible to the colonizers, wolves have been identified with every evil—unless they are invested with every grace.

The second aspect of the conflict brings us to the timeless rivalry that characterizes wolf-human interactions. Throughout recorded history, the conflictual site of interaction with these invisible beings has been livestock. These outsiders sometimes eat the livestock we are raising. The phenomenon probably dates back to the Neolithic era. In the Paleolithic, even though wolves and humans hunted the same types of prey, the comparative density of ungulates and predators, along with the potential alliances (one could follow the tracks of a wolf pack to find prey, or feed on a carcass killed by another species), must have given our interactions with wolves a different character, leaving still-perceptible traces in the value attributed to wolves by contemporary hunter-gatherers who live in contact with them. During the Neolithic era, certain sheep-rearing societies, having domesticated the mouflon of the Ural Mountains some six to ten thousand years earlier, must have seen the first wolves approach these animals, which had become docile and gregarious owing to domestication. Since then, during the last six millennia, technological approaches to pasturing have been invented to limit predation: from Navajo Indians through Alpine shepherds to Kirghiz nomads, humans have devised zootechnical solutions intended to make cohabitation between farmers and wolves both *possible* and viable—although this did not necessarily make it peaceful or cordial.

Wolves sometimes direct their hunting behaviors toward livestock, animals that humans raise for milk and wool as well as meat; hence the particularly exacerbated rivalry. This ecological competition for the same resource is quite probably the reason that our conflictual relations with wolves have been perpetuated and radicalized.

Wolves are thus identified as harmful pests owing to interspecies competition with farmers and hunters. We can be assured that this is a quite widespread ecological situation: two species enter into confrontation because they share the same ecological niche. The question comes down to the way the confrontation is interpreted and modeled. What ontological map can we draw of it? Are we looking at a theft in which an owner is plundered by a criminal? But who has established interspecies property rights? Is the confrontation a war between populations fighting over territory? Is it a simple amoral ecological interaction between two superpredators?

From this standpoint, we cannot compare the wolves' return with that of just any predator or wild animal: wolves are *apex predators*, that is, once they reach maturity they themselves are not the prey of any other predator. As superpredators, they are the only animals in European ecosystems that vigorously occupy the same nutritional level as *Homo sapiens*, at the pinnacle of complex food chains that start with the primary producers (or decomposers), go through the primary and secondary consumers, and end up with the superpredators. Symbolically, wolves share with us the summit of the alimentary pyramid: they are our *equals* from an ecological standpoint. That is, they are our rivals, from the mythological perspective according to which humans are destined to enjoy preeminence and mastery over all the other species on earth. The ecological status of wolves makes them metaphysical operators: their very existence calls into question the foundational Judeo-Christian myth according to which we are the elect and thus take precedence. It is this background myth that the present study sets out to question.

If the task ahead is to propose a model for the way Western humans understand their historic conflict with wolves, we can deduce the type of confrontation that brings together competition for resources and demonization of the enemy. War as a territorial conflict between peoples is the pertinent model here, by analogy, for example, with the conflicts between American colonists and American Indians during the eighteenth and nineteenth centuries. Guided by the paradigm of transcendent sovereignty, the colonists enacted a politics of regulation, control, and extermination toward the indigenous peoples (especially the Amerindians of the Great Plains). These peoples were demonized for being invisible and quite simply incomprehensible; they also competed with the colonists for the land and its natural resources (for example, bison).

This analogy does not entail a Romantic identification of wolves with American Indians; it pinpoints a homology between *relationships*, rather than a resemblance between the parties to a relationship. It allows us to reinterpret the recurrent crises in our interactions with wolves according to the political model of ethnological misunderstanding and diplomatic crisis.

The analogy with the conflict between peoples (competition for resources and demonization) supplies us with a hypothesis for a new model, a new map; the next step is to test its relevance by observing its theoretical and practical effects on the problem that concerns us. The model for the conflict, then, is competition for resources with an invisible stranger, competition that provokes a diplomatic crisis. The misunderstanding can be conceived as an inability to interpret an *ethos*, an inability to communicate in a common code or to develop adaptive modes of interaction.

Presented in this light, the only solution we can bring to the problem consists in restarting peace talks and bringing better diplomats to the table. The model for the new mode of interaction with wolves is *diplomacy*. The mode of interaction, or the path of action, that can be deduced from this approach is that of *negotiation*.

This approach would lead us to set up an apparatus for dialogue at the interface between the human world and the world of wolves. Such an apparatus would be staffed by diplomats trained to "think like wolves," just as Aldo Leopold advocates "thinking like a mountain." The challenge is to avoid interpreting the indices we find in human terms, whether we are wolf-haters, with our anthropomorphism and our guns, conceptualizing wolves as harmful predators, or wolf-lovers, with our anthropomorphism and our binoculars, respecting wolves as hidden gods and as pretexts for all sorts of symbols. At both extremes, everyone fails at the outset, by failing to see in wolves a different way of being alive, a different way of seeing and traversing the world.

The challenge, then, is to adopt an experimental attitude that entails *profiling* wolves, in order to communicate on the basis of key points shared between the ambient worlds of wolves and humans. For this task, there is always a need for mixed-bloods, interpreters, hybrids, bastards, werewolves. This means beings that are folded in two.

Chapter 1

The Diplomatic Model

The word "diplomacy" comes from the ancient Greek δίπλωμα (*diploma*), which means "folded in two," or bent double. A person operating on a borderline must be folded in two, contorted so as to be partly in each camp, thus enabling communication through the sharing of a hybrid code. Such a person serves as an interpreter, acting as a membrane at the interface between two heterogeneous entities. The history of Western explorations offers numerous examples. Among the exemplary figures, at one extreme there is Sacagawea (1788–1812), a Shoshone woman (said to have been won in a game of chance by a French trapper, Toussaint Charbonneau) who became an interpreter and guide for the Lewis and Clark expedition and who was in large part responsible for the success and the *peaceful* progress of that journey. At the other extreme, there is La Malinche, whose role is more ambiguous: an Aztec slave offered to Hernán Cortés, she became the Conquistador's "Doña Marina."[1] Translating between Nahuatl (the Meso-American lingua franca) and the Mayan language of the Yucatan, she made it possible for Cortés to turn the peoples under Aztec domination against one another and thus to take possession of an empire.[2] The diplomat is bent double, between two languages and the ethos associated with each, between two systems of interest: this is what makes her or him apt to be a negotiator and an interpreter, able to operate on any collective front with clear borders—between humans and wolves, but also between livestock farmers and ecologists, between European agencies and public opinion.

From this concept-map constituted by the diplomatic model, the elements indispensable for an effective interaction can now be deduced: a diplomatic relation entails a negotiation aimed at solving problems of cohabitation between communities, without violence. This relation requires an agreed-upon common ground, interpreters, a common language, and means of exerting pressure. The question is how one party can undertake a diplomatic mission that at minimum establishes contact and enables conversation with another party—in other words, how a given party can establish communication, transmit a message, and indicate limits.[3] Such communication requires nothing more and nothing less than a language folded in two: in the case of wolves and humans, a language that is literally lyc/anthropic: it will use shared signifiers (frightening stimuli, territorial signals, and so on) so as to aim at sharable signifieds (notions of territory, or stimuli that indicate distances to be kept).

Arguments for the Diplomatic Model

The Historical Model

The diplomatic paradigm for conceptualizing our relations with wildlife requires recourse to a history so ancient that it has become "natural": it depends on the historical structuring of an animal model that was quite probably established at the dawn of Western civilization, in a symbolic edifice that is hard to interrogate, for it is identical to the naturalist West itself. While a "naturalist" in ordinary English is an amateur observer of nature, a natural history buff, here I adopt the stipulative meaning given to it by French anthropologist Philippe Descola, according to whom "the counterpart of animism is . . . naturalism. For the naturalist's schema reverses the formula of animism: on the one hand, articulating a discontinuity of interiorities and a continuity of physicalities and, on the other hand, reversing their hierarchical order, with the universal laws of matter and life providing naturalism with a paradigm for conceptualizing the place and role of the diversity of the cultural expressions of humanity."[4] It coincides with an ontological map rooted in Neolithic agro-pastoralism, a map that in certain respects we have never left behind, a map that locates evil in wildness while imagining a divinity focused on creating human beings and producing resources that allow these beings to proliferate.[5]

The philosopher Paul Shepard may serve as our guide as we deconstruct the hybrid of metaphysics and ideology that may have terraformed our earth, and in isolating the historical event (the Neolithic revolution) that structured our relations with animals:

[With the Neolithic era,] the cosmic play changed, shifting from chance to strategy, from a state of grace in the face of nature's generosity to a swap, from a ritual gift to a negotiated benefit. Clearly, the "new" relation to nature (which corresponds to three one-hundredths of human time since the beginning of the Pleistocene) led to the need for control. The idea of having control over bodies, pests, predators, plants, animals and microclimates is a familiar one, but it is relatively new to human minds and it can lead to intoxication with power . . . if shepherds have the power to kill lions and wolves, they will be inclined to do so. Wild things henceforth occupy the position of adversary; they take up space, sunshine, or water. . . . As soon as people began to kill wolves to protect their sheep and to crush grasshoppers to protect harvests, wild nature was transformed into an adversary and wild forms became the enemies of everything that was tamed, just as in a war between two enemy armies. The realm of power is a continuum, extending from the control of people to the control of all the rest: the only alternatives are surrender or domination.[6]

This is what justifies the diplomatic paradigm in a first phase: we have to acknowledge the state of affairs Shepard outlines, which has historically been a state of human conflict with wildness since Neolithic times.[7] But the diplomacy in question is not a shortsighted initiative aimed at winning a war by other means (we shall return to this point in part 3). The very means adopted, the act of becoming lycocephalic—learning to think like a wolf (and, more broadly, like a wild being)—is an attempt at bringing adversaries together in order to achieve a state of existence in which human relations with wild beings are not conflictual but rather based on an understanding of our mutually constitutive coevolution. This understanding underlies an active quest for *mutualisms* (relations beneficial to both parties involved) and healthy commensalisms (relations beneficial to one party that neither help nor hurt the other party)—and all this not by reverting to the Paleolithic era but by inventing new relations.

The Geopolitical Argument

Animals in the megafauna category share an ecocomplex by regularly entering into contact to signal their respective intentions to one another. Contact is omnipresent. But our contemporary societies—owing partly to the Neolithic legacy, partly to that legacy's crypto-religious inverse counterpart, which defines wildness as intact and sacred on the model of a paradise lost—refuse to make such contact with wildlife, even though to do so would be to express our common belonging to nature, conceived here as a biotic community.

As an essay by Stephen H. Fritts and others in *Wolves: Behavior, Ecology, and Conservation* makes clear, equating wolves with wilderness is a vestige of the period during which wolves were eradicated, on the basis of a mistaken postulate that wolves can survive only in territories free of humans. Although some wolves in Canada, Siberia, and Mongolia have probably lived without ever sensing or seeing a human being, "most of the world's wolves live somewhere near people. They encounter the signs, sounds, and scents of civilization in their daily travels."[8] The density of human populations in the areas occupied by wolves varies from one to two hundred inhabitants per square kilometer. The situation in France will probably alter those numbers.

Living in contact with significant human density, as wolves do in Europe, implies behavioral adaptations on their part.[9] In Spain and in Italy wolf activity has been seen to shift toward nighttime, except for foggy or rainy days. Erkki Pulliainen has shown that Finnish wolves have learned to move around houses and to cross highways without being seen by humans.[10] Luigi Boitani for his part has documented an Italian pack that established its den in an abandoned house, a phenomenon whose symbolic dimension crystallizes the figure of the interstitial wolf.[11]

When confronted by foreigners, a society turns either to soldiers or to diplomacy. But the foreigners in question here are not our enemies. The new paradigm of cohabitation, then, ought to be diplomatic. By inflecting the persona of the "diplomat"—which has already been redefined for other purposes by Bruno Latour, for example, in *An Inquiry into Modes of Existence*[12]—toward interaction with wolves, we can escape the alternative that offers only a choice between sanctification and eradication.[13]

The task of negotiating with wild beings entails transmitting messages, setting limits, and indicating prohibitions. The underlying purpose of this approach, from both the ecological and the philosophical standpoints, is to create a situation in which humans will once again be able to live with wild predators. Negotiation is the basis for forging new alliances. It implies a change in paradigm, but also, in practical terms, it implies forming teams that can intervene in zones of conflict with the predators; team members will serve as our diplomats, negotiating firm boundaries and facilitating cohabitation on mutually beneficial terms.

Becoming Lycocephalic:
Thinking Like a Wolf, Having a Wolf's *Head*

Cynocephalic symbolism generally serves to call attention to savagery and bestiality. Present in the tales and legends of travelers and explorers (for example, Ctesias, Megasthenes, or Marco Polo), these "men with dogs' heads . . . wage war obstinately, drink human blood and quaff their own gore if they cannot reach the foe."[14] These figures coincide with the timeless mythical figure of the therianthrope, a human-animal hybrid.[15]

The mythological motif of shapeshifting is omnipresent in traditional cultures and contemporary fictions: from Anubis with his canine profile to the dislocation practices of the Tungusic peoples of eastern Siberia and northern China and metamorphoses into lions with wolf-like faces among the Gouin hunters of West Africa.

The therianthropic mytheme of the werewolf designates a zone of indistinction, a hybrid zone that subsists, in representations, between the human and animal worlds, whether animals are mapped as savage beasts or as gods of nature. This zone exists in effect as a transcendental plane for experimentation, a *terra incognita* transformed into a *no-man's-land* by the ideologies of the radical break between human and animal; we must rediscover and map this zone if we are to engage in viable interactions with the wild world—interactions that escape both the pest control model (biopolitics) and the model in which animals are sanctified or recast as museum specimens.

The symbolics of the werewolf, half-man and half-wolf, conveys and perpetuates the repudiation of the wild world by the ontological map we have inherited from the Neolithic era: the werewolf is condemned as a symbol of bestiality onto which all of humanity's worst tendencies are projected.

The challenge, then, is to decolonize and de-Christianize the way the werewolf is imagined, and go on to invest its image with new content. On the terrain of figures with mythological import, a silent battle is being fought over the unconscious motifs that catalyze or prevent changes in civilizational paradigms. As long as wolves and wildness are spontaneously associated with inhuman bestiality in the archetypes we share, every diplomatic paradigm will remain an isolated initiative, under fire from deeply rooted unconscious resistances. Like a paper origami figure, the *counter-natural* figure of the werewolf has to be unfolded and refolded along different lines, so that we can invent and make real the hybrid silhouette of a werewolf-diplomat, a full-fledged participant in a nature that is ecological, evolutive, and technocultural, a nature whose concept remains to be invented.

If the werewolf figure deserves to be reconquered and reversed so we can conceive of a diplomatic model, the process will require transforming its stigmata into marks of nobility, and transforming the caricatures produced by Neolithic metaphysics into battle flags announcing a new bond.[16]

Thus I shall have to redeploy lycocephalic symbolism in order to flesh out the conceptual figure[17] of a werewolf-diplomat on a mission to the border with the wild world: an agent capable of practicing alterphenomenology, capable of seeing, thinking, and communicating *using a wolf's head*, that is, functioning in a cognitive mode approaching that of a wolf. The problem is not whether wolves possess rationality, but whether human rationality is plastic enough to decode and track the mental operations of alterrationalities.

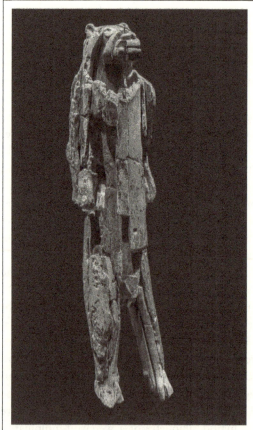

Credit: Lion Man of the Hohlenstein-Stadel, Aurignacian statuette carved from a woolly mammoth tusk, 32,000 BCE, held by Ulmer Museum (Germany)

Figure 1. The Lion Man of the Hohlenstein-Stadel: A Mythic Precursor of Zoocephalic Diplomats

This zoocephalic figure probably played the role of a mythic intercessor between the human and animal populations cohabiting in the biotic community of the Pleistocene. The statuette's pre-Neolithic character raises major problems of interpretation: it also frees this symbol to be put to new uses. *Note*: Current interpretations incline toward assigning the figure a feminine sexual identity. In zoomorphic diplomacy, the work of women has often made it possible to emancipate ethology from the phallocentric prejudices projected onto animals by male observers.

The diplomat is a shapeshifter, *versipellis*, to use Pliny the Elder's neologism in thinking about the werewolf:[18] he "turns his skin inside out" to make possible an interaction between two ethological systems that are incompatible a priori—two ambient worlds, two modes of existence.

On this basis it is now possible to formulate the characterization of wolves that can be inferred from the diplomatic model. A wolf is no longer a wild beast, a "harmful organism," or a sacred animal; wolves become ecological and ethological partners. They constitute *negotiating* partners in the context of a diplomacy conceived as the art of building relationships between coexisting ethological systems.

Diplomats are thus called to respond to an enigma that transcends the interests of human groups: *How* can humans cohabit with wolves in a way that is actually beneficial to all?

Interhuman Diplomacy as a Matrix for Concepts

As soon as these relationships have been mapped out in diplomatic terms, the physiognomy and modus operandi of interactions can be deduced. As a map that lays out the paths of action, the diplomatic model indicates that what is required is no longer regulation, extermination, domestication, or contemplation, but negotiation.

Once this proposition has been formulated, an essential aspect must immediately be spelled out, in order not to yield to the conciliatory approach that would take the formula literally. There remains a fundamental difference between the negotiating entities—it is not a matter of negotiating between equals, or between entities that are "alike." It is obvious that wolves are not the "same" as humans (or they can be seen as "differently the same," to adapt Bernard Charlier's elegant expression[19]). But it is not a matter, either, of negotiations between dominant and dominated parties: it is a matter of negotiating from world to world, from one way of existing to another.

The ontological map produced in the Neolithic era secretes radical objections to the idea of diplomacy between human animals and nonhumans. That map suggests, for example, that a relation of *equality* is required to engage in diplomacy. And yet, to begin with, the state of equality cannot be assessed among living beings: there is no scale that would allow us to judge who is equal to whom in the *bios*, where every life form constitutes a sort of perfection without any model, norm, or canon. Mustn't the two parties nevertheless be equal *under the law*? No, in reality, it is enough for the opposing party in a negotiation to *resist* and *insist*—in other words, it suffices that the opposing party can neither be crushed or scorned. Cortés did not recognize Moctezuma as his equal under the law, but he still had to be a diplomat, since he could neither conquer nor ignore the Aztec people present on their lands. Is it required, then, that the interlocutor be rational, conscious, capable of speaking, in order to negotiate as a diplomat? This is one of the key points of the problem, but no, it is enough for the negotiator to be ratiomorphic (capable of processing sensory data), social, territorial, and intelligent. Doesn't the opposing party have to *want* to negotiate, ultimately? No, it suffices that negotiators be capable of receiving messages.

Nevertheless, such a negotiation is necessarily asymmetrical: the practical role that human diplomats must play differs in scope from that of their wolf counterparts, because human aptitudes for negotiation are of a different order. Still, the lack of asymmetry does not in itself rule out construing an interaction as a negotiation. As François de Callières (1645–1717), a French theoretician of negotiation, showed, diplomacy has to be conceived as *asymmetric negotiation*.[20]

As Callières saw it, diplomacy lay in an "asymmetric anthropology," for diplomats maintain a degree of self-control and an ability to reflect that kings and others in power rarely possess. The analogy with the situation we are considering is local but pointed: what distinguishes human diplomats from their nonhuman counterparts is that their capacities to reflect, create representations, and control their own reactions are of a different order from those of wolves. This situation implies responsibility more than privilege.[21]

Callières's text is moreover an excellent manual for educating the werewolf-diplomat in the art of "earning the good graces" of the wild world. According to the author, negotiators must have an education appropriate to their function: they must know the common languages, the lingua franca of ports (in our context, they must have the means of communicating with animal worlds); they must be familiar with the power relations and the sites of confrontation, the precise interests of each party to the conflict (rural populations, herds, wild biodiversity, livestock farmers, society as a whole), the way relationships are structured, the incompatibilities and the *possible* arrangements. Diplomats must know the history of negotiations with the foreigners involved (encompassing forty thousand years of cohabitation with wolves), the representations we humans make of wolves, and those *they make of us*.

This gnoseological attitude is what we can expect from a werewolf-diplomat; such an attitude would make it possible to carry out effective asymmetrical negotiations. Our "science of negotiation"[22] will rely above all on the weapons of lycocephalic reasoning and ethological persuasion.

The Forms of Pacts and Agreements

Theorists of negotiation distinguish two basic types: cooperative and contributive. The first consists in seeking a specific agreement, articulated around quantifiable interests.

A cooperative negotiation may lead to failure or to agreement. But the quality, the robustness, and the durability of the agreement depend on the type of agreement reached. An agreement is maximally robust when it is based on mutual gains (popularly known as a "win-win" outcome). In a situation of competition for resources such as the one we are considering, the agreement may be based instead on a win-lose model and thus be unstable: this is the way in which French shepherds and sheep farmers interpret the current status quo, to their own disadvantage. The instability is maximal if both members come away from the agreement as losers. When the contending parties are forced into lasting cohabitation, rather than being brought face to face during a single localized meeting, these last two models should be ruled out, for their outcomes are highly unstable and ephemeral, and they generate more crises than they resolve. This is precisely the case that interests us, and it implies the need to seek a lasting modus vivendi.

To resolve conflicts in a case where cohabitation is destined to last, *contributive* negotiation offers an exemplary model. This form of negotiation implies *awareness* of the need to establish a lasting relationship of high quality between parties that will be living side by side over the long term. It dismisses the illusion of a win-win agreement based on strictly material interests. The criterion for success in this type of negotiation, the feature that guarantees its robustness, is that neither party succeeds at the expense of the other. In this model, we shift from a logic of adversarial behavior to a logic of partnership.[23] This partnership makes sense in light of the ecological advantages offered to French ecosystems by the wolves' return. Within an ecosystem, large carnivores ensure regulation from the top, thus reinvigorating the entire food chain. In Yellowstone, ecologists are discovering the effects of *trophic cascade* produced by the return of wolves: these indirect ecosystemic effects are positive for biodiversity (multiplication of nesting birds, revitalization of ungulate populations by top-down regulation, regeneration of forested riverbanks, and even the return of beavers, who transform riverbeds and thus landscapes).[24] Current debates in ecology focus on the effective role of large predators in reinvigorating a wide swath of wild biodiversity. The importance of wolves and other large predators in conservation ecology is being acknowledged; these actors may prove to be decisive elements in the resilience, robustness, and vitality of ecosystems from which they have been eradicated.

If their role indeed proves crucial, wolves will undoubtedly be classified among the key species that are capable of restoring the adaptive potential of ecosystems and of ensuring "total biodiversity" as a future ecological goal entailing cohabitation among living beings.[25]

Casting Doubt on All Values

Werewolf-diplomats can take inspiration from the diplomatic activity described by Bruno Latour, while pushing this conceptual figure to the extreme limit of its hybrid radicality. Even though their lycanthropy is unique, these diplomats retain certain features of Latour's pan-human diplomat: "A diplomat is not someone who pacifies, but someone who casts values into doubt, including the values of those who have sent him."[26]

Diplomats cast values into doubt, all values, especially the most deeply rooted, the Neolithic values that have terraformed the West. Similarly, they must cast doubt on the values attributed to wolves, always, by intercessors who imagine them: a taste for wildness, hatred of everything human, refusal to communicate, cruelty in predation. Similarly, the werewolf-diplomat works for a shared world, but not in the mode of seeking the universal, which remains the cosmopolitical ideal of Latour's diplomat: "That said, it is true that a certain horizon of universality remains. There isn't really any reason to do without it, in any case, since it's the goal we've all inherited. The hope for a shared world accompanies the diplomat: he goes to the negotiation in an attempt to save something of this idea of a shared world, knowing full well that this world is one that must in fact be made."[27]

The werewolf-diplomat intends to save something of a shared world, but something other than a human-centered cosmopolitical universal. Werewolf-diplomats work for a world shared in the mode of eco-ethological association, mutualism—a form of biotic community, in other words, that goes beyond the human universal, while including it. In ecology, the term "biotic community" designates biocenosis as the set of relations among the animal and vegetable species present in a given context. But by methodological choice it omits the human. In his land ethic, Aldo Leopold broadens this concept to include the human species thus caught up in relations of community with all other living beings.[28] Here, I mean to confer a political dimension on this ethic. The biotic community, grasped in its complex trophic relations, the interplay of its niche constructions, its constant symbolic interactions, is the geopolitical cohabitation I am seeking. Relations among groups in a single species, like those among species, reflect a continuous cohabitation on Earth, going back to the first appearance of life forms, and it is in the orbit of this whole that it becomes liberating to conceptualize the relation to wildness.[29] From the eco-ecological standpoint, one can identify a series of positive modes of cohabitation: commensalism, mutualism, the "dear enemy" effect, behavioral symbiosis: these are the geopolitical categories in the diplomat's arsenal, corresponding to different levels of pact and accord.

Chapter 2

Seeking King Solomon's Ring

A Vehicular Language

The fact remains that to negotiate is first of all to engage in dialogue, to palaver, to parley. If there is no common language, how can diplomacy be carried out? Is the language of guns the only recourse?

ST. FRANCIS SPEAKING TO A WOLF

In the Judeo-Christian tradition, this problem is solved on a mythical plane by the introjection of a Word that transcends regimes.

It suffices to recall the wolf of Agubbio as depicted in 1877 by the painter Luc-Olivier Merson with a halo illuminating his coat; this wolf wandered from house to house as a friend and neighbor.

The anecdote is central to our redeployment of the figure of the human-animal diplomat: Francis of Assisi, who spoke the language of the birds and beasts, stands as the *impossible* archetype of the werewolf-diplomat. Around 1220, *Il Poverello*, as Francis was known, was within the walls of the village of Agubbio.[1] A ferocious wolf prowled outside the walls, devouring humans and animals every day; the inhabitants no longer went out unarmed. They asked Francis for help. He set about to do the work of a diplomat: he went out alone, unarmed, to negotiate. In dialogue with the animal, he asked for peace, for he had understood that the wolf was neither malicious nor gratuitously cruel; he ate only out of hunger. Francis worked out a simple agreement: the village residents would feed the wolf, and the wolf would no longer feed on them. The agreement was presented to the villagers; accepted by the two parties, it reestablished an entente cordiale between humans and the wild beast.²

What makes Francis an impossible model is that, in this hagiographic anecdote, what the human and the wolf have in common, the vehicular language, is the divine *Word*. Only a creationist or mystic model would allow the Word to spread even to the mouths of animals. At most, we may retain from Francis an intuition that would become critical later on,

Credit: St. Francis, Stefano di Giovanni de Consolo, known as "Sassetta," *St. Francis and the Wolf of Gubbio* (1444), "Retable de San Sepolcro"

Figure 2. St. Francis: The Impossible Diplomat

The intercessor is represented in a classic intermediary position between the parties in conflict. The geopolitical dimension, the cultural misunderstandings, and the heightened emotions, are made quite visible in this panel, mimicking a zoocephalic diplomacy that Christianity structurally forbade itself to allow, through its anthropology of election and its ecology of stewardship (Callicott, "Genesis").

the idea that a common code ought to make it possible to understand that, in a situation where humans interpret animal behaviors as forms of cruelty and savagery, the behaviors may in fact have intelligible ethological explanations devoid of moral connotations; an example can be found in the problem of *surplus killing*. St. Francis is thus the first in the line of werewolf-diplomats, but he is a phantasmatic precursor, for he negotiates with an instrument that we lack: the Holy Spirit, which, according to the Epistle to the Corinthians (12: 8–13), confers the gift of "different kinds of tongues." We need to pursue our investigation in order to pinpoint an immanent, non-anthropomorphic common code: cognitive ethology and biosemiotics will be our Word.

LANGUAGES DISTINCT FROM SPEECH

If wolves do not share the Word, this does not mean that communication is impossible: animal communication is omnipresent, and cognitive ethology as well as behavioral ecology offer increasingly subtle accounts of this phenomenon every day. There are languages distinct from speech.

To make negotiation with wolves possible, one needs to have access to a wolf language. But how do we determine what language or communicative code is proper to wolves and to animals in general? One source of inspiration for our inquiry comes from a zoosemiotic perspective theorized by Thomas Sebeok, with the goal of adapting linguistic instruments to research on animal communication.[3]

What we are seeking, since we do not have a shared vernacular language, is a vehicular language. A vehicular language is a language that is often simplified, serving as a means of communication between populations that use different codes of communication. A lingua franca, like the one that was spoken beginning in the Middle Ages in the cosmopolitan ports of the Mediterranean by Massaliote sailors and Venetian merchants, Barbary pirates and Castilian *tercio* mercenaries.

This essentially utilitarian language, endowed with a limited lexicon and a virtually nonexistent grammar (verbs are used in the infinitive, without forms indicating mode or tense), remains perfectly effective for enabling simple interactions, defusing the sort of conflictual misunderstanding between strangers that is induced by total incommunicability. The problem is always the same: at the border of my world, I meet a stranger, foreign in language and in ethos—which makes it impossible for me to understand the meaning and function of certain of his or her actions. Am I seeing a greeting or an attack? Is this an enemy or a friend? What does this person want? How am I to react in our interaction? The lingua franca allows me to put these questions to the sailor who is landing, and thus to make something like grounds for understanding possible.

To conceive of a vehicular language between humans and wolves, it is necessary to identify a level of analysis common to the two modes of communication: beyond their differences, they both constitute *codes*. The problem then becomes one of coding and decoding. It was Warren Weaver (1894–1978) who proposed to model language as a system for encoding information, and translation as a system for decoding: an emitter codes and sends information to a transmitter, who must decode the message on the basis of a common code, or one that is compatible.[4]

Shared Ethograms

The question of what humans share with animals is an ancient one. In the Western tradition, it has been structured in three phases. First, by the Neolithic metaphysics mentioned earlier. Next, by Aristotelian philosophy, in the form of the liminal and integrative model of the faculties of the soul (vegetative, the unconscious bioprocesses common to all; sensitive for members of the mobile animal world; and intellectual for humans); this model spreads out living entities in a centrifugal pattern over a continuous, rising, animated spectrum, divided into stages of development. And, in the third stage, by Christian anthropology, which pours the whole privilege of possessing a soul into humanity alone, shoving animals off into the field of matter, or, later, into that of machines, while projecting all the human perversions onto animal figures, just as humans project their own highest qualities onto God, according to the theurgic schema proposed by Ludwig Feuerbach. This summary is of course extremely schematic, and the enduring Christian culture multiplies, with its proteiform variations,[5] its heretics and its heresiarchs, the figures of interaction with animals, of which St. Francis, the patron saint of ecologists since 1979, is the symbol.[6]

This schema was to be undone by Charles Darwin's world-changing idea: the thesis of *common descent*, or common ascendency, according to which the commonality between humans and animals is what persists through the historical differentiation of the species—it is what is shared by those who have a common origin; and what is shared owing to convergences induced by similarities in the ecological conditions of life.

We shall not linger over the cosmological and anthropological impact of Darwin's discovery,[7] but we can identify in his book a very clear formulation of the new inflection given to the problems we are facing. The passage is found in Darwin's third great synthesis, which constitutes one of the precursor texts of modern ethology:

> No doubt as long as man and all the other animals are viewed as independent creations, an effectual stop is put to our natural desire to investigate as far as possible the causes of Expression. By this doctrine, anything and everything can be equally well explained; and it has proved as pernicious with respect to Expression as to every other branch of natural history. With mankind some expressive behaviors, such as the bristling of the hair under the effect of extreme terror, or the uncovering of the teeth under the influence of furious rage, can hardly be understood, except on the belief that man once existed in a much lower and animal-like condition. . . . He who admits on general grounds that the structure and habits of all animals have been gradually evolved, will look at the whole subject of Expression in a new and interesting light.[8]

Fur bristling, teeth bared: here is the wolf, here is the human, their common essence demonstrated: here is the werewolf.

Darwin makes intelligible this shared fringe of behaviors, glimpsed by Hildegard of Bingen, through the idea of a common ascendancy that allows comparative analyses. The transformist theory of natural selection, which postulates an evolution of life forms starting from a common origin, positions all living beings on a single tree,[9] thus in a relation of differential proximity that isolates a necessary genetic and ecological link among life forms. The *ratio* between commonalities and differences is thus proportional to the historical distance with respect to the splitting that separates the two branches of the phylum from which the two life forms emerged (adjusting for differences in the pace of evolution), and proportional to their later transformations with regard to similar or different economic conditions. This new cartography of living beings makes intelligible both the deep genealogical interconnectedness of the species and their obvious differences.

In terms of the current investigation, this shared fringe may be morphological, physiological, and/or anatomical, but also and especially behavioral. In his two final syntheses, Darwin defended the thesis—foundational for the ethology to come—according to which his theory of natural selection did not postulate the heritability of physical characteristics alone, but also that of behavioral traits. This Darwinian distinction is crucial, for it allows us to explode the traditional distinction between physical features (related to biology) and mental features (related to culture). Darwin went on to thematize the idea of inherited natural behaviors as the only idea capable of accounting for certain enigmatic human actions—for example, baring one's teeth.

The late Darwin was a brilliant empirical decipherer of behaviors. He established catalogs of signals through which mammals communicate their emotions. He observed, for example, that the rearward orientation of the ears in an animal in combat constitutes an adaptation, for it is present only in the carnivores and ruminants who fight *with their teeth*. He proposed the concept of "antithesis," which we know now in an improved ethological formulation, to account for the fact that expressive behaviors with oppo-

Figure 3. Charles Darwin: The Zoomorphic Diplomat of Common Lineages

As a strategic move, the struggle for symbols calls for a reversal of the caricatures derived from Neolithic metaphysics so that they become glorifying titles. Decolonizing the imaginary of the werewolf implies transforming stigmata into battle flags. The monkey's body, here, is not the sign of a fall, but of an election, an opening of the richness of living beings to the human reign. "Humanity is exalted not because we are so far above other living creatures, but because knowing them well elevates the very concept of life" (Wilson, *Biophilia*, 22). Here is a credo for zoomorphic diplomats.

Credit: Caricature published in the magazine *Hornet*, 1871

site motivations have common forms, but forms differentiated by *maximal amplitude* (a dominant wolf walks with his head and tail high; a submissive wolf keeps his head and tail down; a wolf waiting to assess the situation holds his tail at the midpoint).

These are the foundational premises of ethology, for this latter, as the science of animal behavior, is possible only in the orbit of Darwinian theory. To be sure, observation and descriptions of animal behaviors existed long before Darwin, but they could not be called ethology, for the latter requires the use of its own method and a battery of concepts that resituate each animal in its own phylum.[10]

Classical ethology is a science of behaviors that uses observation to isolate specific and relatively stable behavioral sequences and transcribes them in "ethograms." But these behaviors are not described simply as such, in isolation; they are characterized as fundamentally related to comparable behaviors in other species.

To grasp this dimension, we need to go back to the methodological stroke of genius on the basis of which Konrad Lorenz founded ethology. Lorenz had learned the methods of comparative anatomy from Ferdinand Hochstetter, a brilliant anatomist and physiologist in Vienna's medical school; as Lorenz tells the story in his intellectual autobiography, ethology consists in transposing those methods from organs to behaviors: in other words, behaviors are to be viewed as organs.[11] Lorenz was proposing a specific theory of behavior in which species were already conceived in Darwinian terms: a species is thus a population of cross-fertilizing variants that maintain kinship relations with other species. What individual members have in common is already present, underneath, for one does not choose one's family. Lorenz's ethology, based on an anatomical model, is a science of behavioral differences overlaid on a common ground. In the tradition of interpreters and diplomats, the place of St. Francis, who extended the Word to animals, is taken by Konrad Lorenz, the founder of modern ethology, as his book *King Solomon's Ring: New Light on Animal Ways*, attests.[12] Solomon's magic allowed him to dialogue with every form of life.

Seen from this perspective, every animal species develops its own gamut of individual and social behaviors. An ethogram represents the entire set of stable forms of behavior inventoried in an animal species. The term "ethogram" was introduced in 1936 by the ornithologist Gerrit François Makkink, in a monograph on the avocet.[13] This detailed catalog presented the behavioral sequences of the species in purely descriptive terms, excluding any anthropomorphic interpretations as much as possible. It had a pedagogical

Figure 4. Konrad Lorenz: The Diplomat on His Way

Through his method of sharing daily life with animals free to move about the grounds of the Altenburg manor, Lorenz inaugurated a cognitive diplomacy founded on mutual impregnation, participant observation, and daily negotiations. Far from the mechanistic accents of some of his conceptualizations, he lived in political cohabitation with other living beings he considered companions, on the alert for any diplomatic misunderstanding.

Credit: Photograph Éditions Wild Project

function, moreover: it helped to train the eye, enabling naturalists to identify relevant mobile segments and break down the perceived life of an animal into behavioral sequences. The concept of an ethogram is ambiguous, in the sense that, through methods of horizontal comparison (what behavioral sequence is shared by the entire species?) and vertical comparison (what sequence changes when a given species is compared with related species?), it seems to reintroduce an Aristotelian zoology in which each species is determined by an essence: a gamut of instincts that is its own, identical in all members of the species and therefore rigid.

But it was by instituting ethograms that more recent ethology has been able to go beyond them, showing, thanks to advances in primatology, how individuals, in differentiated social and affective contexts, modulate, inflect, and subvert these sequences, in a historical and social tinkering analogous to human behavior.

As a comparative science of behaviors, ethology readily supplies *comparative* ethograms that pinpoint common behavioral sequences common to species that are distinct but that have analogous modes of behavior and recent genetic divergences. A table that establishes a comparative ethogram of the hunting behaviors of the major predators, across genus and species lines, is particularly pertinent to our study.[14] If the ethogram of wolves can be compared to that of lions, why would it be impossible to find ethological commonality between wolves and humans (unless we are respecting the absolute borderline presented by the Neolithic ontological map)?

It should by now be clear that this zone of "commonality," this "sharable" zone, which is of practical and communicative importance for relations between the way of life of wolves and that of humans, can be conceived in terms of an ethogram. My hypothesis is that there is something like a hybrid zone shared between the ethogram of wolves and that of humans, a zone of overlap that is the condition of possibility of an age-old ability to communicate. This is the condition on which animal diplomacy depends.

The problem is inextricably bound up with the question of human-animal difference. We shall have to try to untangle these transcendental knots in order to advance practically through the question of commonality.

From the difference in *nature* between man and beasts postulated by the Aristotelian-Christian *scala naturae*, we have moved on to repeated theorizing of a "difference in degree." Darwin's formula, the new unquestioned battle flag of those who deny human-animal difference, is sometimes formulated in terms of "quantitative" rather than qualitative difference. Under its generous appearance, this formula contains opaque logical implications that are almost as toxic as the ancient claim of difference "in nature."

In fact, we encounter a vestigial conceptual error in speaking of a difference in degree, or a quantitative difference, to characterize the relations between animals in general and the human animal. This conceptual ruse implies a de-essentializing of the difference, to be sure, but in so doing it surreptitiously reestablishes a hierarchy of the species on a vaguely Lamarckian scale aimed at showing the complexification of life forms. This ruse indeed subverts the *scala naturae* (once seen as discontinuous, it has become *continuous*), but by making it *perennial*. For there can be differences in degree *only* on a graduated linear scale along *a single* common axis. There can be differences in quantity only according to a *shared* and *unique* standard of measurement.

Now the common scale on which one distinguishes degrees is built by humans in such a way that humanity always turns out to be on a higher level, as the most developed form (for example, regarding intelligence, culture, sociability, morality, creativity, or language). This arbitrary and unique standard fails to grasp the *fundamental divergence* that constitutes the structure of living beings and produces in all directions alterrationalities, altermoralities, alterintentionalities, and altercreativities. For there is in fact no common scale, no standard of common measure: every life form is an instance of perfection without a model, divergence without a canon.

Perfection traditionally means total correspondence with an ideal model. From the perspective I am proposing, each species can be conceived as perfect, but in a paradoxical sense, that is, perfect without regard to any ideal model. To grasp this point, it is important not to take "perfect" in the ordinary sense. A life form is not perfect in the same sense that an intentionally constructed object may be perfect: it is the product of a blind process that is devoid of any engineering intelligence. The use of the word "perfection" is an attempt to qualify the extraordinary complexity—integral, adjusted, interwoven, and functional—of these living beings, among whom we count ourselves, even though *no one* conceived them.

We are dealing here with perfection in an almost aesthetic sense of the term, a sense that combines the Platonic values of the Bauhaus (what is useful is beautiful) with the Kantian theory of genius (genius sets aside previous norms and invents its own). No trajectory of genetic transmission is identical to any other; no biotic community is identical to any other as an ecological milieu constitutive of a species; thus no species, no life form, can constitute the norm or standard for any other. No form of intelligence can constitute the scale on which the intelligence *of others* can be evaluated.

The purest model of model-less perfection can be found in the post-classical conception of a work of art (that is, a work evaluated in the absence of any normative canon for the period). Since a Romantic work of art is one that creates its own norms, every work is unique, thus an exception to the norm, yet it is perfect by its own standard, the one that it secretes and receives in the pure singularity of its constitutive relations with the external world—here, the ecological milieu.

Model-less perfection means that each life form is organically linked by a historical shaping that cannot be equated with the series of biotic communities that its genetic flow has traversed during its historical evolution. This genetic and ecological perfection cannot be understood in a technical sense, for species are not products of an optimal and instantaneous design that would adapt plastic materials to current ends; rather, they are age-old makeshift constructs, cluttered with useless vestigial features, transformed by an evolutionary process destined to subvert a construction that is already there. Every species co-constructs its own norm (nest-building)—and each species is momentarily perfect according to that norm.

But "model-less" does not mean incomparable, for analogous genetic bases and ecological conditions of life constitute common matrices and decisive convergences among species from the standpoint of their modes of existence, or ways of life (on the model of parallelisms in evolutionary biology). Among the various animal species (*Homo sapiens* included) there are family resemblances (phylogenetic proximity) and convergences of "class habitus" or niche (functional ecology).

Comparing an animal species to the human species is thus not necessarily an anthropomorphic gesture; if the comparison bears rigorously on aspects of modes of existence that are meaningfully shared from a genetic standpoint (synapomorphies), or that result from evolutionary convergences or reversions (homoplasies), it is rather a matter of biomorphism, which takes as its model not the human but rather a *matricial mode of living beings*. Thus predatomorphism takes predation as its common model for the mode of existence or form of life.[15] In this sense, too, there are (among others) mammomorphisms that justify comparisons on the level of mammals, and also omnivomorphisms that render intelligible our scattered relations of kinship in modes of existence (and not kinship in terms of species as genetic pools) with bears or crows.[16]

But what, then, is the epistemological nature of the difference between the human animal and the other animals? The difficulty comes from the fact that the number of epistemological types of differences is not infinite. I shall suggest here that among living creatures what is at stake is a difference not in nature or degree but in combinatorics and combinations. By combinatorics, I am referring to the fact that living beings constitute assemblages of certain shared modules, integrated into differing mosaics. A given species shares certain of its modules with another, and different modules with a third. Modules are to be understood here as integrable elements that exist at the genetic,[17] molecular, organic, and behavioral levels. It is in this sense that we can speak of animal combinatorics. As combinatorics of features that are sometimes inherited, sometimes convergent, living creatures share the same tesserae, with which they form original mosaics. But each combinatoric, the first source of differences, is subject to combination. Combination means that these differing modules never exist as such, in isolation: they are always included in organic, genetic, and behavioral complexes that interpret them and inflect them to the point of making them unrecognizable.

Credit: Caricature of the Thomas Henry Huxley, "On the Relations of Man to Other Animals," in *Man's Place in Nature* (Ann Arbor: University of Michigan Press, [1863] 1959), p. 83.

Figure 5. Thomas Henry Huxley: The Diplomat of Taxonomic Cohabitation

One more caricature brandished as a battle flag. Huxley is not only "Darwin's bulldog": he is also a first-rate naturalist, specialist in primate morphometrics. He was the first to study the differences between humans and monkeys empirically, opening the way to the ontologically revolutionary reclassification of *Homo* in the order of Primates (espousing Carl Linnaeus against Johann Friedrich Blumenbach).

If Darwin proposed the theoretical hypothesis of common descent, it was Huxley who, through his empirical studies in anatomical comparison, ended up with the thesis according to which humans descended from the same source type as chimpanzees, through elegant reasoning: "In sum, I now take it as proven that the anatomical differences between marmosets and chimpanzees are much greater than those between chimpanzees and humans. So that, whatever causes have been sufficient to make a same source type evolve, here into a marmoset, there into a chimpanzee, these same causes have been sufficient to make mankind evolve from the same source. As for knowing whether natural causes can produce these transformations or not, I shall not take on that question; I am satisfied to leave it in the powerful hands of Mr. Darwin" (Huxley, Preface, vii–viii).

He thus discovered a diplomatic axiom, backed up by empirical data: "Man . . . resembles [the lower animals] as they resemble one another—he differs from them as they differ from one another." For formulating this simple but constitutive idea that dismisses comparison between two disproportionate sets, he deserves to be counted in the ranks of werewolf diplomats.

Thus two brothers endowed with a common quality, but caught up in complex networks of differences (character traits resulting from different socializations, from psychically metabolized events), do not resemble each other when they are assessed separately. The tendency to make extreme demands on oneself may present as self-deprecatory culpability in one brother, as imperious arrogance in the other. The same quality is subverted by the complex, diverted by the psychobiological context. When we meet the brother or sister of a close friend and find the sibling endowed with a very different character, we may suddenly understand the subtle combination underlying a singular feature of our friend: the trait is combined in the complex of each sibling's personality in such a way that it is recognizable in its emergent form and made visible only when the two family members are in each other's presence. Living species resemble one another in the way brothers and sisters resemble one another, that is, they are made up of combinatorics of often similar traits, inflected by the way they are combined. So the method of comparison becomes intriguing: looking separately at one or the other cannot help us. We have to examine the two similar entities at the same time, to determine by subtraction what they have in common under the complex wholes. Let us use colors as an analogy. Studied separately, one appears green and another mauve: they present themselves as different, without common features. But if we examine them side by side, we can see that the mauve is a combination inflected on the basis of a shared blue combined with red, whereas the one that looks green conceals the same blue inflected toward green by combination with yellow. It is by examining *the emergent difference* between the two similar entities that we can isolate something like a common matrix, which is present as such in neither, since it is always already combined and inflected.

From this standpoint, the metaphor of fraternity among living beings, introduced in Darwin's work and anticipated in certain Amerindian cultures (such as the Lakotas'), takes on new analytic scope. It is in this sense that one can envision a *type* of difference among life forms that is a matter neither of nature nor of degree, but rather of combinatory and combination. We are dealing with an element of a biomorphic method.

Biomorphism:
Analogy without Filiation and Genetic Homology

How can we conceptualize commonalities in life forms if each one is defined as model-less perfection? A potential solution to this problem lies in the concept of biomorphism, surrounded by its isotopes: predatomorphism, omnivomorphism, and mammomorphism. This concept is the basis for a comparative method that emphasizes ecological proximity, which—through convergence or inheritance—implies ethological proximity: in other words, the method calls for a deep comparison of analogies without regard to filiation, as well as homologies relying on shared genetic bases.[18]

An analysis of this order has been suggested by biologist William Timberlake, a specialist in animal behavior who has proposed to categorize comparisons of behaviors on two levels, high or low, according to the ecological and genetic dimensions of the comparisons.[19] He classifies those that display both a high genetic relation and a high ecological relation as "micro-evolutionary," and those that display low genetic resemblance and high ecological resemblance as "ecological."

We shall learn more about the wolf life form when we acknowledge that its eco-ethological conditions of existence are not absolutely unique, but that they are shared in part, as can be shown by superimposed Venn diagrams—for example, by those of humans, who are also social predators of large game, associated with family clans, and destined to a life of feast and famine. Such behavioral analyses of species remotely related in genetic terms were anticipated by as questionable a thinker as Oswald Spengler, isolated by Desmond Morris in the most creditable pages of *The Naked Ape* (1967), and established by Paul Shepard in *The Only World We've Got*.[20]

We are no longer dealing with anthropomorphism but with a form of biomorphism based on predatomorphism and mammomorphism: it is inasmuch as we are mammals that we can understand mammals, and inasmuch as we are predators that we have modes of existence in common with other predators.

More fundamentally, in biomorphic terms, on different scales, we share with the world of mammals (and animals in general, to a certain extent) the major initiatory phases of existence. We are born, we are cared for, we play and learn; we experience joy in seeking what is good for us, fear of what is bad, affection for those close to us, aversion for others, tranquil indifference, the vibrancy of desire, and something like amorous encounters; we carve out our lives, our niches, our milieus; we may be parents, we may belong to a collective, leave a collective, form political relations with others, grieve the loss of those close to us, eventually go into decline ourselves, have more past than future, see the young rise, figure out how to interact with them, and die. This biomorphism of the life cycle indicates a profound proximity. Our existential trajectories have common segments. In one sense of the word "life" (the one found in the expression "That's life"), we have the same life.

These segments differ in terms of the eco-ethological refinements of the various animal lineages, refinements to which only a few thinkers have begun to do justice. Paul Shepard's work on the history of the human eye shows that the structures of the eye's sensitivity, its powers and its limitations, have to be understood as a combination of ancestral features inherited from our sedimented past, from nocturnal pseudo-lemurians, fruit-eating monkeys, tree-climbers, upright runners on the savanna, followers of tracks (which are hieroglyphics), down to the readers of these lines.[21]

On certain points, humans are closer to wolves than to our closest genetic relatives, chimpanzees, for behaviors are also constrained by the ecological conditions of existence, and behaviors create local parallelisms in life forms, just as two trajectories may be parallel and very close to one another over a certain distance, then suddenly diverge in their singular curves.

THE RIGHT TRANSLATION

The question of a common code could be resolved by an attempt to translate animal behaviors into human language. But this solution would maintain the distance between humans and "foreign" beings that has been widely criticized by anthropologists, and it would prevent a genuine comprehension of the foreign by the translator. The problem is not for us as translators to find a perfect correspondence in our own language with what we see in the life of a foreign being, but how to impart into our own language the terms, the ways of dealing with life, the attitudes, of a foreigner, so that this material comes to enrich our own idiom with new and otherwise inaccessible meanings.

It is not simply a matter of translating the meaning of animal behaviors into a human language, then, but rather of operating a double and symmetrical translation: "a good translation." The anthropologist Eduardo Viveiros de Castro has put forward a decisive intuition: "Good translation succeeds at allowing foreign concepts to deform and subvert the conceptual apparatus of the translator such that the *intention* of the original language can be expressed through and thus transform that of the destination."[22] For anthropologists, this comes down to the fact that the theoretical *breakthroughs* in their science have consisted in incorporating and metabolizing the very concepts of the autochthonous peoples they are observing: shamanism, totem, mana, potlatch, and so on.[23]

If we are to be werewolf-diplomats, we have to allow categories of the animal mode of existence to pass into our language, in order to account for certain of our own behavioral tendencies. Not in terms of words, but in terms of observable behavioral peculiarities. The passive-aggressive response to the feeling of weakness in the curmudgeon; generosity as a surplus of vital force in a dominant but nondominating individual; the specific neurological joy of any driving, vital quest that heightens awareness and perceptivity, a feeling different from the dopamine-driven pleasure of drowsiness after a big meal; curiosity about what is new and unexpected on the part of omnivores and creatures with a sense of territoriality—all these are animal matrices deposited in us by evolution, and inflected by the added inherited strata that define us. Thus disperser wolves give their name to human behaviors that are otherwise hard to conceptualize. To be at bay; to be sly as a fox; to strut like a peacock; to get into a cockfight: we understand that these formulas describe, map, and interpret key elements of human behavior better than any other *anthropomorphic* metaphor, because they isolate segments common to the animal and human modes of existence. For "cockfights," any formula that would try to capture a latent but visible conflict, a conflict exclusively between males, a conflict in which domination is symbolic and goes through a whole series of symbolic tactics, destined to be observed by the opposite sex, would be less clear: the animal metaphor makes the human behavior intelligible.

Paul Shepard hypothesizes that during the long Pleistocene era, it was by observing animals that humans, through a mirroring effect, came to discriminate among their own characteristics and emotions, and learned to externalize them in known, perceptible, shared models: the irascible woolly rhinoceros gave a name to the indescribable character of some man; the slender antelope gave a name to the graceful walk of some woman, in a past when the concept of grace had not yet been formulated. As evidence, Shepard takes the omnipresence of formulas in English that describe human behaviors through animal (zoomorphic) metaphors.[24] One can be anthropomorphic *if and only if* one is at the same time rigorously zoomorphic. In this sense, we have always been diplomats, for we have allowed animals to serve as models, in part, for our inner profiles, to give form to who we are, just as anthropologists allow indigenous categories to redefine their comprehension of themselves. Ethologists and students of animal psychology, rather than trying to translate animal behavior into the language of our human subjectivities, or into that of scientific objectivity (stereotypical behavioral sequences, conditioning), could benefit from their own proximity to animals, from the subtlety of their own observations of behavior, as they undertake the *inverse* translation of new animal categories into human languages, in

Figure 6. Charles Le Brun, *Manuel de physiognomonie*, 1668

The proximities between animal and human species must be sought in several directions, in relation to phylogenetic kinships and ecological analogies, shared competencies and common modes of existence: we are bird apes, fox apes, sometimes ant apes.

order to make visible previously unobserved facets of both our inner lives and our social lives, thereby helping us further define ourselves as human beings living in a diffracted common animality.

As this process advances, the new animal categories are expanding human life, enhancing our lives by welcoming ways of understanding ourselves via animal models, as opposed to remaining obsessed by what is "proper" to our human "selves." The complex and subtle behaviors of nonhuman animals, under the microscope of cognitive ethology, seem to be murmuring something yet to be determined in our lives.

Accessible and Decipherable Stimuli

We have seen in what sense animal and human behavioral matrices share common features. In practical terms, however, we need to establish the fact that a shared zone in the ethogram allows communication only if it makes it possible to use shared *signals*, to signify *categories* that are shared between the two life forms.

To understand this phenomenon of interspecies communication, we can return to the way Konrad Lorenz presented his modus operandi for inserting himself into an animal ethogram, thus making communication possible according to a hybrid code, asymptotic to the code proper to the animal species. In his autobiography, Lorenz explained how he taught young jackdaws, living under the family roof in Altenburg, to come down from an upstairs window and join him in the garden: the method, going back to the ancient tradition of mimicking bird calls, consisted in modulating, under the right conditions, the *contact-establishing cry proper to their species*. In 1935, Lorenz published a programmatic text titled "Der Kumpan in der Umwelt des Vogels" (The companion in the world proper to the bird), in which he set forth what is now known as the classic method of ethology.[25] He explained that each animal utters *stimuli* intended for other members of the same species, each one of which is a social initiator (a better term would be "inciter") perfectly adjusted to a receptor in the animal.

Thus the environment, through the conditions of living that it implies, constitutes a source of signals for each animal.[26]

In order to make viable communication possible, then, the whole problem becomes how to isolate and master the modulation (emission and encoding) of *stimuli* that are, for the species in question, *social triggers accessible to the receptor in animals and decodable in their own behavioral code*. Let us note that this insertion in the ethogram has already been used and mastered with wolves in what is called "summer tracking," through induced howls. This technique mimics scientifically the principle of an old Amerindian hunting trick, which consists in passing oneself off as a wolf in order to approach a herd of bison. This timeless hunting ploy can serve as a model for interspecies communication.

Credit: George Catlin, *Buffalo Hunt under the Wolf-skin Mask* (1832–1833). Gift of Mrs. Joseph Harrison, Jr., 1985.66.414, Smithsonian American Art Museum

Figure 7. Two Amerindian Hunters of the Plains: Intertwined Diplomats

For some Amerindians of the plains, wolves are "hunting masters." Like Mongolian nomads, these Amerindians say that in a past outside of time, wolves taught them their most basic hunting techniques. Some ethno-ethologists relate this phenomenon to the roughly two hundred thousand years of the Pleistocene era during which Paleolithic humans, cohabiting with the largest predators and hunting alongside them, closely observed the predators' complex individual and collective hunting behaviors (this seems to be indicated by their zoomorphic wall paintings) and thus learned their effective cynegetic tactics through mimicry. One of these ruses was reproduced by the painter George Catlin during a lengthy voyage devoted to painting the ways of life of these First People before they disappeared.

Inserting Oneself in the Ethogram

Catlin's tableau is a symbol of werewolf diplomacy, but it is also an enigma. At first glance, its meaning seems immediately accessible. Armed with our human modules of attribution of intentionality, which look everywhere for answers to the "why" question and track the hidden intentions behind the behaviors, we understand that for the two Amerindians it is a question of getting as close as possible to bison in order to hunt them.

But then the question inevitably arises: How does it make sense to disguise oneself as a *wolf* to approach bison? To disguise oneself as a predator in order to approach the prey? This enigma, which depicts the hunting behavior of Amerindians as absurd, is a sign that we are no longer werewolf-diplomats: we don't understand, we cannot know, we have forgotten, how the rest of the world behaves. We no longer know how to decipher the signs. For most of us, the murmuring forests are mute.

Here is what might be the key to the enigma, told from the viewpoint of an imaginary Amerindian etho-eco-evolutionist werewolf-diplomat. Coevolution between wolves and their prey on the plains induced a primordial shaping of hunting and defensive behaviors: wolves hunt only the most vulnerable ungulates, and they have to tire their prey during the hunt.

To identify the weakest among their prey, wolves have to evaluate the length of their stride, their gait, their breathing, their behavior, their degree of serenity, the sovereignty of a slow trot, the vitality of resplendent leaps.[27] This necessity can be correlated with another ethological dimension: predators have a fairly low success rate (about one in ten attempts for wolves, still less for the Siberian tiger), and they readily turn toward one of the herd's other prey when the hunt becomes too difficult. We can infer that, in an arms race, the means for discouraging the predator symbolically, and thus psychologically, are as effective as the means for struggling physically against the predator (by fleeing or driving it off).

Wolves thus need to make their prey *flee* to evaluate them. Observers of this process have noted that, in the ethogram of the wolf, in its ambient world, the flight of ungulates is a *stimulus* that *incites* wolves to pursue their prey. After tracking and identification, pursuit is the first phase of wolf predation.

As evolution is prodigious in creative solutions that tweak structures established in the past, certain prey have acquired an aptitude that uses this behavioral structure on the part of the wolf *to their advantage*. They are able to play on the relative rigidity of this hunting technique, which has become "instinctive" in wolves, to trick their potential pursuers. Some of the elk of Isle Royale (in Lake Superior), observed by David Mech, have developed a tendency to confront packs that can include as many as fifteen or sixteen wolves.[28] If they manage to remain calm, to maintain eye contact with the predators, to avoid panic and flight, they are generally not attacked. Facing an immobile animal staring at them, wolves tend to seek other prey. We can hypothesize that this phenomenon manifests an evolutionary origin of courage. The behavioral sequence that consists in standing fast for some time in the face of a threat, showing (or pretending) that one is *not* afraid, constitutes a potentially selective behavior, for it may inhibit attacks by certain predators. While it contains a hereditary matrix, the positive reproductive differential of its carriers may lead to an evolution in behavior. The capacity for self-discipline, self-mastery, which has long been jealously claimed by human animals as a sign of their superiority (a sign of their capacity to surpass or master the animal in themselves), thus may have been selected in other animals at other points of evolution.[29] This behavior may have a hereditary base and be completed by individual experience, or it may result from passive apprenticeship, or both, in unknown proportions.

To master the fear induced by the presence of a predator means to stand fast against the impulse to flee. Ethologists offer numerous stories and pictures of prey that keep their composure for several minutes, sometimes several hours, before the chilling patience of a pack, then literally lose control, allow panic to take over, flee, and are eaten. There would be an adaptive advantage to the moral virtue of courage, which in cases like these constitutes not a thoughtless acceptance of danger but the most rational attitude possible: a symbolic shield with a psychological effect, against fangs. Thus bison have been able to establish a defensive behavior that consists paradoxically in not fleeing, but rather remaining serenely in place, confronting wolves, when flight would very probably seal their demise.

By contrast, bison flee from Amerindian hunters, for they know that remaining in place does not protect them, and that only flight and speed can save them from the wooden birds that implant themselves in their flesh and from the thunderbolts that kill from a distance. This is why, in order to come close to a bison, the Amerindian werewolf-diplomat disguises himself as *a different predator*: a wolf.

When you (a bison) have acquired an adaptive behavior that consists in facing up to a predator whose attack is incited by your flight (a wolf), then another predator, from whom you normally would flee (a human), if he is disguised as a wolf, can come close to you, very close. The bison species (lycocephalic diplomats themselves, on this point) has acquired an evolutionary trick to use against wolves by not fleeing their approach; humans in turn *trick the trickster* by becoming wolves.

Cloaked in a wolf skin (a stimulus for the visual receptor) and with his odor disguised (a stimulus for the olfactory receptor), advancing among the herd, the zoocephalic Amerindian diplomat chooses his targets the way the alpha male of the wolf pack would choose them. At the heart of the herd, the hunter stops almost underneath his target, and releases a single arrow from his bow, not into the shoulder but straight to the heart, so the bison will fall down dead at once. A male merely wounded would roar in pain, panic would set in, and the hunter would be trampled.

The Amerindian hunters depicted by Catlin (figure 7) use a complex behavioral schema characteristic of bison, the result of the historical interweaving of shared lives on the plain, to approach the animals; they insert themselves into the bison's ethogram.

The evolutionary mechanisms involved in this arms race are much more delicate than a simple economic optimization of cost-benefit relations: the differential reproduction of variant individuals carrying specific traits is what actually induces the transformation, but these traits are not direct, obvious, isolated improvements. The behavior is not monogenic: it is not the mechanical effect of a single gene. It is the effect of a genetic complex, inflected by development, that plays a role in a whole series of other aspects of life.

Bison in fact do not stare at wolves by following a stereotypical behavioral sequence encoded as such in the genome. Rather, a bison with an inheritable behavioral matrix (unknowable to us, for now) that predisposes him to be, for example, courageous, stubborn, serene, or placid in the face of a predator, has a positive differential reproductivity and transmits this trait. Selection bears on the behavioral matrix and not on the mechanical and stereotypical act. Moreover, the matrix in question can be engaged through pleiotropy in many other behavioral tendencies; it will shift the animal's entire behavioral complex. And we do not know in what rigorous sense these traits are "advantageous": the theory of evolution, from this standpoint, is a theory of ambiguous advantage, of erratic advantage.[30]

> The foundational concepts of ethology and the earliest experiments provided a rather determinist picture of signals. The picture today is much more "probabilist": a signal can produce various responses, some of which are nonetheless more probable than others. A consequence of research on communication among the higher vertebrates, the idea of "hidden dimensions" has gradually taken hold, the idea that information external to an external signal may modulate the signal's effect.[31]

It is the appearance of emotion in the living creature, and then of thought, that permits this passage from determinism to possibilism: the information received passes through the complex parliament of emotions, memory, and thought, and thus the response varies, because it is diffracted in the individual prism in a complex and locally unpredictable way (although strong tendencies are manifested in statistical terms).

Frans de Waal explains brilliantly why evolution has been able to bring emotions to light as guides for action,[32] to solve the problems posed by behavioral sequences of the stimulus-reaction type, which are genetically encoded in part, as we see more clearly in insect life. It is because emotions allow for a more nuanced treatment of experience—as soon as you are caught up in ecologically complex relations. Confronted by a predator, if you have a rigid behavioral sequence, the adaptive response (to escape by leaping away, for example) will be faster than if you have emotions; thus this is the response valorized by selection. But life always introduces complexities. Imagine facing a predator on the edge of a cliff when you are accompanied by your offspring. Here rigid sequences commanding your behavior (jump!) are less refined than emotions, which simply give indications. Emotions allow you to react in a nuanced way to complex situations: your fear incites you to flee, but your parental affection incites you to stay in place, and another fear (of falling) intervenes to prevent a stereotypical reflex that would be fatal. Feelings can enter into compromises, in a parliament of emotions from which a more subtly adapted solution to a complex problem may emerge. The appearance of emotions in living beings, some 700 million years ago with the earliest brains, probably functioned as a "crane," in Daniel Dennett's sense, that is, an evolutionary arrangement through which living beings lift themselves up *on their own*, in immanence, toward emerging heights of behavioral refinement, of which our noblest attitudes are examples.[33] Lorenz speaks of the "parliament of instincts" and later of emotions and thought, a "parliament" that is nothing but a strange, complex recursive loop adding representations of stimuli and emotion to the stimuli and the emotions themselves: fear plus the idea of fear induces the question: Am I right to be afraid? I am afraid this predator is going to kill me, but if I don't want to die, must I heed my fear? Or should I stand fast before the predator so as not to call up his hunting instinct by running for my life?

It is clear that ruses in the exchange of signs are not exclusive to humans: they pass from animal to animal, are shared, and are played off against one another. This age-old communication is what establishes the possibility of the werewolf-diplomat.

An analogous diplomatic ruse that consists in passing oneself off as a wolf, but this time in the company of wolves themselves, allows ecologists to count wolves during the summer. Wolf specialists and, in France, the National Office for Hunting and Wildlife, practice the technique of incitational howling: "The investigations are carried out by using wolf calls to provoke responses in order to localize the 'meeting places' where wolves gather during the post-reproduction period."[34] To determine if a pack has in fact produced cubs during the spring, the method entails approaching the den, out of sight and out of the olfactory range, and producing wolf calls. Like Lorenz's calls for his jackdaws, this cry is inscribed in the ethogram: it penetrates though an adaptive receptor and constitutes a decisive social signal decipherable by wolves, who respond in a chorus to the human howls. The cubs are probably lured first into responding to the humans, but the adults then join in the collective song. They are presumably signifying to what they take to be another pack that they are there and in control of the territory.

Chapter 3

Understanding and Influencing Behavior

Understanding Behavior

SURPLUS KILLING AS AN ECO-ETHOLOGICAL ENIGMA

Comparing the ethograms of humans and a given animal species allows us to identify a zone of commonality, a fringe of shared behaviors. Identifying these behaviors may allow us, first, to *understand* the behavior of the animal in question, that is, to decipher it on the basis of the relevant code. We may then be able to interact with the animal and to influence its behavior by transmitting messages to it that it can understand, messages adjusted to its perceptual window, and decipherable according to its own code.

To address the issue of comprehension, we need to return to the problem of diplomatic misunderstanding with which this investigation began. The ethno-diplomatic misunderstanding arises at bottom from a problem of mutual communication, an inability to grasp the meaning—the signification and the function—of a stranger's actions, and an inability to interact with that stranger according to the lines of force of his or her behavior, for want of a code for communication and for want of a common *ethos*.

Ethno-diplomatic misunderstandings among human peoples will serve as our analogy for grasping both the failures and the successes of human interactions with wolves. Misunderstandings are archetypal phenomena characterizing exploratory and colonial expeditions.

"Frontier" literature is full of recitals of deadly ethnological misunderstandings, during the encounters between the first colonizers and American Indians. A traditional example has to do with the at once playful and martial Indian practice of the "counting coup" as proof of courage. For the Plain Indians, during a clash, a counting coup signified touching a man or taking away his shield. Bringing off a successful counting coup had more value than killing an adversary. The incompatibility between the outlooks of opposing warrior groups is apparent in the stories of Charles Eastman (1858–1939), a Sioux whose maternal grandfather was a US Army officer.[1] The ethological and diplomatic misunderstanding on the colonizers' part consisted in interpreting an inoffensive counting coup as an actual aggression; thus such coups could cause flare-ups and unleash mutual massacres. Lack of understanding of the foreign ethos, phantasmatic interpretations that led to ill-adapted modes of interaction: the behavioral sequence characteristic of ethnological misunderstandings is found unmistakably on the ethological level as well. This model seems relevant to our attempt to explain some of the most decisive contemporary interactions with wolves.

The misunderstanding produced by a Sioux "coup" is analogous to the misunderstanding over the wolf behavior known as "surplus killing"; this term is applied when wolves attack a flock of sheep and kill many more animals than they can eat. Predators have often been found to leave four to seven dead sheep behind;[2] what shepherds see is the spectacle of a useless massacre, in which the eviscerated but uneaten corpses evoke the picture of a wolf that "kills for sport," a far cry from the wolf that is represented by its defenders as "ecological" in its management of resources. This phenomenon has been a mystery for a long time, and our ignorance of its meaning and function, added to the traumatic experience for the shepherd, has given rise to anthropomorphic condemnations: wolves are thought to be "cruel," "sadistic," "terrorists." As with Indian "coups," the impossibility of deciphering the behavior has led to an erroneous interpretation arising from a unilateral code (the anthropomorphic attribution of sadism to wolves), in other words, to unconditional condemnation on the basis of inappropriate moral judgments (cruelty as a vice). This describes the Gubbio wolf before Francis came on the scene.

A pragmatic interpretation of the Sapir-Whorf hypothesis can be brought to bear here: "The limits of your language are the limits of your world." Within our traditional language there is no way of accessing the world in which wild wolves dwell. The only way to extend our limits is to work on this language in order to draw a new map that identifies bridges and passageways where we now see only borders and broken places. Doing this work in an ethological perspective may help resolve one of the deepest mysteries at the origin of the diplomatic crisis between wolves and shepherds: surplus killing.

This behavior on the part of wolves is intelligible only in the light of an eco-evolutionist ecology: their hunting behaviors constitute relatively stereotypical behavioral sequences established on a genetic basis that have fostered their adaptation in the coevolutionary "arms race" with their *original* prey.[3] We know, for example, that the flight of prey is a *stimulus* that incites attack behavior in wolves (while it is the immobility of prey seen from behind that constitutes a stimulus for attack on the part of tigers).

Similarly, the return to calm in its environment constitutes a stimulus for stopping the killing in wolves adapted to hunting wild ungulates, at the point where a wolf is alone with the slain prey. This is attributable to the fact that wild ungulates have acquired collective defense mechanisms that consist in *dispersing* when wolves attack.

Conversely, sheep have been selected by humans to be gregarious and fearful. Their gregariousness makes a shepherd's work easier: under the influence of fear, the herd clusters together, preventing individuals from wandering away or from falling off rocky embankments. During an attack, however, the panicked sheep clustering around the initial slain prey maintain the wolf in a behavioral state that *calls for* predation, so that, owing to the maintenance of the stimulus for hunting, the situation induces further killing.[4] In their individualizing ecosystems, wolves sometimes carry out surplus killings when their wild prey are immobilized in the snow, or when they cluster in large numbers. The wolves then come back later to eat the remainder in the following days, and the prey is often shared by other predators such as coyotes, along with crows and other carrion-eaters.

As Paul Shepard describes the situation, "predator and prey are the means of a dialogue that the prairie carries on with itself."[5] This implies coevolution of intelligence in the arms race between wolves and ungulates, a phenomenon thoroughly documented by Harry J. Jerison.[6] But today's wolves, having evolved to hunt complex, intelligent game, animals with structures for flight and defense adapted to predation by wolves, now find themselves facing animals selected by humans that have evolved much more rapidly in the opposite direction, losing their former aptitude for defense and flight. Today's sheep, by their docility, gregariousness, and guilelessness, their incapacity to flee or to defend themselves, are profoundly ill-adapted to wolf hunting behavior. Artificial selection has made sheep ethologically deficient in the face of wolves. Let us note that the coevolutionary interplay of wolves and ungulates on the prairie has gone on for several million years, while domestic sheep have been evolving for only six to eight thousand years.

How Surplus Killing Reveals Our Relations with Living Beings

We can argue, then, that in its current form the *ecological relation* between sheep and wolves, in the absence of coevolution, constitutes an eco-evolutionary aberration. This claim is supported by the fact that wild sheep are not intrinsically defenseless in the face of predators: wild urial sheep, ancestors of today's sheep, were prodigious acrobats that could gambol about on rocky outcrops that are inaccessible to their predators. This is a species that has claimed rock walls as its habitat. Urial sheep fled from wolves on cliffs, while domestication has limited their domestic descendants to sites of *human* locomotion, that is, on plains—and these are *also* sites where wolves cause havoc. Human pastoralism has thus created a new conflictual relation between wolves and sheep, through a displacement of ovine populations for the convenience of their management (herding sheep whose ancestral reflexes lead them to clamber about on rocks but whose domestication has made them too fearful to come back down is one of the most complicated tasks faced by shepherds in mountainous terrains). The real origin of surplus killing, then, lies in the displacement of ovine populations onto the plains and the orchestrated loss of their defensive strategies.

The emotional intensity induced in livestock breeders by these situations then takes on another dimension: that of responsibility. Pastoralism has assumed responsibility for these animals that it has deprived of their instincts and defense mechanisms; forgetting this latter point, pastoralists believe themselves morally justified in fighting off predators, engaging in a *just war* with the enemy. Wolves call into question the model of "direct positive action" on living beings. This model, theorized by Georges Haudricourt, is directly correlated with ovine pastoralism:

> Sheep raising as it was practiced in the Mediterranean region seems to me . . . the model of direct positive action. It requires continuous contact with the domesticated being. The shepherd accompanies his flock night and day, leading it with his crook and his dogs; he has to choose grazing grounds, anticipate watering holes, carry newborn lambs over rough spots, and finally defend

his sheep against wolves. His action is direct: contact with hand or stick, clods of earth tossed with crook, dog nipping at a sheep to guide it. His action is positive: he chooses the itinerary that he imposes on his flock at all times. This can be explained either by the "overdomestication" of sheep, the tamed animals having lost their instinctive qualities of self-defense and behavior, or else by the transplantation of animals who formerly lived in mountains whose rocky cliffs protected them from wolves and whose altitude assured them of permanent access to food.[7]

The model of direct positive action implies a relation to living beings that requires, first of all, making them dependent so as to make them manageable; this induces, in a second phase, the pastoralist need to lead and protect them. Critics of the modern relation to nature condemn it as despotic control, but they rarely look far enough back to see the camouflaged prerequisites of that control: the modern relation to nature requires that the otherwise autonomous beings destined to be led and protected be heteronomized, that is, rendered eco-ethologically dependent and kept immature. This is the essence of pastoral domestication.

The dimension of responsibility implied by the model of direct positive action has been analyzed by Catherine and Raphaël Larrère in their work on the domestic contract,[8] and it presides over Raphaël Larrère's interpretation of environmental ethics in the context of the wolves' return to France.[9] This approach entails a finely graduated hierarchy of the moral obligations we have toward different types of animals, which have to be distinguished: some belong to the realm of environmental ethics (wild animals), others to the realm of breeding (domestic animals); the latter take precedence over the former, owing to the very fact of the responsibility we have contracted toward them. This is the most subtle and most realistic formulation of the problem in terms of an ethics taking into account a plurality of living beings.

But responsibility is a double-edged sword. If we are responsible for the sheep we have disarmed, we have to reckon with the fact that our war against wolves is the product of our own action. It is hard to imagine that it existed prior to pastoralism; we can assume that we humans triggered it. This is what leads Paul Shepard to hypothesize that the beginning of our war against nature can be located in the Neolithic era, understood here as the era in which pastoralism involving direct positive action developed. If we ourselves have created the ecological conditions that lead wolves to kill sheep, it becomes more difficult to justify our sacred right to *destroy* them when they do so.[10] After all, not all animal or plant domestications produce dependence and vulnerability as clearly. Haudricourt evokes an alternative model, that of indirect negative action: "not all domestic animals resemble sheep. In the Indochinese countryside, buffalo are 'guarded' by children, but a child will not defend his flock against a tiger; it is the flock, knowing how to defend itself, that will prevent the tiger from taking off with its 'guardian.'"[11]

This is a very pure inversion of the Gévaudan case, which we shall analyze later on,[12] in which the custom of letting young children guard the flocks at night catalyzes wolf attacks on humans. The inversion reveals two profoundly different relations of humans to animals, and to living beings in general. It is not a matter here of putting Neolithic pastoralism on trial, but of exploring why and how surplus killings bring to light our most ancestral relations to other living beings. A wolf's attack on sheep is not merely an emotion-arousing local drama, it is the sign of a breach in our ontological relation to living beings from time immemorial, a relation that turns out to be based on our direct positive action. This model of action, traceable to the Neolithic era but probably extending all the way to the most contemporary scientific agronomies and zootechnologies, rests on the basic idea that actively heteronomizing the other living beings of our biotic community has no long-term effects—that it is allowed by the neutral plasticity of nature. To mold an animal to one's own use, to rob it of its natural defenses for the benefit of livestock farmers, to make massive transformations in the complex relations among living beings, independently of their own spontaneous behaviors and specific requirements, becomes the natural form of human action.

At present, a whole series of agricultural initiatives, from permaculture forest-gardens to refinements of agroecology and the "revolution of a single blade of straw," seems to be converging toward a return to indirect negative action in a reaction against the green revolution, which has put technoscience at the service of direct positive action.

The fact that direct positive action has ecological consequences tends to be acknowledged only when this action takes on sufficiently massive proportions to make its effects apparent to all. But in reality such action has *never* been without consequences, in the sense that it is likely to have been the source of one of the most structuring ontological events of humanity in the Western Hemisphere: by displacing domestic animals and making them accessible to predators on the prairies, by depriving them of their defenses, direct positive action inaugurated a war against a whole series of species that did not accept the yoke of domestication; it discriminated between friends and enemies, a distinction that gives meaning to the concept of politics, for the philosopher Carl Schmitt.[13] For the heirs of this operation, through centrifugal force, pastoral metaphysics has turned nonhuman living beings into slaves, allies, or enemies.[14] Once ecological partners in the complex exchanges of life that characterized the onto-ecological forms of subsistence of hunter-gatherers, nonhuman living beings have been relegated to the category of docile resources (for example, sheep and chickens) or helpers (for example, horses and dogs), or else, deemed of no use to humans, they have been stigmatized as vermin, pests or, worse, as predators, deemed harmful to our supremacist exploitation of biotic communities.

We can recognize here a motif that has been subject to much analysis, starting with that of Lynn White Jr., on the environmental ethics that grew out of Judeo-Christianity.[15] But this discourse, perceived as original, may well be simply a late sub-product of a much older metaphysical architectonics, never written down, that was both the cause and the effect of a mutation in the ecolo-economic subsistence relations between humans and the rest of the biotic community. Metaphysics is intrinsically ecological. By coding what is domestic as a resource (and no longer a gift or an exchange), by rendering it fragile, the Neolithic era with its direct positive action triggered a conflictual relation between humans and all other living beings, coding the latter as "savage"; echoes of this conflict are still audible in the contemporary stigmatizing connotations of the word "savagery." This relation of ecological competition, of mutual harm, of resistance to the yoke, was coded early on as *war*; more recently, victory on the part of humanity has been theorized as progress and civilization. It is undoubtedly time to determine the real stakes, the errors, the misguided wanderings of this war from which we have never recovered; it is time to determine whether the war warrants continuation. For the Neolithic ended not because it took a wrong turn but because it *triumphed*. Our dominance now seems to have such potency, though, that we can allow ourselves to question its foundations. "Wild" animals have been vanquished to such an extent that we look at them today with more empathy than fear. We can also question the well-foundedness of our conflictual relation with nature, because in its latest forms this relation is unquestionably destroying the biosphere and endangering our existence on the earth: this relation thus gives us an opportunity to see, through its failure, the constructed character of our most foundational ontological map. A metaphysics can be repudiated if it renders the world uninhabitable.[16]

We can question this relation, finally, because we can seek to be something other than a species rigidified in a fundamentally aggressive-defensive attitude toward our companions in the biotic community, perversely devoted to controlling them, degrading them, destroying them, and then nostalgically regretting them. We have probably inherited this attitude of resentment toward what is wild and coded as untamed, along with the drive to control it, from ancestral traumas imposed by the environment, the result of Neolithic famines and epidemics that were induced in turn by the specialization of food supplies subject to the vagaries of climate and their effects on harvests, and by the demographic explosion. These traumas were absent during the Paleolithic era, when life expectancy was, by a strange paradox that deserves analysis, probably greater than that in the early Neolithic era.[17] These traumas probably sparked the coding of the relation to the biotic community as war with the environment: they induced the phantasmatic vision of the human past prior to civilization as original distress (something that bears very little resemblance to the lived experience of our primate cousins, or of hunter-gatherers), a condition that had to be transcended through more elaborate control of domesticated beings and firmer domination of wild ones. They introduced an existential pattern that was to become our own: that of a closed human society, stressed by ecological relations that it does not control, incapable of conceiving of its ties to other living beings except as alienating domestication, domination of the untamed, and Arcadian delight in a nature pacified by this control.

Wild and Domestic

Jocelyne Porcher is an anthropologist of animal breeding; her position on the question of cohabitation between livestock and wolves, and our moral obligations toward sheep, opens a window onto part of this pastoral metaphysics. She postulates that domestication is a contract in which the animal gives itself up, along with its freedom, wholly or in part, in exchange for certain considerations. As part of the respect farmers owe their animals, they need to ensure a better life than the animals would have had in the wild.[18] But it is already problematic for humans to claim to know that domesticated life is better for an animal than life in the wild, presumptuous to answer the question of what life is worth living on behalf of other animals. Porcher argues that animals in the category of prey spend their entire lives in fear, and that domestication ensures them *quietude*, a quality of life that justifies domestication and pays, in part, the debt owners incur for putting them to death. The return of wolves would thus prevent livestock farmers from fulfilling their part of the *contract* toward sheep, that is, providing a life of *quietude*, preferable to a life of fear. "The debt that we owe to farm animals imposes on us the need to make a choice. First respect the farmers and protect the sheep, offer them peaceful living conditions by not living in fear of wolves, and then find a place for wolves, if it is possible."[19]

There are two rather significant confusions in this reasoning. First, it is not for a sheep as such that one can choose between a wild life lived in fear of wolves and a domestic life in the peace and quiet of the stable, but rather for a sheep already transformed by that domestic life: it is the peace and quiet of the stable that has led the pugnacious wild mountain sheep to evolve into terrified prairie sheep. Wild mountain sheep certainly live on watch for wolves, but not in fear; they have instincts for flight and for self-defense; they face up to the threat. Enclosing them in confined spaces, to offer them a quietude that they have not asked for (they did not come of their own free will into the Neolithic enclosures) does not necessarily bring them better lives—if the question can even be raised in these terms. The first historical confusion thus consists in hypostatizing domestic animals, in naturalizing their dependence and their vulnerability, characteristics that would require us—if we were to adopt the most ethical attitude—to protect them from a life lived in fear of wolves; while in fact we ourselves, over several thousand years of artificial selection, have created these beings that are defenseless in the face of predators. Should we postulate that our moral duty is to lock up the antelopes and the impalas on the savanna in order to offer them a better life than the one we fantasize that they are leading in fear of lions? Our tendency to consider as natural the dependency that the Neolithic era induced in animals, and to deduce from this that we have paternalistic responsibilities, is characteristic of the pastoral metaphysics dating back to that very era.

The second historical confusion of Porcher's reasoning consists in interpreting the wolves' return as a new danger with respect to the quietude we owe sheep, a quietude attributed to the domestic contract of sheep farmers from time immemorial. But this position neglects the fact, here, that wolves were absent from the French countryside for only some fifty years, and that during around ten thousand years of pastoralism, that is, for the near-totality of its history, shepherds and sheep *cohabited* with wolves. In other words, that peaceful life of sheep protected from the threat of wolves *never* existed during the very long period of preindustrial pastoralism.

Porcher actually takes preindustrial pastoralism as her model for an ethical relation to domesticated animals. In this respect, her loud and clear voice is very important for bringing reason, human reason, back to a whole facet of breeding that has become monstrous as it has been industrialized. But where the relation of sheep to wolves is concerned, one cannot take as a model the breeding practices that prevailed prior to the industrialization of the nineteenth century and at the same time attribute to those practices virtues (protecting sheep from the fear of wolves) that never existed, and that are precisely belated corollaries of the industrial era.

Once again, we see that even in the most empathetic, the most respectful, the most ethical formulations with respect to animals, the pastoral metaphysics derived from the direct positive action practiced in the Neolithic era creeps in: here, it consists in obscuring the initial gesture through which overdomestication of certain animals deprives them of autonomy, and subsequently seeing them only as vulnerable creatures requiring human protection and guidance. Once that first gesture is concealed, the most ethical, the most decent attitude, in effect becomes that of assuming a relationship of *stewardship* toward nonhuman beings. And it makes it possible to deem that, in farming, putting an animal to death is justifiable if and only if the farmer gives the animal better living conditions than it would have in the wild. It is true, to be sure, that for most domesticated animals domestic life is better than wild life; but this is the case precisely because in these animals traits have been selected that have made them ill-adapted to living in the wild, and not because they have always been ill-adapted. Something rings false in Porcher's domestic contract: there is blindness with regard to the evolutionary dimension, a sort of ahistoric naturalization of the animals' status, resolutely wiping out the difference between wild and domestic, as if goats had been goats and sheep sheep from time immemorial.

Aside from the particular issue of the relation to predators, Porcher's stance in favor of livestock farming allows her to bring out some rather profound intuitions concerning contemporary relations to animals: "In our societies, wild/domestic representations have been inverted to a great degree. 'Wild' animals are no longer red in tooth and claw, cruel and without law, but have become free, socialized and intelligent, unlike domestic animals, who are no longer gentle and peaceful beings, but . . . imbecilic things that we can exploit like raw material. Wild animals are no longer foils, they are models."[20]

This idea points up rather well the post-Neolithic transition that we are undergoing now, and the *tensions* in it that are being revealed by the wolves' return. For, in the current conflict, the wolf-hating farmers deploy a discourse that maintains the picture of wild wolves as bloodthirsty, while domestic animals are deemed morally superior because they are tranquil, pacified, civilized. A more urban movement tends to imagine the inverse, construing wild animals as superior because they are free and pure. But these two positions, seemingly opposed in every way, are simply two sides of the same coin. The cult of wild nature has arisen as a reaction to the seeming domestication of human life by the Neolithic metaphysics, the effects of which are experienced as constraints on vital instincts. The metaphysics arising from the cult of wild nature idealizes living beings as freed of the limits seemingly imposed by a generalized pastoral history. The myth of the Wild perpetuates an obsession with the Neolithic enemy; it takes the form of a metaphysics of beings in chains who want to break out. A new ethological philosophy is required if we humans are to come to terms with our animal nature and our place in the biotic community in a new way, leaving behind both the ontological map of the Neolithic pastoral metaphysics and its belated reactive inverse, the cult of wild nature.

What makes this an extraordinarily difficult task is that those ontological maps have no "outside": a discourse on animals that would escape both of those attractors has not yet been formulated, although a few lineaments can be spotted in a-Neolithic writings and practices, by humans scattered here and there who have lived as singular animals in relation with other animals.

According to American Indians, there was nothing "savage" before white people arrived with their idea of domestication. That idea created its opposite. Before domestication, if *nothing* was "savage," what did life look like? How did its vital forces operate? Exiting from Neolithic metaphysics implies un-domesticating oneself, to be sure, but without becoming reactive savage beings, Romantic savages, neo-pagan savages versed in primal screams. In other words, without becoming the sort of savage that domesticated humans have invented. The latter valorize a shedding of constraints that is needed only by constrained beings. Undomesticated animals are wild without brutality, without constraints to shed. They are life forms devoid of chains.

Wild is the provisional label I am giving to the life form of living beings not shaped by the pastoral metaphysics: wild is the term that will characterize the mode of existence of a-Neolithic human and nonhuman animals.[21] Wild is the term for the savage expunged of the connotations of savagery, primality, and purity that the myth of the Wild has projected onto animals. Wild describes nonhuman animals as we have never known them to be, in relations to humans that have not yet been theorized, and that are certainly not relations of outside control or of self-surpassing.

Animal diplomacy is an attempt to approach the meaning of what I am calling wildness by experimenting with concrete forms of cohabitation that simultaneously avoid both the control of a dominator and the idealization of nature as a free and pure sanctuary.

We can see how the complex history of our relations to other living beings obscures the analysis that might be made of the meaning of our concrete interactions with animals, for example, in the case of surplus killing. Nevertheless, the lessons of this inquiry so far suggest that artificial selection is in large measure the cause of the eco-ethological asymmetry in the relation between wolves and sheep that lies behind surplus killing. Wolves and domesticated sheep belong to ethological systems that do not meet in equilibrium but rather in a state of reciprocal decomposition. The fact remains that contemporary livestock farmers cannot and must not be held responsible for the effects of Neolithic pastoralism: we have made sheep defenseless; we have to love them that way. In consequence, we have to find solutions that are adapted to effective cohabitation with wolves. Certain species of rustic sheep nevertheless defend themselves better against wolves. And technological developments in farming, when they are intelligently conceived and adapted to the presence of wolves (smaller flocks, increased surveillance, nocturnal grazing, defense arrangements, and so on), are capable, thanks to ten thousand years of accumulated experience, of making predation tolerable for pastoralism and of redirecting the attention of wolves toward wild prey on a broad scale. Such techniques, neglected since the eradication of wolves in the twentieth century, deserve to be resurrected, in order to reimagine a resilient pastoralism. The ethologist Jean-Marc Landry concludes: "In the face of wolves, we need to institute a system of prevention that shatters the behavior of surplus killing in order to limit the damage."[22] Experiments in diplomatic ethology that find a way to limit this phenomenon would in fact significantly limit the losses attributable to wolves and thus lower the corresponding emotional inflation. This is the archetype of a diplomatic mission.

What Does "The Savage" Become in the Anthropocene?

From an ecopolitical standpoint, the Anthropocene[23] marks the emergence of a *close and generalized* cohabitation of human societies with the other living beings. Nonhuman living beings are no longer elsewhere, in an inaccessible, intact, hostile or pure outside, that is, in a *wilderness*: they are *among us*. More than nine-tenths of the emerged lands of the planet have in effect been "anthropized." In the Anthropocene, polar bears are among us, since we are the cause of the warming that is shrinking their faraway habitats; the orcas of the North Pacific, playing in heaps of plastic debris, are among us; the Australian bats, through which the Hendra virus transits to reach us, are among us.

The concept of the Anthropocene has at least the advantage of reminding us to what extent human life is caught up in feedback loops intertwined with those of other life forms, thus making us more vividly aware of our interdependence. If there are no longer any living beings at an unbridgeable distance, left intact, does this mean that wildness has disappeared? Must we conclude that all forms of life or matter are now comparable to co-constructed hybrids, like laboratory mice or the atoms trapped in Bose-Einstein condensates—or, at best, comparable to "recalcitrants"?

It is not because wilderness has disappeared that wildness no longer exists. We need to rethink wildness so as to protect ourselves against the complacent notion that the human species has become a geographic force such that the entire planet is hybridized in relation to us, so much so that nothing is inaccessible, forbidden, or foreign to us any longer.

For there is a resistant form of wildness in the Anthropocene; it can be accessed, however, only by way of a detour—for example, by way of a cultural zone for which the naturalist opposition between nature and culture, wild and domesticated, is meaningless.

In Amerindian sign language (the vehicular language that allowed the different tribes of the Plains to communicate with one another), there is a gesture that means, translators tell us, "by oneself."[24] This same gesture is translated by "wild." It is this gesture, for us a slight thing with no past, no history, that will serve as our guide for developing the concept of wildness we need in the Anthropocene. Does "by oneself" signify "isolated," "kept at a distance"?

My hypothesis is that this formula can take on meaning for us only when we return to the biological reality of a certain overdomestication achieved through direct positive action. Indeed, in a first phase, the "by oneself" proper to wildness could be defined in contrast to this overdomestication.[25] In the latter practice, reproduction of a given species is controlled through the selection of just *one or two* isolated criteria that have advantages for a *different* species: our own. In this way, animals of the domesticated species undergo hypertrophy in certain traits, atrophy in others. This phenomenon has led, for example, to the Belgian Blue cattle, a recently developed race of bovines with hyperdeveloped musculature attributable to a mutation in the myostatin gene, a mutation carefully selected because it reduces the percentage of fat in the body and makes it possible to recuperate more fine cuts of meat in the butchering process. But calves of this variety can no longer be born without systematic caesarians (carried out laterally on standing cows, rather like unzipping a suitcase), for they can no longer pass through the cervix of the Holstein cows that serve as surrogate mothers. Biological mothers no longer bear their own calves; the mother's life is too precious. As many as ten caesarians can be carried out on a single surrogate during her lifetime.

In an initial sense, unlike their domestic counterparts, animals on their own, "by themselves," are not subject to selective pressures that benefit a *different* life form that is *exploiting* them. All selective pressures refine the undomesticated animal's features to its *own* advantage and for its own use. Thus the vigilance of antelopes is selected to benefit their own species, not to help lions.

In a second sense, wild animals on their own, unlike overdomesticated animals, are products of *creative selection*, a concept developed by Konrad Lorenz according to which every lineage of living beings, through its insertion into a biotic community, is constantly subjected to a *multiplicity* of simultaneous different and even contradictory selection processes. Domestic animals illustrate what happens when creative selection disappears: overdomestication entails hyperselection focusing on one or two traits (milk production, racing speed, production of flesh). Once the animals' survival and reproduction are guaranteed by the farmer, the deleterious pleiotropic effects of these mutations are not eliminated by natural selection. As a result, these animals can tend rapidly toward pathological phenotypes that are nonviable and profoundly ill-adapted to the wild life from which the animals originated.[26] Their resilience is radically reduced, their adaptability to other life patterns collapses, and the refinement of their social and display behaviors disappears.[27] Conversely, wild animals are subjected to multiple pressures, and their phenotype has to be understood as the virtually optimal proposition of evolution for conjugating *heterogeneous* requirements. This is, in a sense, what underlies the impression of grace and enigmatic perfection that is produced when one observes a titmouse, a wolf, or a yew. The phenotype perceived has to be understood as a creation emerging from the ecosystems traversed by the being's lineage over millions of years, in the form of a viable solution to multiple intertwined selective pressures.

Creative selection generates a supple interdependence within a complex milieu. Selective pressures are manifestations of the constitutive relations of a living being with the biotic community. These relations are multiple and intertwined in such a way that the living being is connected with numerous other living beings and phenomena: climates, parasites, other species, niche variations, beings with which it shares its food supply, its prey; beings with which it has a relation of mutuality.

Consequently, to be "by oneself" does not consist in being autonomous, in the sense of being *disconnected* from the entire biotic community, as in the modern understanding of autonomy, which is haunted by the debatable figure of the liberal imagination consisting in a pure individual free of any chains linking him to alienating affiliations. To be "by oneself" here consists in being autonomous in the sense of being *well connected* to the entire biotic community, that is, connected in a plural, resilient, viable manner in such a way as to avoid depending totally on an exploiter who selects and protects, or on a changeable resource, or on an irregular niche. The only true independence is *balanced interdependence*: an interdependence that *liberates* the being from dependence focused on a single parameter.

To sum up this "by oneself," on one's own, in English, I shall thus continue to use the term "wild," in the sense of untamed, resistant to being selected for the purposes of a different species and resistant to oversimplified selective pressures, savage but without all the connotations layered into the civilized critiques of savagery and into the Romantic sacralization of wildness.

There is, finally, a third dimension to the concept of "by oneself." To be "by oneself," on one's own, is not simply to be recalcitrant. The concept is manifested in the wild evolutionary-ecological dynamics present among us today, which do much more than "recalcitrate": *they inhabit*. Beings "on their own" inhabit territories as do their fellow living beings, including ourselves, with their own geopolitics, their own sense of territory, their own way of occupying the land, of mapping the key points, of being *at home*. It is this irreducible *inhabiting* practiced by others that is abolished when the notion of hybridity is generalized.

Cohabiting with beings "on their own" is different from claiming that everything is hybrid in nature and culture. What is at stake in this era of troubled cohabitation is precisely how to avoid obscuring or suppressing the eco-evo-ethological singularity of the life forms that are *among us by themselves*: savages without savagery. It is not because the common buzzard enters into strange mutual relations with highways, feeding on carcasses spewed out onto the shoulders and clearing the roads in the process, that buzzards become guinea pigs. It is not because blue tits actively seek out cigarette butts to make their nests—for nicotine has anti-parasitic properties that protects their eggs—that they become hybrids of humans or domestic animals. Blue tits are among us on their own.

Wildness is a process. It is a complex of eco-evolutionary dynamics whose particular feature is that they are not advantageous to anything but themselves. Wild beings are "at home" on the earth; they inhabit it in a constant and multivalent transactional and coevolutionary articulation with human life and human activities, in a multiple and vicarious interdependence, that is, a balanced interdependence that is the hidden name of independence.[28]

A wild being is thus no longer an isolated and intact being, it is rather a being that is *by itself*, that is *on its own among us*. Everything that, among us, in us, and apart from us, remains by itself, deserves a concept so it will not be rendered invisible and thus be mistreated. Let us call it wild, or cohabitant.[29]

In the metaphysics of stewardship, according to which God gave the earth to mankind, wild animals are only undesirable guests, sometimes tolerated by humans. In the Anthropocene, understood in an overly constructivist sense, wild animals are no longer anything but co-constructed hybrids lacking any real alterity. But the Anthropocene understood in the ecopolitical sense proposed here designates only the generalization of a de facto cohabitation with the life forms that are among us while remaining autonomous, independent, "other."

This Anthropocene calls for a different relation to the biotic communities, to the ecological assemblages of species that are on the margins of the dominant economic relations of exploitation or production, and thus scarcely coded as resources, once called savage, or harmful. What is called for now is to recode them as cohabitants, and guests, knowing that we ourselves are not hosts but rather *fellow guests*. We are all, we and they, heterotrophic and autotrophic, *invited guests* at the table of the sun, since that star supplies all the energy here below. Devouring sun-energy is the original ecological problem of every living being. But when eco-evolution has dispersed the genetic flows into infinitely varied species inclined to eat one another, combined in multiple niches that are nevertheless superimposed on the same space, the eco-evolutionary problem has become that of *sharing the sun*. From this standpoint, wolves, deer, beech groves, and perhaps even entire ecological systems are caught up in constitutive relationships: they are diplomatic partners that cohabit with us from the standpoint of their own geopolitics, in this age-old enterprise of living beings caught up in eco-evolution.

Wild beings in our current era, stripped of the trappings of savagery and isolation, thus emerge as *among us by themselves*. Every being that is among us by itself is wild; all such beings call on us to look at them and relate to them in new ways. This is what I call *diplomacy*. Animal diplomacy[30] can be presented as another paradigm for relations to biotic communities (including indiscriminately the synanthropic and wild species, but not directly the domesticated species) in the Anthropocene era. If wildness is by itself among us, we can no longer keep it as a difference, nor can we sanctify it, just as we can no longer justify controlling it or heteronomizing it in order to dominate it. We have to cohabit with it in all its difference: we have to practice diplomacy. Because we are necessarily in contact with wild beings, but because they are by themselves, diplomacy appears to be a modality of relationship particularly well adapted to this new manner of inhabiting territories together.

This new manner begins with the recognition that certain living beings have a quite particular manner of being among us: the feral manner. This is the case of wolves. A wolf is an Anthropocenic animal par excellence. The problem of cohabitation with it is emblematic of the ecopolitics required for tomorrow.

First, because "he who can do the most can do the least": if we succeed in cohabiting with the most stigmatized, the most hated, the most terrifying beings, the hardest to manage, our clearest rivals in the trophic pyramid, then we *shall be able* to cohabit with the others. Then, because wolves are the archetypes of the harmful, and as such they challenge our construction of living beings as beings that must serve us or else *disappear*. And also because they are hardest to control: cryptic animals, invisible, dispersers, incredibly mobile, and tireless colonizers of new territories as well.

Finally, because they have long embodied a certain myth of wilderness, and because their actual behavior, as interstitial animals that make their dens in our hollows and our fallow lands, hints at how we might exit from that myth, in order to redirect our conception of separate coexistence with wild life in terms of diplomatic cohabitation.

Acting on Behavior

Living by Focusing on Tigers: An Example of Ethosophic Cohabitation

Insertion in a large predator's ethogram is a human technique for communication, for luring, or for dialogue; it has been used in various cases of territorial conflict with animals, in order to make cohabitation possible.

An example of this asymmetric communication can be found in a masquerade played out in the Sundarbans region of India. This area, consisting of mangroves at the mouth of the Brahmaputra River, has been invaded by the last surviving man-eating tigers. The behavior of these felines—their taste for human flesh—remains unexplained.

Several dissuasive methods have been tested in order to preserve the human inhabitants of the region.[31] In 1987, an initiative was proposed to limit the dangers during humans' displacements in nature. The tiger should be conceived here as an avatar—in the Hindu sense of incarnation—of the wolf of Gubbio. The presence of these large predators that attack and terrorize the outskirts of human cities calls for a new diplomatic initiative.

Saints being in short supply, ethology comes into play to formulate a diplomatic mission. The goal is to pinpoint a common code for the purpose of making peace, but this time using a mode of communication that is the inverse of Francis's, namely, deception. It has been established empirically that tigers tend to attack prey seen from behind. In ethological terms, this observation can be translated as follows: the behavior of distancing, or the presentation of the back of a neck, constitutes a *stimulus* that incites an attack. (While this presentation does not necessarily trigger an attack, its absence seems to inhibit attack to a significant extent.) Analogous forms of this behavioral schema are found among other large predators.

The ethological ruse thus consists in *depriving* the tiger of his stimulus to attack. If we observe the human body from a predator's viewpoint, the silhouette is virtually identical from the front and the back; it is extremely hard to tell the difference. The sole distinguishing feature is the face, which contrasts with the back of the head through its color and its texture (skin versus hair) and through the geometric facial features inscribed on it. Developmental psychology has amply shown that human infants recognize the face as a structure, independently of the support: it constitutes a *Gestalt*, so much so that a sketch presenting two circles and a straight line automatically "makes" a face for the human brain. Sensitivity to the structure of a face also seems to be present in predators: a "facelike" arrangement constitutes a *Gestalt*, a pregnant form that enters the brain's window of perception. Seeing it as a telling form against an indeterminate background, a predator can decode its meaning. We can hypothesize what this means to an opportunistic predator: the prey is "facing off," preparing to defend itself; to attack will require an expenditure of energy and impose a situation of risk. In fact, we know that tigers succeed in actually killing only a small fraction of the prey they hunt.

Figure 8. Three Woodsmen: The Were-tigers of the Brahmaputra Region

Several stories told by inhabitants stress the way masks work like "charms"; they say that the tigers they meet follow them for a time and then become obviously confused and demoralized by the trick, and they retreat back to the jungle. It is impossible to imagine the tiger's perplexity after he has circled, camouflaged in tall grass, around a woodcutter, patiently carrying out his hunting ruse only to find himself once again confronted by a face.

Credit: Photograph Éditions Wild Project

Thus the ethological ruse of our diplomats acts out the Hegelian definition of technology, which "turns nature against itself": it consists in placing a *mask* over the head of a passerby, a fisherman, a woodsman, that gives him eyes in the back of his head.

This quite inexpensive initiative, generalized to an entire population, seems to have had a non-negligeable effect, for tiger attacks decreased significantly during the period under study.[32]

This initiative is potentially of great ethological value: neither guns nor traps but *masks* become the zoocephalic diplomat's improbable defense weapon against tigers, because these simple objects fit elegantly into the tiger's ethogram. Thanks to what has been learned about tigers' attacking behavior, face masks produce a maximum of pragmatic, ecological, and political effects with a minimum of force.[33]

The Diplomatic Competencies of Wolves

To address the challenge of comprehending animal behavior, I propose the following hypothesis: the fact that we share the same genetic history (as mammals) and specific ecological conditions (as carnivores with complex hunting behaviors, and thus with intelligence and sociality) implies broad swaths of common life, and makes it likely that we share certain common categories. On the practical level that is our focus here, the most telling example lies in the category of *territory*, which we can presume to be shared—not in the form of ideas but rather as customary ways of proceeding, or vital practices—in the ethograms of different but related species, including humans. In this regard we can draw a mammomorphic analogy between the phenomenal and vocal territorial markings of wolves, the trail signs left by bonobos,[34] the sonic territories marked out by sparrow songs, and the practices of natural signs left by humans (stone mounds, knotted branches, rock formations such as Inuit *inuksuit*, and so on).

A diplomatic mission situated at the border between the animal and the human worlds must thus be able to engage in dialogue from a position of strength starting from shared categories. Wolves do not recognize physical barriers (highways, fences); these do not constitute stimuli adapted to their perceptual window and are not decipherable in the categories they possess and comprehend, any more than they understand the boundaries of a national park. But wolves do possess and comprehend the category of territory, in the sense that they possess a way of life with customary behaviors and practices that delimit, mark out, and isolate a given territory in the abstract space of the environment, distinguishing its inside from its outside. We can take this, then, as the first key diplomatic competence of wolves. It is omnipresent in the wolf ethogram, where it has a structuring function: wolves constantly patrol their own territorial borders. "Territoriality is a very special form of contest, in which the animal need win only once or a relatively few times. Consequently, the resident expends far less energy than would be the case if it were forced into a confrontation each time it attempted to eat in the presence of a conspecific animal."[35]

This definition of behavioral ecology contains the essence of the diplomatic method applied to wolf predation on sheep: once territoriality has symbolically imposed some form of pact and agreement, it limits actual conflicts and the intensity of the energy that would be expended in a foot-by-foot defense of the resource. The diplomatic ideal comes down to signifying territoriality so forcefully that constant confrontation is spontaneously inhibited—exactly as this occurs in the animal world, between wolf packs, for example, when territoriality is established. In an initiative undertaken by biologist Dave Ausband, this idea has been applied to the practical management of wolf packs by establishing invisible boundaries of smells that mimic the presence of a rival pack.[36] These borders effectively *structure* the wolves' geopolitical space by limiting border crossings by members of other packs present in the area. This experimental initiative with its astonishing results is the archetype of a diplomatic approach; we shall analyze it and its philosophical implications later on.

Territory is a category shared by wolf and human ethograms. We can even hypothesize that our conceptual representations of property, borders, land registers, and geopolitical territories are simply refinements developed in the course of evolutionary divergences and cultural radiations, on the basis of "territory," a matricial ethological category shared from time immemorial.[37] It is a fundamental category of the prehuman and literally lycanthropic language that brings together the categories shared by the wolf and human ethograms—a were-language, as it were. We share categories and ways of signifying. We ought to be able to use them.

The question, then, is how to let a wolf know what the limits of his territory are, *just as one pack signifies the limits of its territory to other packs*. And we need to do this in a more complex way: because our territories overlap, we have to be able to signify to wolves the limits in the *uses* of those territories.[38] Not by default, but precisely because it is a type of limit that wolves understand: any other measure would be bound to fail, because it would not be using the right language.

The second key diplomatic competence of wolves, beyond their capacity to decode and respect territorial limits, is their inductive intelligence. It has been demonstrated that wolves are sensitive to punishment, in the sense that they never allow themselves to be caught a second time in the same trap; they never repeat a dangerous act. This is what allows us to demonstrate that wolves are very sensitive to the operant conditioning that Pavlov discovered in domestic animals, a sensitivity that must have originated in their wild ancestors.

A wolf is a very inductive and thus prudent predator. This means that it is constantly learning from experience: it remembers associations between *stimuli* and orients its behavior in relation to this acquired information.[39]

This inductive intelligence is of particular interest, in part because it was discovered relatively recently, and because it stands in contrast with the characterization of animal life that has prevailed at least in the West since

Credit: Anonymous engraving

Figure 9. Georges Leroy: The Diplomat of the Animal Enlightenment

A hunter and a philosopher, Georges Leroy contributed to the *Encyclopedia* being prepared by Denis Diderot and Jean le Rond d'Alembert, with articles on topics such as falconry, instinct, and mankind (moral). In 1768, under the pseudonym "Naturalist from Nuremberg," he published a collection of essays on animals, *The Intelligence and Perfectibility of Animals from a Philosophic Point of View*, in which he explored the forms of animal intelligence in relation to their various ecological lifestyles. "The continual necessity of rapine, the habit of bloodshed, and the daily feeding on the torn and bleeding carcasses of animals, seem unlikely to give the wolf a very interesting moral character; and yet, except in cases of rivalry in love, wolves do not appear to be actually cruel to one another. During the time of their association they defend one another, and the maternal tenderness of the she-wolf is so intense as to render her wholly insensible to danger" (26–27). Leroy speculates that the form of intelligence he detects in wolves originated in the diversity of collaborations among individuals, a diversity that tends to generate new ideas on a continuing basis. Contrasting herbivores to wolves, Leroy uses the example of stags: "The stag is one of those animals which, by constitution and the natural inclinations resulting therefrom, by their food, and their relations with others, are not thrown in the way of acquiring many ideas. The stag has no difficulties to surmount in procuring his food. . . . neither love, nor the societies into which they form themselves during the winter, are to them very fertile sources of ideas (38, 41). Leroy's magistral intuition was that ecological situations (mode of nutrition, social relationships) imply differing developments of cognitive activity.

the modern era began. One way to think about this contrast is to consider a tautological reminder present in the French language: *la bêtise de la bête*, the stupidity of beasts.

This formulation implies that beasts are mechanistic creatures incapable of intelligent learning. Until quite recently, the seemingly limpid but in fact obscure category of "instinct"[40] has allowed partisans of a radical distinction between humans and animals to grant the latter a certain intelligence on the one hand (nest construction, hunting strategies), while denying it on the other (as innate behaviors, instincts for nesting, hunting, and the like are automatic programs for action devoid of intelligence; they are genetically coded adaptations).

By abandoning the concept of instinct and by highlighting the difference between inherited behavioral sequences and individual and cultural inventions, along with the hybridizations between these two factors that constitute the hidden core of behavior, contemporary ethology has amply demonstrated the presence of inductive learning among nonhuman animals.

The problem comes down to communicating what has been acquired through learning structures established in genomes. The capacity for inductive learning is an inherited structure specific to wolves; it is possible and desirable for humans to exploit that capacity not to tame or domesticate wolves but to signify various limits to them and to teach them to make certain associations.

This possibility is what led Antoine Nochy, Jean-Jacques Blanchon, and Jacques Deschamps to develop the outline of a new plan for managing wild wolves in France:

> To the extent that wolves are ubiquitous, with an incredible plasticity of adaptation, it is time to understand that we have to enter into relations with them to bring about an evolution in their behavior. And the key element in the evolution of wolves—and wolf packs—entails intervening specifically in situations that disturb our society. In other words, [we ought] to fire on them only in a situation of attack. And to stop shooting "from far away and from nowhere." What happens to a single wolf happens to the pack, which has its own experience and culture. The use of scientific trapping would allow the services of the State to stop shooting systematically outside of contexts of attack, and, through capture, finally put the State back in the position of political manager of wolves and make it a producer of essential biological knowledge about animals that could

change their behavior in relation to that of humans and of the resources in the territory they occupy. When that happens, it will be a matter of protecting human territories and signifying this to the wolves.[41]

Guns can be a solution to the problem of signifying territorial boundaries only if one can be sure that the wolf in question is effectively terrorized, and that the shooting is firmly linked cognitively by the wolf to the attack.

The problem then becomes one of "changing the animal's behavior."[42] This ethologically fecund option has remained obscured by the ancient way of conceiving of animals and mapping their place in nature, a conception that closed off several paths for action. From that traditional standpoint, a machine-beast cannot be taught; indeed, a wild animal, sacred in itself, *must not* be educated: it would be desecration, domestication, to seek to change its behavior. It is only when wild wolves are conceived as eco-ethological partners, their mode of existence as just one among many, in a nature in which we humans, too, strive to participate, that one can develop the idea of transforming their behavior through teaching: through the biomorphic window that is the common zone we share.

To do this, pursuing our search for a common code, we need to have stimuli that wolves are capable of understanding and associating with limits.

A Range of Defensive Measures to Try Experimentally

These two diplomatic competencies, wolves' grasp of territorial limits and their inductive intelligence, allow us to envision practical measures that fit into the wolf ethogram.

One such measure consists in nonlethal capture: catch-and-release.[43] In the present case, this measure amounts to capturing wolves in the vicinity of flocks of sheep at the moment of their attempted attack, using "easy-grip" traps equipped with protective rubber coating. The wolves are then released immediately onto the site, after being fitted with a GPS collar and after biological indices have been collected noninvasively to evaluate their state of health, individual identity, and diet. This approach has a quadruple advantage: it triggers a trauma in the captured wolf that will constitute a powerful deterrent to intruding on the territory of flocks of sheep; since it is not lethal, it allows the wolf, once released, to transmit its experience to the pack it is rejoining; it also allows us, by way of the geolocalization device, to obtain reliable scientific information about an animal with whose behaviors we are no longer familiar; finally, it makes it possible to pinpoint any individual wolf that continues to attack the flocks despite the trauma induced by capture and to set up preventive arrangements targeting the particular animal that has made sheep its habitual prey, and not just any wolf at random, as the latter approach risks fragmenting the pack.

In the long run, this multifunctional arrangement has a precise goal: getting wolves to avoid the zones of livestock farming that have been rendered unfavorable by the defensive measures: "It is a matter of intervening and entering into relations with the animal precisely and systematically in the situations that disturb society—essentially when flocks are being attacked—so as to make the animal's behavior evolve, by rendering hostile the immediate perimeter where human activities are taking place."[44]

The effectiveness of this initiative to limit attacks has not been definitively established, but there are good reasons to believe it can play a significant role in keeping wolf packs from coming too close to flocks. Above all, it permits the development of knowledge that is lacking today about the distribution, the way of life, the ecological dynamics of these animals, and their way of establishing their territories among us.

But a whole series of experiments remains to be imagined and assessed from the perspective of zoocephalic diplomacy. The most ecologically effective initiatives have probably not yet seen the light of day. Jean-Marc Landry's work, remarkable in its ethological finesse in this connection, is currently being tested: members of a flock of sheep are fitted with a repellent device (chemical or auditory) that is triggered by a rise in the animal's heart rate. The point is to teach the wolf by operant conditioning to experience a sort of fear of the flock.[45]

The ethological principle behind this experiment is based on lycocephalic reasoning that follows very closely what might be taking place in a wolf's mind. Landry, putting himself in the place of a wolf, within its internal history of learning from experience, understands, first of all, that a simple experience of fright will not suffice, for the wolf will not associate the incident with the flock. Wolves cannot be taught to fear sheep, for they are already familiar with them and know that they can approach them without risk. Frightening a wolf once will not make up for all the times in the past where it has been able to approach a flock without being harmed. Landry's hypothesis is that a new stimulus must be created, diffuse and of unknown origin for the wolf, but associated with the flock in a steady and continuous fashion (the "discriminating stimulus" might be a yellow scarf around the neck of every tenth sheep, associated, for example, with a permanent ultrasonic stimulus diffused by a collar). The discriminating stimulus will allow the wolf to make a connection between *this* yellow flock and the terrifying stimulus, whatever it may be, every time it approaches the flock, so that the wolf will associate the discriminating stimulus with the terrifying stimulus. Every flock with yellow scarves will remind it of the past shocking experience. The expectation is that this arrangement will become embedded in the wolf's way of reckoning with the world. The technical feasibility of this approach remains problematic, however, which is why this type of experimentation has to be supported and expanded.

At the same time, to gain a better understanding of the relations between wolves and flocks in the French context, Landry has launched a long-term research project, the CanOvis initiative.[46] It rests on a protocol for capturing previously invisible data that involved using nocturnal video equipment (for 188 nights in all) near flocks in zones where predation is common. This project is a diplomatic enterprise aimed at understanding the real-life complex interactions between a flock, guard dogs, and wolves: "In varied and complementary contexts, the first two seasons of observation have allowed us, *by having access to the night world,* to document a large number of particularly interesting situations, even highly unusual ones, given the current state of knowledge on the subject." These data ought to make it possible, little by little, to "build a new way of looking at flock protection and wolf behavior (predatory or not)."[47]

Some of the data concerning the behavior of wolves in contact with flocks are particularly intriguing. First, it becomes clear that wolves "occupy the territory."[48] Packs quite often regularly pass peacefully in the vicinity of flocks, and the flocks show little interest. This phenomenon challenges the stereotypical picture of a starving wolf that cannot prevent itself from devouring the first sheep in sight. Thus predation appears to be a deliberate operation, requiring particular conditions—and it is on these conditions that researchers need to focus.

More importantly, the wolves that do attack flocks seem to do so not as part of a pack but alone or in pairs. These wolves concentrate on a flock for hours on end, scrutinizing it and biding their time. They make repeated attempts to attack, often unsuccessfully. The dogs drive them off but do not dissuade them: in other words, they keep the wolves at a distance by their action, but they never produce a sufficiently disagreeable stimulus to induce, through negative reinforcement, a tendency in wolves to *remain* far from the flocks.

Finally, the wolves involved in attacks seem to be mainly young ones (this can be observed on one of the videos on the IPRA site): "Certain wolves seem inexperienced: among these insistent wolves, most appear bold but ultimately not very effective."[49] This is one of the hypotheses to be explored. If confirmed, a discovery of this sort would allow us to look at the problem of culling in a different, ethologically informed way. Landry in fact shows the dangerous character of random culling. Let us take a so-called complex wolf pack, consisting of three generations: the breeding pair, the offspring of previous years, and the current year's cubs.[50] Taking out the cubs has no effect on predation. Killing one of the parents introduces the risk of fragmenting the pack and thus of multiplying individual raids on the flock by wandering young wolves deprived of collective hunting tactics: "loss of parental hunting experience," "destructurization," "increase in dispersers, increase in breeding pairs."[51] If young, immature apprentice wolves are the ones who indeed produce depredations among sheep, then these are the ones who ought to be targeted specifically for culling, for they establish behavior patterns that may well last and be transmitted to subsequent generations.

The question of defensive measures then becomes much more pointed. It becomes a matter of looking for *dissuasive* measures explicitly adapted to wolves that are solitary, probably immature and inexperienced, measures that will not only drive the wolves away physically on a given occasion but will also discourage their interest in flocks on a lasting basis.

Landry shows, moreover, that the number of wolves *is not* a factor in the amount of depredation: according to him, the number of wolves present is ultimately not correlated with the number of attacks.[52] This is an interesting point, in that it contests the logic of the current management strategy, which postulates that culling an arbitrary number of wolves each year (thirty-six in 2015) will mathematically lower the number of sheep killed. This logic appears to ignore the complexity of the phenomenon.

The remaining problem lies in the capacity of wolves to become habituated to repellents. After a few unsuccessful attempts, they spot the mechanism, observe that no harm comes to them, and take the risk of returning to the attack. A shepherd from the Var region has described the series of initiatives he tried: putting perfume on the sheep, leaving a radio on all night, remaining present himself, and setting off firecrackers. Each of these tactics worked for a while, until the wolf or wolves in question became aware of the deception and outfoxed the shepherd.[53]

In an important article, conservation biologist John Shivik and his collaborators show how nonlethal techniques of pack management are nevertheless superior to lethal ones in several respects: theirs is a strictly diplomatic argument.[54] First of all, nonlethal techniques prevent the counterproductive collateral effects described earlier. By maintaining the social structure of the packs, they preserve the wolves' territoriality, thus potentially inhibiting other predators, including other wolves or stray dogs, from coming in to attack the flocks. Above all, these nonlethal tactics favor the cultural apprenticeship by means of which wolves transmit their distancing behavior with regard to flocks from one generation to the next.

Drawing on experimental data, the authors also show the effectiveness of a defense mechanism that produces very strong light and random stressful noises (some thirty different recorded sounds are used, to maintain the effect of neophobia—wolves fear what they do not recognize—and to prevent habituation) when the presence of a predator is detected in a given zone. This arrangement, known as Movement Activated Guard (MAG), if it were adapted to French conditions, could contribute further to limiting predation. To be sure, these methods require experimentation and effort on the part of farmers, and they incur costs.

If it is excessive, then, to claim that the presence of wolves irremediably condemns ovine pastoralism (sheep and wolves have cohabited, after all, for the last eight thousand years), it would be complacent to suppose that the presence of wolves does not imply a significant transformation of technical practices and tools. In the current difficult socioeconomic situation of sheep farmers in France, it is understandable that the need to change is particularly burdensome: the conception of living beings that prevails in our societies does not easily accommodate the notion that an animal can force workers to change their manner of working. Still, it is not fair to place all the responsibility for the sheep-raising crisis, or the social crisis in ovine pastoralism, on wolves, for these crises arose before wolves returned to France.

There are still questions to be answered concerning the effective potential of a given measure to frighten wolves (how many times must the conditioning be repeated to be operative?), the extension of the induced behavior (does the wolf associate the fright with the attack, with the flock, with all flocks? What rule for behavior does the measure create in the wolf's mind, in terms of cognitive ethology?), and the duration of the measure's effectiveness (how much time does the wolf need to learn that the measure is a repellent?).

Credit: Photograph Éditions Wild Project

Figure 10. Jean-Marc Landry: The Diplomat Specializing in Subtle Stimuli

What Jean-Marc Landry has isolated in his experimental work on defense measures is the need to take into account, simultaneously, a behaviorist approach that does justice to the power of conditioning and a mentalist approach that credits wolves' intelligence and memory. If wolves have a long experience of tranquil proximity to flocks, how can a frightening experience distance them? With what will they associate that experience? This is where the idea of *discriminating stimuli* comes in.

Inventing Defensive Measures: What Superstimuli for Wolves?

The theoretical problem that unifies these experiments comes down to learning with precision what constitutes a territory for wolves themselves, how they see it, think it, experience it, so as to experiment further not only with stimuli but with "superstimuli" that can interact even more effectively with the animals.

The concept of superstimulus has been proposed by Niko Tinbergen in a monograph on herring gulls.[55] By carrying out experiments on young gulls, he discovered that the most effective perceptible sign to incite begging behavior was not the image of the mother's head itself, but an abstract geometric combination that accentuated the significant aspects of that image (contrast, form, position), in this instance, a thin stick with two black lines at its tip (accentuating the contrast with the red dot at the end of the gull's beak, a reference point for begging behavior). This stick brought forth more begging behavior on the part of young gulls *than the mother's beak itself.* This is an example of the sort of superstimulus that will have to be devised and tested in order to interact with wolves according to their own ethological code.

It is a question of opening of a space for experimenting with defensive measures[56] that are not necessarily lethal. Such measures must be based on superstimuli to convey meaning and to become imprinted; they must produce effective experiences of fright and deep associations of ideas. It will be important to test multiple techniques so as to compare them, try them in combination, isolate the most effective and economical methods. Certain techniques have already been tried by shepherds, but these empirical tests need to be replaced by more efficient experimental protocols. A synthesis of calls by the dominating pack, a synthesis of pheromones worn on sheep collars or located near a flock, defensive collars filled with pepper worn by one sheep out of ten, ultrasound sirens, portable megaphones activated at the moment of an attack when the dogs start to bark, light-shedding flares, salt-pellet-shooting rifles, and so on: the goal of this diplomatic experimentation is to invent integrated technologies that would solve several problems at once and could be inserted intelligently into farmers' practices and into the biodiversity that supports these practices.

These defensive measures need not be lethal. For legal reasons, in the first place, and also for moral reasons, but above all for practical reasons—for nonlethal frightening is the only way to spread the message in a profoundly social species that is capable of collective learning. In the absence of additional data, we must provisionally accept the empirical rule according to which *what one wolf knows, the whole pack knows.*[57] As it happens, in a pack the cubs learning hunting culture today are the dispersers of tomorrow and thus the future alpha wolves, hunt leaders, and teachers of the next generation, which will disperse once again. Nonlethal defensive measures would thus allow for spontaneous diffusion of the solution by the natural world itself, with no need for a constant defense, like the one required by water pressure on a dam, to be imposed on animals construed as machines and deemed incapable of understanding or learning: it would be a matter of allowing the social dynamic of wolves to spread the message. It is very unlikely, of course, that this approach would eliminate all attacks, for the wolves will try again if they sense a breach, but it could limit attacks enough to lower the pressure on shepherds so that cohabitation would be conceivable. Shepherds need means to signify to wolves the limits of their hunting territory. Wolves are opportunistic: if attacking sheep becomes painful, frightening, traumatizing, they will attack wild prey instead; it will be more strenuous, but safer. In other words, the goal is to transform the cynegetic cultures of packs toward a virtually exclusive hunt for wild prey. Do such hunting cultures exist, or are they only a figment of human imagination? This question requires an epistemological detour concerning the forms of human knowledge about animal knowledge. This will be the object of part 2 of the present book.

Chapter 4

Animal Political Philosophy

Diplomatic ethology is not solely a matter of finding practical ways to manage human interactions with wild animals; it also allows us to formulate problems of political philosophy that pertain to human-animal relations. And taking a detour through political philosophy will in turn help us identify the most appropriate technical solutions to the problems that arise in concrete relations between human actors and the wolves that have reappeared in France, solutions of which biofences, or "odor barriers," will serve as the paradigm.

One way of approaching the philosophical dimension of human-animal conflicts is genealogical: the contemporary problematics surrounding human-animal relations can be said to result from the dispersal of nonhuman animals into spheres previously considered exclusively human (morality, law, politics), a dispersal analogous to that of wolves into French territory.[1]

By the end of the twentieth century, spurred by the work of researchers such as Peter Singer[2] and pressure from animal protection associations, nonhuman animals had entered into the sphere of morality: owing to their ability to suffer pain and to receive benefits, they became moral patients requiring consideration as such. This access to a sphere previously reserved for humans opened up a breach through which animals have colonized the realm of law, owing in large part to the work of Tom Regan, who conceptualizes mammals as "subjects of a life."[3] This encroachment on the realm of law then opened up a new breach through which animals have entered politics: moving beyond passive measures of legal protection, defenders have claimed active rights as political subjects on animals' behalf; in *Zoopolis*, for example, Sue Donaldson and Will Kymlicka have developed the notion of "animal citizenship."[4]

The question then becomes: Up to what point will the animals follow us onto the Ark so we can "save" them? And must *they* follow *us*, or must *we* exit from the Ark in some fashion? For the question of animals' access to the political sphere raises conceptual problems that appear insurmountable.

The fact is that the conceptual apparatus of modern political philosophy stipulates that, for access to the status of political subject, one must proceed by way of a contract. Now, a contract requires speech acts to express demands and negotiate status. The struggles for the emancipation of minorities over the centuries have relied on this approach: the *empowerment* of minorities has allowed them, by making vigorous use of speech acts, to stake a claim to civil rights *on their own behalf*, and thus has enabled them to enter politics. As Gilles Deleuze has argued, the vicissitudes of these movements have shown "the indignity of speaking for others."[5]

Here is where the aporia of the introduction of animals into politics becomes visible: nonhuman animals cannot *speak* for themselves. The risk is thus that ventriloquism will persist: humans will continue to speak for animals, granting them political status while continuing to maintain them *in their place*. This objection has already been raised to some of the approaches we have considered, even though the objection does not challenge the relevance of those theoretical efforts to advance through a whole series of fundamental problems (from everyday relations to domestic animals to the conditions of breeding and slaughtering). *Zoopolis* is in this respect at one and the same time the generous pinnacle and the ventriloqual limit of the project that consists in granting animals civil rights and a citizenship that they do not claim for themselves, that is, emancipating them behind their backs.[6]

Power Relations or Legal Relations

As a way of bringing animals into politics, a wholly different approach can be imagined: rather than imposing on them the conceptual structures of human politics, one could join them in the interactions of *animal politics*. Such an approach entails calling into question the claim that one must enter into a contract in order to acquire civil status.

To make the paradox of *diplomacy with wild beings* thinkable, we need to untangle the entire conceptual apparatus of modern political philosophy. As we have seen, this philosophy equates contracts with logos, making it possible to establish legal relations as the sole alternative to power relations. Western modernity is based on a dichotomy: the relation to another being may be grounded in law or in power; there is no third way. A legal relation comes about with beings that are capable of recognizing and following conventions and rules formulated in words, that is, with human beings exclusively. A power relation operates where all other beings are concerned: those that do not speak can only be encountered in a generalized struggle governed by what is depicted in caricatures of Darwinism as the law of the jungle. "Survival of the fittest" is the name of this power relation, the exclusive relation with all those that do not understand law. The mytheme of the "progress of civilization" that prevails in our societies can be summed up by this dynamic: it anticipates continuing human victories on the front of power relations directed *against nonhumans*, in an exercise of power that is *justified* by the need to maximize legal relations *among humans*. The motif of the "war against nature" among the Moderns, projected into the past all the way back to the Neolithic and fantasized as emancipation, via a technological struggle, from an original state of distress, arises from this *dichotomy in all relations to an other* that is constitutive of our political ontology.

This dichotomy is the basis of the ontological error on the part of the Moderns with regard to animals, and the goal of the present chapter is to show how the dichotomy functions with regard to wolves. Wolves do not speak and do not enter into contracts, in the sense of the social contract, but we are nevertheless not condemned to relate to them solely in terms of power. The alternative lies in "animal diplomacy," in the philosophical sense being elaborated here.

Contemporary ethology and eco-evolution have begun to demonstrate that relations among nonhuman animals themselves are not limited to power relations, to struggles for survival. Political relations between human and nonhuman animals can exist because, in the animal world, conventions, symbols, and geopolitics exist—in a nonmetaphorical sense, as we shall see.

Once the existence of these phenomena has been demonstrated, it is no longer appropriate to impose the conceptual apparatus of modern political philosophy on the animal world; rather, we can enter into a form of political relations with animals that coincides with their own political forms. We can animalize politics: this is what animal diplomacy means. It is a different way of bringing animals into politics, while at the same time bringing human animals, symmetrically, into the Great Politics of the biotic community.

For while wolves do not enter into contracts, they nevertheless have political—that is, symbolic—behaviors; they have geopolitical behaviors through which they establish boundaries and hierarchies; they have *conventional* intra- and interspecies behaviors. If animal diplomacy is not to be merely a metaphor, the analogy has to be operative, that is, it has to bear on the critical points of the phenomenon under consideration. The type of diplomatic relation one can have with animals must of course include the possibility of communication, as we saw in chapter 2 (palavers), but it must also entail the possibility of *conventional* relations among the entities involved (wolf packs), in a biomorphic sense that we shall seek to pin down.[7]

The Symbolic Lives of the Other Animals

Wolves are animals that manifest conventional behaviors in the sense that they understand limits that have a symbolic dimension: they interact with these limits, and they are capable of producing such limits themselves. The scientific advances of cognitive ethology and ecology, articulated with the urgent questions of conservation biology, are making it possible to draw a new map of the Western world in its relations with animals.

Beginning with the works of Rudolph Schenkel[8] and continuing through abundant refinements, wolf ecology has shown that the act of feeding is eminently ritualized in wolves. Whereas each individual in the same pack can in principle feast anarchically, that is, in no prescribed order, on flesh won in a hunt, there is in fact a complex etiquette through which each one inhibits the expression of personal hunger and waits his or her turn, without it being necessary every time for the dominant members to claim their priority by a direct assertion of power (even though ritualized gestures of dominance and submission are frequently repeated in order to reaffirm the hierarchy). The belief according to which dominant wolves are always "alphas" that have won their supremacy by force is a bias induced by observation of packs that have been artificially reconstituted; in fact, the dominant wolves are most often the breeding pair.[9] The ritualized gestures within a pack show the existence of an animal etiquette in its conventional and symbolic dimensions; they make visible the capacity of wolves to react to information that has been retained in memory and *established as rules*, as behavioral norms; this is quite different from a power relation constantly brought back into play by confrontation. The field of rules and norms, in a sense other than, but homologous to, the human sense, is extending its horizon to include nonhuman animals.

Animal Heraldry

At the other extreme from the metabolic processes of wolves, we find an even more decisive manifestation of their symbolic life: the practice of marking via excrements (urine and fecal matter) and glandular secretions sets up signals that communicate with wolves in other packs and with animals of other species.

During a tracking session in Hautes-Alpes in the winter of 2015, I discovered a wolf trail by associating a cluster of indices that allowed me to identify it: a rectilinear path, massive lozenge-shaped footprints made with powerful claws, and, further on, the droppings of a large canid, in which fragments of bone and ungulate pelt were all clumped together. It was noteworthy that these leavings were deposited on the path with extraordinary regularity, roughly every sixty to one hundred meters, in small amounts.

The symbolic function—here, territorial—of these droppings is clear: wolves excrete symbolic matter as if they are acting according to a geopolitical aim of sovereignty that allows them to express the limits of their territory without getting involved in actual conflict. It must be noted that alongside every third pile, roughly speaking, a few centimeters away, various mustelids (weasels and skunks, probably) leave their own droppings, as if in a dialogue between flags, from one frontier outpost to another. We have lacked the skills to translate. To the extent that wolves' territories overlap readily with those of mustelids, and to the extent that the territories of wolf packs are exclusive only in relation to other wolves, these droppings point to a complex geopolitics in which each dropping signifies different things to different readers.

Thus a wolf of the same pack sees a mark that he is on his home ground, as he presumably acquires information, to varying degrees, about the identity, age, sex, sexual availability, health, and even emotional state of the previous wolf, and identifies the regime of a littermate. A wolf from a rival pack sees an area marker that must not be crossed on pain of death. Most of the time, a "foreign" wolf will stop in front of that immaterial boundary—invisible to us—and then run along a parallel borderline, if he is claiming the adjacent territory. This behavior leads to the phenomenon of the "fragrant bowls" that have been well documented in Yellowstone: each pack marks the external borders of its territory more intensely than the interior, drawing a sort of geopolitical map whose sign system is made up of odors.

The borders of these territories run in parallel, separated by a slender no-man's-land. The result, transcribed onto human maps, is striking: we see almost geometric forms embedded in a puzzle analogous to maps of human nations.[10] Researchers in Yellowstone National Park have shown that when a pack ventures onto the territory of a rival pack, it "suspends its marking," which indicates that its members know they have crossed a border. Moreover, it appears that dispersing wolves do not react to borders in the same way as packs do: the behavior of packs differs according to their intentions (are they preparing to fight, or simply traveling?) and according to how powerful they feel. Here is a whole slew of complex conventional behaviors that have only recently been identified by contemporary ethology.

Moreover, these behaviors are not simply intraspecific; other mammals read different things in them. If we borrow the expository tactic in cognitive ethology known as the "animal soliloquy,"[11] we can hear mustelids such as weasels and martens saying: "To be sure, you are at home here, Sire Wolf, but we also have a certain right to claim our own territory on top of yours, as long as we do each other no harm." (Of course, this formulation is both speculative and inadequate to translate the real dialogue that these animals engage in through their droppings.) As for understanding what roe deer or fawns read there, the mystery remains intact, awaiting study by more astute naturalists, more subtle heralds.

It is fascinating to realize that for many mammals, wolves especially, the excretory function, and more precisely their excrement—that is, what is par excellence unusable, from a metabolic standpoint—has taken on a function of political signaling, one that is highly important and even constitutive of their social identity: it can be called animal heraldry. This is a particularly elegant case of exaptation, a case in which an eminently useless feature becomes eminently functional; the most trivial feature becomes the most "noble."[12] It is a remarkable symbol of evolutionary creativity, with its circular economy in which ceaseless tinkering can recruit and "exapt" even the most useless forms, making droppings the building blocks of a communication system. Here, excretory behaviors fulfill the essential functions of human heraldry: wolf droppings are territorial banners that—like flags, and unlike walls—constrain no one, but that signal territorial limits; excrement constitutes the complex coat of arms of a particular group and a particular individual, designating a family of brown bears or a clan of white wolves, spelling out the status of *absent* subjects with a blazon of odor. From this standpoint, a tracker is a herald in an unknown land, sniffing every dropping, seeking in its form and location—quite visible on a white rock in the middle of the track, on a promontory alongside a rushing stream—the coat of arms that announces the presence of an invisible animal, its species, its stature, its own geopolitics on the territory. The tracker, as we have seen, can be a diplomat.

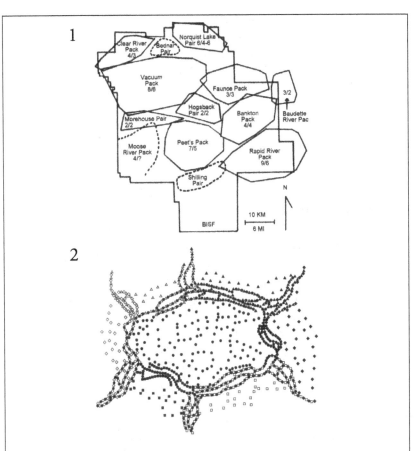

Credit: No. 1, map, Fritts and Mech, *Dynamics, Movements, and Feeding Economy of Newly Protected Wolves*; no. 2, model, Peters and Mech, "Scent-Marking in Wolves"

Figure 11. Lupine Geopolitics

1. Geographic distribution of the territories of thirteen wolf packs in northwest Minnesota in 1975–1976. The first number indicates the size of the pack in the winter; the second, its size in the spring.

2. Model showing the distribution of odor markings through the territory of a wolf pack (black dots) in its relation to six other bordering packs. Each of the different symbols represents the markings of a neighboring pack. The paths of the markings are represented by a thin black line. The shape of a bowl induced by the most intense markings of each pack can be seen on the borders of their respective territories.

The intentional and signifying character of this heraldic function is particularly visible in an animal such as the Eurasian lynx, which has the catlike habit of burying its droppings or covering them with snow or earth, following an enigmatic sense of hygiene or modesty. However, the droppings it leaves on the borders of its territory are never covered over: this shows that the animal (whether the behavioral sequence is hereditary, intentional, or both) distinguishes among the various functions of excretion and recognizes the specificity of the heraldic dimension.

What Is an Animal Convention?

It can be argued that this terminology simply belongs to the order of anthropomorphic metaphors. Reluctance to speak about symbols and conventions in the animal context seems to be part of the naturalist ontology (in Philippe Descola's sense), according to which only those beings that have an inner life, as evidenced by speech, possess conventions, these being dependent on symbolic activity. This way of arranging things seems to me to belong to the past.

In a first sense, what a wolf excretes is a "sign" according to the definition proposed by the philosopher and semiotician Charles Sanders Peirce: "something which stands to somebody for something in some respect or capacity."[13] But what type of sign is in question? Peirce identifies three: icon, index, and symbol. An icon (for example, a cross) represents its object through actual resemblance, while an index represents its object not through resemblance but through a real (causal or inductive) connection with the object (fever is an index of illness).[14] In the case of droppings, the relation between the object and what it signifies belongs to the "index" category if the information drawn from it is, for example, the identity, the sex, or the emotional state of the creature that left the mark.

But if the meaning drawn from the droppings is a border taken as a limit, then the relationship is no more indexical than it is iconic. An excremental dropping has no resemblance whatsoever to a border or boundary marker, nor is there an indexical connection. We are compelled by the process of elimination, however reluctantly, to see symbolism in this relation. Strictly speaking, of Peirce's three possible relations only the symbolic is available—the one that was supposed to belong exclusively to humans. Peirce specifies in his *Elements of Logic* that a "*Symbol* is a sign which refers to the Object that it denotes by virtue of a law, usually an association of general ideas, which operates to cause the Symbol to be interpreted as referring to that Object."[15] The symbolic rule may have been formulated a priori, by convention, or constituted a posteriori, by cultural habit. A wordless "no entry" sign is neither an icon nor an index, but a symbol. Upon examination, given the information gap between the material object (an excrement, a scraping) and the signification (interpretation of the object as a geopolitical marking of a border), we are clearly dealing with a symbol, but in an animal sense, one that nudges the expectations of the traditional definition toward something that is not yet conceptualizable.

For there to be something like a symbol, nevertheless, the receiver must be endowed with symbolic thought. One could argue ad infinitum about the concept of symbolic thought, for it is a term that "sings more than it speaks," to borrow an expression from Paul Valéry: it serves more often as a sign of distinction than as an analytic instrument. To say that there are major differences between the aptitude for symbolism of human animals and that of nonhumans is to state the obvious. Nevertheless, the definition proposed by Roberte Hamayon, an anthropologist specializing in shamanism, is pertinent here: "The distinguishing feature of symbolic thought is that it connects its objects with things external to them, in such a way that these objects can evoke things other than themselves."[16] In these terms, the geopolitical reading of wolf droppings enters surreptitiously into the field of symbolic practices. This suggests that the concept of symbolic thought as a site where a typically human form of signification emerges is a concept whose frontiers and properties have yet to be stabilized.

I propose, then, to conceptualize the phenomena under consideration here—convention, symbolic thought, geopolitics—in a more formal way.

By convention, I mean to designate shared knowledge that, if accepted, has normative effects on behavior, effects such as limitation, incitation, or inhibition, without any physical (or conflictual) *power relations* coming into play. The odor border is conventional in the sense that, unlike a fence, it prevents no one physically from crossing over. Its effects depend not on its material properties, but rather on the *information* that it transmits—this is what I call its "symbolic" functioning.

By symbolic thought, I mean to characterize the aptitude—possessed to at least a minimal degree—to grasp a situation in which a material entity is endowed with a signification that *exceeds* its exclusively material properties (and that thus arises from a certain arbitrariness of the sign) once it is received as information in a relation between a sender and a receiver. Symbolic borders thus map spaces; in the cognitive experience of wolves, this means that symbolic delineations are necessarily superimposed on the sensorial landscape being traversed. These are mental maps in the strong sense. A map is not merely an internalized, structured representation of an external space, like those that have been observed in certain rodents thanks to the ingenious experiments of the psychologist Edward Chace Tolman:[17] a wolf's map is the internalization of an external space onto which a conventional *signaling system* has been applied—in other words, it notes geopolitical frontiers.

By geopolitics, finally, I mean to evoke the emergence of complex territorial entities that are based on conventional limits and require symbolic activity on the part of nonhuman animals, who enter in this way into *political* relations, in the sense in which their decisions in relation to the borders that structure spaces have effects in their *collective* interactions at various levels (within the pack, between packs, between species, and so on).

There are, then, political and conventional relations among wolf packs, and it is into these relations, in the wolves' own dynamics, that humans can insert themselves in order to signify territorial limits and thereby influence the wolves' behavior.

This is what I call animal diplomacy: entering into a political relation with animals that is not a power relation, one that relies not on their capacity to enter into a contract, since that capacity is lacking, but rather on their capacity to engage in conventional behaviors.

This perspective allows us to question in new ways the two approaches that have structured the relation between humans and wolves since the latters' return to France in 1992. In a situation of contact with the animals, a whole sector of the rural world encompassing ovine pastoralism has come to demand management by force: the most moderate voices seek regulation through hunting, while others call for total eradication. The consensus is that only force can resolve a conflict with creatures that lack the capacity to enter into contracts, according to the ontology of the Moderns. Contact is unavoidable: these animals cannot be "zoned," confined in wilderness sanctuaries (for example, in national parks), because of their process of dispersal, which in the French ecological context of widespread ecofragmentation, inevitably brings them close to human activities.[18] The only alternative to power relations, then, is a diplomatic approach.

As it happens, reliance on power relations with wolves (regulation, extermination, speaking with the language of guns) proves counterproductive. It is not a question of criticizing all use of firearms in defense of a flock: shooting to frighten predators as well as defensive shooting are measures as reasonable as they are necessary. But such measures have to be distinguished from shooting to "cull" the animals; when culling is practiced independently of situations of attack, it tends to disperse wolves randomly into vast new territories. Quantitative studies by biologists in the American context have shown that killing wolves is apt to produce the opposite of the desired effect: it can *increase* wolf attacks on flocks of domestic sheep,[19] and it also augments the wolves' birth rate.[20] In addition, by killing an animal at random, one risks fragmenting the pack, causing it to lose the skills used in organized hunting that allow its members to feed on vigorous wild fauna; the result of random culling is thus increased predation by more solitary wolves on flocks, where hunting is much easier.

WOLF GEOPOLITICS

Among the ethological initiatives that have been presented as diplomatic, one in particular stands out for its sophisticated grasp of both the shared category of territory and the common code that needs to be elaborated in order to communicate with wolves: I am referring to the *biofences* introduced by biologist Dave Ausband of the University of Montana. Ausband's scientific investigation brings together ecology and ethology from the perspective of conservation biology.[21] Ausband started from the problem raised by the predation of wolves on livestock in Idaho and Wyoming. Humans—government agencies, in this case—were responding to these attacks by culling predators. The individual wolves involved in the attacks were targeted (which already reflects a more refined policy in ethological terms than the random culling practiced in France). Nevertheless, these deadly shootings, while they might be effective in the short run, ultimately fail: the predation begins again. Nonlethal methods of flock protection, for their part, have not yet proven themselves, and they require much more human presence. Starting from the observation that wolves use markings (urine, droppings, scratch marks) to "establish their territory in the landscape and avoid interspecies conflict," Ausband hypothesized that markings of the same type deposited by humans could be used to influence the movements of wolves in Idaho. So he and his team have deployed 63.7 kilometers of biofencing (consisting in a bouquet of odors mimicking the markings of a powerful pack) in a space involving the territory of three packs. This method is derived from experiments undertaken in Africa aimed at keeping feral dogs out of villages, with excellent results. Following the animals by means of signal-emitting collars shows that there has been a telling limitation on border crossings—in most cases, no crossings have been observed, only a few attempts. Most importantly, in one instance Ausband deployed a biofence between the meeting site of a pack and a flock of sheep located 1.6 kilometers away. During the four preceding summers, the flock had been attacked. During the summer after the biofence was put in place (2010), there were no attacks. However, the following year, the border was crossed once again. Apparently, if it is to last, the arrangement has to be renewed. Ausband concludes that these experiments should be continued on a large scale.

Given wolves' adaptability, it is clear that no miracles can be expected. Still, if experiments like Ausband's can be repeated, improved, and combined,[22] solutions based on a sophisticated ethology and on animal diplomacy may make it possible to reduce predation on flocks to a degree that would be *tolerable* for pastoralism.

This is an example of a *geopolitical* operation: using conventional border markers that do not involve power relations, just the way wolf packs do, in order to avoid conflict. This process allows humans to insert themselves into the animals' political ethogram rather than imposing human political forms from the outside.

This approach can also be viewed as a way of grasping the specific social affordances of wolves. Affordances are the properties of a being or a thing that allow another being to enter in specific social interactions with it, the potential ways in which it can be grasped. Such offerings are behavioral bridges between dissimilar beings. Véronique Servais, an anthropologist of communication, has shown how social relations with animals do not necessarily arise from our projections onto them of human social inclinations; they may arise from forms of openness to social contact conveyed by the animals. In her descriptions of strange interactions between humans and dolphins, she notes: "It is astonishing, moreover, that an animal like the dolphin can convey so much social openness to the sensibility of a primate. They have the property of arousing emotions coordinated with a particular mode of relation."[23] What wolves convey, toward us primates are *geopolitical overtures*. These overtures become fully graspable when we adopt a zoocephalic perspective. As a species, wolves are prodigiously rich in overtures that allow political interactions, having to do, for example, with the ways territory is used. The sociopolitical offerings of domesticated dogs are not magical inventions of domestication: they are simply extensions of wolves' widely underestimated political inclinations and potentialities for interaction, even with other species.[24]

The role of diplomats is thus not to expand human politics so as to include the biotic community, but to take into account the fact that there

Credit: Photograph Éditions Wild Project

Figure 12. Dave Ausband: The Cartographer Diplomat

As primates, human beings are endowed with a weak sense of smell, making them blind to the subtle territorial structures and messages encrypted in the odors of animal droppings. Dave Ausband's initiative was based on an attempt to enlarge our diplomatic aptitudes by experimenting with a sensibility to nonhuman ways of delimiting territory and then materializing that sensibility in *biofences*. Starting with vials of animal odors, the researchers construct a bouquet of complex odors designed to *inform* the behavior of wolves through the play of olfactory lures. The biofence project exalts both human and wolf intelligence: humans seek to trick wolves even though they know the animals are too intelligent to react to anything but a subtle message that will spark the curiosity of these predators, challenging their pride as sovereigns of a territory and arousing their hierarchical instincts. Like a magic lantern, the vial contains an entire pack (that is, multiple odors blended together to signify to beings within sniffing range that a numerous and powerful group has passed by). In biofences, the odors are not merely smells, they are stimuli signs, geopolitical symbols, presences extrapolated by wolves' imagination, territorial markers, challenges posed, reasonable borderlines. They constitute a signifying olfactory landscape. For humans it comes down to using a foreign dialect and foreign cultural practices, in order to pacify our relations with our cohabitants on the earth.

is already something resembling the political in that community: it is not a matter of including nonhuman animals in our own political structures of representation, but of the human animal becoming open to animal politics. The role human diplomats can usefully play toward animals does not lie in acting as their ventriloquists, but rather in identifying forms of a common language; not expressive forms (what are they asking for?) but "impressive" forms (what messages can we get across?), while looking for mutually beneficial ecological interactions without a relation of vital dependency. Biofences constitute a model for the practice of werewolf diplomacy: their ethological subtlety allows them to isolate the hybrid fringe where communication between dissimilar rationalities can occur, taking into account another species' way of relating to space. The likelihood that such arrangements will prove pragmatically effective reinforces the need for experimental work on the key points of the ethograms in question, in search of solutions where a minimum of force can produce a maximal effect in human relations with wild animals, without recourse to exhausting and futile impositions of force.[25]

It is sometimes objected that there is a form of hypocrisy in the biofencing project—that it purports to be initiating a dialogue while in fact it is simply *deceiving* the animals. There are three responses to this objection.

The first one is simple. The biofencing approach is not based on a belief that we can pacify our relations with a large predator; we must not invoke a phantom of the wolf of Gubbio and the confounding naïve belief that it propagates, the belief that sincere dialogue and good will—which do not even resolve conflicts of interest among humans, after all—could resolve conflicts between humans and nonhumans. For the problem is first of all pragmatic: we must imagine measures that render cohabitation *concretely* possible.

Secondly, as I shall show further on, the moral problem intrinsic to diplomacy is not that of its means but of its ends: if the goal of diplomacy is to win a war by other means, the biofencing approach indeed seems *immoral*. But if the goal consists in permitting mutualist cohabitation, the measure becomes morally conceivable.

Thirdly, and this is the most important response, biofencing measures can be understood as deception only if the human agents have not become *decentered*. True wolf diplomacy is *perspectivist* (in the sense of Amazonian perspectivism, which we shall analyze at the end of part 2): that is, it adopts the ontological attitude that consists in recognizing the *effectiveness* of the attitudes toward one another displayed by the beings engaged in interaction. An eloquent example of perspectivism can be found in advice given by Runa Puma Indians of Ecuador, as reported by anthropologist Eduardo Kohn: "Sleep face up!" Kohn is warned in a forest hunting camp. If you sleep on your back with your face visible, a jaguar passing by will see you as a "self like himself, a *you*—he'll leave you alone." But if you sleep on your stomach with your face hidden, you'll be seen as meat, and the jaguar won't hesitate to attack. The identity of the human actor ("self" or meat) changes according to the way the jaguar looks at him or her. As Kohn says, "How other kinds of beings see us matters. That other kinds of beings see us changes things."[26] In other words, the point of view of others transforms our very identities, and thus the form of the relation between us. Here, then, is the pragmatic lesson of perspectivism for wolf diplomacy: in practical interactions with other forms of life, we are what we are because we are *recognized as such* by the other.

Now, from a wolf's perspective, in the wolf form of rationality, what do we resemble, we humans defending our flocks? Most likely something like a *powerful wolf pack*, one that is currently occupying the territory and with which it is preferable not to come into contact. Setting up odiferous markings that serve as indices of a large and frightening pack to keep wolves at a distance from human activity is thus paradoxically an honest perspectivist signal. The dialogue involved is a perspectivist one in which we act *in such a way that they see us as they must see us* if peaceable cohabitation is to be possible. Biofences are not deceptive; they allow us to sleep with our faces up, as it were. In the long run, these practices of diplomacy are likely to lead to the establishment of the sort of ethological equilibrium characteristic of natural systems, like the etho-ecological phenomenon known as the "dear enemy" effect.[27] This phenomenon, well established empirically, characterizes the situation in which two neighboring populations of territorial animals experience a significant decline in their mutual aggressiveness as soon as territorial borders are clearly and firmly established. Once this status quo has allowed each party to get used to its neighbor, the individuals in each group expend less energy and time in defensive behaviors toward the other group, while behavioral aggressivity toward non-neighboring outsiders—control groups, as it were—remains similar to what it was before.

Measures of werewolf diplomacy designed to produce the "dear enemy" effect can thus be seen as sketching out future maps for immanent cohabitation of diverse life forms.

The Rights They Grant Themselves

These reflections on the conventions of life that appear to exist in the social and political behaviors of wolves opens up a space for problematic questions concerning animal rights. Much contemporary literature in this area is vigorously investigating the matter of what rights we should grant nonhuman animals. This process entails bringing animals into human political structures, and the endeavor certainly is an important one. But it would be useful to investigate also, in matters of cohabitation, the rights that animals grant *themselves*, and in what biomorphic sense rights are in question. This second endeavor, proper to the diplomatic approach, is complementary to the first: it consists in imposing on oneself an excursion into the invisible "right" of others. This makes it possible to interpret conflicts with non-humans as *conflicts of rights* between foreign "systems of thought and law" manifested by beings cohabiting in a single territory. The very formulation of this hypothesis is made fantastical by the ontological infrastructure that leads us to live and think as though positive rights existed only in the state of society that is reserved for us, while all other living beings remain confined to the state of nature, where the law of the fittest reigns—in other words, non-law. By acknowledging that wolves manifestly and consistently use intraspecies "conventions," and perhaps also *inter*species conventions when territorial marking is involved, we open up a breach in this edifice.

When predation on a flock is coded as the harm that a being of non-law commits on livestock construed as property under human law, one can interpret the conflict that pits wolves against pastoralism in a different way, in the light of the foregoing analyses. To do this, we shall take an analytic detour through a discussion of conflicts between human cultures in terms of the heterogeneity of "systems of thought and law" by the historian of prehistory Alain Testart. Testart's description of the encounter between English colonizers and Australian Aborigines is enlightening in this regard:

> When the English made contact with the Australian Aborigines, around 1800, everything began with good intentions and good humor. But when the Aborigines, considering that new game, sheep, were good to hunt like any other prey, killed a few animals from a flock, the owner called it *theft*; the government had a few Aborigines arrested and hung *as a matter of justice* for thievery; and, again *as a matter of justice*, since revenge is *the law* in the Aborigine world, the Aborigines turned their bows and arrows

on a few shepherds; after that, armed expeditions were organized to punish those *abominable crimes* that targeted peaceful citizens, guns giving the English an advantage over their adversaries that requires no comment.[28]

Wolves probably have a casual attitude similar to that of the Aborigines regarding the ownership of livestock: sheep are not possessions, they are game. Are we dealing, in the wolves' case, with a "different social system," and if so, how can that system be described? It has been established that, in the wolves' "system of thought and law," there are powerful normative conventions: members of higher rank in the hierarchy are known to have precedence in access to meals, the offspring of the dominant pair are fed and protected, territorial borders are recognized and respected in myriad ways—and wolves appear to deem that nothing belongs to another predator except what that predator can *protect*.

This is a different concept of what it means to keep and to take: not the archetype of non-law (except with respect to our law), but a *different* law, for which we can find ethnographic equivalents, moreover. Testart concludes: "It is not that men are malicious, it is that different social systems, which are simultaneously systems of law and systems of thought, lead to different ways of legitimizing rights for different groups, and these rights enter into conflict."[29]

According to Roman law, one actually possesses only what one has acquired legally; thus, when a wolf takes a sheep, it is stealing, thievery. In our imagination, that wolf is often viewed as a furtive criminal, a sneaky burglar, an out-and-out scoundrel. Under our Roman law of property, the wolf is *indeed* a thief. But there is a cultural misunderstanding here. The wolf's logic is analogous to *different* practices of keeping and taking. We can envision, anecdotally, a different historical analogy. Following Christian law, monks used to say, for example, that the Scandinavians who came through on their longboats were criminal looters. But Viking common law, spelled out implicitly in the *Konnungs skuggsa* ("Practical rules for traders going off to sea") seems to express a different code, a different norm, which could be formulated as a decree: "You actually possess *only what you can protect.*" Everything else in effect belongs to any being that has the strength and skill to take it. It is perfectly legitimate, in this Viking moral code, to take what is badly protected by others: for what you are unable to protect does not *belong* to you. Thus looting is not a crime against Viking law but its untroubled expression.[30]

This analogy is not to be taken literally. It consists simply in a first incursion into what we shall later call an animal ethnography, in an effort to understand certain aspects of other ways of being alive by analogy with elements of human historical and cultural diversity. Here is the strange law of wolves, which they seem to recognize themselves: powerful and normative conventions within the packs, subtle and complex relations with other species, but a denial of property rights concerning prey that is not protected by rival predators from outside the pack. Wolves, then, are not malicious; rather, in wolf-human interactions we are seeing one system of thought and law enter into conflict with another. An Englishman stealing a sheep in Australia in 1800 is certainly a criminal, but what about an Aborigine, cohabiting on the same land, who had been operating under his own system of rights before that system was challenged—if he downs a sheep in the outback with an arrow, is he a criminal? Is he not acting in the name of a different right? The point is not to show that the Aborigine is not a thief, but that he is not *lawless*. By analogy, we can also construe the wolf's refusal to recognize livestock as property as a form of law, a form that tells us something still enigmatic concerning the rules of cohabitation that remain to be imagined.

Among the Siberian hunter-gatherers studied by Roberte Hamayon in *La chasse à l'âme*, an animal killed and taken away by another cannot be said to be "stolen" in the forest, for "hunting is associated with the notion of sharing, which goes beyond the group of participants and extends . . . to everyone who is hungry; everyone can share, on the spot, meat left by a hunter expecting to come back for it—that hunter will make up for it later. The notion of sharing excludes thievery; there is unanimous agreement that theft is absent from forests, inconceivable among the indigenes."[31] What is interesting here is a system of human vernacular law that excludes the idea of theft, despite the appropriation that follows upon capture.[32] This law extends to other human hunters, but sometimes to nonhuman predators as well, in speech or in practice. Indeed, the idea of reciprocity among large predators, human and nonhuman, who leave each other, intentionally or not, remainders of prey to be consumed, is omnipresent among hunter-gatherers. The ecological commensalism that is de facto present among predators is established in *law*: one cannot condemn someone who feeds off our hunt behind our backs, for this is a shared right (although the hunter can try to prevent it by hiding the meat or taking it away). Prey, even killed, is a *common* good.

So where does the diplomatic misunderstanding begin? As is often the case with questions that concern us, somewhere around the nebula constituted by Neolithization, understood here as the shift to an agropastoral mode of existence. Roberte Hamayon isolates the differences in customs between the Siberian hunters and related tribes that have changed their way of life in favor of domestication and pastoral livestock farming. The activity of hunting treats living beings as circulating in feedback loops, whereas the activity of raising livestock deals with living beings as "goods to be transmitted,"[33] making the idea that an animal can be stolen *conceivable*.[34]

From this analysis we can draw a hypothetical interpretation of continuity throughout the species. If we can establish a subtle continuity between the law of shepherds and the law of Tungusic people (through socioeconomic mutation), and another continuity—the duty to share, which excludes the very idea of theft in forests—between the law of hunters and that of their predatory commensal cohabitants (bears, tigers, wolves, lynxes, crows, eagles, and so on), then it becomes possible to think that we are really dealing with *continuous* variations on the spectrum of law: metamorphic variations that do not consist in a binary opposition between a positive human law (on the order of pure convention) and a natural animal law (on the order of pure power relations), with a difference in nature between the two. Through subtle metamorphoses, the spectrum of law comes to include even nonhuman animals, and the law that connects certain hunter-gatherers to the other animals in their environment is sometimes *closer* to animal law than to the Neolithic pastoral law (of which we are the heirs, and which we institute as the exclusive norm for law). The question of a right of property concerning animals thus reveals the lines of fracture of our Neolithic conception of living beings, once we hypothetically situate wolves, hunter-gatherers, and pastoral peoples on the same comparative spectrum.

This analysis aims less to make a point than to render exotic—to upset, via concurrent narratives—the architectonic structures of our political conception of the way humans relate to nonhumans.

The wolf's refusal to recognize the right of property over the livestock of humans must not be overvalued, but it must not be ignored, either. It is not a matter of giving all systems of law equal status a priori, but of recognizing that one cannot interact with a foreign system if one has not well understood one's own. And in so doing, the acknowledged ability of wolves to recognize conventions, gather information, and learn limits creates an opportunity to envision the establishment of a hybrid system of law, one whose pact would certainly not be countersigned by wolf packs, but would be vigorously established by ethological arrangements of markings, defenses, and means of deflecting the wolves' attention.

This type of analysis, undertaken from the wolves' standpoint, compares a wolf's right to eat a sheep to the human right to possess one for the purpose of eating it. The wolf's perspective is spectacularly dramatized in a fable by La Fontaine titled "Le loup et les bergers." The fable is interesting because the wolf is not a figure used to represent a human type (as are grasshoppers, ants, and so on, in other well-known fables); the fiction that consists in having an animal speak amounts here to showing what that animal's viewpoint *could be*, in its genuine eco-ethological singularity (a predator in competition with the human animal for the meat of herbivores). But let us let the fable speak for itself.

The Wolf and the Shepherds

A wolf of most humane complexion—
Here below quite the rarity—
Indulged, one day, in a profound reflection
About the conduct cruel that he
Engaged in—of necessity, of course.
"Oh, how they hate me! . . . Who? . . . Perforce,
Everyone, I'll be bound! Ah! Woe is me!
. . .

Credit: La Fontaine, *Complete Fables of Jean de La Fontaine*, book 10, fable 5, illustration by Gustave Doré

Figure 13.

And all for some rotting old sheep, or some
Foul, snarling dog, or some scum-ridden ass,
Victims of my carnivorous taste! Alas,
  Alack! I fear the time has come
To change my diet. Not the merest crumb
  Of meat—alive or dead—shall pass
My lips! From this day forth, nothing but grass,
Though it may kill me! For, is it not worse
To be so loathed throughout the universe?"
Just then he saw a lamb fixed to a spit,
Roasting, and shepherds making free with it,
Chewing and chomping on its flesh. "Oh, my!"
Says he. "How wrong I was to vilify
  Myself for killing them, and yet
Their guardians and their hounds, before my eye,
  Treat themselves to lamb *en brochette*!
What kind of fool was I? No, gods above!
What they can do, I can do more thereof!"
   . . .
  Our wolf spoke true. Where is it written
That our race feasts on beasts—un-conscience-smitten—
Who sup as in the Golden Age they did,
But that, contrariwise, we still forbid
  That they eat us—hacking us, carving,
Boiling us to their taste? The wolf is wrong,
O shepherds, only when he is not strong.
Must he live hermit-like? Must he die starving?[35]

PART TWO

DIPLOMATIC INTELLIGENCE

FOR A WOLF SCIENCE

Chapter 5

Orienting Wolf Pack Cultures

How to Postulate What Cannot Be Observed?

Through their search for specific invariants, zoology and ethology have been concentrating for a long time on what members of a given species have in *common* (Karl Lorenz has made both vertical and horizontal comparisons). For wolves, this concentration has been accentuated by the extreme difficulty of observing them in nature. R. O. Stephenson, a biologist, notes that the Nunamiut, an Inupiat people in Alaska, are well ahead of the ethologists in observing wolves: owing to the singularity of the ecological context they share with wolves (desert-like steppes where one can see far away), they are familiar with individual animals and their peculiarities; they know the habits and customs of particular packs. Stephenson thus contends that the questions raised by Western ethologists assume "too little variability in animals, behavior, and environmental conditions." While scientific ecology brings an approach that is essential for biological knowledge of wolves in terms of population dynamics, "some unknown and potentially significant aspects of wolf behavior and ecology may be obscured if we do not guard against the tendency in our discipline to blindly follow general laws."[1]

Our infrastructural understanding of animals has remained Aristotelian. The prevailing belief holds that knowledge of their "essential nature" (the defining characteristics of the species) suffices to allow us to study an animal's behavior: in other words, the individual is assumed not to deviate from its species-specific traits. This assimilation of essence to species is exemplified in a striking way in the use of the term "instinct" to explain an animal's behavior. We look at animals in the light of the following syllogism: we humans make decisions, whereas animals act on instinct; now, instinct is species-specific; thus to know one wolf is to know all wolves.

If our traditional scientific approach to wolves is limited, in comparison with that of the Nunamiut, for example, it is because this approach continues to consider wolves in strictly quantitative terms, as populations and as organisms; it neglects the qualitative dimensions presented by packs as regional cultures and by individuals with their own behaviors. It treats animals in mechanistic terms, for this is the only way to quantify the data and subject it to mathematical analysis. Now, with the increased prestige of material science, quantification has come to be taken as the foundation for rigorous discourse. This assumption sometimes obscures the essential aspects of the problem, however, for the simple reason that they are not quantifiable.[2] For the case that concerns us, this creates false enigmas: Why are certain pastoral zones that have little exposure to wolf packs centers of attack, while other zones are not disturbed? Models seeking quantifiable biological causes have failed to find any; this may well be because the role of regional culture proper to a given pack—cynegetic culture—has been ignored.

The problem of the strict ecological model, constructed to address the problem of the pressure of predation, is that it is a *physical* model: it postulates that to counterbalance the pressure of predation, one must respond by an equal and inverse pressure—the pressure of protection or regulation. This latter has to respond symmetrically, point for point and at every turn, to the pressure of predation, like a dam against the current. However, this is not the most appropriate model to use with wolves, for our relation to wolves is not one of mutual physical pressure, but rather one of information exchange. It would be fruitful to pass from the exchange of energy to the exchange of information, from a physical model to a living model. The problem is not one of opposing potential predators by providing continuous protection against them, but of establishing defensive measures *that convey information to them* and thus bring about a spontaneous and intelligent response to the pressure of predation.

In the end, we need to assume the practical consequences of what everyone, from shepherds to wolf-lovers, repeats endlessly, in what is perhaps their only point of agreement: *wolves are intelligent.*

In one instance, the use of a radio collar to follow a female wolf in Idaho isolated a strange phenomenon. She belonged to a pack that attacked domestic livestock. One day she was driven out by another female who took her place as the reproducer (alpha female), in the kind of straightforward power struggle that is the wolf form of politics. After a year of dispersal, the first wolf turned up in another pack, one that had never attacked the livestock that was omnipresent in its environment. She became its alpha female, and within a year her new pack was found regularly attacking domestic sheep.

On the basis of this anecdote, we can propose the hypothesis—one that is not entertained in today's ethology—that each pack has its own hunting culture (Jean-Marc Landry evokes "hunting traditions"), one that includes modes of cooperation (distributed or centralized governance, coercion or free rein allowed to individual initiatives), strategies (encircling, lying in wait, diverting), and the prey on which its members focus preferentially, comprehending the prey's behavior and defensive tactics accordingly (*stotting* in the case of pronghorn antelopes, *charging* in the case of musk oxen, the *frighten and run* approach practiced by bison).

These pack cultures could not be observed under experimental protocols or with reliable statistics and interpretive data; we have only anecdotes, stories, and surmises, nothing that the behavioral sciences recognize as reliable scientific data. In a scientific epistemology, what cannot be objectified does not exist. As anecdotes cannot be objectified, they are viewed as belonging to an anthropomorphic sensibility.

But where experimental science has no data, knowledge can advance, oddly enough, in the terra incognita of the unobservable: by logical deduction alone.

How can we allow ourselves to make a speculative hypothesis that is unsupported by the data of the best observers in the field? The history of science offers one means, an instrument of invention, that consists in a logical deduction leading to a necessary but not obvious conclusion, on the basis of *documentable* premises that make it possible to do without empirical data, at least provisionally. This reasoning was advanced in 1930 by Imanishi Kinji, a Japanese primatologist, and reproduced by Frans de Waal:[3] if there *is* a capacity to learn in a species, then there *will necessarily be* group cultural traditions in a highly social species; this is a logical consequence, no matter what empirical research is capable of observing or interpreting. Let us start from this deduction as a working hypothesis.

Wolves have unquestionable capacities to learn. They hunt animals that weigh up to twenty times more than they do, and they use multiple food sources; such activities require an apprenticeship that is provided by the pack.[4] These cynegetic cultures have been taught to the wolf cubs and adolescents by the "head of the hunt," often male and female reproducers. The cubs grow, learn, and disperse. They establish dynasties in other territories, propagate their pack cultures, and introduce changes in them.

The advantage of this perspective lies in the hypothesis that one can orient regional cynegetic cultures in wolf packs by signifying to them that it is harder to get their nourishment from flocks than from wild prey. It is heuristically appropriate to leave behind the mechanistic model of an animal that, famished and blinded by its instincts, attacks the first prey it comes across, without discernment. We know that wolves analyze the conditions of attack in detail, that they select their prey and, above all, that as "opportunistic predators they back off every time they face resistance. One interesting phenomenon here is that certain wolves spend a great deal of time near livestock without necessarily attacking it. This is the case, for example, in Montana, along the Flathead River: one pack has a territory there that has encompassed pastures crowded with livestock for decades, and yet has never launched an attack. The pack traverses or bypasses the flock in order to attack elk or deer.[5]

On this basis, we may imagine measures for flock protection that would induce new hunting behaviors in a pack and could spread to a certain extent from generation to generation and from pack to pack, through apprenticeship in hunting culture and through dispersal. We may *imagine* that if such territorial limits had been energetically taught to the two Italian wolves that arrived in the Mollières valley in 1992, their numerous current descendants, who form the core of the several hundred wolves now present in France, would attack flocks less spontaneously; for this message, this regional culture, passes from the alpha wolves to the cubs, who are the future dispersers and the future alphas that will form the future generations. In the field of ethological speculations, one may also ask whether it might not be conceivable to orient the hunting culture of wolves toward wild boar, at least in part. These animals constitute a small part of the diet of *Lupus italicus*, owing to their pugnacity in comparison with that of other, more accessible prey. But an experimental initiative might try to induce a taste for that prey by leaving young boar caught in a hunt near the pack's meeting place. If one could observe this type of shift of predation toward swine, we would see the archetype of an "objective alliance." In fact, the proliferation of wild boar is a fairly serious ecological problem, especially in certain regions like the Var, where wolves abound. If wolves were capable of reducing this population, their presence would be more acceptable, their economic role would be better understood, and the whole guild of large predators, viewed as rival and harmful killers in the terms of Neolithic metaphysics, would be reevaluated in its fundamental ecological function of top-down regulation of ungulates, a function apt to revivify the ecosystems involved.

Research into Animal Cultures: A Methodological Problem

This practical question about hunting cultures reveals an epistemological problem concerning our knowledge of animals: By coding them as natural beings and studying them using the protocols of the biological sciences, what do we miss in their way of being alive? The question of animal cultures has received increasing attention over the last few decades. Beyond the observation of practices transmitted in nonhereditary ways[6] (cleaning apples, in the case of Japanese macaques, or opening milk bottles, in the case of British blue tits), the difficulty we have conceptualizing what is meant by a *cultural dimension* of nonhuman life requires us to reintroduce an ancient and profound epistemological debate: we have to reopen the "quarrel over methodology" in the realm of animal science. The German approach sketched out by Jacob Herder, formulated by Wilhelm Windelband and later (1899) by Heinrich Rickert in *Science and History: A Critique of Positive Epistemology*, is most interesting here.[7]

To the historical model that analyzes singular processes, Rickert opposed a nomological, quantitative, determinist, and predictive paradigm that isolates laws.[8] In this model, each individual case is only one state of the law after the instantiation of a variable by a value in the equation that formulates the law. All cases are covered by the law, which is not a set, like the Aristotelian concept, but a regulated mode of deployment of cases, ordered according to a progression that is precisely a mathematical function: two bodies attract each other as a function of the product of their masses and the square of their distance from each other. Replace the variables mass and distance by any value whatsoever, and you will have described or predicted or explained the gravitational relation of any body whatsoever in the universe with any other body.

In contrast, the competing model has several names: William Whewell calls it paleo-etiological, in his historical study of the inductive sciences;[9] for our purposes, I shall use the term "idiopathic sciences." These are the inverse of the nomological sciences: the latter focus on what happens everywhere, and always follow the same mode of deployment regulated by laws, whereas the idiopathic sciences focus on *what will never happen more than once*—sciences concerned with what, after a single occurrence, never occurs again; sciences concerned with the volatile events of the universe. This opposition is deeply rooted in the theoretical consciousness of one strand of nineteenth-century thought, heir to the triumphs of Newtonian physics, which gave nomology its full amplitude in astronomy, and which was seized upon by Romanticism: "Love what will never be seen twice."[10]

Chapter 6

Toward the Social Sciences of Wolves

Interiority, Variability, Sociality

A crucial fact lies behind this inquiry: over the last few decades, wolves have acquired the prerogative, the sacrosanct status, of "honorary primate." That category has been developed by the primatologist Thelma Rowell to characterize animals that manifest cognitive or cultural aptitudes analogous to those of primates, and that have found their way into the world of culture, subjectivity, and sociality. Dolphins belong to this category, as well as certain birds (especially corvids), and others.

Interestingly, the concept of honorary primate was not laudatory at the outset: it derived from Rowell's theorization, in 1990, of the "hierarchical scandal" she saw in ethology, where primates enjoyed privileged methodological treatment that condemned the other species to be written off as "beasts." Wolf science, however, began to follow the path of primatology a couple of decades ago, especially in Yellowstone. "The way we study primates is rather different from the way classical ethology was carried out, with long-term research, individual-based studies looking for relationships, looking for ways of communication. Classical ethology, on the other hand, focuses mainly on relations with and around food: who eats what, how animals organize themselves around resources, and so forth."[1]

As primatology has gradually adopted the methods and questions of anthropology, wolf science has quietly adopted those of primatology. In a fruitful paradox, this cross-contamination allows us to imagine an anthropological approach to wolves, or, more precisely, the social sciences of wolves.[2]

Recognition of Interiority

We can retrace the path from nomological ethology to historical ethology by focusing on several major themes. Ethologists began to propose new ways of thinking about animal behavior that were intriguing as applied to wolves. In setting forth her methodological approach to the social behaviors of wolves, for example, biologist Jane M. Packard referred to two "schools of thought," determinist and stochastic: "According to the determinist perspective, events in the natural world unfold according to certain predictable or predetermined rules and return to steady states. In contrast, from the stochastic perspective, order is apparent only at a specific time as a reflection of chance events."[3]

We recognize our two protagonists. With a certain diplomatic finesse, Packard meant to retain them both, as complementary approaches to understanding wolf behavior.

This is a first opening to the variability of behaviors, but it is obviously still formulated in the *terminology* of the physical and chemical sciences. For ethology has struggled to earn its stripes as a natural science, and it has had to express itself in terms of the "hard" sciences to maintain its status.

This twofold approach becomes most interesting where questions of dominance arise. Packard referred to the determinist approach to characterize the attitude that postulates that dominance is connected to diversity, but that this diversity is *genetic and programmed*, so that one can predict the dominance of cubs in a litter, for example, by measuring their serotonin level, which is correlated with dominance, according to experimental psychology. But she also documented cases in which there was an inverse relation between two brothers after a fight. A dominant wolf, after being wounded, showed lasting submissive behaviors toward a brother who had previously been the submissive one.

The problem of what is innate and what is acquired is no longer a burning issue, but its operative reformulations are struggling to emerge. The problem covers only a proportion of what we do not know, and an original form that is unknown: What does it mean to speak of behavior at the genetic level? We have no idea. In reality, there are unquestionably hereditary behavioral sequences, observable in juveniles and in adults, but since we never see them *before* the animal develops, we can never determine what has resulted from the process of development and what belongs to the order of genes. At best, we can speak of "instincts for mastering skills," that is, facilitators for a certain type of learning. There are behavioral sequences for exhibiting curiosity, or behavioral matrices that facilitate the acquisition of certain information, the development of techniques of the body.

Packard thus came to pose the problem in terms not of social dominance, which would not be a relevant category (since it confuses the possible effect of a character trait—being dominant in the pack—with the trait itself), but in terms of *self-affirmation*. The question becomes: What individual has a tendency, likely inheritable, to self-affirmation, defined in observable terms such as a regular tendency *not to* refuse the escalation of conflicts? What individual spontaneously refuses the escalation of conflicts induced by the self-affirmation of others? According to Packard, "The personality changes that occur with age and reproductive experience . . . suggest that the patterns described as 'temperament' are a function of the shifting internal state of the individual. Behavioral profiles may be predictable as long as internal states are relatively stable; however, fluctuations occur when external conditions or internal states change."[4]

This is what led Packard, in an interesting epistemological gesture rich in encrypted implications, to ferret out a conceptual nuance differentiating "temperament" from "character." She defined "temperament" as the aspects of personality that change little over a lifetime, while "'character' refers to the aspects of personality that change as individuals mature" and "learn styles for coping with stressful situations." This is a conceptual nuance that comes straight from human psychology. She went on to add: "I agree that this is an important distinction that should be considered in future studies of the individual variation in wolves."[5]

It was once an uphill struggle to show that wolves had distinct personalities (temperament); with Packard, they acquired character, which they could forge themselves. It is not a matter here of an unquestioned anthropomorphism, but of a recent hypothesis developed out of a need to account for empirical data that were *otherwise unintelligible*. To study wolves more appropriately, then, it has become necessary, once again, to describe their individual personalities, to tell their life stories.[6]

This type of sign, although discreet, is decisive: as ethology becomes more and more refined, the empirical data multiply increasingly. The more data there are, the more their variability stands out—and the earlier simplistic schemas—describing pack structure, for example, or the predictability of dominance patterns—break down.

In a paradigmatic case, the ideological figure of the linear alpha-omega hierarchy has been contested to such an extent that it is no longer deemed appropriate to speak of an alpha in wolf ethology; the accepted term today is *breeder*.[7]

Variability: A Shared Prerogative of Living Beings

The more variability is manifested in a species, the more important it is to seek theoretical models that do justice to behavioral variability. We are starting to look to the sciences of a species that has established variability as its prerogative (in other words, the human sciences), as opposed to the natural sciences, whose mononaturalism reduces animals to nomological regularities. Mononaturalists grasp animals in an Aristotelian essentialist zoology, which encompasses instincts and a reified understanding of ethograms as deterministic behavioral programs shared by all members of a species. In contrast, the human species is claimed to be characterized by pure variability: idiopathy, culturalism, the arbitrariness of cultures and signs, absolute cultural and individual variability. Nonetheless, this opposition between multiculturalism and mononaturalism is in constant flux within contemporary ethology.[8]

To clarify the connection being advanced here between wolves and the social sciences, it may be useful to revisit the concept of variability, which is the basis for the breach between mononaturalism and multiculturalism, and whose ontological implications for Darwin's thought have not always been well understood. The metaphysics of variability in Darwin implies that animal and human variability originate in a property that is essential to all living beings. Life itself varies essentially.

Among the metaphysical deceptions and lures of naturalism, we can include the anointing of humanity as sovereign. In this view, nature is repetitive, governed by universal laws, while (human) cultures are diverse, multiple, infinitely varied, and this is what sets the inner life of humans apart. This inner life is not determined by conditions; instead, it is liberated and creative; the arbitrariness of its signs and symbols frees it from the deterministic effect of the environment. But this myth has been shattered by the breach Darwin opened up in the Ark by isolating an ontology of variation at the origin of *living beings*: the variability of human cultures is in no way special, it is only a form of variability catalyzed in a particular species of living beings, the human species. Since Darwin, then, we can no longer contrast multiculturalism and mononaturalism; rather, we need to make room for something that might be called multibiologism, a phenomenon that underlies and facilitates the emergence of multiculturalism.

The variability of wolf behavior, like that of sheep behavior, as noted by observers who are willing to study the animals closely, arises from the ontological fact that living beings as such are variable in their essence. The variability of cultures, including wolf culture and human culture, as contrasted with the unity of "the laws of nature," is only a manifestation of the variability of all living beings. The degree to which variations in human cultures (languages, beliefs, customs, technologies related to the body) have emerged does not set humans apart from other living beings; rather, it takes the shared property of variability to another power.[9] The hyper-variation of human cultures is prefigured in the cultures of wolf packs, for individual variation arises within webs of complex etho-ecological relations, where it plays a historical role, enabled by social apprenticeship, and where it structures differentiated social functions. We can speak, then, of a multinaturalism of living beings, with human multiculturalism being simply the expression of the vital variation catalyzed by the radiation of human cognitive facilities toward the symbolic.

The variability of cultures arises from the embedded variability of individuals, groups, living conditions, and historical processes that exist in sedimented layers of differing durability, creating asynchronies: the variability of humans is one more point of convergence with their biotic foundation, revealing their condition, which is above all that of being alive, and paradoxically, in a second phase, that of being physical and thinking beings.

It is this foundational feature of variability, common to all living beings, that justifies bringing wolf ethology into contact with the human sciences. This is a surreptitious mutation that has ontological implications for the naturalist break between nature and culture, since the old epistemological models of nature no longer serve to characterize beings situated at the interface with physical nature, namely, living beings; we need epistemological models that are idiopathic, qualitative, and historical, with a cultural dimension. Animals make their entry into the Ark of significations and evaluations, bringing the entire biotic community in their wake, as we see in the rise of phytosociology and in the neurobiology of plants. This process does not lower human beings to the status of mere organisms, predictable and deterministic organic bodies; rather, it lifts all living beings, lined up behind animals, to the epistemological and ontological status that had been granted to humanity. And this feat accomplished by human hands elevates human life in a remarkable way.

An Example: Wolf Political Science

This point has been brought to the forefront by the emergence of debates that belong to the realm of *wolf political science*. For a long time, the behavioral form of wolf leadership was stereotyped according to an ideologically biased model positing the dominance of alpha males. This was, for example, the position of the biologist Michael W. Fox in 1980: There is "an alpha male who not only rules over the males but is the leader of the pack. He is the decision maker. Other wolves, even older ones, respond to him submissively and affectionately as would cubs to their parents."[10]

At the other extreme, Erik Zimen maintained in 1981 that "no member decides alone when an activity is to begin or end, or which way or at what speed the pack is to move, or exercises sole power of command in any of the other activities that are vital to the cohesion of the pack. The autocratic leading wolf does not exist."[11] Zimen emphasized that the youngest wolves could sometimes protest effectively against the actions of the leader; this led him to qualify wolves' political mode of governance as a "qualified democracy." Confronted with the variability and detail of the empirical data, ethologists have found themselves needing to incorporate concepts and models into the human and social sciences that could do justice to the subtlety of social and behavioral constructs.

One might also evoke the phenomenon of the "home field advantage." During a conflict between packs, it turns out that the one that possesses and is intimately familiar with the territory being defended is more often victorious than the pack trying to take it over. This strategic concept borrowed from human studies of war and sport singles out yet another point of homology.

The debates in wolf political science are wide open, given the complexities involved in trying to understand what "power" means in the mode of existence of wolves. There is clearly an analogy between certain behavioral relationships in humans and in wolves that leads us to speak of "power": humility in the face of assertive stances, rituals in which a wolf makes itself small, in which the adult behaves like a juvenile and plays up to the dominant wolf—manifestations that, in the life form to which we humans belong, that of complex primates, we call "displays of power." But in what sense can the anthropological concept of power apply to nonhumans? The issue of transporting concepts from the social sciences into ethology brings to light the major theoretical knot of anthropomorphism and its various avatars. It is by analyzing the major disruptions in our knowledge of wolves brought about by the Yellowstone Wolf Project that we shall be able to advance in this inquiry.

Chapter 7

A Laboratory Called Yellowstone

To reach the level of diplomacy as the term is generally understood, the first requirement is an in-depth understanding of the way of life of those with whom one intends to negotiate. As far as wolves are concerned, a renewed and increased understanding has been made possible by the greatest noninvasive wolf-welcoming open-air laboratory in the world: Yellowstone National Park.

Douglas W. Smith is the biologist in charge of wolf science in Yellowstone. He actively contributed to the reintroduction of the species into the park in 1995, after a legal battle that went on for more than two decades. He now coordinates all the scientific projects focused on the wolf population within the park's borders. His book *Decade of the Wolf* is revelatory and emblematic of the newly emerging paradigms for understanding wolves, and animals in general.[1] In his scientific articles, he relies heavily on precise empirical data and quantitative protocols treated in mathematical terms (statistical analyses, DNA decodings, Lotka-Volterra equations adapted to predator-prey relationships). But his book offers a different epistemological tonality: in it, Smith tells life stories. The epistemological transformation of the conditions of *observation*, in the living laboratory known as Lamar Valley, is what has revolutionized our knowledge of wolves: never before have researchers using scientific protocols been able to observe wolf packs with such acuity and continuity. The GPS collars that make it possible to localize the packs, the scopes that allow long distance viewing, the ecological context of Yellowstone, with its flat sagebrush plains situated far from the cover of impenetrable forests, and the diplomatic subtlety of the researchers' observations, are invaluable instruments in this process.

Smith's book, then, is itself a symptom of the expansion of wolf ethology, adding a historical and idiopathic paradigm to the quantitative approach. The mere fact of having a fairly precise *definition* for observation (in the visual sense of the term "definition") that renders the personalities of wolf packs and individual wolves *visible* means that ethology is facing up to the duty of doing history, and can no longer be content to make generalizations on populations based solely on quantifiable information. It is the combination of these two approaches, each enriching the other, that can serve as a model for wolf science.

The Need for a Narrative Epistemology

The first lesson from observation of the wolves in Yellowstone, for Smith, is that the professional life of a wolf researcher is full of surprises and errors: the animals do not supply scientists with "irrefutable facts." "Not only are there tremendous differences in both individual and pack personalities, but each displays a surprising range of behaviors depending on what's going on around them at any given time."[2]

Recognizing the failure of the prevailing nomological models, Smith finds himself in the epistemological situation of needing to reform the basic conception of his own science and consequently of his own practice of knowledge production: intending to bring to light the laws of animal behavior, he finds himself *telling stories*.

The animals' personalities (temperament plus character) contradict theoretical notions: "Beyond all our current theories and speculations, there's an enormous wild card that gets played out time and again in wolf society, and it has to do with personalities."[3] But beyond that, these personalities require researchers to incorporate concepts into the model that are foreign to the natural sciences. "The age of individual animals is also important: in the world of wolves, experience counts for an awful lot."[4]

The nomological dimension remains in place, of course, but wolf ethology now has a twofold character. On one side, there is quantitative zoology and behavioral ecology with a nomological thrust: studies in this dimension are published in scientific journals. On the other side, though, we find a "dark" literature, editorially camouflaged under the rubric "general public"; this literature, embracing the fascination with wolves of the public at large, appears in highly publicized works that deliver the "forbidden science" emerging from Yellowstone: its idiopathic ethology.[5]

To account for the dynamics of a wolf population, the models do not suffice; it is essential to tell the stories of the packs.

On the side of the road that runs along the Lamar Valley, at dawn in the spring of 2015, in the rain, my companions and I used telescopes to observe members of the Junction Butte Pack, who were wandering unhurriedly around a bison carcass. While they were engaging in an odd ballet with two grizzlies, about fifteen crows, and a bald eagle, a senior park biologist who specialized in observing wolves launched into a complex genealogy. The light-colored male lying next to the carcass could be the new breeder. The former alpha, who had fathered most of the pack, had seen his mate die a few winters before. Declining to couple with one of his daughters, he had left the pack in search of a new mate, leaving his relatives temporarily at a loss. His two oldest daughters then gradually welcomed the attentions of two dispersing males who had been lurking at their border, males who had been intimidated and energetically driven off by the father when they had tried to approach. After several months of wandering, the father came back with a new mate, whom he had seduced in another pack; he found his own pack enriched by the two young males attracted to his daughters. One morning a few days later, however, the biologists found the remains of the patriarch's new mate, who had been killed under cover of night, presumably by the two young males, determined to keep the role of breeders and the power over the pack that they had assumed in the absence of the patriarch. The old king left his daughters again, and since then the pack seemed, strangely enough, to be led by the young princely couples.

A story about something that happens only once: this is the newly dominant narrative style, for ethology is becoming a historical science.

Why does nomological science oppose narration? The essential problem stems from the requirement of protocols in scientific discourse. To submit a language to protocols means giving a single, unambiguous, and operationizable meaning (that is, a meaning endowed with quantifiable correlates in a technical experiment) to *all* the concepts that are brought together and formulated in a theory.[6] But language subjected to such protocols cannot be used to tell stories. To "protocolize" scientific language amounts to semantic domestication: it locks up the properties of beings by modelizing and stylizing them, excluding and treating as negligeable anything that does not fit the mold. Structurally speaking, the recourse to narrative produces semantic wilding.[7]

But to explain the dynamics of wolf recolonization, or pack structure, or indeed to answer any of the questions that used to belong to quantitative zoology, we now need to tell stories. At a remove from protocols of quantitative behavioral ecology, whose precise reports on pack size, territory size, and evaluation of fitness purported to allow us, *on their own*, to deduce the development of the system in a determinist manner, we now need to narrate sequences of events, the history of variations on what had been thought to be the norm, on what is in fact, at best, a statistical norm produced a posteriori. We have moved into the realm of an ontology of variation and of population-based thinking, quite remote from the Newtonian nomology built on an Aristotelian zoology of blended essences. Variability and engagement in processes are the essence of life forms, and at a certain level they appear to rule out protocolized language and nomology. The ontological properties of living beings (here, variability) have epistemological implications.

In *Decade of the Wolf*, Smith makes crucial expository choices in order to follow his idiopathic model (an unformulated and probably unconscious model, as Smith had little interest in epistemology as such). His book is rich in stories whose metaphors point to the modes of intelligibility that come into play in efforts to understand wolves. For example, he presents chapters that are explicitly historical biographies of "great wolves," reminiscent of those of "great men" (or women) in human history: the wolf (female 40) who reigned as a despotic queen over the destiny of the Druid Peak Pack, or female 42, the despot's sister and "whipping boy," who eventually became queen herself and proved to be a very different sort of ruler.

The chapters devoted to individual portraits point up the necessity of biography: stories of intrapack conflicts reveal the historical dimension, while descriptions of pack dynamics bring out the sociological dimension, and depictions of pack "personalities" accentuate the ethnographic dimension.

The problem is that as soon as one decides to adopt storytelling as a method of elucidation, one is *launched*. The relation between the language of protocols and natural language in the science in question is reversed. In evolutionary biology and ecology, these relations are complex: protocolized concepts are often brought in by way of anthropomorphic terms (competition, selection, strategy, and so on). In the storytelling approach, the relation is reversed in favor of metaphor. Metaphors become omnipresent, structuring a discourse about wolves that takes the form of a history of wolf packs.[8]

The History of Packs as Dynamic History

To account for the dynamics of pack constitution, then, we can no longer settle for a quantified report on the size of the pack, the number of available prey, and the rate of stress on breeders; we have to tell the story of the wolf dynasty that produced the pack.

The Druid Peak Pack was formed shortly after the reintroduction of wolves into Yellowstone in 1995. It was followed continuously over some twenty years by the same observers, who have become specialists in its political history. Smith and Ferguson write: "The sheer size of the Druid Peak Pack in 2001—along with the fact that they often lived, right out in front of us, what seemed like epic lives, full of struggle and conquest—made for some of the most unforgettable encounters of the past ten years. To those who saw them from the national park's northeast entrance road before the breakup, sometimes twenty or more animals cruising through the Lamar Valley like they were the best and brightest game in town, it will no doubt remain one of the great wolf watching experiences of all time."[9]

These observations have given rise to a different way of understanding the *styles* of animal life: as Smith points out, after the reintroduction of wolves, "the northern range, with its rich resources, was quickly becoming center stage for an incredible amount of action and intrigue."[10] These are the stories I propose to share here.

The emblematic leader of the Druid Peak Pack was Number 40: "An early matriarch of the Druid Peak Pack was the exceptionally forceful, no-nonsense female Number 40, who in 1996 seemed to wrest control of the group from her mother, Number 38."[11]

Smith adds that sometime after this "apparent coup mom left the pack to wander on her own for nearly a year, later returning to the group—possibly drawn back by a nearly irresistible urge to help rear pups born in the spring of 1997."[12] Her daughter tolerated her presence, but somewhat sourly, so that 38 left the pack again to wander outside the park. One night in December 1997 she was killed by a rancher who had mistaken her for a coyote.

For the next three years, Number 40 remained "the undisputed leader—some might say full-blown tyrant—of the Druid Peak wolves. No one challenged her. By all indications one had only to look cross-eyed at this alpha to find herself slammed to the ground with a bared set of canines poised above her neck."[13] Few wolves have been as thoroughly observed as female 40, and she was never timid about displaying her personality. The member of her family who received the brunt of her punishments was her sister, Number 42—an animal whose extended suffering under her cruel sister was depicted in two *National Geographic* television specials, as the "Cinderella wolf."[14] In 1999, Cinderella separated from the pack to dig her own den: Smith's team hoped she was about to give birth. Shortly after her den was finished, 40 visited her sister and attacked her with unusual violence. The latter did nothing to defend herself. She abandoned her den, and no one knew whether she had had cubs, or, if she had, what had become of them.

The following year, strange events led to questions about what ethologists believed they knew about wolves. First of all, 40 gave birth to a litter of cubs in the pack's "official" den. Ordinarily, she would have been the only breeder, as seems to be the norm in wolf society. But 106, a low-ranking female from the pack, also gave birth, in a den in Pebble Creek. Finally, 42 had dug a third den in the opposite direction, where she too produced a litter.

In wolf society, nonbreeder females and males spontaneously take on the role of nurses for the alpha litters: they feed, tend, and protect them. But that year, few members of the pack came to help 40 raise her cubs; she found herself alone with her mate, 21, the very courteous alpha male (that is, the breeder male) of the pack. Female 106, of lower rank, was even more isolated. By contrast, Cinderella (42) was regularly assisted by many adult females, and especially by two sisters born three years earlier, 103 and 105. Six weeks later, when her cubs were somewhat autonomous, 42 and her companions left them behind for an expedition. Wolf experts watched the scene from a distance through their scopes: not far from 40's den, they saw

Credit: Photograph © University of Buffalo

Figure 14. A Pack

the old matriarch herself, and as usual, she lit into Number 42 with what even for her was tremendous ferocity. Then, as if wanting to make up for recent lost opportunities she turned on Number 105, determined to give her a good thrashing as well. Soon thereafter all the wolves, including Number 40, headed back in the direction of Number 42's den site. By this time it was growing dark, leaving those of us watching in the lurch, desperate to know what would happen next. That a lot did happen that night, though, there can be no doubt. The next morning, Number 40 showed up in the Lamar Valley near the Buffalo Ranch, about a mile from Number 42's den site—bloody and staggering, barely able to stand. . . . [A few hours later] this feisty, aggressive matriarch of the Druid Pack—the wolf avoided by most and feared by all—was dead.[15]

No one knew exactly what had happened that night. But the wolf specialists at Yellowstone imagine the following scenario. A group arrived at Cinderella's den, but Cinderella, in contrast to her behavior the year before, was not prepared to let her tyrannical sister approach her cubs; she attacked her dominant sister. As often happens spontaneously in canine skirmishes, the other members of the pack chose sides and joined the battle. But queen 40 no longer had many allies. Her jugular artery was severed, and dozens of deep cuts were found on her body.

If this account is accurate, it would be the first time in the scientific record that an alpha female wolf was killed by her subordinates. But this is not the end of the story. Over the next six days, 42 was observed carrying her cubs one by one, in her mouth, to the traditional den of the Druid Peak Pack, a site that had long been under the fierce control of her sister, Number 40.

Number 42 adopted the cubs of her dead sister and raised them along with her own. More intriguing still, she welcomed into the main den Number 106, the low-ranking female who had given birth at Pebble Creek, along with her whole litter. Alpha females are usually very protective of their den and aggressive toward the rare litters born to others. But three litters, forty cubs in all, were raised in the traditional den during the summer of 2000.

"Clearly the tyrant was out, and in her place had come a far more benevolent leader."[16] In an interview, Rick McIntyre, the expert concerning this pack, noted that 42 did an excellent job of getting the pack to work together. He wondered whether the simple fact of getting out from under the matriarch's yoke hadn't emancipated the lower-ranking females. Number 106, for example, came to demonstrate great leadership skill, "becoming among other things the finest hunter in the pack."[17] In 2005, she remained the tireless and benevolent alpha heading the Geode Creek Pack, which she had helped found.

And the story was still not over: like the history of every dynasty, it went on through the twists and turns of generations, accompanied by echoes of the past.

Four years later, Number 42 was involved in a clash with Mollie's Pack, whose territory was in Hayden Valley, further south. This was her last battle. Her lover, 40's former mate, an important character in his own right, escaped from the battle with his life. "If it was in fact Mollie's Pack that delivered the fatal blow the tale becomes one Shakespeare would love—the queen wolf dead, an act of revenge after all those years following the eviction of Mollie's Pack . . . from the Lamar Valley." And Smith hastened to add, with a nod to his official epistemological postulates: "Of course wolves aren't wired that way."[18]

Thanks to her generous personality and her epic story, 42 was one of the wolves most appreciated in Yellowstone National Park.[19] The story of the Druid Peak Pack has become the tale of a dynasty, a Shakespearean play in which a whole gallery of characters circulates: the cruel, tyrannical queen; the powerful, noble, debonair king; the queen's sister, humiliated but then victorious, who becomes the king's wife and a generous sovereign.

How can we conceptualize these events? We are virtually compelled to do so through geopolitical metaphors, analogies with power relations that we have known and continue to observe, and through telling parallels between the etho-ecological conditions of life of various animals, ourselves included.

Questioned on the genealogy of the Blacktail Plateau Pack, McIntyre remarked: "Like living through a very historic time—the Russian Revolution or the Civil War, maybe—with all these upheavals going on. And you never know how it's going to turn out."[20]

Two crucial characteristics underlie the art Rick McIntyre displays in his observations as a werewolf-diplomat. First, McIntyre is not a professional biologist, so he is not caught up in the normativity of discourse and acts proper to scientific eco-ethology; that is, he can report what he sees without running the risk of having his work stigmatized by accusations of anthropomorphism or mentalism. Second, his prolonged contact with a single group of wolves allows him to develop a historian's methodological approach to wolves' lives.

McIntyre thus advances a powerful intuition: invoking his readings in human history, he hypothesizes that the best model for grasping wolves' geopolitical mode of existence is that of European *feudalism* as practiced at the pinnacle of the Germanic Holy Roman Empire.[21] Wolves are in fact territorial in a particular sense: their borders are effective; their mode of dispersal creates internal and external relations that closely resemble the historical and social dynamics of feudalism, so much so that this would be the most fine-grained interpretive grid available, much more appropriate than the political behavior of eusocial insects or of solitary lynxes. It is a question of feudalism without an overlord between packs, analogous in this respect to Renaissance Italy.[22]

Credit: Photograph © Éditions Wild Project

Figure 15. Rick McIntyre: The Historiographer Diplomat

A biologist technician working for the Yellowstone Wolf Project, Rick McIntyre started getting up before dawn to observe wolves in the park on June 12, 2000, and he kept it up for more than 3,500 consecutive days. Doug Smith said of him that he followed the history of the Druid Peak Pack the way people follow soap operas. A true historiographer, he compiled more than eight thousand pages of meticulous notes, following a rigorous protocol of ethological asceticism that kept interpretation to a minimum as long as possible. ("Number 745 wakes up. He yawns. He lies down again.") Smith reports that McIntyre is quite proud of having written more words than are found in the Bible.

A skeptical reader may object that the metaphors used here are only anthropomorphic projections. But the question is not whether these metaphors are anthropomorphic: the question is how to single out the anthropomorphic metaphors that recur and to determine precisely *which* behavior of *which* species or population they qualify. The recurrence of epic "struggles and conquests" and references to Shakespeare among wolf researchers can be interpreted as an indicator of a wolf lifestyle that calls spontaneously and appropriately for analogies of this sort.[23] In a strange way, the epic and tragic genres are frequently evoked by wolf specialists in describing these life forms spontaneously interpreted as feudal.

The metaphors in question, then, require interpretation in strictly ethological terms, so as to distinguish metaphors that are appropriately enlisted to talk about wolves from those that are not. Anthropomorphism is an analogic method like any other: it borrows the rules of deduction of a given field in order to make predictions in a different field. Do we reproach physicist Fresnel for metaphorizing light as a wave, thus countering Newton's theory of corpuscles? Do we admonish him for being obsessed with waves and accuse him of a fundamental error when he takes waves as models for light? This thought experiment might suggest that the force of the accusation of anthropomorphism in ethology comes from elsewhere: from the need of a certain metaphysics to keep on reaffirming the difference between humans and nonhumans. It may stem, too, from the exasperation of naturalists when they see humans reduce the fascinating singularity of animal life to their own narcissistic categories.

The fact remains that, as an analytic operation (that is, an operation borrowed from specific rules of deduction), anthropomorphism is subjected to the same epistemological norms as any other analogy. Analogies are strictly hypothetic and never thetic: they require that all the axes of a comparison be tested, that all the hidden facets embedded in the original schema and transposed to a different one be revealed.

If I propose to be anthropomorphic here, it is not in order to raise nonhuman animals up to the human level, for we are already on the same ground, nor is it to make them disappear in their singularity by attributing to them a trivially human inner life; it is so that we can approach animals and try to understand them with disciplines, methods, and concepts that are *as elaborate as those that we have developed for ourselves*. And with analogous infrastructural epistemological norms: existentialism (the existence of the animal precedes its essence); the place of cultures, variation, history, multiple embedded layers (individual, interpersonal relations, groups, populations, biotic communities), explanatory pluralism within animals (emotion, cognition, impulse, hereditary behavioral sequences, "instinctive acquisition of a skill"), the impossible reduction to isolated parameters, contextualism, methodological interactionism, and so on.

Anthropomorphism thus becomes a phase in a biomorphic method. It consists in isolating, by analogy, the type of relations or behaviors that one is observing in a given animal, present here and now, through resemblance to human life: it calls this "power" or "seduction" or "play." One deduces heuristically what one might observe in terms of behavioral sequences if the deduction were accurate. The next step is to translate this into a biotic behavioral matrix anterior to the differentiation between what is nonhuman and what is human (or the product of the divergence) and then to apply that matrix to the species studied. Ultimately, these steps should lead to the empirical and experimental questions that observation needs to address.

The problem, then, is how to gain access to the profound difference that is so close to sameness, that intimate otherness, that affiliated foreignness among beings that have been sculpted by the very same forces.

What Is "Power" in the Animal World?

These metaphors are enlightening, then, because they constitute guides pertaining to the questions of cognitive ethology that we need to address to nonhuman animals. If the position of a given individual is characterized in the human ethogram in terms of "power," we need to be able to deduce from this fact observable properties in the ethological forms of human power. Then, once such properties have been isolated, they need to be translated into the behavioral physiognomies proper to animal life. Can they be found in relations among wolves? The great British primatologist Thelma Rowell has theorized the questions of dominance proper to nonhuman primates. Her formulations serve as useful guides for finding out not what dominance *is* among animals in general, but what to look for in animal behaviors associated with dominance.

Rowell argues that we can determine who holds power among primates if we can answer four questions: Does a particular individual receive attention from most of the others with each change in activity? Is that individual at the head of the group with a significant degree of frequency during changes of direction? Does that individual defend the group in situations of conflict? Is the behavior of others "policed" by that individual?[24]

It is by analogy with the ethological form of dominance or leadership in human behavior that Rowell seeks comparable signs in nonhuman primates, structuring the analogy around the spontaneous behaviors and specific requirements that she has identified during years of observation. If no one made anthropomorphic analogies, we would not know what to look for. Once these analogies are isolated in behavioral sequences of nonhuman primates, they can be considered as hypotheses to be tested on wolves. Who frequently leads the border patrol? Who receives discreet attention from the wolves in the pack before they go off to hunt?[25]

As it happens, the hypothesis concerning the individual who is the center of attention at the moment when a change in activity begins has not yet been tested with wolves. Attention shifts very frequently in wolf packs, as a function of relationships and inner states. By contrast, it seems quite clear that it is usually the same individual (almost three times out of four) who leads the column when wolves travel single file. For example, during the mating season, a male generally heads the line; this is understandable enough, given the symbolic stakes around the prolongation of his role as breeder. At the beginning of winter, though, the female breeder is just as likely to lead the column as the male.[26] The importance of the respective roles of males and females is hard to evaluate. Rick McIntyre has remarked that during the 1980s, when more women began to be involved in wolf ethology, what ethologists *saw* in their scopes suddenly changed: the Schenkelian myth of the tyrannical and patriarchal alpha male had to be reevaluated when it became apparent that female breeders played a central leadership role.[27] The next step is to determine the respective decision-making spheres associated with males and females, and the importance of these spheres for the life of the group. For example, the site of the den is chosen by the female, and she also may well lead the hunt, so that from one standpoint her leadership is more important than that of the male. But their respective personalities often result in differences in the intensity of their leadership, as we have seen with the legendary pair 40 and 21 at the head of the Druid Peak Pack. Finally, we must note that at Yellowstone in particular, dynastic power does not pass from the alpha male to one of his sons (for the sons leave more spontaneously in dispersal toward other packs), but from the alpha female to one of her daughters, who remains in the pack and becomes the future alpha. Power here is matrilineal.[28]

For a Metaphorology of Ethological Discourses

Once again, it is not a question of either stigmatizing or glorifying anthropomorphism, but rather of analyzing the *style* of the metaphors invoked for each animal species. As it happens, in cognitive ethology, in their efforts to qualify various animal behaviors—meerkats cooperating with one another, chimpanzees engaged in power plays, bonobos in their subtle sociality revolving around conciliatory eroticism, the serene matriarchy of elephants—researchers very seldom use the vocabulary of *feudal nobility* that we have observed in studies of wolves. The question becomes the following: What metaphors do researchers in the field use spontaneously when, after long years of observations, they try to synthesize what they have *seen*, when they are attempting to make it *intelligible*?

Once we have answered that question, we can formulate another: What *invariance* and what *convergence* of metaphor types do we find, and to which animal species and types of social behavior are they applied? The convergence of metaphors concerning wolves' way of life brings into view the whole continent of animal metaphorology in ethology: it makes it possible to envision a wholesale meta-analysis, through a compilation of ethological studies, in order to isolate the potential recurring metaphors connected with certain species or certain aspects of existence (for example, dominance, territoriality, or display).[29]

What we need is a metaphorology that taps into the secrets of ethological discourse and gives us a better grasp of who animals are, and who we are—an understanding that should in turn make an expanded animal diplomacy possible. This will not give us a body of knowledge as such, but rather new ranges of representation that will let us establish affiliations with life forms in their difference, so as to grasp that difference in its intimate uncanniness.

The anthropomorphism involved in animal diplomacy requires us to go through the asceticism of objectification and prolonged observation; and then the metaphors discovered must be reread with preconceptions suspended. For example, speaking of a "noble" or "aristocratic" wolf implies suspending the usual understanding of those adjectives. We need to isolate point by point the positions in the behavioral weft of wolves that call forth such an analogy and then situate these positions in more or less neutral behavioral sequences: we need to create an ethogram of nobility. This ethogram will encompass a certain territoriality that entails insatiable curiosity on the part of wolves toward those who traverse their territory, and ferocious collective defenses against rivals: what we call sovereignty in humans. It will encompass social behaviors made up of perilous shared challenges (hunting big game), moments of joy and collective unity as a hunt is begun and when it is completed. It will encompass a way of confronting prey, or rivals, in which the courage of the one who takes the first risk has to be exalted by the pack as a value, since it allows capture or victory. This ethogram will characterize a collective life led without scheming, without premeditation, but held together by loyalty to a family clan, a loyalty that may conflict with a desire to reproduce and to found one's own pack. Thus if the authority of the alpha breeders becomes intolerable, lower-ranking wolves, often offspring or siblings of the alpha wolf, will undertake a risky voyage in order to establish their own dynasty.

On the Two Anthropomorphisms

This does not mean that we have to project human social structures naively onto other animals; rather, it means identifying behavioral tonalities in the animal world that also exist in the human world, and that are encapsulated in conceptual characterizations (the chimpanzee politician for Andrew Whiten, the wolf aristocrat for Rick McIntyre, the erotomaniacal bonobo diplomat for Frans de Waal, the industrious self-sacrificing bee for Karl von Frisch).[30]

It is noteworthy that these are not the same metaphors as the ones conveyed by our fables; the latter exhibit a less elaborate anthropomorphism, one that does not go through the complex dialectic of ethological objectification and retranslation into human terms, the convergence of metaphors in a direction provided by specialists in daily observation of the species in question. If we speak of a proud, haughty eagle, it has to do with the morphology of the bird's face, where the strong brows and deep-set eyes correspond to what we read as pride or haughtiness in a human face. To attribute these qualities to an eagle is to make what Lorenz calls "an unfounded interpretation," one that finds in the crystallized morphology of the creature's face, as in a dolphin's "smile," human facial expressions associated with certain attitudes or emotions.

Thus there are two types of anthropomorphism. The first is the one that intervenes spontaneously and interprets mistakenly, following Lorenz's model. This is a cognitive bias of the human mind. The second constitutes a heuristic methodological phase, based on analogic reasoning, in the protocol of ethosophic research that I call biomorphic. It implies questioning key metaphors, those used to characterize a certain type of behavior or species; the next step is to refine and purify the characterization by deducing the properties that one *ought* to see and comparing them with the precise form of behaviors that one *can* observe. The difference between the two is simple: it's the difference between a journal entry and the Bible! We would have to fill as many pages of notes from daily observation as there are pages in the Bible to be able to trust our metaphors as comparable guides to the comprehension of animal primordia. For those of us who are not field ethologists, we would do well to place our trust only in the metaphors of researchers who have carried out the lengthy work of observation.

The spontaneous anthropomorphism that produces unfounded interpretations is a human instinct triggered by the terror induced by the silence of the rest of the living world; this form of anthropomorphism saturates the world with human meaning in order to make it intelligible, to bring it out of its mutism, out of the pre-language sovereignty that does not experience the absence of language as a lack the way we primates do. We seem to have a need to speak in the presence of animals, to speak to them, to speak among ourselves about what they do: to bring them into the human order, the semantic order of verbal signification.

At the other pole, that of the methodological anthropomorphism we are considering here, inspired by the great ethologists, *a silent asceticism* is required: one has to contemplate in silence over long periods of time, resisting the desire to interpret what the animals under observation are doing (this is the ethological method for describing behavioral sequences) for as long as possible while suspending the desire to *understand* (that is, to translate, to betray). In the silence of observation, where projection is also silenced, one can ultimately do justice to what *may* be happening.

In Fact, Close Observation of Animal Life Is Extremely Difficult

Discussing the work that primatologist Thelma Rowell has devoted to the ethology of sheep, Vinciane Despret offers a fine analysis of the incredible delicacy of the kind of observation required to make *signifying elements* visible. Equipped with the ethological protocols that she had developed during her extensive work on primates, Rowell spent the final years of her career observing a herd of sheep in her garden in England. Refusing to settle for the simplistic topoi that explain dominant behaviors exclusively as battles between males over females, Rowell looked for explanations elsewhere. It is an endlessly repeated commonplace that sheep are stupid, but with infinite patience Rowell managed to bring to light microscopic behaviors that quite probably play a role in a complex sociality: muzzle movements give directions to the herd, but these directions are not followed unless the animal making the movements gains the attention and something like the trust of its conspecific associates.[31]

Here, then, is the secret, the key to grasping animal interactions: the most architectonic behaviors of living being are *not spectacular*. They are subtle, almost bashfully discreet, no more than is minimally required to be evident for members of a particular life form, the beings that exchange them. We cannot see these behaviors, any more than an extraterrestrial would be able to read an amorous feeling upon observing the way a human gaze rests a fraction of a second longer than usual on another human's smile.

This is what can be called ethological diplomacy: it requires that one not *schematically* impose observable features—that is, structural behaviors modeled in other species—and then project them as dominant signifiers onto a tissue of interactions (for example, looking for dominance of the primate type in domesticated sheep). This is not to say that such signifiers are lacking, but that they may take different forms, and, most importantly, they may not be the essential features in a set of behaviors. We humans perform a series of dominance rituals on a daily basis without believing in them: we defer to employers whom we may not respect, while our real respect may be visible elsewhere, in small gestures, in insistent thanks. Dominance, as a structure, must certainly exist on a very wide scale; the problem is what it hides. Among wolves, this structure becomes visible as soon as one spends enough time observing them.

It is a demanding and liberating spiritual exercise to lie in sagebrush for hours on end, a rainproof notebook in hand, staring at a pack in the Lamar Valley until the cold drives you away, all the while noting scrupulously *what you see*, and not what you understand.

A Spiritual Exercise for Wolf Diplomacy That Can Be Tried at Home

The democratization of video devices and the circulation of films on the Internet plays a discreet but major role in the mutations of animal philosophy. The surprising old stories that used to be retold around a hearth and that have been entertained with skepticism by reasonable people are now *visible to all*, on a worldwide scale. Movies, cartoons, YouTube videos, and amateur animal documentaries supply a wealth of stories in which, under our very eyes, nonhuman animals pass their time doing what our metaphysical categories serenely postulate that they *cannot* do. Stories and anecdotes are becoming not the stigmata of ethology but the point of departure for controlled investigations.[32]

Beyond this new resource, professional animal documentaries, whose success has been undeniable since the invention of cinema, conceal major philosophical stakes.

For if there is indeed a narrative arrangement that, generally speaking, refuses to do justice to the silence required by diplomatic ethology, it is that of documentaries. These films often have the related vices of personalizing beings on the model of the human self and of dramatizing animals' existence through the artifices of a crude Darwinism. One can hypothesize that the omnipresent litany of the survival of the fittest, the struggle for life with all its risks and dangers (omnipresent refrains in the *commentaries* embedded in animal documentaries), is not based on an informed Darwinism that teaches us about animals' modes of existence. But we may in fact be contending even more with formal injunctions that emerge from the media support structure itself: to make a watchable full-length film, one has to stage *dramas* apt to move human spectators. Thus we witness the injection of survivalist narrative schemas into the life of an animal that would otherwise be inadequately supplied with incidents meaningful *to us*, with plots that fit into Vladimir Propp's morphology (a hero, an initial situation, a crisis, opponents, helpers, a dénouement . . .). But in fact—and this is the weakness of such films—the dramatic crisis is almost systematically presented as involving the *survival of the fittest*.[33]

At a more civilizational level, the belief according to which the existential tonality of living beings is a struggle for existence can be understood as the projection of the terror we feel when we contemplate the *distress* that we think was ours before civilization developed (the terror we feel at the idea of going back to a time lacking the comforts of modern life), whereas we have become heteronomous and incapable of moving around in such a period with fluidity. This is what constitutes the mytheme of the original distress of the prehuman, a dubious synthesis but one that is deeply rooted in Hobbesian anthropology (according to which humans are wolves for other humans) and in misunderstood Darwinism. Yet if we look carefully at our closest primate cousins, do any of them seem to live in nature as if they were in distress? We need to remember that the Darwinian struggle for existence is meaningful at a certain degree of abstraction: it plays out among variants at the level of populations. It is quite manifest when we are looking at infant mortality; beyond that threshold, animal life becomes simply a matter of living, no longer focused on sheer survival. The lives of wolves are not clouded by the conflict of all against all, but complicated by social relations, the joyful running of the hunt and the sated joy of victory, the burgeoning emotions of love between a young female and an adventurous disperser sheltered from the gaze of a jealous alpha father, loyal friendships, sovereign siestas when a prey ensures a week of feasting . . .

Far from a crude Darwinism, then, everyday animal life is relatively peaceful, and above all quite undramatic in the narrative sense of the term (few initiatory thresholds, quests, complex desires, contradictory memberships, self-centered stakes . . .). When one spends several hours in a row observing the play of wolves, bison, bears, and elk in the Lamar Valley, one can begin to grasp the extent to which the translation of this play into a struggle for survival denatures it: what one sees is more like a slow, wordless ballet incorporating discreet though highly significant acts, undramatic exchanges of gazes and odors, and long periods of détente between predators and herbivores—until the lightning-fast attack. We would need entirely different narratives to try to do justice to animals' manner of being alive.

As it happens, each one of us can carry out a personal experiment in order to try out this form of ethological asceticism, the experiment of observing without adding meaning, describing without understanding. Without leaving ourselves behind, everyone can try this experiment through a simple but radical act: watch a documentary about animals *with the sound turned off*. This can be an experiment on oneself and one's relation to other living beings, toward the goal of an inner metamorphosis. Animal life does not deserve to be coded as a pure struggle for life; it unfolds in partly familiar and partly inaccessible styles and tonalities, capable of teaching us existential ruses.

This hypothesis becomes more powerful when you decide to watch one of these full-length films in silence. Rather quickly, the process may come to seem tedious—at least, in relation to the narrative protocols required by a televised work, and more deeply by the psyche of the Moderns. But after an hour or so, the activity becomes prodigiously interesting: the absence of words that decode and impoverish the animals' behaviors leaves you in the adamic position of the ethologist, an experience offered by the prolonged period of lying in wait, aided by the long-distance scope that offers supernatural intimacy: in silence, confronting nameless behaviors that are connected with no known feeling—the enigma of the ways of being alive.[34]

A similar diplomatic exercise has been developed by American artist Sam Easterson in the form of installation videos, some of which are on display at the National Wildlife Museum in Jackson, Wyoming. The arrangement consists first of all in focusing a discreet, noninvasive portable camera on a wild animal, for example, a wolf or a bison. No commentary, no staging that would organize a linear story according to human codes, little set-up. Just slices of living, nonnarrativized time, not dramatized in terms of survival of the fittest. The video "Running Wild," from 2012, allows a strange shamanic dislocation that displaces the viewer, most notably, for example, into the body of a bison.

Here are some notes you might jot down while watching the video: See myself as a bison in a pond! Hear myself drinking as a bison while seeing my own horns. Hear myself breathe as water drips down from my lips toward the crystalline surface. See the trees reflected in the pond. See my enormous black tongue lick my lips. Gallop: feel each stride strike my patellas. See a young bison flee when he sees my horns; challenge him. Look at hoofprints in the snow, my own: *I* am looking at them.

Chapter 8

On Intentionality

Toward an Animist Epistemology

Intentionality as an Epistemological Postulate

The philosophical problem we encounter here is twofold. To try to understand the modes of existence of other animals, is it appropriate to postulate that they have complex mental lives? And if so, what must the *status* of such a postulate be? Is it an empathetic desire, a moral obligation, an established truth—or a methodological ruse? Philosopher Daniel Dennett has addressed the question not by taking the postulate as an established truth but by asking what effects of intelligibility it would have if it could be demonstrated.[1] The way he poses the philosophical problem seems to originate in part from his deep understanding of the theory of evolution (an understanding perhaps slightly tilted toward hyper-adaptationism). In their structure, their conformation, their most spontaneous reactions, living organisms exhibit organizations and ways of working that appear purposeful. Evolution as such has no purpose, of course, yet living beings *seem* purposeful, so much so that they are more readily intelligible as soon as one questions them in terms of their reason for being. This is the adaptationist way of reasoning, or the reverse engineering approach of a Daniel Dennett.[2] You want to know what this particular organ is? Ask for what purpose a blind but talented tinkerer might have come up with it, and your hypothesis will surely be crowned with success. Some entities in the world have neither intentionality nor purpose but are nevertheless better understood if they are interrogated *as if* they had intentionality and purpose. This is Dennett's "intentional stance."

A first-order intentional system has beliefs and desires. A second-order intentional system is more sophisticated: it has beliefs and desires on the subject of beliefs and desires, its own or those of others. And so on, in a logical chain.

Posing the problems of ethology in terms of intentional systems amounts to a polemical challenge with respect to C. Lloyd Morgan's "canon of parsimony," which "enjoins us to settle on the most killjoy, least romantic hypothesis that will account systematically for the observed and observable behavior."[3] Dennett opposes the behaviorist tendency (which is, here, a style of scientific reasoning, not historical behaviorism): "The claim that *in principle* a lowest-order story can always be told of any animal behavior (an entirely physiological story, or even an abstemiously behavioristic story of unimaginable complexity) is no longer interesting. . . . Today we are interested in asking what gains in perspicuity, in predictive power, in generalization, might accrue if we adopt a higher-level hypothesis that takes a risky step into intentional characterization. The question is empirical. The tactic of adopting the intentional stance is not a matter of *replacing* empirical investigations with aprioristic ('armchair') investigations, but of using the stance to suggest which brute empirical questions to put to nature."[4]

For example, in connection with the well-known 1982 article by Seyfarth and Cheney about the complex communications of vervet monkeys in reaction to three different predators,[5] one can explore whether vervet monkeys traveling alone make their grunting sounds when a predator is approaching. It turns out that they do not; they hide in silence. This is an argument in support of the intentional use of differentiated cries of alarm. Their cries can no longer be interpreted as "anxious yapping," as the behaviorists maintain in the presence of predators such as leopards or pythons. We can see that the intentional stance has nothing to do, here, with an ethical decision regarding animal well-being, with an ideological revolution in the form of granting animals what they had not been granted before, or even with an ontological revolution that would consist in shifting the break between human and nonhuman mental lives elsewhere. It comes down to an epistemological necessity. This is what I call an animist epistemological strategy.

However, trying to isolate intentional behaviors would raise an epistemological problem that Dennett characterizes as a vicious circle: for an original or particularly complex and intentional behavior to be documentable, it has to be repeatable and repeated. Once it is repeated, the behaviorist can always argue that, because it has been repeated, it has been learned by behaviorist operant conditioning.

In addition to this vicious circle bound up with repeatable data, the ethologist confronts a second epistemological problem: how to treat the nonrepeatable data, specifically the *anecdotal data*. In fact, the latter are deceptive and hard to use; they are not representative and thus they are inductively impotent; they are often, however, very "telling." But the regime for administering proof in an empirical science excludes them structurally. To get around this problem, Dennett's thesis is that one needs to use the "Sherlock Holmes method." He is referring to the ruse by means of which Sherlock, in "A Scandal in Bohemia," looks for a photograph hidden by his adversary in a house. He himself hides, asking Watson to toss a smoke bomb and yell "fire!" The adversary heads discreetly toward the place where the photo is hidden. "Similar stratagems can be designed to test the various hypotheses about the beliefs and desires of vervet monkeys and other creatures. These stratagems have the virtue of provoking novel but interpretable behavior, of *generating anecdotes* under controlled (and hence scientifically admissible) conditions."[6]

The following could be some new guidelines for today's ethology: Do not keep receiving anecdotes the way all animal observers did up to the nineteenth century, but do not reject them, either, the way animal psychologists inspired by behaviorism do; instead, generate anecdotes under controlled conditions.

Inventing Nonhuman Soliloquies

To do this, Dennett goes back to Richard Dawkins (*The Selfish Gene*[7]) and borrows an "expository technique" that consists in inventing soliloquies attributed to biological entities.

For example, to test the intentionality of a bird mimicking a broken wing to attract a predator away from the nest and her chicks, Dennett imagines the bird's soliloquy: "I'm a low-nesting bird, whose chicks are not protectable against a predator who discovers them. This approaching predator can be *expected* soon to discover them unless I distract it; it could be distracted by its *desire* to catch and eat me, but only if it *thought* there was a *reasonable* chance of its actually catching me . . ."[8]

Dennett notes that his soliloquy attributes to the deceitful bird a very sophisticated degree of intentionality. "It is unlikely in the extreme that any feathered 'deceiver' is an intentional system of this intelligence. A more realistic soliloquy for any bird would probably be more along the lines of:

'Here comes a predator; all of a sudden I feel this tremendous urge to do that silly broken wing dance. I wonder why?' (Yes, I know, it would be wildly romantic to suppose such a bird would be up to such a metalevel wondering about its sudden urge.)"[9]

The second degree of intentionality corresponds to the ability to have beliefs or desires concerning beliefs or desires. By extension, we grasp the sense of the third degree: beliefs about beliefs about beliefs.

The problem is to how to use the soliloquy method to determine "just how sensitive a bird's cognitive control system is to the relevant variables in the environment."[10]

If a bird tested in this fashion manifests extreme sophistication in the use of the stratagem in relation to the environmental conditions (evidence that it distinguishes among predators, or that it knows it cannot deceive the same predator with the same trick several times in a row), then it will be possible to prove that interpreting its behavior as belonging to a higher order (one that postulates a higher degree of intentionality) is appropriate.

The tactic of creating an expository soliloquy is not a form of poetic license, a guilty anthropomorphic pleasure, or a desire to reenchant an animal world that has been condemned to being defined as mere matter animated by instincts; it is an established epistemological method. It consists in the injection of a first-person narrative as a method for developing experimental ethological protocols that allow us to evaluate the degree of intentionality of other animals.

The Intentionality of Wolves

We can now interrogate the relevance of the search for high-level intentionality in wolves. Mark Rowlands, a Welsh analytic philosopher, lived for more than a decade with a wolf. He drew on this experience to produce a remarkable work depicting the intuitions of a werewolf-diplomat in which he defends an intriguing thesis: according to him, the human primate is a specialist in high-level intentionality, for intentionality is made for deception and strategic interaction in political situations; and we humans are not political animals but rather politician-animals par excellence.[11]

Primatologists Andrew Whiten and Richard Byrne use the term "Machiavellian intelligence" to characterize the high-level intelligence of certain primates that allows them to interact and form complex alliances.[12] Among these primates, chimpanzees being an example and *Homo sapiens* a paragon, interactions are opportunities for "manipulating and exploiting your colleagues—and so acquiring all the benefits of group living while incurring fewer of the costs. Such manipulation and exploitation are based on a capacity for deception: the primary, and most effective way of manipulating your colleagues is by deceiving them."[13] Rowlands deduces from this that, among primates, selective pressures have played a role in the increase in the ability to deceive and to spot deception. On this basis, he sketches a tableau of the social life of primates that require deception in order to counter plots: the aptitude for scheming is omnipresent. Wolves, which are also social animals, "never went down that path." Indeed, "with regard to . . . scheming and deception, dogs and wolves are like children compared to the great apes. No one really understands why apes should adopt this strategy while wolves did not. But . . . one thing is overwhelmingly clear: it did happen."[14]

Rowlands's rhetorical strategy consists in raising awareness of the scale of intelligence on which there is supposedly a simple difference of degree: "When we talk about the superior intelligence of apes, the superiority of simian over lupine intelligence, we should bear in mind the terms of the comparison: apes are more intelligent than wolves because, ultimately, they are better schemers and deceivers."[15]

This allows Rowlands to show that the scale is not neutral and not suited for all animals. Rather, it is modeled on a quite specific form of cognitive functioning proper to a series of species that relate in a specific way to their own evolutionary inheritance: this series includes human beings as well as certain social primates. After making the nature of this scale clear, he shifts it from the cognitive realm, where it seems to be *glorified* by humans, to the moral realm, where these same humans *condemn* it. Thus Rowlands reverses the scale's axiological polarity: what was greatness becomes infamy; what was stupidity becomes moral innocence, thus virtue.

"Perhaps the single greatest contribution apes have made to the world—the single defining contribution for which they will always be remembered—is malice aforethought."[16] By premeditation Rowlands means malevolent intentions, but the term extends to encompass everything.

Rowlands constructs his misanthropic explanation for the genesis of morality on the basis of singular cognitive capabilities that allow premeditation: "Standing on its own, alone in all of nature, we find the ape: the only animal sufficiently unpleasant to become a moral animal."[17] This occurs because the secondary effects of these new powers have to be regulated. Immorality is always the other side of the coin of some power—the power of another being. In Rowlands's view, coercive morality emerges as a need to control malevolent behaviors by norms, in a species in which premeditation has appeared, in which offenses are not forgotten, and in which the capacity for harm among conspecifics belonging to the same group is magnified by Machiavellian intelligence. This is a different genealogy for morality than that of Darwin, Leopold, and Callicott, who postulate a continuity of "social feelings" leading toward a moral feeling.

At the opposite pole, Rowlands argues that wolves are not political animals: rather, they are aristocrats. It is interesting to note the type of experiences he brings up to illustrate this point, and the type of metaphors he uses. These converge with some of Rick McIntyre's observations, in which we have explored the metaphoric content.[18] Rowlands reports that, in violent conflicts, his tame wolf, Brenin, attacked only animals as powerful and aggressive as himself, that he stopped as soon as symbolic signs of submission appeared, and that he showed indifference or "a curious form of goodness" toward those weaker than himself, even if they were aggressive. Rowlands tells the story of a six-month-old Labrador who violently harassed Brenin: the wolf, who could not keep on ignoring the behavior, took the pup's whole head in his mouth to immobilize and calm him.

The author adds: "If you judge Brenin by Kundera's test then I think he actually emerged with moral reputation reasonably intact." Rowlands is referring here to a passage in *The Unbearable Lightness of Being*: "The true moral test of humanity . . . lies in its relations to those who are at its mercy: the animals."[19]

A "moral reputation reasonably intact": for what other animal would one use so spontaneously the anthropomorphic metaphor of moral reputation? Why do analogous lexical fields appear in the writings of other observers of wolves (Doug Smith, Jane Packard, Rick McIntyre, Peter Steinhardt, and so on)?[20] And what does the metaphor reveal, specifically? A feminist sociological critic might see the phantasm of intellectuals, male for the most part, fallen heirs of the aristocracy that they project, but this would be a good way to evade the question—and then again, if that argument were to hold, why would this register be absent from the works of specialists in bees and suricates? It is more probable that wolves' ethological-ethical behavior evokes metaphors intended to make them more intelligible that come from the realm of behaviors Westerners call noble. In other words, certain behavioral sequences are reminiscent of the moral norms and behavioral codes found in the medieval chivalry of Europe and elsewhere: a candid refinement, an absence of grudge-holding, an absence of premeditation, a spontaneous expression of strength in a challenge, panache in the physical pleasure of confrontation, an inability to win by devious methods, a refusal to attack another known to be weaker. These are strange animal primordia.[21]

By contrasting the ape politician and the wolf aristocrat, Rowlands sketches out an unformulated and perhaps unconscious rereading of Nietzsche's genealogy of morality. This becomes obvious when Rowlands spells out the two polarities. "The wolf is art of the highest form and you cannot be in its presence without this lifting your spirits. . . . But if the art of the wolf was something that I couldn't emulate, underlying it was something else: a strength that I could at least try to approximate. The ape that I am is a crabbed, graceless creature that deals in weakness: a weakness that it manufactures in others, and a weakness with which it is ultimately infected. It is this weakness that permits evil—moral evil—a foothold in the world. The art of the wolf is grounded in its strength."[22]

Here Rowlands is evoking the collateral moral effects induced by the differentiated cognitive capacities of the two animals. From his perspective, the moral sphere as a set of dilemmas and contradictory values is only a secondary effect of the evolutionary emergence of cognitive powers: those on whom faculties of premeditation have been bestowed also have received, consequently, as a way of regulating those powers, the duty to pardon.

"A wolf will quickly forgive and forget. But an ape is driven by malice aforethought and is not so easily mollified."[23] It seems likely that the complex character of the emotional life of primates, with their ambiguous emotions (blends of fear and pride, submission and anger), plays a role in the appearance of this premeditation, which must therefore not be taken as a moral failing.

The Shakespearean dimension of the history of the Druid Peak Pack becomes more intelligible in the light of these analyses: it is without premeditation and without "afterthoughts" that the drama between sisters 40 and 42 plays out, in frontal relations of dominance and overt conflicts; unstoppable once they begin, they take on the dimension of a *tragic destiny*.[24]

Despite the caricatural schemas and the problematic misanthropy that we can read between the lines of Rowlands's reasoning, these meditations are valuable for the enterprise they outline: an analysis of human existentials on the basis of the multiple ancestral heritages in human life, and a behavioral approach to different moralities on the basis of eco-evolutionist conjunctures, which human culture will then evaluate according to axiological norms.

This will be the evolutionary history of our intelligence. Why did wolves and other *social* mammals, who have a common ancestor with primates some dozens of millions of years back, not follow the evolutionary path of Machiavellian intelligence? This is a complete mystery.

But we can hypothesize that wolves do not need intraspecific strategic intelligence, do not need to be able to read signs, because their social structures and their behavioral tonality imply little in the way of power plays. And even when such plays take place, the conflicts are face-to-face, symbolic, and they put on display essentially what must be called, for lack of a better term, the *valor* of the animals, in the escalation of a conflict induced by the self-affirmation of each wolf. Which one will yield first and accept a subordinate position? Which one will go the furthest in self-affirmation? But there is nothing on the order of scheming or trickery. The absence of such behaviors has long been seen as an effect of incompetence in the realm of high-level intentionality. But what if it were the inverse? What if the conditions of wolves' political life neutralized the selective pressures that could be applied to the competencies of high-level intentionality? And what if this were a life form that has not undergone an evolution toward scheming and psychology, because its political tonality and its morality, one might say, ruled out an adaptive reward for this type of relation among conspecifics?

In this sense, it is perhaps inappropriate to look for complex intentionalities among wolves: an aristocratic creature does not constantly try to find out what another thinks, does not attempt to act in response to what the other believes that he or she thinks, does not seek to deceive others or to play on the representations of others. Such a creature is a force that acts in the world, on the basis of straightforward behaviors manifesting loyalty, direct measures of strength.

Moreover, these observations make it possible to refine a thesis developed earlier, concerning the importance of not giving in to the new ecumenical myth of "difference in degree," which appears to be the most generous possible formulation toward animals while still being epistemologically human-centered. It is primocentric to seek advanced degrees of intentionality in all animals, as if this were *the* mark of intelligence or consciousness, whereas it is only the type of intelligence and reflexivity characteristic of a primate politician, and rarely its highest moral aptitude. Current successes in animal science of projects that seek intentionality as the form of intelligence in nonhuman animals, as in other projects that seek "self-consciousness" as the form of reflexivity linked to intentionality, reveal this bias on the part of scientists who, in the name of a difference of degree between animal intelligences consecrated by Darwin, impose tests on nonhuman animals in which *only* primates succeed, to the exclusion of alien forms of intelligence and relations to the self that we cannot yet imagine but that constitute the way of being alive characteristic of other animals.

These developments give us a deeper understanding of the privileged relation that *Homo sapiens* maintains with diplomatic aptitudes: we are, by virtue of our eco-evolutionary essence, animal diplomats. But these developments also bring to light the moral ambiguity of these aptitudes. Animals endowed by evolution with a high degree of intentionality are capable of deception. This aptitude implies that we know how to conceptualize the inner lives of those around us. It is in the moral ambiguity emerging from this single cognitive aptitude that the two uses of diplomacy originate. Diplomacy can be used to deceive the adversary in order to win a war, or it can be used to understand the adversary in order to improve relations; in other words, it can be intentionally used for *mutualist* purposes. Humans can thus decide how to use this gift made to primates by evolution. Sorting out the possibilities is one of the major challenges addressed by this inquiry; it will be the focus of part 3.

Chapter 9

A Differently Rational Shamanism

Possible Philosophical Forms of Animism

As a guide to the form of diplomatic knowledge I am seeking to describe, I propose to recruit the epistemological approach implied by animism. Philosophers have begun to focus on animism over the last couple of decades; Philippe Descola in particular has conceptualized it as an abstract *ontological schema*, liberating it both from the traditional way of seeing it (as an archaic vestige of human thought limited to prescientific peoples) and from the traditional way of studying it (in terms of its expression in singular cultures: the Achuar, the Makuna, the Chewong, and so on).[1] Thanks to Descola's presentation, animism has become a basic ontological attitude that scholars can venture to adopt, if only for the purpose of formulating *hypotheses*. Along with anthropologist Eduardo Viveiros de Castro,[2] Descola has freed up animism to serve as a philosophical paradigm.

This liberation is essential for reflections on the ontological schemas that we shall need to envision for the future. Descola, who has been very circumspect in determining the *normative* implications of his anthropological theory where questions of political and practical ecology are concerned,[3] evokes the limits of naturalism in a recent book, *La composition des mondes*.[4] According to him, these limits are made visible by the destructive effects for which naturalism is in part responsible and that are mortgaging the inhabitability of the earth. When Descola envisions the future, he concludes that scientific realism is an ontological schema that warrants inflection: not that it is false—what could be the standard of truth for an ontological attitude?—but that it appears outdated. For Descola, descriptive anthropology

149

becomes a guide for a new normative philosophy of nature *without* Nature. He suggests allusively that shifting our current naturalism toward a "diffuse analogism" might be a solution, if not perhaps even the only solution, given that analogism is a state that precedes scientific realism in historical terms (it was present, for example, in the episteme of the European Renaissance); thus it is closer to modern Western thought than animism, which is, for us, not only an alien ontological form but also an *inverse* of scientific realism. Descola does justice here to the subtlety of his categories. But is it really inconceivable that the eco-etho-evolutionist philosophy of *living beings* that we need could require shifting our scientific ontology toward a diffuse *animism*?[5]

This diffuse plural animism can be understood here as a form of ethocentrism, that is, an ontological and epistemological attitude postulating that "everything acts." This form of animism, which I shall deploy further on, is called for today by a whole panoply of emerging knowledge. For example, plant neurobiology is seeking to show that neurons, in the strict sense, are not the *only* cells capable of ensuring "neural" or cognitive functions:[6] although plants possess no neurons, they manifest aptitudes that are *in certain respects* analogous to animal behaviors that we call intelligent. Here again we are seeing an attempt to give new meaning to a concept that neurobiology had locked down (in this instance, "intelligence"). Far from daydreams about plants' tastes in music, this branch of botany is the only one capable of accounting for phenomena of which we have only recently become aware. The natural sciences have also revealed their limitations in attempts to account for the ability of certain trees to defend themselves in an adaptive manner against aggression by herbivores, as well as to communicate the danger to neighboring trees; we shall look at this case more closely later on. But, closer to the hard data of biology, these reconfigurations have been made visible by biologist Matthew Gilliham and his team with the very recent discovery that plants make effective use of a neurotransmitter that is well known in animals (Gaba, short for gamma-aminobutyric acid) in situations of ecological stress (drought, salinity, acid soil, and so on).[7] Botanists have long believed that Gaba played only a metabolic role in plants, since, in the absence of neurons, Gaba could not function as a *neurotransmitter*. This self-evident "fact" has just been disproved. Gilliham has discovered that a *signaling mechanism* is present in plants. Gaba procures a signal for a protein in the plant's cellular membrane that alters electrical activity and allows the plant to react to transformations in its environment. The implication of this discovery in terms of *plant* neurobiology is clear: it is not necessary to have nerve cells in the strict sense to carry out operations that are nevertheless interpreted as a form of intelligence. The ontological deck of cards has been reshuffled.

Is it a coincidence that we are dealing here with the same molecule in animals and plants? Gaba may stem from a common ancestor, or its two manifestations may be convergent (that is, may have evolved separately). We find here the two fundamental models that justify a generalized ethology, in which the biomorphic comparison allows us to grasp the singularities of living beings: as combinatorics of traits that are sometimes inherited, sometimes convergent, living species share the same tesserae, with which they form original mosaics. To say that a plant "defends itself against aggression" is no longer a dubious anthropomorphism, once we have rigorously understood by this that the plant is reacting to an external stress by internal neurotransmitters, which trigger reactions selected by evolution that are able to counteract the aggression.[8]

The bond is woven ecologically in ourselves as well, since we know that certain human medicines act on proteins linked to Gaba in our brains, and that they often come from plants that synthesize Gaba—a phenomenon for which we still have no explanation. It is through this sort of discovery that deep interconnections among living beings have been made visible, interconnections that require concepts yet to be formulated in any science so far conceived, leaving us to face mysterious moments of awareness. Yet mystery enlarges space. Consequently, its political effect is to make space: space for the other living beings in our political ontology.

An ethocentric animism would be a useful tool, then, from the methodological standpoint, and it is also called for by the field of environmental history, one of whose historiographical postulates consists in establishing ecological entities as *agents* of history, on the same basis as human individuals and groups.[9] The basic problem comes down to determining rigorously what type of animism we need in order to think *better*. It is not a matter of postulating souls everywhere, in a complacently archaic way, but of asking ourselves to what extent there is an increase in intelligibility if we postulate intentional dimensions in new places, as Dennett does. But it is also a matter of asking to what extent some effects of cohabitation are enhanced and some effects of destruction lessened if we postulate different forms of agency, ethologically and scientifically documented, here and there. The whole problem comes down to opening an inquiry into the type of animistic agency with which the world is richly endowed.

This philosophical attitude is known as "generalized ethology." Ecological systems warrant the proposal of a hypothesis according to which "everything acts"—from the pyrophilic pine trees that favor forest fires, to the crows that guide wolves toward their prey, to the acacia that secretes tannins so as to disgust those who graze on them, to the forest of Sainte-Baume-en-Provence that has its own way of maintaining the hygrometry it needs to prosper. A generalized ethology that allows and requires this diplomatic cohabitation, this attention to the system of signs: this is a highly rational animism![10] The error of the reductionist positivists, or physicalists, arises from a belief that Darwin's triumph lay in proving that the living world is *devoid* of purpose and meaning. This is a profound misunderstanding: the theory of evolution postulates that what is devoid of purpose is the *process* that elaborates the profusion of types of purpose and meaning that are present in the living world. To understand the behavior of things—any thing, all things—is to understand how they behave among themselves, so we can understand how to behave toward them, how to construct our relations with them, how to use our powers, and how to avoid letting them divide us or keep us apart. In an ethological cosmology in which everything acts, the privileged mode of action is diplomacy.

A philosophical revalorization of animism has been proposed by Australian philosopher Val Plumwood:[11] her philosophical animism aims to open "the door to a world in which we can begin to negotiate life membership of an ecological community of kindred beings."[12]

The significance of Plumwood's position resides in her search for the conditions of logical possibility of an ethics that would automatically make room for nonhumans. One of those conditions implies that "recognizing earth others as fellow agents and narrative subjects is crucial for all ethical, collaborative, communicative and mutualistic projects."[13] This attitude entails leaving behind the myth of mindlessness according to which we are the only beings supplied with minds; we can accomplish this not by producing a *conceptual* analysis of what minds are, but by undergoing the direct experience of being a mind *among others* in a world already packed with minds (mindfulness). The material world becomes mindful, in a creative philosophical enterprise verging on fiction, an enterprise undertaking to develop "stories that create much greater transparency of these [inter-active] relationships in our day-to-day lives."[14] The ultimate object of this approach, which calls for a literary and political dimension, comes down to "making room" for the other beings on our earth.

As a philosophical attitude aiming to transform the fabulations through which we recount life, there is nothing more fantastic in this animism than postulating the existence of "monads," of a cosmic "will to power," or of a Being transcending existing beings. Animism can become a research hypothesis in ethosophy and in the philosophy of ecology, at a far remove from its stigmatization as an atavism of the human mind or as animalist sentimentalism. Nevertheless, there is another sense of animism that we need to examine in order to grasp the specificity of the diplomatic approach.

Tracking as a Way of Experiencing the Biomorphic Convergences between Humans and Wolves

We are now ready to approach the epistemological stakes of a diplomatic wolf science.

The recent model of ecology is quantitative and objectifying. It thus brings into play certain effects of intelligibility while excluding others. But contemporary ecology could be enriched by a parallel and more comprehensive, or "comprehending," approach. To experimental reasoning about the animal mode of existence, we need to add a hermeneutic dimension, by way of natural language. To *understand* a human, we have to put ourselves in that person's place, see through her eyes, coincide with his form of life. But how do we do this with an animal? If we are to *understand* its behaviors, it will not be through an interhuman theory of mind, it will be because its behaviors are biomorphic: they have to do with the fact of being a living organism. Thus the best strategy for understanding animal behaviors entails looking in a new way at the vital events we share with animals, seeking to extrapolate the signification we would give those events if we were experiencing them ourselves—if we were in the particular animals' place in the complex economy of living beings, in their own ecological niche with their own genetic past, in their own mode of existence shaped by their ongoing relationships.

This comprehensive approach, grounded in "etho-eco-evolutionary" empathy, can be traced back to technologies of knowledge characteristic of hunter-gatherer societies, or to pastoral societies in close contact with wolves. The fundamental element of this approach is tracking.

Tracking is a way of experiencing nature that probably originated in hunting practices. As a contemporary practice, however, it has much broader and more fundamental uses. In a world where *Homo sapiens* has interacted for several hundred thousand years with a rich and omnipresent fauna, tracking appears above all as a *geopolitical* practice addressing basic questions such as these: "Who *lives* here? And how do these beings live?

How is territory constructed in their world? On what points do my actions affect their lives, and vice versa?"

This is the dimension of tracking, then, detached from its relation to hunting, that we shall explore here. The eco-fragmentation that is destroying animal habitats on a massive scale is not simply an effect of huge infrastructure projects; it is above all an effect of our ignorance about the invisible configurations through which animals inhabit these spaces that we thought we had claimed for ourselves.

Simple initiatives, inconsequential for humans, are reviving habitats that our land uses have mutilated. Examples can be found in the "Backyard Wildlife Habitat" program, which demonstrates how gardening practices can recreate spaces of cohabitation that increase biodiversity (for example, planting a certain flower that will attract butterflies, or building a certain type of nest platform or birdhouse that can serve as a landing spot for a migratory bird heading north).[15] This is one of the directions taken by the "reconciliation ecology" project.[16]

The question of tracking thus becomes once again what it may have been throughout the Pleistocene era, when coexistence with a rich and abundant fauna required knowing *how* to cohabit with it, what habits to avoid disrupting, which ones to transform, what powers to come to terms with and what borders to respect: a fully developed diplomatic geopolitics of the biotic community.

To understand an animal, we must put ourselves in its place, see through its eyes. This is precisely what tracking allows us to do. Find the key points of biomorphic convergence by following *in the tracks* of the animal—for example, a wolf. Find the problematics that are vital (in a different sense) in themselves. Analyze the features we have in common: try to get out of the vital human stance so as to coincide with the animal in another place. Follow a side trail, for example. Certain animal trails are sites of indistinction between humans and animals, for at first glance we cannot tell whose trails they are. A given trail is often shared, shaped, and marked without distinction by several species, including humans, and it is with the same pathbreaking vision, and for the same reasons, that each group chooses its paths. Deer trails are open invitations; those of wild boar become challenging when the rough cover becomes denser, because these trails are lower to the ground. Chamois trails are often too vertical, for these animals live like birds in three dimensions, with vertical paths being just as natural to them as horizontal ones. Wolf trails are optimal for long strides. Among the large animals, there are communal stakes where movement is concerned; there are analogous ways of moving about, a similar search for an already-broken trail, for an optimal passageway, for a stream to quench thirst or just to enjoy running water, for sun to warm the skin after the chill of the valley, for a vantage point looking out over the valley that allows one to get one's bearings and to see what may be coming, for shade against the noonday sun, for a detour to get around the peak. A wolf trail always takes the path of least resistance. And this is why a human will always follow an animal trail (of a certain size), and why, on and by virtue of that trail, between that human and that animal there is no distinction, a fact that proves, in the essential lived experience of following it, the proximity of the two. Humans and wolves see through the same eyes; they are mammals that open up a path with the same stakes and the same way of thinking and deciding. This biomorphism, which seeks the common matrices of modes of existence, is based on a complex cluster made up of shared neurological bases, shared eco-ethological conditions, a certain community of feeling and thought—an intrinsic community of vital problematics. This is what is manifested by tracking.

Let us conjure up a tracking game: a track in the clay soil of a stream bed. All one can see are traces of *Canis lupus* in the mud. But with other eyes, we shall try to reconstitute a trajectory, to extrapolate a course of action, a way of moving, a bundle of intentions, which tell us about a way of inhabiting a place. The intense emotion felt in tracking, stronger in a sense than what one feels upon seeing the animal directly,[17] comes down to seeing *with the other's eyes*. To follow the animal's trail, we are obliged to *move inside its head*, in order to understand its intentions, to walk with its paws to understand its displacements. Here we see the front feet, pressed parallel into the clay: it stopped, right here where we are, to look around the landscape, sniff the scent of the sheep grazing below. There, it inspected its realm with a royal gaze; here, a scraping, to indicate to other packs the border that they will not cross without having to fight or be challenged. All this structures thought, in an action-science in which every hypothesis orients our steps and our gaze in a new direction.[18]

Shamanic Dislocation as a Method

The methodology of tracking has a deeply rooted point of intersection with shamanic rites: *dislocation*, which consists in the power to shift one's mind into the body of an animal—often a feline, a wolf, or a vulture. This *sensation* of seeing through an animal's eyes, procured by tracking, is moreover perhaps in part at the origin of the imaginary extrapolation that consecrates dislocation as a supernatural power. The fact remains that this form of shamanic dislocation underlies the practical method of a rigorous science devoted to the large predators.

The dislocation required for tracking makes it possible to develop proactive hypotheses aimed at finding these elusive animals we know as wolves and understanding how they organize their territory in relation to human activities. Tracking in fact requires that we first determine what zones to examine. On maps, by comparing official and unofficial data on the places where sightings or traces of wolves have been found, we have to triangulate the possible positions. Then, by imagining how wolves configure their territory, we have to choose our axes of displacement while optimizing speed (forest trails following crests, for example), relative tranquility, access to prey, access to drinking water, and so on; it becomes possible, by this strange wolf feng shui, to make hypotheses about key points where we have a good chance of finding tracks. With this method, working with others, I have been able to surprise three wolves on their familiar paths, along with countless sets of tracks, during a nocturnal tracking session in the Var region in southeastern France.

But this practice is not only credited by naturalists; it is the methodological basis of the scientific ecology of wolves in contexts where more costly methods (radio-collaring, spotting from a plane) are not accessible. American ecologists who specialize in wolves have of necessity become competent trackers; some have produced practical manuals for reading wolf tracks that would do indigenous forest dwellers proud.[19] The use of tracking also confers a diplomatic dimension on some intelligent initiatives made in conservation biology. In 1993, an initiative aimed at conserving large predators, "Yellowstone to Yukon" (Y2Y), formulated a goal that is characteristic of the project of rewilding developed by biologist Michael Soulé.[20] Rewilding consists in maintaining protected natural core zones, ensuring corridors between these zones, and making sure carnivores are present to ensure the integrity of the trophic pyramid. The goal of Y2Y was to make it possible for the large North American predators (wolves, grizzlies, pumas, and so on) to move all along the mountain chain that goes from Alaska to the Rocky Mountains—what American ecologist Cristina Eisenberg calls "the carnivore way."[21] It turns out that the survival of the large predators depends on the dynamics of dispersal over very great distances: the animals need to be allowed simultaneously to avoid exhausting the supply of prey in their territories, to ensure genetic mixing, and to colonize new areas in the face of change, especially climate change. However, the corridors in question tend to be cluttered with human installations that carve up the territory (countless fences, highways, railroads, fields, cities, and suburbs) with no concern for animal displacements, creating serious obstacles to dispersal. This is one of the invisible but powerful causes that led to the disappearance of large predators from the region in the twentieth century.

To assess the actual conditions of this north-south corridor, Karsten Heuer, a biologist and the director of Y2Y since 2013, made an epic trek on foot in 1998, following the tracks of grizzlies. Questioned about his motivations, he replied: "I decided to find out if this thing that I was so excited about was actually workable on the ground. That was the birth of the idea to trek—to try to be one of those animals, a grizzly bear or a wolf

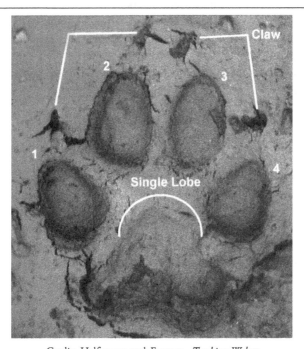

Credit: Halfpenny and Furman, *Tracking Wolves*

Figure 16. Elements of Identification of a Wolf Print (scale 1:1)

The print is longer (9–11 cm) than it is wide. It has an oval shape, unlike the rounder canine shape. The claws are strong and pronounced. The interdigital pads include a pronounced lobe in front, and sometimes three small lobes behind. The spaces between the front pad and the interdigital pads are larger than in dogs. A straight twig can pass between the front and side pads without cutting them (claws not included). Nevertheless, identification almost always requires incorporating additional information: the complete cluster (two anterior, two posterior); the track, often rectilinear (where the animal's stride [*allure*] can be read); the context (human and nonhuman allies).

or wolverine, trying to make these movements from one reserve to another, and see not just the physical barriers that might exist, but also the political, economic, and value-based ones among the people."[22] During 188 days of hiking, covering some three thousand kilometers, Heuer put himself in the place of a grizzly, tracking the animals' traces, looking for the trails they took, isolating the points where their movement was blocked by human infrastructures and points where small adjustments could facilitate the bears' displacements. He was able to determine that the corridor in question did not have to be invented, it had already been in place for several thousand years: he had followed the grizzlies' traces from one end to the other. In the process, among other things, he helped show the extraordinary effectiveness of passages on or under roads to allow the animals to disperse, as soon as those points were imagined in a diplomatic way, in harmony with the animals' way of configuring space.[23]

A Methodological Shamanism

In the earlier discussion of tracking, we noted the animist theme of shamanistic dislocation as an ability to shift oneself into an animal's body. This ability plays a decisive role in the epistemology required by the diplomatic approach. It requires us to pay attention to what nonscientific ways of understanding of the world can teach us about interactions with living beings.

The parallel with shamanism is not arbitrary, for shamans are specialists in mental interactions with nonhumans. Wolf science is based on understanding, but it is not an understanding that is grounded, as it was for Wilhelm Dilthey, in the notion that we share a common *humanity*.[24] Instead, it is an understanding that rests on a biomorphic foundation. But passing from one species to another cannot occur spontaneously and effortlessly, for the gap between life forms implies a change in one's perspective on the cosmos: this is something the Amerindian approach teaches us. A comprehensive wolf science thus has to be *perspectivist*. Perspectivism is an anthropological concept developed by Brazilian anthropologist Eduardo Viveiros de Castro, starting from the symbolic system constituted by Amerindian (and more specifically Amazonian) shamanism.

Amazonian perspectivism is an ontological and epistemological attitude present among many New World peoples, who share the idea that the world is "composed of a multiplicity of points of view. Every existent is a center of intentionality apprehending other existents according to their respective characteristics and powers."[25]

In this approach, for example, Amerindians suggest that jaguars look at blood the way humans see manioc beer; vultures look at rotten meat as humans see grilled fish. Read as a parable about the inversion of disgust and delight, this observation reveals one of the strengths of perspectivism: through such metaphors, it is able to grasp, from within, the relation that other beings maintain with shared entities. The parable accounts for their taste for and delight in things that disgust us. On this point, it captures the biological truth that evolution develops, in each species, an appetite for what constitutes its own diet, for what it finds "really and truly" desirable, however repugnant others may find that diet.

Now, this cosmology is straightforwardly pragmatic: "Amerindian shamanism could be defined as the authorization of certain individuals to cross the corporeal barriers between species, adopt an exospecific subjective perspective, and administer the relations between those species and humans. By seeing nonhuman beings as they see themselves (again as humans), shamans become capable of playing the role of active interlocutors in the trans-specific dialogue and, even more importantly, of returning from their travels to recount them, something the 'laity' can only do with difficulty. This encounter or exchange of perspectives is not only a dangerous process but a political art: diplomacy."[26]

The point of convergence between shamanism and wolf diplomacy is obvious here: the fundamental political challenge is how to manage relations between ourselves and the others, and this implies recognizing those others as agents, or, in a certain sense, subjects. The fundamental technical problem then becomes how to set up arrangements for effective communication.

The character of the werewolf, in animist symbolic systems, is highly perspectivist. In *How Forests Think*, Eduardo Kohn evokes a similar jaguar character as a guide for understanding the complex interweavings between human communities and the symbiotic life of forests themselves. The forests in Ecuador's Upper Amazon, he says, "are full of *runa puma*, shape-shifting human-jaguars, or were-jaguars as I will call them. *Runa* in Quichua means 'person'; *puma* means 'predator' or 'jaguar.' These runa puma—beings who can see themselves being seen by jaguars as fellow predators, and who also sometimes *see* other humans the way jaguars do, namely, as prey—have been known to wander all the way down to the distant Napo River."[27] It is insofar as he considers himself *seen* as a puma by a puma, or that he sees his fellow humans as prey, that the Amazonian were-jaguar acquires his hybridity: the body is only a cloak, a secondary feature that does not define the identity of a being—the essence of every being is defined by its *perspective* on the world.

The perspectivist figure of the runa puma is what gives its ultimate meaning to the zoocephalic diplomat being portrayed here. Wolf diplomats are werewolves owing to their *hybridized perspective*. The hybridization of a werewolf's body is only a metaphor for a much deeper hybridization of perspectives on the world, that is, on the relations that the hybridized figure maintains with the others. Seeing from a wolf's point of view, thinking like a wolf through the process of tracking and the quest for ways to communicate limits, entering into interactions with wolves in which the diplomat is considered *by them* as a wolf (in the howling that incites to action or in the use of biofences) effectively transforms the diplomat into a werewolf. To go back to the dizzying play of Amazonian perspectivism, we note that the werewolf diplomat sometimes sees himself as being seen by wolves as one of their own, negotiating borders as they do. Sometimes the werewolf even sees humans the way wolves see them.

For this hybridization of perspectives is not only an internal (perceptual or cognitive) phenomenon: it has practical and political effects. In fact, perspectivism offers more than the possibility of hybridizing perspectives in one's imagination. Above all, it posits that the point of view of a given being has an ontological effect: that is, it produces effects on the identity *of the others* involved in an interaction, and on the *form* of the relationship. Thus it is effective in *political* terms. We saw this phenomenon taking shape in part 1 of this book in the discussion of biofences. Here we reach the core of the extraordinary philosophical originality of perspectivism.[28]

Taking our inspiration from this aspect of perspectivist cosmology, we can understand why a perspectivist diplomat deserves to be called a were-diplomat, that is, a hybrid. It is precisely because the cognitive and practical arrangements such diplomats have to put in place to practice their art are techniques of metamorphosis. But metamorphosis must be understood here in the perspectivist sense, as it has been formulated, for example, by Philippe Descola, as "one of the means that animist ontology has invented so that subjectivities that are analogous but ensconced in incommensurable bodily garb can nevertheless communicate without too many obstacles."[29] If we are materialist enough to think that we are not ensconced in bodily garb but constituted by it, cohabitation nevertheless requires that we become animist enough to borrow these means of communication with subjectivities that are in fact analogous but simultaneously incommensurable. To this extent, "metamorphosis is not a change in ordinary form, but the culminating stage in a relationship in which each participant, by modifying the viewing position that his or her body imposes, strives to coincide with the perspective from which he or she thinks the other sees himself or herself." Metamorphosis is thus a technique that consists in a "displacement of the angle of approach that one is seeking to take on 'in the skin' of the other by espousing the other's intentionality." When it is successful, "humans no longer see animals the way they usually see them, but the way the animals see themselves, that is, as humans, and shamans are perceived as they do not usually see themselves, but as they wish to be seen, as animals."[30]

This strange conception of metamorphosis is represented ritually by fascinating objects known as transforming masks. The hinged masks of the Kwakwaka'wakw Indians of the coastal regions of the American Northwest are good examples: they conceal a movable mechanism that makes it possible to open an outer animal face over an inner human face (sometimes with multiple levels).[31] The contemporary artist Sanford Williams, from the Mowachaht tribe, reinterprets this tradition freely, making masks whose imaginary power is gripping.[32] Taking our inspiration from this artistic freedom, we can shift the meaning of the transforming mask and establish it as an emblem of the practice of were-diplomacy. This practice consists in working out transforming masks *to wear oneself*, with the help of evo-eco-ethological knowledge and skills, and sensitivity to other ways of being alive. Cobbling together one's own transforming mask, making a mask that can be fully manipulated in order to accede, via this metamorphosis, to alterrationalities—the rationalities of nonhuman living beings—constitutes the inaugural *spiritual exercise* of were-diplomacy. This is what makes such metamorphoses politically effective, in a second phase: that of imagining pragmatic techniques for reconciling behaviors, in view of mutualist cohabitation.

Following the example of peoples who have remained in close contact with large predators, wild-animal diplomacy invites us to return to relations that are more pragmatic because they are more spiritual.

There is one other sense in which were-animals constitute diplomatic characters. The were-animal is a clarifying mytheme for anyone interrogating relations between humans and nonhumans. Leaving aside its seductive and Romantic appearances (primal letting-go and return to an original wildness, as opposed to the neurasthenia and polish of civilization[33]), were-animals can be analyzed terms of an ontological schema, in Descola's sense. The were-animal is a cryptic creature that becomes perfectly intelligible in terms of animism, analogism, and eco-evolutionism: it is a vestige of animism, inflected in medieval analogism, and reinvested by modern science. This chimera acquires its origin from the animism of hunting societies, along with some of its constitutive features: shamanistic dislocation, in the characteristic form of *versipellis*, or skin-shifter; in folklore, we find the recurrent theme of an animal skin as an *operator* of transformation (one puts on the skin to transform oneself, for skin is a garment cloaking something that is capable of alteration—a plastic physicality). To this cryptic creature, animism may add a pact with the devil, interactions with the moon, or a healing dimension. Finally, eco-evolutionism invests the mytheme with the idea of a bestial presence inside everyone; every human is condemned to this presence and thus has a moral obligation to rise above it—or else to turn it loose so as to be more "authentic." A penetrating historian might seek to date the appearance of each of these features in folklore in relation to their belonging to these three successive ontological schemas in the constitution of the were-animal mytheme.

Credit: Creation of Sanford Williams, inspired by the artistic tradition of the Amerindians of British Columbia

Figure 17. Wolf-Human Transforming Mask

And here is our cryptid, our yeti, our Sasquatch. It is a chimera not because it does not exist, but because it hybridizes more than wolf and human bodies; and more than perspectives, it hybridizes ontologies.[34] This is what makes it possible for the were-animal figure to constitute an *ontological smuggler* of perspectives that call our naturalism into question. A composite figure that traverses ontologies and captures new features in the process, it can be reinvested to counterbalance the contemporary monopoly of the naturalistic schema in our relations to living beings and allow us to circulate among the worlds.

The Double Epistemological Play of Diplomacy

Diplomacy implies a cognitive ethology freed from objectification that nevertheless does not abandon the quest for knowledge. Perspectivism is both a cosmology and a method; it simultaneously postulates the *singularity* of the other's point of view and the *accessibility* of that viewpoint through a decentering always skeptical of its own explanatory hypotheses. Postulating an animal perspective belongs to the long tradition of Jacob von Uexküll's work on the *Umwelt*, a being's environment or surroundings, and it runs up against reasonable behaviorist objections. Do animals have intentions? But, with the help of Daniel Dennett's concept of the "intentional stance," it is possible to advance along this path. Postulating alterintentionalities and alterrationalities allows a surge of knowledge and understanding.

Eduardo Viveiros de Castro isolates the contrast induced between the epistemology of animism and that of naturalism, which he calls "ours": "Our epistemological game, then, is objectification; what has not been objectified simply remains abstract or unreal. The form of the Other is the thing. Amerindian shamanism is guided by the inverse ideal: to know is to 'personify,' to take the point of view of what should be known or, rather, *the one* whom [*sic*] should be known. The key is to know, in Guimarães Rosa's phrase, 'the who of things, without which there would be no way to respond intelligently to the question of 'why.' The form of the Other is the person."[35]

Perspectivism thus consists in universalizing what philosophers of mind call "the intentional attitude." Far from reducing intentionality to zero in order to objectify the world, perspectivism postulates that the world is never better understood than when it is seen through the lens of "a systematic and deliberate abduction of agency."[36]

In Amerindian objectivism, moreover, nonhuman living beings are not the only ones who are enriched with minds: so are the gods, the dead, meteorological phenomena, artifacts, and so on. This is one of the many points on which the diplomatic perspectivist approach differs from its Amazonian model. But, most importantly, we need to ask what the word "person" signifies in the Amazonian approach, where "personhood" is conferred on nonhumans.

Castro, among others, proposes this response: "Animals and other nonhumans having a soul 'see themselves as persons' and therefore 'are persons': intentional, double-sided (visible and invisible) objects constituted by social relations."[37]

Let us note that this definition conceals a strange form of anthropocentrism, in which reflexivity plays a constitutive role (I see myself as something, therefore I am that thing). However, when we try to grasp it as a power proper to living beings, perspectivism becomes by contrast capable of giving a deep and liberating meaning to the concept of "person."

In the Amazonian context, the concept "person" certainly does not refer to the architectonic definition in Western philosophy formulated by Boethius the Scholastic, the definition that underlies the contemporary ordinary and legal uses of the world: *naturae rationabilis individual substantia* (individual substance of a rational nature[38]). What does "person" mean, then, from the Amazonian perspective?

A traditional anthropological attitude that interprets animism as an anthropomorphism that projects the *human* form on all other living beings would be guilty of ethnocentrism. In fact, "the human" is a category created only recently in the modern West,[39] a category that does not exist as an *objectified concept* earlier or elsewhere; thus it cannot be projected onto the animists. But then what do animists project? One possible response to this question has been made visible by Georges Canguilhem and Hans Jonas in their philosophical work on life forms.[40] These authors attribute a distinctive feature to living beings as contrasted with inorganic matter: living beings constitute a configuring center, an irreducible point of view on the world endowed with an internal space that is the site of dealing with information from the "outside" world. In other words, each living being constitutes a pole that shapes its own experience, that secretes and transports its own evaluations, its own values: starting with the paramecium, a single-celled ciliate that distinguishes between predator and prey, between what it needs to flee and what it needs to seek out, between what is toxic and what is appetizing *for a paramecium*. By contrast, the mineral world has no center, no pole, no point of view on the world. In this sense, each organism is "the measure of all things": the very fact of existing brings to light the high and the low, the hot and the cold, the good and the bad, *for that organism*. These pairings are the original form of what we call values, imagining that they are the absolute prerogatives of humans. They are the basis for the life-sustaining normativity of every living being. It hardly matters whether a given organism *sees itself* in these terms: all organisms *live* this way, even without self-awareness, and they appear this way to humans who know how to look at them. And then, since each organism is constituted by relations that link it to others, the contextual viewpoint of one group plays a role in establishing the plural identity of the organisms with which it interacts, and thus in the material form of the relation.

This is how I interpret what the animist perspective means by "person" as applicable to other living beings. Animists do not *project* onto nonhuman living beings the presumption that they operate from an irreducible standpoint that inflects the nature of others, that each one is a configuring center and polarizer of values. Rather, animists *recognize* this prerogative, which is several billion years old. Animism conceived in this way does not entail projections (one can speak of projections in this context only from a reductionist standpoint that has already postulated the *absence* of this reality); animism entails a serene acknowledgment, a taking into account, of an existing reality. If this interpretation, or recomposition, of perspectivism is even only partially apt, perspectivism can be seen to possess a philosophical, epistemological, and ethical fecundity from which every diplomatic approach deserves to benefit.

Epistemological animism understood in this way is something quite different, then, from a retrograde anthropomorphism, or a superstition about the existence of spirits, or a simple exaptation of our models of the human mind onto nonhumans: it is a way of formulating the essential ontological saliency of living beings with respect to nonhuman living beings, a saliency that the traditional anthropological approach did not grasp.

As an element of a method, it ought to allow us to enrich our approach to the living phenomena of biology in a scientific context to come in which we will have understood the limits of engaging in objectifying epistemological play that aims to conceptualize living beings in general and animals in particular. For science does not have a fixed essence; it can adjust its approaches and its methods so as to encompass and make room for this aspect of living beings. Still, the difficulties of making this approach operational remain intact in scientific experimentation: so far, very few *animist experimental protocols* have been invented.

An Indigenous Detour

The potential enrichment allowed by the use of a perspectivist and animist method within traditional science shows up in a spectacular sociological enigma that has thwarted biologists for a long time. The enigma began with the death of more than two thousand kudu antelopes in the Transvaal in South Africa. They had been placed in a preserve rich in vegetation, analogous in every way to the savanna. There were no bite marks, no signs of illness. No external element seemed to have been involved. The leaves of the acacia caffra, abundantly present in the preserve, are the kudus' preferred food. But dissection showed that the animals seemed to have been intoxicated by their daily diet. To solve this riddle, a researcher in zoology, Wouter Van Hoven, had to carry out an intellectual operation characteristic of Amerindian perspectivism; in other words, he had to adopt an ontological attitude that consists in recognizing the presence in other beings of an irreducible point of view on the world, and consequently acknowledging that they are *for themselves* something other than what they are *for us*. If all kudus (sometimes known as "masked antelopes," owing to their geometric facial markings) are prey *for us* (in other words, unthreatening to us), for the acacia caffra they are *predators*. Now, what do *we* do when we face a predator? We react with a feeling of stress that triggers defensive reactions. Here, then, is the acacias' secret. From their own perspective, *they are prey*, and they possess defensive arrangements that evolution confers on prey—defenses that ordinary scientific ontology could not have suspected.[41] The biologist thus brought to light the physiological ability of acacias to *react perceptibly* and quickly—in just a few minutes—to the stress induced by grazing on its leaves, by an increase in the degree of tannin present in their leaves, so that the aggressors turned away, poisoned.[42] The experimental arrangement imagined to prove the phenomenon required pure perspectivism: the researcher came up with the idea of using a thin stick to lash the leaves vigorously, and he was able to measure this discreet defensive reaction, which was followed by a lowering in the degree of the poison, an hour or so after the attack ended. Because the kudus were in an enclosed preserve, thus unable to migrate from one clump of trees to another, they were condemned to feeding from the same acacias. These trees, trapped in a situation of continuing aggression, were condemned to raising their defenses continuously, and the level of tannin became so toxic that the antelopes died. In the savanna, in fact, it is by traveling from one grove to another, over great distances, that antelopes can wait until the levels of toxic tannin decrease in their earlier prey (and this fact confirms that the acacias' actions are actually *reactions*: the rise in tannin levels is only temporary, and the level returns to normal a short time after the aggression ends). These trees can be seen as covert assassins, authors of the perfect crime, since to the eyes of the Moderns they appear inert and incapable of reacting.

This case does not merely illustrate the perspectivism that is an essential adjunct to the natural life sciences: it also requires an animist epistemology. Van Hoven discovered the surprising fact that, even without being attacked themselves, trees in close proximity to a tree that has been attacked show signs of stress and defend themselves. Following the hypothesis that trees communicated danger through volatile signals, he tested the air captured in a bag that hermetically sealed off the branch of a lashed acacia and isolated the presence of specific molecules. He was able to show that acacias subjected to aggression synthesized volatile ethylenes that warned their conspecific neighbors, so that the latter also increased their tannin levels even before they were approached by herbivores.[43]

To account for phenomena of this sort, we need new etho-evolutionary concepts of "intelligence," communication, and purposeful behaviors. Alterrationalities—forms of intelligence that require us to dismantle our old conceptions of intelligence—are beginning to appear here and there in life forms where they had not been expected. The kudu case issues a powerful call for plural and diffuse animism as an epistemological attitude or even an ontological schema that is worthy of enriching tomorrow's scientific worldview.

This detour through the indigenous path of the animist concept thus suggests the extent to which our understanding of living beings can be enriched by understandings found in nonscientific cultures. What is at stake is our ability to envision a mode of knowledge that re-enchants life forms, moving away from the objectification of nonhuman living beings that amounts to a dementalizing epistemological move. But this re-enchantment is not that of the shaman; it does not require that we personify every agent. Re-enchanting the world does not consist in ontologically supplementing matter with souls, but in re-enchanting the *mode through which experience is grasped*, that is, the mode through which we acquire knowledge, by de-objectifying the object of study without any loss of knowledge, aiming at greater intelligibility and thus improved cohabitation. Re-enchanting the world consists in hybridizing animist and scientific epistemological practices: hypothesizing agency by inference *and* rigorously examining possible ways of being an agent. It is not a question of finding out what entity has or lacks a soul: since we do not know what a soul is, that question would be pointless. The problem is how to find out what concepts have to be postulated or invented—concepts such as alterintentionality, alterrationality, communications, and interiority—as applicable to nonhuman living beings in order to understand these beings better in their own specific forms of existence. This is what methodological animism would look like.

Far from the traditional opposition between a positivist attitude in which knowledge disenchants (cloaked in the supposedly lucid courage to live in a world that has been objectified to death) and an attitude that renounces knowledge in the name of aesthetic and affective effects of a fantasized supernature, what is at stake here is understanding that re-enchantment is necessary *to know better*, and it is *because one knows better* that enchantment happens.

In the diplomatic approach, this "personification" of shamanic epistemology takes the precise methodical form of an "intentional stance" as a working hypothesis that allows effects of intelligibility that are necessary for achieving access to the singularity of the living world.[44] Dennett understood very well that a refined comprehension of living beings enabled by an enriched Darwinism would reveal the existence of alterintentionalities—intentionalities without consciousness, without self-reflection—and sketched out typologies of these forms,[45] but that task remains to be completed.

I am not proposing a critique of quantitative ecology (a functional ecology of populations and communities), nor even a critique of the behavioral ecology inherited from sociology that has integrated the model of the selfish gene and is based on neo-Darwinist research hypotheses: the latter is unquestionably relevant, as one approach among others, in the still unstable nexus of theoretical viewpoints that is the eco-etho-evolutionist understanding of life forms. I am arguing rather that we need to couple the prevailing scientific epistemology with a complementary animist epistemology: parallel and constructed approaches, sometimes hybrid, sometimes accentuated on one side or the other. Every philosophical paradigm of life forms requires this dual approach, precisely because life forms have an ontological singularity that Dennett and Shepard have both identified: they are full of reasons without having been created by a reason.

This unresolved metaphysical enigma calls for a twofold approach if we are to do justice to quantifiable and determinist—or at least probabilist—objectivity, as well as to the irreducible agency of living phenomena.

Rigorously speaking, it is the epistemology of an eco-etho-evolutionist shamanism that is to be our guide to the diplomatic approach. This is the point where epistemology becomes indistinguishable from a body of spiritual exercises. Becoming an animal diplomat requires spiritual exercises if one is to gain access to the vast life of the *bios* from the vantage point of the small life of a species, and the microscopic life of a self. Let us consider, as examples, the asceticism of an ethological description without interpretation (verbs and dashes), an extensive analysis of animal documentaries with no soundtrack; examination of Sam Easterson's video installations; tracking; directing ontological attention to relationships and ethical care for relationships; acquiring a dual naturalist and animist epistemology; exploring active knowledge of evolutions and coevolutions, in the ecology of relationships and communities and in evolutionary psychology; then exercising sensitivity to the poetry of ways of being alive.

Diplomatic Influence

The link between werewolf diplomacy and shamanism is manifest in other ways as well. The mytheme of speaking the "language of animals" as a shamanic power is omnipresent in animist and shamanic cultures. In his 1992 autobiography, Archie Fire Lame Deer, a Sioux stuntman turned medicine man, evokes a power of this order: "I had the *zuzecha* power, the 'power over snakes.' I could control a rattlesnake by waving eagle feathers over it."[46] At first glance one might write this off as mystifying charlatanism, whereas it is actually an exercise in diplomatic ethology. The author himself offers a quite candid eco-evolutionist explanation: "Eagles, hawks, and even roadrunners eat rattlers. In a fight between bird and snake, the snake always loses. So when a rattler senses the movement of feathers, it does not coil to strike but stretches out, trying to get away. Then I could grab the snake and pick it up."[47]

This art is widespread in Amerindian cultures: its mystic and symbolic dimension is woven secondarily into the aptitude for diplomacy, which rests on a fine-grained understanding of eco-ethological relations. Thus the Hopi of the Arizona mesas use two large eagle feathers to inflect and orient the behavior of snakes in the Snake Dance ritual. They use feathers because these are key stimuli used by eagles on rattlesnakes, which react in a nonaggressive manner; precise movements of the feathers induce precise behavioral attitudes, learned by the dancers during lengthy exercises carried out in the animals' company. This type of art, or aptitude, is another form of werewolf diplomacy: an animist cosmology can call it "speaking the language of animals," being medicine men, or being shamans: such labels are equally relevant.[48] It involves a very specific form of knowledge, one that requires either experience in vernacular ethology or else knowledge of eco-evolution; in both cases, one gains access to a form of dialogue and a form of *influence* that is neither control nor mastery.[49] Ethological knowledge makes it possible to create magical effects.

Grasping the difference between influence and control, moreover, is the key to an a-Neolithic ethic that is manifested here and there in the relation of certain peoples to living beings, as it is in some of our own marginal relations with them. In reality, it is sometimes more a matter of impotence than desire that some of our practices privilege influence to the detriment of control; but certain eco-existential situations leave us de facto facing the impossibility of control: the ecological crisis, death, the quest for happiness as a symptom of one's inability to be fulfilled despite living conditions of abundance and peace. The inability to control constitutes the metaphysical anguish of the heirs of the Neolithic map; it is what, intimately, *terrifies* them. As it happens, shamans are specialists in managing what is unmanageable and aleatory:[50] they influence, they try to take on a little power to influence without seeking to dominate. Thus they act and present themselves as agents, whatever the degree of submission may be; they respond to the unmanageable by generating the sensation of doing something, and by recapturing and appropriating what has happened. They are specialists in influence.

Influence constitutes a different relation to reality: to be sure, it is a form of letting go and acceptance with respect to something that does not depend on us, but at the same time influencing is action. Influencing is indeed a positive action designed to stabilize the meaning and status of the metastable entities we are confronting, and to open up paths for further action; it is an action designed to weave a bond wedding us to what is happening and to make us recognize, often, that it is bigger than we are. It is a way of entering into dialogue with something that surpasses us, without resigning ourselves as we confront the impossibility of control, and without trying to minimize or vilify the thing that surpasses us *in order to* control it.

But diplomatic influence is no less effective than control, even though it is less spectacular, for it follows the course of everyday life. Its model of effectiveness indeed consists in borrowing *the very force of other beings*—borrowing, not appropriating. This means that it operates without making these beings dependent, as in a certain practice of over-domestication, which takes over the cycles of engendering animals and seeds by making them heteronomous, incapable of reproducing themselves and of prospering on their own. Diplomatic influence as a form of relationship entails producing a maximum of effects with a minimum of force, by a delicate inflection of the flows that surround us. The delicacy of this inflection is found in the surplus of diplomatic intelligence (in terms of information and conception alike) that guides this action.[51]

The compass for this type of action points to a clear destination: it is a matter of integrating ourselves into autonomous and resilient dynamics that include us, ground us, and surpass us, ecologically, energetically, and symbolically; influencing these dynamics in order to find what we need, without endangering their continued existence or their potential for evolution and deployment—a matter of composing ourselves with them to the point of revitalizing them through our actions.

To be sure, control has its advantages; I am not about to produce an elegy to impotence. It is not a matter of rejecting wholesale the relations to living beings of Western culture, any more than of idealizing autochthonic philosophies indiscriminately. The goal would be to open, with infinite patience, a delicate inquiry that would give things their due, in order to envision the hybrid ontological maps of the future. Before it became obsessional, control as the mode of action inherited from the Neolithic metaphysics of direct positive action freed us on countless points from mutating in contact with recent constructions in political economy toward forms of social metabolism mechanistically enjoined to reify and kill everything.

Control can be rational and reasonable, when it bears upon the life forms that, in us and apart from us, *can* be controlled without harm: when it applies its direct positive action without mortgaging systemic dynamics; when it does not heteronomize its objects for the purpose of controlling to the point of making them dependent, vulnerable, and unstable. But the heart of the problem is not control itself; it comes down to the fact that control, as an unshakeable *norm* governing human relations to living beings, secretes *paranoia* about the *absence* of control. And this paranoia applies henceforth to what we *cannot* and will never be able to control, that is, to the essential aspects of human existence: our relations with those we love;

death; inclusion in the ecological complexes that are our very foundation; our evolutionary past, which *resurfaces* in us at every moment, providing the matrix for our primary emotions, our constitutive desires, our ways of thinking, our sense of being alive: the changing seasons, and the ecological dynamics under our feet, all the way to the biosphere.

For these, we have influence: we have the art of diplomacy—the kind of diplomacy in which fine-grained knowledge, an enlarged sense of self, an art of composing relationships, allow us to coexist in harmony with those entities, in ourselves and apart from ourselves, that do not want to be domesticated.

Chapter 10

On Tracking

We have concentrated, so far, on the practical dimension of tracking; if we now adopt a radically different scale and examine its role in the lengthy process of hominization that went on for several million years, we can surmise that tracking played a major role in the shaping of human thought. Some of the most distinctive cognitive abilities of *Homo sapiens* may actually be products and collateral effects of the selective pressures that bore on the activity of tracking prey. This hypothesis, if it were to prove valid, would confer on animal diplomacy a dimension that goes far beyond the simple eco-ethological practice: it would become the forgotten name of the original powers through which a primate *became* human.

As a species, *Homo sapiens* is the complex product of coevolutions with the other species encountered during its own evolutionary trajectory as it passed through various eco-complexes. Species can even be described as emergent properties of constitutive relationships in the eco-complexes that the genetic flow of populations has traversed.[1] Every species is the history of a unique drama. Dolphins are absolutely singular, as are termites, wolves, and all the rest. What is there in the trajectory constitutive of *Homo sapiens* that made us into this particular intriguing species? One of the individuating phenomena of hominization lay in the transition of a primate species to a predominantly fruit-based diet more than two million years ago, in a certain forest eco-complex in Africa; in a second phase, the genetic flow of this species led its members to become primarily carnivorous omnivores in a savanna eco-complex. This historic combinatorial, a fructivorous primate that became carnivorous, is a singularity of the human species. It allows us to understand certain of our distinctive features with more acuity than zoological comparisons do, for the latter tend to overemphasize our phylogenetic proximity with our primate cousins.

The Evolution of Intelligence

In his field studies of the tracking practices of the San ("Bushmen") hunter-gatherers of the Kalahari, the anthropologist Louis Liebenberg developed a hypothesis about the role of tracking in the emergence of human cognitive capabilities.[2] I propose to borrow his hypothesis and take it further, inflecting and extending it to the logic of animal diplomacy.

Liebenberg's reasoning starts with a correlation between a certain type of foraging (*persistence hunting*), the cognitive abilities it requires, and the process of hominization. A wide range of data suggests that the genus *Homo* hunted actively at least starting with *Homo erectus*, which appeared about 1.9 million years ago. Numerous tool marks made by butchering operations have been found on parts of the prey that would have already been eaten by others if the carcasses had been left untouched. Thus there is little doubt about the existence of active hunting. But how was it carried out?

When we imagine our prehuman ancestors, we tend to picture them catching large game by throwing stones or stakes hardened in fire. But given the athletic and defensive capacities of the large ungulates, this hypothesis is implausible. Bows and arrows, although these were the most polyvalent weapons, appeared much later, probably after the emergence of *Homo sapiens* (the earliest bows found are around seventy-one thousand and sixty-four thousand years old).[3] Stakes can be thrown effectively only from a distance of ten meters or so. Before the invention of the spear-thrower and the bow, it is unlikely that *Homo*, given the vigilance of its prey, could get close enough to large ungulates to kill them.[4]

This is what leads to Liebenberg's postulate that the hunting technique used most widely throughout most of the history of the genus *Homo* was persistence hunting—a technique that can still be observed today among certain hunter-gatherers, most notably the San of the Kalahari. This practice consists in seeking out fresh ungulate tracks and following them in pursuit of the animal—which keeps on moving when it smells or hears something on its trail—and persisting for *several hours*, until the animal is immobilized by its own hyperthermia and is then at the mercy of the hunter. The large ungulates on the savanna in fact have means of regulating body heat induced by effort that are less effective *over the long run* than those of humans (like the large felines, the large ungulates have thermoregulation mechanisms that are more effective for sprinting). Thus, by inducing an increase in body temperature in the animal to the point where it can no longer flee, a hunter can get close enough to attack. Tracking can easily go on for eight hours, as many as twelve in rare cases. The animal is then killed at close range by a lance thrust through the heart.[5]

The hypothesis that persistence hunting was the original practice finds further support in one of the most spectacular phenotypical singularities of the genus *Homo*: the gradual loss of fur, which established the genus as "the naked ape." This development may be interpreted as an adaptation to the thermoregulation by perspiration that is required by the endurance race proper to persistence hunting. The endurance race seems indeed to be still visible in the *Homo sapiens* phenotype: biomechanical adaptations that favor equilibrium and speed and that optimize balancing motions point in this direction. If the effects of these selective pressures, present over hundreds of millions of years, are still visible *in our bodies*, we can hypothesize that they are also still present in our minds, a locus just as defining as our bare skin. For in fact, to engage in this kind of hunting, it is obviously necessary to be able to run for a long time, but it is equally necessary to run *in the right direction*. The animal being pursued is typically *not* in the hunter's field of vision: the hunter sees only its tracks. Thus, along with the runner's bare skin and body type, natural selection must have also favored the ability *not to lose the trail*.

This hypothesis opens up a reflection on the cognitive techniques proper to tracking over long distances (systematic tracking and speculative tracking, as defined by Liebenberg), which we shall look at more closely further on.[6] First, I should like to reflect on what happened *before* these techniques were developed, in the evolutionary chain of events that led a certain primate to the food-producing act of tracking.

Liebenberg's hypothesis supposes that humans appeared and developed cognitively from the standpoint of these tracking abilities because they settled into an ecological niche in which foraging required *speculation*. For fruit-eaters, this was not necessary, any more than it was for carrion-feeders. A persistence hunter's way of finding food, unlike that of a kudu, a lion, or a boar, *required* speculation in a technical sense: it required a process of investigation bringing together the three fundamental inferences of human logic: abduction (the formulation of hypotheses), deduction, and induction. The original forms of knowledge production would thus have to be sought in the Pleistocene, with, as catalyst, the phase when the manner of acquiring food veered toward hunting. Can the requirements of hunting really be at the origin of fundamental aspects of human thinking?

Seeing the Invisible

There is no need to correlate our intelligence exclusively with that of the other primates, for they are not trackers, as *Homo erectus* (or *ergaster*) must have been for some two million years. The simple fact is that we were fruit-eating creatures that became carnivorous trackers, that is, *visual beings* condemned to seek *invisible* things. The eco-evolutionary combination that underlies our cognitive identity as living thinkers is the encounter in a life form between our past as social fruit-eating primates (with a weak sense of smell, powerful eyes, and a well-honed theory of mind, that is, an ability to speculate about the meaning hidden behind the visible behavior of our fellow humans) and new ecological conditions implying new selective pressures: bipedal life on the savanna pushed certain primates to become omnivores with a bent toward meat eating, which *requires* tracking. This is a key to the mental powers of the combinatorial animal we know as human.

For that, it was necessary to awaken the "eye" that sees what is invisible, the eye of the mind. Our coevolution with our new prey induced the establishment of original cognitive competencies. Thus the key event was not the fact of eating meat (even though that played a role by contributing protein, which was probably needed to feed an increasingly voluminous brain), nor was it hunting as predation and devouring (even though that played a role on the phenotypical and ecological levels); it was *tracking*. It was under the sensory-motor conditions of tracking, that is, during the *search* for an animal rather than its killing, that our neuro-perceptive anatomical matrix, emerging from our evolutionary history, immersed in a new ecological environment and encountering conditions never seen before, was to bring out ethological behaviors that led to the development of a certain swath of human intelligence: thinking in the strong sense, thinking as inquiry.

The vast majority of terrestrial carnivores were originally endowed with powerful, discriminating senses of smell. Hawks, to be sure, are predators in which sight dominates, but their cynegetic problems are very different from those of bipeds: the distancing offered by an aerial view implies that the quasi-optimal evolutionary solution amounts to favoring visual perception, for the view from on high makes it possible to see prey from far away, and to track it *by sight*.

Let us look at the ecological conditions in the life of a terrestrial carnivore. It strides across its territory without advance knowledge about the location of game; it comes across a "trail" and follows it until it finds its prey. The animal's aptitude to reach the prey via the trail is directly under selective pressure. The trail consists in visual and olfactory stimuli. For those who hunt by smell (canids and felines, for example), olfactory stimuli suffice to trigger identification of the animal, by igniting neurons. The odor alone allows an animal to know in what direction another animal is traveling: it is where the intensity of the stimulus is strongest. The experience familiar to many of us that consists in tracking down a bakery by following the smell of warm bread down the street makes it clear how few abstract cognitive operations are required for "hunters" to get their bearings and estimate their chances in tracking by smell. The boreal lynx, when it tracks a snowshoe hare in the snow and crosses a windswept trail, chooses the wrong direction 50 percent of the time: it is not very good at reading the *meaning* of the trail with its eyes, when olfactory signs are absent.

Now, we humans are terrestrial carnivores, but without a powerful sense of smell (fruits and leaves do not require this, since they do not flee); our sight is powerful, but we are stuck on the surface; even a vulture's sight would not suffice to pierce the cover of woods or the roundness of the earth. So here is another way to formulate our hypothesis: the singular vital problem of the genus *Homo*, the origin of its cognitive specificity, toward which selection has progressively refined adaptive solutions, is how to track food without sensorial adaptations suited for that task. In us, because we are vision-oriented fruit-eaters who have become carnivores, visual performance has to be supplemented by that of the inner eye.

If humans are visual predators, it is the relation of their own form of vision to that of their ungulate prey that governs their relation to tracking, that is, to obtaining food, during a very large part of their history. For while humans can see well enough to follow a trail, their vision is not penetrating enough and its range not broad enough for them to hunt by sight alone. The human condition thus entails having eyes that are good, but that are tied to the ground, and a sense of smell that is not highly developed; this condition creates a platform for the forms of tracking that are probably at the origin of a portion of the capabilities of human thought.[7] Slow runners with weak noses and eyes stuck on the ground, humans can catch an animal only by following it over long distances without seeing it. In other words, they have to follow its tracks. It was the power *and* the limitations of human vision that allowed the emergence of the mind's eye, the most powerful eye, in its radiation of cognitive effects, that any living beings have developed to this day. In comparison, wolves do not have the same sensory-motor schema. Their sense of smell is highly developed. What do wolves *see* when they spot a deer track? This is a very difficult question on which opinions are divided. Is a wolf able to decode the origin of the track? That is, does the sight of a track launch, by igniting certain neurons, a full image of the prey whose trace is the present/absent symbol? For me, the question is, rather: Does the wolf need such an image? Ungulate hooves secrete odors, and, unlike a human, a wolf sees the ungulate more clearly with this odor than in the mental image set off by neural ignition at the *sight* of the mark. A strong smell has an analogous evocative effect on us, moreover, even with our much more limited olfactory sense. Let us postulate, then, that wolves follow the track of a smell more readily not because their eyes are incapable of seeing it, but because the olfactory track is more *alive*. It is because the traces of odors are less alive for us, less evocative, that humans had to heighten the symbolic power of *evocation* from the dead trace in the sand alone, and thus heighten the assemblages of neurons that create the mental image in an abstract manner. In this way, something like a proto-symbol came into being, erected as such by acts of interpretation that read *more* in a trace that can be seen in it by the naked eye.

Let us consider a track in the sand. For the visual hunter, the track demands to be read, to be translated, that is, to be interpreted as a sign. The hunter is compelled to look for the imprint, which familiarizes him with the phenomenon of a sign, a present element that points to something simultaneously present and absent, and constitutes certain premises of symbolic faculties: the need to learn to *read* tracks, that is, to interpret them. Anyone who has had the experience of bending down to see deer tracks in a forest remembers learning how to decode the animal's direction according to the asymmetric form of the track. The quantity of information contained in this ideogram can be prodigious: species, age, sex, direction, state of health, individual identity, emotional state, activity in progress.

In tracking, we witness the potential rise of decisive cognitive abilities that are centered around the power to see the invisible, such as the animal's destination, or a sequence from its past. Tracks in a straight line, for example, indicate that the animal is headed toward a specific destination. When the animal returns to its den, its trail is thus often a straight line; if the trail meets other, older traces of the same animal, we are approaching its den. For the animal wanders to forage when it sets out, but it knows perfectly well where it is going as it heads back. A good tracker can read the trail of a predator that has hunted, then rested during the hottest part of the day, eaten a little more meat, and set off again.

> Looking at some lion tracks, Karel Kleinman, a Bushman tracker who worked in the Kgalagadi Transfrontier National Park, pointed out that the lion (a male) that was lying in the shade of a dune, got up and trotted a short distance, stood still, then trotted off at a steady pace in a specific direction. He explained that the lion had heard a female in the distance, got up, and trotted higher up on the dune, where he stood still to listen; he then trotted off to go and find the female. Kleinman drove his vehicle around some high dunes to find his way to where he predicted the lion had been going. He picked up the tracks and followed them to a spot where the lion had encountered two other lions, a male and a female. The tracks indicated that the two males had been fighting over the female, after which one of the males went off together with the female. The original set of tracks only indicated a male lion that got up, stopped, and continued at a trot. But the way it moved showed that it was not hunting, since it was not trying to move stealthily to stalk prey. Rather, it stopped to listen to something in the distance, and then moved off at a steady pace. The way it moved indicated that it was attracted to a female.[8]

Tracking thus consists in reconstructing and extrapolating a history of animal activity that is much richer than what is shown by the traces themselves—which give access to the invisible. The tracker thus sees what is invisible in the literal sense of the term, like a doctor making a diagnosis.

Practical manuals on tracking are categorical: identifications made at first glance are often false. A good tracker has to internalize the sign, place it in a series, in a critical or supportive constellation with other signs, before determining the identity of the prey.[9] Tracking thus requires systematic investigation, and a systematic suspension of judgment until enough signs have been obtained to confirm the identification. "Decisions made after a quick glance are often erroneous. Trackers need to take time to study new signs in detail when they are first encountered."[10]

Statements by trackers are marked by a recurrence of such references to the need to reflect, to take one's time before reaching a decision. A systematic suspension of judgment is necessary in the field; it is an integral part of the exercise. We may well wonder about this: If tracking is a foundational activity, and if suspension of judgment is necessary, what might this have induced in everyday cognitive tasks? We could hypothesize that this is one of the origins of the view according to which suspending judgment is a mark of sagacity. Relating the visible to the invisible, which is a cognitive challenge characteristic of humans, requires suspension of judgment. Finding something absent on the basis of what is present is the challenge of hunting. A similar problem arises in attributing intentions to other members of one's species—determining an invisible intention on the basis of visible behavior, reconstituting a past action on the basis of prints. It is as though these two ecological conditions of life (those faced by tracking animals and those faced by social animals) had induced selective pressure on the capacity to reconstitute, mentally, the invisible links between visible fragments established as clues. This is a specific cognitive problem that may well have made us human. Sherlock Holmes is only an extreme form of the social primate tracker.

The activity of tracking can take two different forms.[11] Systematic tracking consists in following the animal trace by trace. This type of tracking suffices over short distances, but successful tracking nevertheless often requires the ability to read, interpret the tracks, and suspend judgment. As we have seen, *Homo* became a runner and practiced persistence hunting. Over long distances, there is always a moment when the trail is lost (owing to rocky soil, a river, a crossing point for many animal trails): here the second type of tracking, *speculative*, becomes necessary.

From this standpoint, it may be that evolution not only favored our capacities for systematic tracking but also those for speculative tracking:

> To reconstruct the animal's activities, the tracker primarily gathers empirical evidence in the form of spoor and other signs. Speculative tracking involves the creation of a working hypothesis on the basis of initial interpretation of signs and knowledge of the animal's behavior and the terrain. With a hypothetical reconstruction of the animal's activities in mind, trackers then look for signs where they expect to find them. The emphasis is primarily on speculation, looking for signs only to confirm or refute expectations. When expectations are confirmed, hypothetical reconstructions are reinforced. When expectations prove to be incorrect, trackers must revise their working hypothesis and investigate alternatives.[12]

The tracker formulates possibilities, nourished by positive and negative feedback. Here we can see in what serious sense Liebenberg believes he is justified in seeing in tracking something like an origin of science. Although he does not spell out the distinction, it is obviously not a matter of science as a historically dated emergence, but of specific cognitive aptitudes required by a particular form of inquiry, called "rational," and of their methodical articulation. The first competencies involved in speculative tracking are the formulation and testing of hypotheses. Speculative tracking in fact consists in creating a working hypothesis that bears on something inaccessible to the senses, something invisible. Next, one has to *deduce* what evidence one *ought to* be able to observe empirically if the hypothesis were true. Then one has to search for that evidence on the ground to test the hypothesis.[13] As it happens, the articulation of these three basic inferences of human logic (abduction, deduction, and induction) coincides precisely, in this order, with what the pragmatist logician Charles Sanders Peirce calls the scientific method, or the method of inquiry.[14] Endurance hunting as a form of foraging by mammals, with its implication of cognitive capacities, is thus the starting point for an inquiry following Peirce's method—inquiry being understood here in the pragmatic sense of processes that entail searching for trustworthy beliefs and articulating the inferences of human logic in a precise order.

The role of hunting-related selection processes spread over many thousands of years, in the emergence or the orientation of certain human cognitive aptitudes on the order of logic, would be worth examining systematically. Epistemologist Ian Hacking hypothesizes that, while the styles of scientific reasoning can be dated historically, logical capacities themselves are prehistoric.[15] For example, proof by contradiction seems to play a decisive role in tracking: "It is also important for trackers to recognize when there are no signs at all. When the terrain is very hard, trackers need to be able to tell if the animal would have left some signs if it did in fact pass that way. This is important since trackers need to know when they are no longer on the trail. If the tracker can see that there are no signs where there should have been signs, then the animal probably followed the other route."[16]

The ecological conditions proper to the tracking practices of a primate hunter may have been of pedagogical value for certain inferences concerning, for example, the absence of signs, along with the everyday familiarity of a primate hunter with logical problems of this order (here there ought to be tracks, for the mud is friable; but there aren't any, so . . .) could have played a facilitating role in the acquisition of reasoning.

With Liebenberg, we witness an evolutionary history of the emergence of certain aspects of human thought: it suffices to assume that selective pressure was exerted on the matrix of cognitive faculties required by tracking, for us to see these faculties as the matrix from which, by exaptation, the abstract thought of human inquiry took shape.

Empathic Dislocation

In speculative tracking, once trackers have grasped the general direction of the trail and know that there is an animal route along this axis, a river, a key point, they will leave the path to go directly to that key point and rediscover the path from there. They have to visualize how the animal is moving from the animal's own point of view.

> Tracking involves intense concentration, resulting in a subjective experience of projecting oneself into the animal. The tracks indicate when the animal is starting to get tired: its stride becomes shorter, it kicks up more sand, and the distances between consecutive resting places become shorter. When tracking an animal one attempts to think like an animal in order to predict where it is going. Looking at its tracks, one visualizes the motion of the animal. What is perhaps most significant when tracking an animal and projecting yourself into the animal, is that you at times *feel* as if you have become the animal—it is as if you can *feel* the motion of the animal's body in your own body.[17]

This knowledge of an animal is thus not just inductive knowledge of its habits, its behaviors, its ecology; it is also an ability to transpose oneself into the animal, as it were, in order to make hypotheses. From this viewpoint, we can see how the cognitive abilities proper to tracking in an animal lacking a powerful sense of smell might blend with the ability of social primates to master a theory of mind, that is, an ability to postulate the existence, in others, of intentions, beliefs, and desires with respect to intentions, and to decode them. In primates who have become hunters, the theory of mind extends beyond that of their own primate fellows to encompass *that of their prey*. We may hypothesize that *Homo* finds its cognitive singularity in being a social interpreter oriented toward tracking, that is, that members of this genus will use the gifts they have received by selection as primate psychologists, to interpret other living beings in addition to their conspecific fellows. Tracking catalyzes the psychological and social interpretive faculties as it exapts them toward activities of zoocephalic diplomacy.

Speculative tracking consists in following an imaginary route, sparing oneself the effort of examining every single trace, by visualizing the path of the animal through the bush as if through the animal's own eyes. Experts in speculative tracking have their eyes fixed on the horizon; they do not look at the ground, they dream it. That is, they look for signs on the ground only where they have *projected* the presence of those signs. "What would I do if I were you, animal, but you in depth, with your desires and your aversions, your rhythm and your world?" That is the question the experts ask themselves as soon as they lose the trail, so they can orient themselves anew.

The articulation in a given primate of speculative tracking abilities and a theory of mind suggests that the activity of seeking out prey coincides with a form of shamanic dislocation, in the sense of a displacement of the shaman's mind into the animal's body. It is in the everyday act of tracking, under selective pressure, that we might locate the source of human theriomorphy, the immemorial power in humans to merge with the rest of the animal cosmos: the ability to become the wolf who hunts, or the antelope who chooses his path. For Liebenberg, the bodily dislocation needed for persistence hunting allows us to account for the adaptive value of empathy. He bases this intuition on what Nate, a Bushman tracker who was one of his interlocutors, explained to him about what is required before tracking begins.

> Nate explained to me that a tracker must continually "test" his own body against that of the kudu—looking at the tracks of the kudu, the length of its stride and the way it kicks up the sand indicates how tired it is feeling. You must compare your own body with what the kudu is feeling. . . . It is your subjective feelings that monitor your own condition against that of the kudu—failing which you may die of hyperthermia. This example demonstrates the value of empathy in the success of the hunt and therefore the adaptive value in terms of natural selection.[18]

This metamorphosis, even in its most empathic form, is not a Romantic daydream; it is, along the axis of our hypothesis, an ability acquired under selective pressure during the evolution of the genus *Homo*. We can see here in what sense werewolf—or zoocephalic—diplomacy, as an attempt to gain access to the rationalities hidden inside other animals, and more broadly to the internal logic of living and nonliving beings (including oceans, mountains, and skies), rests on prehistoric aptitudes that have in part created humans in their cognitive singularity.[19] We are werewolf diplomats, empowered to grasp how *everything behaves* and confronted with the moral necessity of determining what to do with our power.

The werewolf is not a form manifesting our reduction to a primitive bestiality; it is the highest form of our relational intelligence.

An Exaptation of Tracking Skills

Tracking, as a daily habit and a vital necessity, that is, a practice based on cognitive capacities selected over several hundred thousand years, was able to put in place the cognitive capabilities that are the exaptive preserve of the faculties of *human thought*. By exaptive preserve, I mean that our current capabilities are offshoots of uses of mental organs selected during the process of evolution. The entire set of complex, heterogenous selective pressures that operated on human cognitive competencies during hominization managed to preserve traits that were not selected to do what we do with our minds today but that render our own mental activities possible, from mathematics to art and philosophy.[20] In evolutionary biology, two types of traits can constitute exaptations: first, traits selected for an initial function and made available for a different function by an unexpected change; but also, and this is most interesting, architectural traits induced by the emergence of a selected trait that are available for the acquisition of a function. The more complex the organ, the more it manifests collateral architectural constraints. The brain is a singularly complex organ whose capabilities have been selected by evolution; it is permanently available for a redefinition of its uses. Stephen Jay Gould traces this intuition back to Darwin:

> Darwin, who was not a strict adaptationist, recognized . . . that the brain, though undoubtedly built by selection for some complex set of functions, can, as a result of its intricate structure, work in an unlimited number of ways quite unrelated to the selective pressure that constructed it. Many of these ways might become important, if not indispensable, for future survival in later social contexts (like afternoon tea for Wallace's contemporaries). . . . Most of what the brain now does to enhance our survival lies in the domain of exaptation.[21]

Tracking certainly induced selective pressures on the origin of cognitive capacities, elements of which are still used in a virtually identical way today, while other elements and their architectural constraints have made other unprecedented uses possible.

Here we are making the hypothesis that something like a "law of evolution" exists: virtually every trait that is subjected to intense, interwoven, and prolonged selective pressures, instituted in this way as a superior capability, ends up exceeding its original function by taking on unforeseen new and inventive uses (provided that the organ is not hypertelic, like the hummingbird's beak). For example, the blowhole, a respiratory organ, has been put to communicative use in cetaceans (nostrils speaking dialects); an acoustic oil that also serves as ballast in sperm whales refines the perceptual definition of sonar technologies. The same thing holds true of cognitive capabilities in the search for food among the ancestors of *Homo sapiens*. If natural selection exerts pressure to bring into being some sort of "superpower," that power will end up serving additional purposes, being available—exaptable—for other inventions and combinations. In this light, innovation is a collateral effect of an overabundance of strengths induced by selection.

The whole matter of reading signs thus appears to stem from the natural habit of reading tracks as signs of the invisible in what is visible. At bottom, the current life form of any species exemplifies a subversion and hybridization of ancient habits in tension with the new vital problems transmuted by the emerging eco-historical context—the evolving result of a form of tinkering. But the basic material is essential, and in our context the material in question is the cognitive capacity to engage in tracking by reading signs and mentally reconstituting what is absent. Interpreting and reconstructing are both omnipresent activities in tracking. They appeared well before the existence of any text. Writing becomes much less enigmatic in the light of a life form that engages in tracking, that is, in reading signs. The use of symbols becomes easier to grasp, for a track, as a clue, is an intermediary between the iconic association of ideas (smoke and fire) and symbolic reference (words and things); a track serves as the transition. Thanks to tracking we can envision the conditions of possibility of the appearance of symbolic thought, the spoken word, the written word—as avatars of an animal's pawprint.[22]

During the territorial explorations of the various *Homo* species (probably *erectus* first, then *sapiens*), the colonization of new environments led to a wide array of foraging techniques (harvesting shellfish, fishing, trapping, enriched harvesting in ecosystems with more diverse vegetation), ending up in the Neolithic with the revolution constituted by plant domestication and food stockpiling. The diversification of foraging practices initially reduced the pressure on tracking abilities, with the result that these abilities became available for other uses. This situation of functional vacancy is characteristic of exaptation. It constitutes the "freeing" of a trait for an unanticipated change in function or use. But the matricial form remained. In the combined form that makes up the human animal, the module for tracking behaviors is present in the palimpsest, but later transformations have made it almost unrecognizable: "Part of the strangeness of human experience and history is the capacity for directing the restless psychic force of the meat-mind upon the nonprey world, to experience forests and fields in some strange sense of pursuit and capture."[23]

Our cognitive identity, then, seems to have come in part from the exaptive reserve deposited in us, in the form of selected behavioral and cerebral abilities, by our sedimented ancestral inheritances. We have seen the abilities of hunter-gatherers (sign-reading, inquiry), and those of social animals, destined to collaborate and to live collectively (theory of mind, abduction of agency). We should also look at the contributions of our fruit- and leaf-gathering primate forbears, with their attraction to colors, their aptitude for memorization (the thousands of seeds hidden and found again by jays exemplify the major cognitive strength selected); their power of categorial discrimination among subtle differences (between a medicinal plant and a poison, for example); their capacity for induction (the ability to generalize a property found in one class of plants, and to seek that property among related plants); and perhaps even the use of concepts (in the original form of giss as used by early twentieth-century birdwatchers[24]) and their joyous curiosity about any new form.

But we also have to add "tinkering abilities," which probably introduced to human cognitive faculties the understanding of solids. The linked technical operations required to end up with a complex product (double-faced silex blades) are probably the exaptive reserve for the imaginary chains of actions that serve as means for reaching a projected end (planning) that also characterize human intelligence. This lengthening of practical and theoretical chains of reasoning is supported along parallel lines by language as a prosthetic memory for previous thoughts, crystallized in words, whereas they would be easily forgotten without symbolic support. Matricial cognitive and affective elements originating in the hunting life constitute combined modules of our history as social primates, ending up with the still enigmatic integrative complex that we are.[25] The selective pressures that weighed on our animal ancestors, the liberation of selected capabilities toward new uses that escape natural selection: these are the conditions of possibility of zoocephalic diplomacy—and of my own effort, in this text, that is an effort to exhume that diplomacy.

The very long human cynegetic history has been obscured by Neolithic agriculture, which changed humans' relation to the search for food. The Neolithic era corresponds to only three one-hundredths of human time, but it catalyzed the spread of the mental matrices that emerged from the hunting-and-gathering period and sent them in unprecedented directions, allowing the invention of new uses for hands, minds, and desires. The fact remains that the hundreds of thousands of years of the human animal's intensive quest to sustain life undoubtedly shaped our inner framework in a profound way. *Ecce homo*: a hunter in a world without prey.

Tracking and the Existential Motif of the Quest

If we follow this hypothesis, tracking constitutes a primal and omnipresent activity in the genus *Homo*, forgotten by the Moderns although it is a foundation of our cognitive condition. How then could it not be also constitutive of part of our *affective* matrices?

Temple Grandin, a specialist in animal behavior and a zoocephalic diplomat of the highest order, analyzes in this way the emotional power that nourishes our most varied projects, under the auspices of the hunt in the human evolutionary past. Thanks to recent advances in animal neurobiology, she translates this power into a state of neuronal attraction manifested in the very desire to seek, and not simply the pleasure one has in finding. She proposes a zoomorphic theory of the deep meaning of the human quest, mythicized in Western chivalry, Nordic legends, detective fiction, and probably all adventure literature. For her analysis, on the order of what we have called a "good zoomorphic translation," she turns to animal life to seek behavioral singularities that shed light on our own.

Grandin relies on the experimental results of Jaak Panksepp, a neuroscientist who developed the concept of a "SEEKING circuit" or system (his capitalization) to characterize the neuronal system that is activated in living beings when emotions of "intense interest, engaged curiosity, and lively anticipation" procured by the search for food are manifested.[26] These emotions are present in all animals during the search for shelter, for a sexual partner, and especially during the search for food by predators. Thinking about humanity, in light of the neuro-zoological concept of the SEEKING system, is a biomorphism and more specifically a predatomorphism. This does not mean interpreting animal behaviors by projecting human affects onto them, but rather interpreting human behaviors by projecting onto them behavioral matrices that have been identified and understood in other animals.

Panksepp's discoveries are crucial in this regard, for he associates this SEEKING circuit with something profoundly new: "Researchers used to think that this circuit was the brain's *pleasure center*. Sometimes they called it the *reward center*. The main neurotransmitter associated with the SEEKING circuit is dopamine, so they thought dopamine was the 'pleasure' chemical."[27]

It has been discovered that what guinea pigs stimulate to obtain a synthesis of dopamine is not the pleasure system but the SEEKING center of the brain: "What the self-stimulating rats were stimulating was their curiosity/interest/anticipation circuits. *That's* what feels good: being excited about things and intensely interested in what's going on—being what people used to call 'high on life.'"[28]

What is true for the quest for food in general is accentuated for predation, in particular, because the context of predation implies that food is challenging to obtain. We can hypothesize that a predator with a behavioral basis that induces ludic joy in the hunt thereby possesses an adaptive advantage that may be emphasized by selection. More generally, as Darwin saw, evolution tends to inscribe in us pure joy in doing things that are good for us (here in the sense of things that augment *fitness* in one way or another). Panksepp shows that hunting activates the same network as the SEEKING system: curiosity, interest, anticipation) with the same agreeable sensations, the same joy, in the quest.[29] It is this emotion associated with the search for food that has been exapted in our daily hunts, detached from killing and from any food-seeking function. "Humans enjoy any kind of hunt: they like hunting through flea markets for hidden finds; they like hunting for answers to medical problems on the Internet; they like hunting for the ultimate meaning of life in church or in a philosophy seminar. All of these activities come out of the same systems in the brain."[30]

The decisive argument that shows the gap between the pleasure circuit and the SEEKING circuit is the temporality of activation: "This part of the brain *starts* firing when the animal sees a sign that food might be nearby but *stops* firing when the animal sees the actual food itself. The SEEKING circuit fires during the *search* for food, not during the final locating or eating of the food. It's the search that feels so good."[31]

Dopamine can thus be characterized as the hormone not of pleasure but of seeking.[32] Tracking as ardent seeking: this is the biomorphic essence of human quests. The complex set of emotions including interest, anticipation, attentive curiosity, inexhaustible energy, and attentional blindness would be an exaptation, thus a deviation, from a cerebral circuit whose original function was to interest us intensely in what was important for our survival: following and finding the fleeing animal. "We stay alert and alive in the vanished forests of the world."[33] Among herbivores, the emotional framework of the quest for food is probably less intensified from the standpoint of desire, less directional, owing to the omnipresence of a food supply that does not flee.

The exaptation of our SEEKING system adds spice to our lives: it establishes, in the folds of our brains, our quests, our projects, our vital strength, our ability to accomplish great things.[34] This behavioral matrix is zoomorphic in the sense that is it through scientific attention to the refinement of a behavioral and emotional complex *in animals* that we end up understanding better who *we* are given the evolution that links us to them. The SEEKING system constitutes one of the animal primordia. Grandin thus proposes a zoomorphic theory of the joys of the quest: Don Quixote is the example par excellence of continuous activity, to the point of incandescence, of the SEEKING module of the animal brain.

Grandin is a great werewolf diplomat: she accounts for who we are by doing justice to the great strength of animal life in us, its subtle multivalence, far from any simplistic physiochemical determination. She does not strip us of our humanity, she revivifies it. She makes visible the mystery of being a body, far from the reductionism that confuses bodies with machines and takes perverse pleasure in degradation. She keeps us from forgetting that we are first of all bodies engaged in the spiritual experiences of existence: love, fear, existential anguish, the most elevated thoughts, research and curiosity, desire, peace.

Here is the strength of an analysis of human life in biological terms: it is manifested when one can make intelligible the highest, most subtle aspects of human existence without degrading them. The spiritualist attitude accepts the explanation of hunger or sexual desire as biological phenomena, but proposes to see the higher, refined, inspiring emotions as belonging to a disembodied spirituality. In contrast, we can consider that a Darwinian eco-etho-neurobiological approach to human existence is justified only when it makes the highest affects of existence—grace, the experience of freedom, quests—intelligible in a nonreductionist way.[35]

Tracking today thus takes on a new dimension. We are no longer simply contemplating a folkloric natural practice; we are invited to return, as Shepard proposed, to its roots in the Pleistocene. Far from entailing a vague Romantic experience of naked life in the woods, this return consists in allowing our human biogram to resurface in us, coincident with the original act of tracking, which can be understood to have shaped part of our cognitive and affective capabilities, and thus part of who we are. It allows us to experience what happens, then, when the long human past comes back to us and coincides with the present moment.

Being Read by Others

Although tracking has been blended into our evolutionary history as an original salient feature, it does not institute a position of human transcendence within the realm of living beings, the position of reader who is not read, the only interpreting consciousness of a living realm otherwise blind to itself. Tracking along paths implies being *trackable*. Often, bent over in front of a spoor, trackers will look up upon hearing a vulture's cry. They check the bordering brush in vain, prey to the circular paradox of tracking. Who is watching you while you are studying a footprint? Of what amused gaze are you the nonchalant object, that is, the prey? The objectifying relation to living beings is surreptitiously inverted in the heart of the forest.

The first moment of awareness amounts to understanding that one is sending signs. This is what prods us to disappear. Become sagebrush. Rub ourselves with odiferous leaves, flatten ourselves against the hillside, high up above the valley, and wait, until, for the rest of the world, we are no longer anything but sagebrush in a stand of sagebrush. Then something may happen.

The second moment of awareness comes down to understanding that we are being read. An experience during a tracking session in Yellowstone National Park will allow me to evoke the full extension of the life of signs in the animal world. Walking in Yellowstone is a promise of encounters. In the Lamar Valley, all along the Yellowstone River, I undertook to explore a zone explicitly described by the local park rangers as animated by "bear activity." Two bison carcasses stood out on the plain, and powerful carnivores were fighting over them aggressively. I kept walking along a crest, in the wind, so that I risked surprising a grizzly at every turn. A pronghorn antelope was walking in front of me. I tried to reassure it, and to encourage it to keep moving about a hundred steps ahead, in the direction of the path, so it would be my scout: its sense of smell was so superior to mine that I would read in its behavior, its ears, its tension, its gait, the presence of a grizzly that I could not smell on my own. But the antelope had its own ideas. Further on, I located crows calling and triangulated the zones of vulture flight so I wouldn't come across a carcass and whoever was defending it. This is when I wondered: What do the other animals read in my behavior? I was decoding in their attitudes what they knew about the surrounding world, but weren't they doing the same thing? All those long moments in the sagebrush where a pronghorn scrutinized me, when a bison studied me, or when an upright black bear looked me up and down took on another dimension: I thought they were interested in me—were they in fact reading something that interested them concerning something *other* than me? A whole research program opens up: Portmann's phanerology in reverse. An ecosystem in the informational sense of the term is thinkable as a circuit in which signs are exchanged and information shared.

Do bears and wolves read the presence of prey in the flight of crows? Bernd Heinrich, the ornithologist who specializes in the corvid family, reminds us that hunters read the presence of bears in the cries crows make near the prey. Liebenberg explains, for his part, that Bushmen trackers are capable of interpreting the meaning of jackals' cries. A jackal produces different sounds to maintain contact or to signify that it is following the track of a hyena or of a large predator (the call diminishes in intensity and ends in a dry cough). According to the trackers, this cough is a sign of its fear, combined with its excitement at finding already killed prey. If the cry is uttered only once, the jackal is following a hyena: it has given up on the trail, for it knows that hyenas leave nothing on their carcasses. If the cry is repeated, it means that the jackal is on the trail of a leopard or a lion: it knows that the trail will lead to meat in profusion. Voluntarily or not, the jackal sends signs, to fellow jackals but also to anyone else who knows how to decipher them: this allows hunters to avoid lions at night and to imagine their hunting strategies.[36] We must add to this the phenomena analyzed by biosemiotics, and those noted by phanerology; the "honest signals" that birds (usually males) send to the females by their dazzling plumage; those that antelopes send to lions concerning their vigor; and all those animal masks like the wolf's, which accentuates contrasts, externalizes the expressivity of wolf existence in the service of a subtle social and political life—the face of a wolf is no less a face, but it is more than a face, it is a mask.

As we have seen, evolution ultimately exploits anything and everything at hand—excrement, body odors, volatile ethanols in the case of trees, feathers and display features of all types—to cobble together instruments that can be used to signify and communicate. This process is visible not only in terrestrial creatures but also in marine mammals, who are endowed with forms of communication very close to human language—signal variety, clan dialects (among orca), multiple functions of vocalization, and so on. In animal documentaries we are prepared to see dolphins use something like click languages. But odontocetes have esophagi that do not communicate with their respiratory channels: no air passes through their mouth, only water and food, so their mouths cannot emit any sound at all. What we interpret as vocalizations are in fact modulations of frequencies induced by the animals' blowholes. The extraordinary refinement of their signals, in terms of rhythm, frequency, and sound combinations, is produced by that organ, homologous to human nostrils. Blowholes correspond to the nostrils of the terrestrial ancestors of the cetaceans; these organs migrated to the top of the skull to facilitate respiration on the surface while the eyes remained under water. It is important to understand that, when it became a sea animal, the ancestor of the cetaceans lost its system of communicating by mouth; so a system of production of subtle signs was recreated on the basis of the blowholes alone (helped by the evolution of phonic lips in the odontocetes). This same system allows the emitting function of echolocation. With the equivalent of a nose, then, evolution pieced together an arrangement for *modulating* extremely elaborate sonic signs.

Evolution seems to create arrangements for *signifying* with whatever exaptable element comes along, as if it were such an efficient find from the evolutionary viewpoint that the phylogenetic flows converged in that direction.

To live is to be generous in signs. This means giving signs to all, in self-defense, without desiring to, without their being appropriable: this is the phenomenological definition of a pure gift. Giving and receiving signs, in exchange, is the foundation and the nature of the great vital politics that weaves living beings together in the biotic community. Here is the generalized ethology that postulates the omnipresence of sign systems and the necessity of inserting oneself in them. From this standpoint, the practice of tracking appears symmetrical to the practice of geopolitics: it is not simply a matter of reading signs, but of being read by others at the same time.

PART THREE

THE DIPLOMATIC PROJECT

AN ETHICS OF RELATIONS

Chapter 11

The Power That Is Diplomacy

Our detour through wolf epistemology has shed light on the cognitive salience of human intelligence that constructs us *spontaneously* as werewolf diplomats.

Human intelligence has a "super-adaptivity"[1] that allows humans to raise problems that are not those of their ambient world, problems that stand apart from needs and necessities. In the end, this is what allows humans to formulate *new* problems: human thinking constantly comes up with new enigmas and deals with the terra incognita that these enigmas open up and shape. In a way, other animals also have diplomatic cognitive capacities, but the "super-adaptivity" of human intelligence, as original a cognitive trait as the sonar capacity of bats, is what allows humans *to try to formulate* problems that are proper to other forms of life. This capability unlocks access to alterrationalities, as humans contemplate the behavior of other animals and indeed of all complex beings.

This super-adaptivity is what establishes the possibility and the irreducible asymmetry of the diplomatic project I am defending here. Having sketched out a natural history of human diplomatic capacities from the standpoint of its cognitive underpinnings in tracking, I shall extend this history here from the standpoint of the capacities of humans to relate to other species. The American anthropologist Pat Shipman maintains that the specificity of *Homo sapiens* lies in the universality, the intensity, and the particularity of its connections with other animal species. She argues that these relations played an especially decisive role in the process of hominization that has made us what we are.[2] In her view, for example, the shift to a carnivorous diet—a key event that took place more than two million years ago—reoriented our attention to other animals, increased our interest in them, even to the point of fascination with these creatures that had been of lesser interest when our diet was essentially plant-based. Our competition with the large predators, combined with our relative physical weakness, made our intellectual ability to observe, interpret, understand, and predict animal behavior the feat on which the selection process that led to the various aspects of the contemporary human mind presumably exerted the most pressure. In this view, our relations with the other animals were what made us human.[3]

Thus it is conceivable that, starting from the very origins of *Homo sapiens*, we have been specialists in animal diplomacy, defined as the ability to grasp the modes of existence of other animals in detail, and to insert ourselves into their ethograms. The explanation lies in cognitive abilities favored by natural selection, traditional and then scientific eco-ethological knowledge, combined with a philosophical asceticism that takes the form of a decentering that allows us to come closer to other ways of being alive.

In comparison, the cognitive abilities of the other animals can be understood, following Temple Grandin's intuition, according to the "gifted autistic" model. Grandin, who holds a PhD in animal science and is a "high-functioning autistic," defends the thesis that animals are geniuses in the same sense as certain autistic persons are geniuses: blind to what is for most of us self-evident, incapable of carrying out certain mental operations that are trivial for other species, they are nevertheless capable of reaching perceptual dimensions invisible to others, and they are virtuosos in mental operations that the rest of us cannot perform. For example, birds such as the jays in oak forests who hide huge quantities of seeds and fruit to prepare for winter—they are said to be saving up "treasure"—have an ability to memorize that far exceeds our own, yet they are unable to solve certain problems that are child's play to us.[4]

Cognitive abilities are creations of evolution: as such, they are subjected to the selective pressures associated with the mode of ecological life of the species that possesses them. Symptoms of these pressures include the curiosity of omnivorous species such as foxes, the problem-solving capacities of the corvids, the prodigious memory of species that hide oleaginous fruit (such as squirrels and jays). But in the history of living beings it has happened that a complex of selected cognitive functions has turned out to be available for hitherto unprecedented, unanticipated uses. For selection does not account for everything: certain capacities, selected and accentuated for certain advantageous uses, can undergo exaptation—they can change their uses and functions and serve unexpected purposes.

Credit: Photograph © Rosalie Winard

Figure 18. Temple Grandin: The Diplomat of Animal Genius

The ideas of this high-functioning autistic professional with a doctorate in animal science have led to a breakthrough in our understanding of animal intelligence. Grandin defends the thesis according to which animals are geniuses in the specific sense in which some autistic persons are geniuses: blind to what is self-evident to the rest of us, incapable of performing certain mental operations that we find easy, they are hypersensitive to visual dimensions that we cannot see and virtuosos in certain mental operations that far exceed our abilities (see Grandin and Johnson, *Animals in Translation*). In the process, she assigns a new and highly original task to zoocephalic diplomats, that of isolating what an animal sees and thinks in a specific context, on the basis of the singular physical underpinnings of its genius. In order to "solve the mystery of animals," she puts herself bodily in their place and analyzes what they have been able to see and infer from their own cognitive world, anamorphic with respect to ours, as if seen in a distorting mirror. Her zootechnological contribution has profoundly reformed the protocols for handling animals destined for slaughter, introducing "a more ethical system." (Grandin's best advocate in France has been Vinciane Despret; see especially Despret, *What Would Animals Say If We Asked the Right Questions?*)

The super-adaptivity of human intelligence comes from our zigzagging evolutionary history (the combined ancestral inheritances of our sedimented past) and from the complex exaptations that this history has induced: as social primates, we are experts in the theory of mind. During the process of hominization, the addition of meat to our diet led to the exaptation of our theories of mind toward *other minds*: those of animals to be hunted,[5] as well as toward the subtle behaviors of vegetation to be harvested (where and when certain plants grow, with what they are associated in the vegetable and animal communities, and so on).

The absence of specialization in the omnivore's diet, which invites us to keep finding new food sources in newly explored biotopes, as crows and foxes do, has oriented us toward the acquisition of an intelligence capable of interpreting the behavior of other living beings, formulating the key to their specific ways of living, deciphering their *codes*. The timeless ruses of hunting, the use of decoys, the tacit knowledge on display in prehistoric wall paintings,[6] the animal myths, all these are faint traces of an art that is now forgotten or instrumentalized. In the history of the primate-wolf-crow that we are, cognitive capabilities have thus been combined and exapted, during our natural and cultural evolution, in such a way that humanity has acquired the empathic intelligence of a werewolf diplomat.

This is a form of animal greatness in the human. Humans do not have to raise themselves above their inner animal, or become in their essence something other than animal, to achieve this greatness. We see in what sense the figure of the werewolf, as a hybrid, coded as a brutalized, degraded form of the human in the pastoral metaphysics that emerged from the Neolithic era, deserves to be flipped over and made a figure to be honored: it is as an animal combinatorics that humans are what they are, with all their forms of grandeur and all their ambiguities.

By animal greatness in the human, I mean to point to powers that are valued as lofty, noble, and superior, powers that must not be interpreted as signs of election through which the human would be elevated above the inner beast, but rather as gifts inherited from the animal ancestry embedded in us: diplomacy and good intelligence, empathy and parental love, curiosity about what is other or alien, pity for the vulnerable, forgetfulness of self, powers of love and connection that extend even beyond the borders of our species. These latter powers also belong to animals: to the original wolves who became our dogs, to the original felines who became our housemates, and even today, among wild animals, these powers are spectacularly evident, for example, in *Delphinidae* (orcas, dolphins, and the like), creatures that regularly cross the boundaries of their species to come splash us with curiosity and sometimes with affection.

We need to dismantle the idea that everything that is great in humans represents a transcending of nature, that everything lofty represents a pulling away from a stupid, evil biological matrix. Human greatness does not lie in a domination of the flesh by a supposedly purer spirit—it lies in a *specific way* of being the animal that we are. Symmetrically, human greatness does not consist in degrading what is elevated in humanity; rather, it entails resisting a reduction to instinctual behaviors, a reduction whose misanthropy animalizes the human in order to depict it as savage, whether to rejoice in this or to stigmatize the degradation. There is greatness in animals (let us recall the enigmatic behaviors of Wolf 21 in Yellowstone), and from that greatness stems, strangely and by quite twisted paths, our own. Realizing our greatness results from understanding and accentuating our healthy vitality as living beings, and not from exerting control over a body supposedly condemned to bestial impulses or mechanical instincts.

The philosophical anthropologies of the last two thousand years seem to have been defined by the discreet but invariant speculative strategy that consists in defining the human by its difference from what characterizes other living beings, even though these latter are increasingly seen to share more and more of the oldest prerogatives of humans. But the philosophical anthropology of the twenty-first century would do well to take a different path, that of defining the human not by *difference* but by affiliation and constitutive relations. The act of defining by distinguishing seems almost a logical necessity: it is in fact, however, a political act. One can just as well define the specificity of something by the singular manner in which its relations with others are knotted together. In the relational ontology that I shall develop further shortly, our relations are our foundation; with respect to them, we come second. What constitutes us as human, then, are our constitutive relations with nonhumans: our past evolutionary affiliations and our present ecological relations.[7]

Of the Two Diplomacies

Our aptitude for diplomacy is not of the same order as that of other animals. Diplomacy is a form of *power*, and the use we make of it is potentially twofold. Every power can be envisioned from opposing ethical perspectives. The super-adaptivity of human intelligence confers on us great power, thus also great privileges—and great responsibilities.

The human practice of animal diplomacy, as a competency going back into time immemorial, has known a variety of uses over the millennia of human history. During the Paleolithic era, it was probably practiced by hunters in a relation to the nonhuman that was on the order of a complex exchange with a "giving environment."[8] In the Neolithic era, if we follow Paul Shepard's hypothesis, the relation changed, and animal diplomacy was no longer a means for enlivening exchanges, but an extension of a war against nature *by other means*.[9]

We can indeed instrumentalize this power to affirm our supremacy over living beings, or, conversely, we can consider that possessing these diplomatic competencies is not a privilege that allows us to set ourselves *above* the animal kingdom but rather a *responsibility* that leads us to put in place a nondestructive diplomacy aimed at reinvoking our ancient mutual relations, and to imagine and institute new ones.[10]

We find ourselves at a philosophical crossroads that requires in-depth analysis. In the current state of our inquiry, choosing to privilege that reading of power in terms of responsibility would be wishful thinking, the prerogative of an ecological sensibility. This choice has to be reinforced by argumentation, especially given the legacy of a Neolithic metaphysics that views progress as a matter of dominating nature.

I shall try to show that the perspective that consists in using the power in question to ensure a continuation of the war against nature by other means entails a profound structural misunderstanding of our place in the biotic community. This misunderstanding consists in postulating that human beings and nonhuman living beings are bodies foreign to one another, separate and in conflict. But this postulate breaks down if we take into account the evolutionary history of our species as primate-wolf-crow evoked above, and the environmental history of our local relations with wolves in the biotic community. This is what prompts me to propose a detour through the history of wolves seen as preying on humans, a detour that will lead us to an understanding of the entities currently in presence as the products of a relation between wolves and human populations. We cannot think of ourselves as at war with other living beings because we are caught up with them in constitutive relations. The approach that puts the accent on the *relation* between the parties involved, rather than on each party in isolation, will make it possible to understand real diplomacy as an art of revitalizing relationships, as opposed to an instrumental diplomacy understood as a ruse of war between adversaries.

Chapter 12

We Have Invented the Wolf

"Wolves" Do Not Exist

One of the diplomatic misunderstandings that presides over our conflict with wolves, beyond their real impact on pastoralism, has to do with their representation as man-eating beasts. As with the ethnographic misunderstandings evoked earlier, the difficulty of observing wolves, our deficient ethological grasp of how they live, and the trauma associated in humans with the idea of being devoured, have given the question of man-eaters a decisive and highly mediatized affective scope that has tended to dominate the debate about wolves, to the detriment of the more subtle problematics that are really at stake. Nevertheless, the intensity of this association reveals structures that underlie our relation to the large predators and to living beings in general, structures that allow us to envision reforms in our relation to wildness, if only we can manage to dissipate the diplomatic misunderstandings.

The debate is structured in a more or less binary fashion. On the one hand, for several decades a fringe of protectionist discourse regarding wolves has been presenting the argument that these animals do not attack people. In the face of this widely publicized claim, researchers who are more academic and less committed to protecting these animals, upset by the simultaneously ideological and ill-informed thesis, seem to think that they can set in motion a crusade for the truth rather easily by maintaining that, yes, wolves do attack people[1]—that is, wolves have attacked people and may well do so again.[2]

Now the claims made in this binary debate—wolves attack humans / wolves do not attack humans—are neither true nor false. They are not supplied with the minimal conditions of clarity and rigor that would allow them to be tested for their truth value. If one were to assert that "keraks are maranivores," one would be in an analogous situation, for the two terms of the assertion are logically underdetermined. The same holds true for the two claims cited earlier: neither is true, for "wolves" do not exist any more than "humans" do.

The Enigma of the Two Wolves

To make this phenomenon visible, let us make a detour via an enigma. It has been established that Amerindian and Inuit societies, which have regular contacts with wolves, judge that wolves do not attack humans.[3] Now, the archival work of the historian Jean-Marc Moriceau clearly reveals a large number of attacks on humans in France.[4] Overall, accounts of such attacks are significantly *more numerous* in Europe than in all of the Americas.[5]

Here is the mystery: How can wolves be man-eaters on one side of the Atlantic and not on the other? And yet we are dealing with the same species: *Canis lupus.*

To solve the mystery, we may begin by postulating that the Amerindian archives are defective—that, lacking reliable sources, the Amerindian oral narratives are unable to supply solid data on the degree to which wolves were dangerous in the past. Beyond the epistemological ethnocentrism of this postulate, the hypothesis is dubious: Amerindian oral narratives do retain traces indicating how dangerous other animals have been for humans (grizzly bears, mountain lions); why would these have disappeared for wolves? In addition, we might suppose that, if the danger from wolves were real, this is precisely a point that would not be lost or neglected in oral teaching. The mystery deepens when we look at certain specific tales. In Alaska, the Tanaina Indians say that wolves were at one time men and are therefore brothers. One tale advises a hiker lost in the forest to call on the wolf to help him find his way.[6] In contrast, when we look at "Peter and the Wolf" or "Little Red Riding Hood," we find fairly pure inversions of the mytheme "lost in the forest." What is lifesaving on one side is life-threatening on the other.

The second hypothesis for resolving the enigma comes down to evoking the power of representations. In this view, the positive or negative presuppositions about wolves inflect the interpretation and ordering of the data. For example, one can place less emphasis on attacks when wolves are brothers to humans; attacks can be interpreted as natural necessities or products of human error. If wolves are seen as devils, then attacks will receive greater emphasis and a different interpretation.

This hypothesis does not suffice to explain the contrasting data, but it allows us to shift the question toward the origin of these representations themselves.

Representations as Products of Ecological Relations

Let us hypothesize that the *cultural representations* of wolves can be classified according to the ecological relations that wolves maintain with human populations.

Luigi Boitani classifies the different types of representations of wolves in terms of the modes of production of human societies, from both a diachronic and a synchronic standpoint. He thus asserts that "human cultures whose main subsistence was hunting and war shared a positive image of the wolf in all historical periods and geographical areas," whereas "shepherds had a negative image of wolves because wolves were the main threat to shepherds' economic survival." Finally, the modes of subsistence based on sedentary agriculture gave rise to "a positive view of the wolf, or at least an ambiguous attitude."[7] In populations where sheep-raising is practiced extensively and where there is considerable wolf presence, wolves are hated (this was the case in medieval Europe, as it is in modern Europe). In hunter-gatherer societies, wolves are models and brothers, rarely rivals vis-à-vis prey, though they can become rivals, a shift that leads to hunting in order to regulate the pressure (for example, ritual killing of pups among the Athabascan). When deer populations are destroying the crops, the wolf may be adored as "a great god" (Japanese *ookami*), as was the case during the shogun era.[8] Certain wolves were thus lured by food to drive away the animals that were damaging crops. Mongol pastoral societies, which had a lucid sense of ecosystems, were ambiguous about wolves: they were powerful spirits that belonged to the ecosystem god, and at the same time rivals that provoked anger when they attacked livestock. It was necessary to defend against them, drive them away, leave nothing to them, regulate them (pups were culled by being tossed skyward; as they fell to their death, they were simultaneously being entrusted to a higher power), but they were never eradicated or despised. Finally, where sheep-raising was the principal life-sustaining activity and a necessity for survival, wolves were essentially hated.

The representation of wolves and the physiognomy of actual encounters could be said to be tied to the ecological conjunction.[9] This variability would be facilitated by the great behavioral plasticity of both humans and wolves. The representation of wolves is the product of a complex ecological situation, translated and refracted in categories and representations; it is not the product of a human (civilizing) essence and a wolf (predatory) essence that would make wolves rivals and enemies of humans. We can see this phenomenon at work in the evolution of a particular culture: the Sami people in the north of Sweden shifted from an attitude of respect for wolves to an attitude of disdain or even enmity after they began to change their way of life and raise domesticated reindeer.[10] On this point, we have to leave Aristotle behind: animal behaviors are not contained and exhausted in an essence, that is, in a gamut of specific instincts shared by interchangeable individuals, nor are they genetically programmed. To know a wolf is not to know all wolves.

A species is not an essence, but a historical population, with a behavioral plasticity that can adapt subtly to circumstances. We cannot know "the wolf," or "wolves in general," any more than we can claim to know humans, as at least one ethnologist has, by saying that their ethogram is that of a rational animal and a political animal.

It is in this framework that we need to interrogate the representations of wolves as man-eaters. Boitani has shown very clearly that representations of wolves are apt to vary as a function of the type of ecological and socioeconomic relations that a human population maintains with the biotic community. But is this an adequate explanation? We need to make this argument even more radical, in order to bring out the diplomatic implications of this ethno-ecological question.

The hypothesis I am defending here consists in postulating that the cultural representations of wolves are not the only products of the ecological relations between humans and the biotic community; *the actual wolves themselves* are also products of these relations: wolves understood as *objective forms of life*, with specific habits, cultures, and behaviors.

Thus we need to understand the human-wolf relationship as a historical conjuncture, independent of "humans-in-themselves" and "wolves-in-themselves" but always as a historical complex that brings constitutive ecological relations into convergence and brings out, from these relations, a specific form of human and a specific form of wolf.

This hypothesis would allow us to solve the enigma constituted by the difference in wolf attacks on humans between the eastern and western sides of the Atlantic. We shall establish this hypothesis through an environmental approach that interrogates the ecological conditions of the relation between French rural populations and wolves in the modern era. Not "wolves in general" but "our wolves," those produced by us, produced by the ecological relations established over the long run of history. Put differently, if "our" wolves are represented and experienced as savage beasts, that could mean that the relations we have established with them and with their prey have *made* them savage beasts, that is, man-eaters, or, more recently, "cruel" predators that kill their prey without feeding on them.

Thus not only have we invented the beasts, in the sense that might be produced by a culturalist constructivism granting a primary role to our symbolic representations in our perception of the world; we have also invented them in the *realist* sense of the term, that is, we have brought them into our landscapes by inflecting their way of acting, their way of life, their ethogram—in other words, by the interplay of our socioeconomic relations with the biotic community.

We Have Invented the Beasts Three Times

From the perspective of wolf science, the variability of individuals, of packs, and of their cultural dimensions has appeared quite clearly. What now needs to be made intelligible is the fact that this plasticity of animal life forms is the product of ecological relations with the *other* species in the surrounding biotic community. And in this respect we humans play an important role in the transformation of animal species, even the wildest. We can inflect behavioral forms. Here we must not understand "inventing" in the sense of producing Frankensteins, nor must we deduce from this, misanthropically, an exclusively human responsibility. By the expression "inventing the beasts," I mean to designate the human social, economic, and ecological operations on which our relations with wolves have been based, operations that are capable of transforming the animals' behavior into conducts that humans condemn *secondarily*—after humans, through their actions, have created the conditions that triggered those behaviors—as monstrous. These behaviors are of two orders. First—and this is the dominant case—the killing and eating of humans; second, the case of more recent concern known as *surplus killing*, misinterpreted as sadistic and cruel predation on defenseless sheep.

The existence of the man-eating wolf in the French landscape between the fifteenth and the nineteenth centuries is well documented. Here we shall concentrate on the healthy wolves[11] responsible in toto for 1,857 attacks between 1421 and 1918.[12]

Moriceau's study foregrounds the way the man-eating behavior of wolves can be understood in relation to the ecological, economic, social, and demographic conditions put in place by humans. "Wolves' attacks on humans have revealed something to us about the way human societies function and have served as a bio-indicator regarding the management of rural spaces."[13] As a rural historian, Moriceau shines the investigative spotlight on human societies. But if we shift our gaze slightly, we can shift our focus from the impact of wolves on societies to the impact of these societies—and in particular of the choices they have made regarding "the management of rural spaces"—on the behavior of wolves. In other words, the data provided by Moriceau's study make possible both a history of rural societies and a history of wolf societies, from the standpoint of the constitutive relations between humans and nonhumans.

The Bestiality of the European Wars

The origins of the invention of the modern "beast" can be traced to the chronological correlation between the peak periods of "beast" attacks on humans (identified as such by contemporaries and grouped in time and space) and the wars in which French territories and their European neighbors were engulfed. The first "beasts" that appeared between 1596 and 1600 in regions of Bourbonnais, Brittany, Bresse, Touraine, and Maine followed the wars of religion that ravaged these territories over half a century. The beasts of Orléans and Touraine, in 1691 and 1695, were inscribed in the context of Louis XIV's wars and a serious economic crisis. This economic crisis, not coincidentally, also induced some of the most serious epidemics that the kingdom of France had ever known. The correlation between beasts and wars, with their economic impact, manifested the first phase in the creation of "beasts": a connection between necrophagy and anthropophagy, that is, habituation to human flesh as a food source.[14] Some wolves became necrophages opportunistically, when humans left corpses where they had fallen in combat, unburied, at the mercy of carrion-eaters.

The human habit, which some might call "bestial," of leaving cadavers to rot on the ground created a new ecological relation with the wolf populations in the vicinity, one apt to influence their behavior: here was one step in the invention of the wolf as beast. The induced habituation to human meat, perhaps a certain taste for it, along with the ease of acquiring this resource as compared with the difficulty of hunting down vigorous ungulates, constituted a major factor in the historical appearance of man-eating behavior and the figure of the man-eating wolf. In certain Amerindian cultures, the funerary ritual that consisted in burning human remains on raised wooden platforms may have entailed arrangements designed to prevent necrophagy as a first stage of anthropophagy.[15] The ecological relations that certain hunter-gatherers maintained with wolves seem, from this standpoint, so controlled that the hunter-gatherers could formulate beliefs symmetrically inverse to the figure of the Big Bad Wolf. Their cooperative affiliation with wolves, where Occidentals today see only devouring, takes on a profound form in a Yakut poem:

> When you are in the Other World,
> Take a Wolf as a Friend,
> For he knows the Order of the Forest.[16]

Socioeconomic Features of Pastoralism in the Gévaudan Region

The Gévaudan case crystallized the figure of the man-eating wolf in French culture.[17] The scope of the attacks and the publicity they drew at the time from a press with less to focus on after the wars established this historical episode as a collective trauma. The archetype of a diplomatic misunderstanding, the story sealed the fate of the French relation to wolves in the modern era. It will be useful to analyze the episode in terms of the ecology of relationships, on the basis of Jean-Marc Moriceau's data.

We know that wars had drained France's rural regions, including the Gévaudan, of the adult male population, producing a new socioeconomic situation that fostered a second phase of the objective invention of the wolf as "beast." Since few adult males were available, children took over the shepherding tasks. And children were preferentially attacked by wolves, a fact that contributed to the construction of a representation of wolves as particularly monstrous. Of the 1,561 victims counted between 1421 and 1918, 1,310 were less than twenty years old.

Moreover, the statistics reveal the clear overrepresentation of herders among the victims of wolf attacks: of 345 cases counted in the Gévaudan region between 1764 and 1767, 176 were shepherds. Here we see the cluster of socioeconomic conditions that presided over a new phase in the invention of the "beast": when frail children were watching, far from the scattered dwelling places, over bovines that often weighed "ten times more than the young herders," the physical disproportion between the protectors and the protected "offered the wolf a quite different perspective."[18]

A third factor in the invention of the wolf as "beast" was the alteration in geographical conditions. In the regions in question, the rural landscape was highly fragmented. During the period covered by Moriceau's study, the forests in France reached a low point: massive clearing during the Middle Ages, accelerated during a period of economic growth in the twelfth century, had led to the systematic destruction of wildlife throughout the territory corresponding to the kingdom of France. As in other historical situations, the reduction in wildlife and the fragmentation of the habitat contributed to the destruction of wolves' natural prey, thus starving the wolf population, or at least leading these opportunistic predators to fall back on a more accessible prey than the now-rare ungulates, thereby reinforcing their anthropophagic behaviors.

The man-eating wolf was thus produced by a cluster of related factors, including the eco-fragmentation and the human overpopulation that reduced the numbers of wild prey and the generalization of child labor in response to poverty.[19] The fact that wolves focused their attacks on children thus must not be understood as a sign of cruelty on their part, but as revealing a relational ecological structure in the biotic community: transforming the relations of human populations to the *bios* transforms animal behavior, as in a network where everything is connected.

Three principal factors—the dispersal of bovine agropastoralism, the specialization of children in bovine protection, and the destruction of wolves' natural prey—thus constituted the framework for an ecological relationship that gave rise to a generalization about the anthropophagic behavior of wolves, of which representations of the Big Bad Wolf are simply derivatives.

We can henceforth affirm, then, that certain wolves attack—in eco-sociological situations *induced by humans*, very specific and very controllable situations—*certain* humans who can be viewed as prey. Humans, by their behavior, have coproduced the Beast of the Gévaudan, and the others, by putting in place an agropastoral model of the child shepherd, induced by the socioeconomic distress of the European livestock farmers of the time.

Our initial enigma—how to explain the different rates of wolf attacks on humans in Europe as opposed to Amerindian lands—is thus resolved by taking into account the differential ecological relations instituted between humans and wolves. The Amerindian populations participated in a relation that probably inhibited the possibility of predation. The human-wolf relation precedes each of its terms. If the relation changes, the essence of the terms change: we invent—not in representations, but in forests—a new type of wolf, a real wolf that is more inclined to attack humans.

Ovine Pastoralism and Technological Itineraries

Solving the puzzle of the different rates of wolf attacks on humans allows us to begin to resolve the correlated contemporary enigma: How to explain that in France our wolves regularly attack livestock, whereas in other parts of the world wolves spend time around livestock and come into close contact without attacking their potential prey?[20] In Montana, for instance, near the Flathead River, one wolf pack has a territory that includes pastures full of livestock, and there have been no attacks in thirty years. They pass through the herds or go around them to chase deer and elk. How are we to understand this?

The question is not *whether* wolves attack sheep, but rather how to grasp the constitutive relation that produces predation. In the analysis of surplus killing, we have seen that through artificial selection the process of domestication produced a type of sheep unable to defend itself against wolves and whose group flight behaviors catalyzed their own slaughter.

We can extend this analysis by considering the role of rock formations. When we read in the press that a wolf attack has killed several hundred animals, most of the time this means that in their haste to escape the sheep have been killed by falling off a rocky cliff.

Are wolves really the killers in such a case? More rigorously speaking, it is the wolf-sheep ethological relation, modified by domestication, that produces this sort of drama. The pastoral tradition has selected sheep that have retained a flight reflex orienting them toward rocky cliffs for their own protection, like their *mouflon urial* ancestors. But domestication has deprived modern sheep of the nerve and the biomechanical competencies that had allowed them to scamper about sure-footedly on steep rocky slopes. Their panic, their awkwardness, their gregariousness, all pleiotropic effects of the docility produced by selection, leads them to fall en masse into the abyss.

An approach by way of ecological relations leads us to recognize an ambiguous form of human responsibility (ancient, inherited, unattributable) in dramas in which we cast the wolf as the sole enemy. The diplomatic approach is designed to make any assignment of responsibility ambiguous: when we are caught up in ancient relationships, like two old nations, two ancient peoples, the history of our ties is so deep and complex that there are no more isolated responsibilities—we have to acknowledge that we have made each other what we are, interwoven ourselves with the others, in order to take seriously the diplomatic project of living together.

If domestic sheep are much more vulnerable in the face of wolves than their ancestors, there are nevertheless great disparities with regard to types of pastoralism. It would be false to claim that it is possible to annihilate wolf predation on domestic herds *completely*: all pastoral societies in contact with large predators are subjected to attacks, though to very different degrees, and sometimes almost never. The question is whether it is possible to render such attacks tolerable, that is, to limit them sufficiently so that they do not endanger pastoral activity as a whole. Beyond strictly defensive measures, the difference between the technical itineraries of agropastoral activities is what allows us to answer that question. The relations between pastoral practices and the presence of wolves are what create wolves that eat sheep or wolves that do not take much interest in sheep. Thus we need to ask what situations are correlated with attacks and, by contrast, which ones inhibit attacks?

The current economic situation of certain agropastoralist spaces plays a major role in the propensity of wolves to attack herds. The geographer Farid Benhammou thus asserts that "the lack of a labor force and of appropriate pastoral equipment (more rainwater catchments, better clearing of brush, restoration or construction of huts allowing more human presence) increases the risks of predation."[21]

The evolution of livestock breeding toward a specialized system, with a smaller labor force, occurring in territories that are less and less cultivated and occupied in very different ways (certain zones being abandoned in favor of a concentration of herds in others) favors wolf attacks on sheep. A related factor is "an increase in sheep as opposed to cattle" in several sectors of the southern Alps, owing in part to the European incentive system.[22]

Moreover, for the last twenty years livestock breeding in France has been confronted by a structural crisis owing to international competition in the marketing of lamb and sheep meat.[23] This competition is all the more difficult for the farmers because the French are eating less and less mutton. This critical situation is producing new pressure on farmers, so much so that "in the dry zones of the Alps, in the Jura and in part of the eastern Pyrenees, agricultural associations have encouraged sheep farmers to give up the use of shepherds in the interest of profitability."[24] The requirement that production costs be maximally reduced for a minimally profitable activity is a matter of economic rationality. However, from the ecological standpoint, this requirement means putting in place conditions favorable to predatory behaviors on the part of certain wolves. The increased size of herds and the reduction in the number of herders, in a context of rural depopulation and reforestation, are particularly pronounced in the Vésubie sector of the Alpes-Maritimes department, an area that has been highly affected by wolf attacks. And to this are added "the technical difficulties of setting up protective measures (regrouping in nocturnal parks is locally difficult owing to slopes; the forest cover complicates the work of sheep dogs)."[25]

The analysis of local situations allows us to solve the enigma of the differentiated attacks on herds. The prevailing economic conditions and livestock farming practices, along with the topological situations, institute a *singular economic relationship* with wolf packs that inflects the wolves' predatory behaviors.

If agropastoral practices can establish conditions favorable to predation, this implies that they can also set up *unfavorable* conditions. The influence of practices on relationships shows the very considerable plasticity of the constitutive ecological relationships, and thus of wolf behaviors: in other words, it is a question of changing practices in order to transform relationships. In certain situations these changes can be achieved with very little effort. The cases of the Écrins National Park and the Queyras Natural Regional Park are very interesting in this regard. The data Benhammou has collected show how wolf behavior changes as soon as the ecological relation changes, that is, when livestock-raising practices change: "The herd the most often attacked in 1999 [in the Monges mountains] saw the attacks of predators diminish and almost disappear in 2002. This was a herd for which the three preventive measures (two sheep dogs, nocturnal regrouping, and a shepherd's helper) along with the construction of a hut and a rain catchment had been provided for the August pasture."[26]

The decreased rate of attack following the establishment of an integrated set of protective measures seems to confirm the theory of the optimal nutritional regime: the strategy adopted by a predator consists in managing the best compromise between gains in energy and costs of acquiring food, by selecting the most profitable species as prey.[27] A decrease in the profitability of the main prey results in increased opportunistic behaviors on the part of predators: they seek and find prey elsewhere. Several sheep farmers, most notably those in contact with the wolf pack of the Glières plateau, indicate that they have not experienced any attacks in the several years since they introduced measures compatible with their enterprises (shepherd's helpers, sheep dogs, nocturnal enclosures). Nevertheless, the situation is not that easy to resolve everywhere.

Eco-fragmentation

The availability of wild prey, apt to lighten predatory pressures, is another important explanatory factor for attacks on domestic sheep.

Such predation is very weak in places where wild fauna is abundant and in good health.[28] It is dominant in milieus where biodiversity and large fauna have been destroyed by human activity. In Romania, Poland, and Finland, predation on sheep has dropped sharply since populations of wild ungulates have been reintroduced.

This availability is largely dependent on the degree of fragmentation of the landscape: that is, the degree to which the surface of the available habitats has been reduced, and the degree to which the isolation of these habitats has been increased.[29] These two processes have a direct impact on the size and viability of populations, in particular the large ungulates that make up the preferred diet of wolves.[30]

In addition to fragmentation, the edge effect studied by landscape ecology may account for the fact that wolves turn to domesticated ungulates when they do not succeed in meeting their caloric needs. Edge zones are the external fringes of habitats. These are intermediate zones between two biotopes that combine the conditions of the two ecosystems (interior habitat and matrix). With a decrease in the size of habitat fragments and the multiplication of linear transportation infrastructures, edge surfaces increase. These zones favor generalized species (such as wolves) at the expense of specialized species, the latter being more closely dependent for their survival on a particular milieu. This is what landscape ecology calls the edge effect: species living in the interior milieu see their vital domain diminishing, a phenomenon that limits the number of individuals.

Moreover, the edge effect multiplies the opportunities for contact between wolves and domestic herds, since the edges bring the forest cover of the ecotone—the transition area—into contact with the matrix, which consists essentially in zones of pasture in the Alpine regions that concern us.

Finally, landscape fragmentation has an indirect impact on the size of wolf packs and thus on wolves' hunting techniques. In eco-fragmented spaces, which imply shrunken territories, wolf packs are often "simple" (a breeding pair and one generation of descendants) rather than "complex" (with more than one generation of descendants and other aggregated individuals). But the success of a "simple" pack in hunting wild ungulates is compromised by the small number of individuals able to participate. Predation pressure thus bears preferentially on domestic ungulates, which are easier to attack.

Moreover, the limited size of packs, owing to landscape fragmentation, potentially increased the number of dispersals. It has been demonstrated that solitary wolves are most often the ones that attack domestic herds, since it is easier for them to do so than to hunt wild prey.

We see here the set of conditions through which the relation of human populations with the biotic community, by virtue of human economic and ecologic activity, transforms the behavior of other beings in the web of life. Predation on humans, massive predation on herds: these are not essential, necessary, and inevitable wolf behaviors but rather products of a complex environmental history in which humans, forests, and animals are caught up, inseparably.

As populations, lineages, and individuals, wolves are changing, complex historical effects of the ecological relations they maintain with the biotic community that includes them. Humans, as a species and as societies, in their behavior toward other living beings, have no "essential" advantage: they too are changing, complex, historical effects of their own ecological relations to the biotic community. The heart of the problem, far from the comfortable Aristotelian discourse about the essence of one species or another, is situated at the level of the complexes of eco-sociological relations, and it is on the foundations of these relations that we now need to base our inquiry. Diplomacy is no longer that of one camp *against* another; if it recognizes that the two camps are only the recent endpoints, produced secondarily via the same constitutive relation, it becomes diplomacy as the art of revitalizing the relations themselves.

Chapter 13

Constitutive Relations

Our inquiry has allowed us to see that the living entities we have isolated (both species and individuals) are constituted by long and complex historical ecological relations that rule out any opposition between human and nonhuman, nature and culture. We humans, as living beings, like North American or European wolves, are the historical product of a nexus of ecological relations with the rest of the biotic community and with abiotic conditions, and in particular with species caught up in the same ecological features that have given rise to us and continue to accompany us today.[1] This understanding makes it possible to give the idea of diplomacy defended here its full weight and specificity: true diplomacy among living beings is a *diplomacy of relations*. This gives a new dimension to the recurring enigmatic formula according to which "we are nature."

By diplomacy of relations, I mean a diplomacy based on an ontology and an ethics of relations: that is, on a conception of the world according to which we are a web of relations with the biotic community, a web in which seeking what is good for one group implies seeking what is good for the relation itself. It is a diplomacy of conciliation and reconciliation.

It is the opposite of a diplomacy of *entities*, which is based on a substantialist ontology and ethics of terms, according to which what exists are above all separate things, humans and wolves, savages and civilized creatures, beings of law and beings of matter, and according to which one must prioritize what is good for the set of beings to which one belongs (species, country, social class) over what is good for relations, which are viewed as secondary.

To make this opposition more comprehensible, I need to sketch in briefly the change in the basis for the map of the world: the transformation of the conception of the world and of experience from a perspective centered on things to a perspective focused on relations among things.

This transformation leads to what the philosophy of ecology calls a *realism of relations*. This form of realism stipulates that what is most real in reality are not the entities we isolate by perception and thought (individuals) but the dynamic relations that constitute these entities in a process of individuation. The entities, or *relata*, are secondary and derived with respect to relations. We find two well-developed versions of this ontological thesis, one in Gilbert Simondon, in the wake of Gaston Bachelard (a realism of relations in which relations "have the value of being");[2] the other in the philosophy of ecology from Paul Shepard to Arne Naess and J. Baird Callicott (a realism of ecological relations in which these relations are anterior to every living being).[3] Taking this realism of relations seriously will allow us to resolve the aporia posited earlier regarding the diplomatic approach: Why cannot that approach be summed up as a continuation of the war against nature *by other means*?

If We Are Knots of Relations and Not Separate Camps, What Does Diplomacy Look Like?

From a historical viewpoint, ecology has been from the outset a science focusing on relations. The inventor of its name, Ernst Haeckel, defined this emerging science as follows: "By ecology, we understand the whole science of the organism's relationship with the surrounding outside world, which includes in a broader sense all 'existential conditions.'"[4] We can find this definition almost word for word in contemporary manuals of ecology.

But it is in philosophy that we find the most enlightening formulations of this extreme vigilance concerning relations, raising them up to the rank of being. With his philosophy of relations, the arduous exercise of thought and imagination in which philosopher Gilbert Simondon invites us to participate amounts to learning to conceptualize every being as a knot of relations. In his terms, "The method consists . . . in considering every real relation as having the rank of being." It is by following this conceptual pathway that Simondon ends up with the most enigmatic formulation of his theory of relations: "The individual is not properly speaking in relation with himself or herself, nor with other realities; he or she is the being *of* the relation, and not the being *in* relation, for a relation is an intense operation, an active center."[5]

No being is in relation with other beings, for that would imply that the individual preexists as a term, secondarily put into relation, or at least that one could isolate the individual from any relation to consider the individual separately.

It is extraordinarily difficult for the mind to decode experience in a relational form, and to unlearn or minimize the "thing-ist" reflections that decode experience as a set of separate entities. The valorization of relations easily becomes a gratuitous slogan that obscures the real stakes: to accede via the operations of living thought to a *logic* of relations. This logic requires a major effort in ontology, which professional philosophers have only begun to undertake;[6] it will allow us to give a rigorous sense to the concept of relation and to the types of relations that are constitutive of the different types of beings. Still, it is possible to use an ontology of relations on a provisional basis. Its guiding principles are basically the following: what constitutes the essence of a being (that without which a thing would not be that thing) is the historical process of its relations—if the relations are transformed, that essence is transformed; if they disappear, it disappears or is transformed.

For Simondon, "a relation is a modality of being; it is simultaneous with respect to the terms whose existence it ensures."[7] Relations already ensure existence, but they neither precede nor constitute it. Paul Shepard's philosophy of ecology, endowed with an extraordinary attention to the historicity conferred by evolutionist thought, goes further, in a sense, in the radicality of this idea as applied to ecology: it postulates, in what appears to be a logical paradox, that the relation is *anterior* to the entities involved.[8] In substantialist logic, it is necessary for something to exist for it to be subsequently set into relation. But this logic is flawed by an essentialist belief that obscures the *process* by which living beings come into existence. The Darwinian approach to species as populations undergoing gradual transformation is what enables us to resolve this paradox, with the same effectiveness as that of the chicken and the egg.

If we take seriously the logic of becoming in evolution, a relation is no longer simultaneous with the entities involved. It is anterior to them logically and chronologically:

> Ecology, in tandem with the new Physics, may even be taken to imply not merely that relationships of things are as real as the things but that relationships are *more* real than things—that

is, that things are just the focus of a complex of relationships, however abstract this may seem. From the perspective of contemporary biology, species adapt to a niche in an ecosystem. Their actual relationships to other organisms (to predators, to prey, to parasites and disease organisms) and to physical and chemical conditions (to temperature, radiation, salinity, wind, soil, and water pH) literally mold their outward forms, their metabolic processes, and even their psychological and mental capacities. A specimen is, in effect, a summation of its species' historical adaptive relationship to the environment. [This is what led Paul Shepard to say that "relationships of things are as real as the things."] . . . One might say that from an ecological perspective relations are "prior to" the things related, and the systemic wholes woven from these relations are prior to their component parts.[9]

The ecological relations between a wolf population and its potential prey precede the specific forms that tomorrow's population will take. The species that our descendants will call *Canis lupus* will be a historic product of these relations. The current hybridizations between coyotes and wolves, for example, induced in part by population displacements related to global warming, are producing a variant that biologists will call by default a "coywolf," and that will perhaps be the source of a future species.

In the contemporary philosophy of ecology, the concepts of "transactor" and "transactional network" developed by the philosopher Donato Bergandi and the biologist Patrick Blandin to characterize intrinsically connected and cohesive entities are probably among the most promising paths for an ontology of consistent relations in tomorrow's ecology.[10] These scholars postulate that relations in an ecosystem are not unidirectional between terms; they are necessarily *transactional*, that is, as conditioned by the nature of the two interacting elements as they are by the nature of the majority of the elements in the set. The concepts of transactor and transactional network consist in postulating, for example, in a holistic and emergentist approach to ecosystems, that they constitute relatively autonomous and cohesive coevolutive entities capable of giving a foothold globally to natural selection, as systems.

But these concepts can be most useful here as they apply to an ontology of relations. Relations are constitutive of individual beings, for they constitute "coevolutive transactions" over the long run between life forms (wolves and deer, for example), transactions that bear many other elements of the system in themselves (what deer eat, creatures in a commensal relation with wolves, parasites, and so on). "What is important," Blandin specifies, "is introducing the idea that coevolutive transactions lead to the production of co-signifying memories (most notably genetic)."[11] These memories are co-signifying because they respond to one another in the present: they are intertwined. The genetic memory that is transported in the tapered body of each wolf responds to the genetic memory embodied in each deer: during the millennia memorized in their bodies, the vigilance of the one is entwined with the ruse of the other, so much so that neither can exist alone, any more than it can make sense alone. Each makes sense only as caught up in a multiple coevolutive transactional network, which must not be essentialized (it is plastic, contingent in its becoming, and it is a trajectory), any more than it must be neglected to the benefit of an atomist individualism. It constitutes the balanced interdependence that is the only independence possible. In it, according to Simondon's formula, each individual is not its own self alone, any more than it is Everything: it is "the being of relations" with those that constitute it, that enter with it into vital trans-actions.

This ontological approach, as soon as we combine the conceptual operations of these various thinkers, gives Tennyson's formula its deep meaning: "I am a part of all that I have met."[12] I am a part of everything I have met because to be is first of all to be the historical product and the activity of a relation with an Other whom one has encountered.

In sum, we now have access to an ontology of constitutive ecological relations (transactional relations constitute the identity of beings), endowed with an eco-evolutive historicity (these relations are transformed as they transform forms of life; they are relatively stable over short periods of time, but they define the deep identity of species over very long periods of time), backed up by a realism of relations (beings are not *in* relation, they are the being *of* relation).[13]

The Survival of the Best Related

The ontology of ecological relations allows us to understand in a different way the term "survival of the fittest" as the basic schema for Darwinian evolution. Beyond the fact that the formula actually comes from Herbert Spencer (Darwin adopted it only later), its tautological dimension has often been evoked: the fittest survive, but how do we know they were the fittest? Because they survived.[14]

An essentially empty signifier adopted as a popular summation of one of the most important theories for metaphysics and philosophical anthropology leaves a great deal of room for ideological interpretations. One of them is quite obviously the discreet condemnation of the floating signifier "fit" by the avatars of strength: the older and sturdier notion "survival of the strongest" has taken over the empty form. In response to the ideological changes of the twentieth century, the strongest came to be understood as the most efficient, then the most effective, then the most adaptable (the most flexible, in neoliberal thinking). This way of representing Darwin's notion has probably had little effect on the development of theoretical biology,[15] but it plays such a crucial role in our collective representation of living beings that it founds our cosmology (our conception of Nature) and our anthropology (our conception of Humanity): *Homo sapiens* would be, for example, the one species that has freed itself from the reign of Nature-as-survival-of-the-fittest, by systematizing care for the weakest. This would be what makes humans stand out, the sign of the species' *humanity* as opposed to Nature's inhumanity (just when did the name of a species become an intrinsic moral value?), and the sign of its exalted status.

To forestall any accusation of ideological progress-ism, the most sophisticated commentators of course add that survival of the fittest has to be understood *as a function of the contingent parameters* of the milieu. In the old and symbolically spectacular experiment undertaken by Georges Teissier and Philippe L'Héritier, making a change in the ventilation of a population cage made flies with nonfunctioning wings *more fit*, that is, better able to survive to sexual maturity and to reproduce, than flies with functioning wings.[16] But the relationship thus discovered did not challenge the basic understanding of aptitude, or "fitness," as performance in competition for resources and reproduction. The emergence of fitness as a quantifiable selective value, defined in the synthetic theory of evolution in terms of the average number of descendants that reached sexual maturity, certainly made it easier to operationalize the concept in descriptive field studies, but from a philosophical standpoint it did nothing to give the notion a clearer semantic content.

This failure can be attributed to the fact that the approach in question is insufficiently ecological, in that it focuses on a weak interaction between two variants and *one* aptitude at a given instant, while neglecting both the multiplicity of interactions taking place at the same time and the effects of niche construction. As soon as the question of the selective value of a variant in intraspecies competition is raised within the real context of the dizzying multiplicity of its relations with the entire set of living beings with which it enters into interaction as well as its relations with all the prevailing abiotic conditions, the problem appears in a different light. Darwin is the founder of ecology in several senses, but above all in the profound sense that he prefigured its intersection with the theory of evolution: he stressed the multiplicity of ecological interactions as the key to the action of natural selection.

The ecological dimension may have been obscured in part owing to an epistemological gap in methods. Once scientists had moved on from the Darwinian consilience of inductions (situating hundreds of *empirical* cases and rules within a network so as to invent laws) to the model of the experimental sciences in evolutionary biology, it was no longer possible to quantify the totality of interactions: the simple closed systems required by experimentation, which had become the ruling method, could observe only the relation between two competing species and a food source (as in the experiments of Georgy Gause[17]), or two parameters: for example, another famous experiment on competitive exclusion involved two species of bedbugs plus variable levels of silicate and phosphate. Differential performances in surviving and reproducing in relation to one or two abiotic parameters tell us nothing about the essential *fitness* of a variant.

But in the original Darwinian perspective, the struggle for survival, another name for the survival of the fittest, does not have direct implications for performance: as Darwin makes clear in his text, it is a question of dependency. He speaks of the "dependence of one being on another," and of dependency with respect to abiotic conditions: "A plant on the edge of a desert is said to struggle for life against the drought, though more properly it should be said to be dependent on the moisture."[18] Dependency with respect to other species and to abiotic conditions reflects a much greater pluralism than its substitute, competition between conspecific variants. Rivalries within a species must not be interpreted in terms of direct competition, in the anthropomorphic sense of the term (conflict, combat, killing, looting of resources): the parties are competing as to the quality of their multiple relations to the rest of the surrounding biotic community.

This breakthrough that reconfigures performance as dependency and prefigures the theme of interdependencies in scientific and political ecology has to be accompanied by a critique of the concept of intraspecific competition in its anthropomorphic usage, and by a viable answer to the question "which is the fittest."

As for intraspecific competition, a pedagogical bias has produced serious consequences for the understanding of evolution. To make the variation-selection dialectic comprehensible, biologists are often obliged to tell a story in which the variation conferring an adaptive advantage is produced in a single generation, thus evacuating the key point of Darwinism: the fact that evolutionary scientists study populations, not individuals. By representing two individual variants, one endowed with an advantageous mutation and the other not, the first triumphing over the second during their lifetimes and in the mode of conflict, the pedagogical motif distorts more than it explains. In fact, individuals bearing variations are not intrinsically positioned as competitors in the human sense of the term: on the contrary, they may very well be in relations of altruism, indifference, or even absence of contact throughout their lives; it is at the level of whole populations, over time, that a population of variants can become dominant, without conflict, simply through the interplay of generations and differential reproduction. One can say, metaphorically, that populations of variants are in competition, in the sense that they show differential reproduction. But populations of variants are abstract entities that allow us to make evolutionary flows intelligible; they are not entities in the strict sense capable of entering into competition in the strict sense.

Even at the level of populations, there is no competition among variants, in the strict sense, for the significant difference lies in differential reproduction: those individuals that do not possess the advantageous mutation do not die *vanquished* by the others, they simply reproduce in *somewhat* smaller numbers; the difference may be imperceptible on the scale of a single generation. There will not have been intraspecies battles, or competition for the same resource, or even a struggle among variants on the existential level. In a major ecological misunderstanding, the relation of predation has become the unconscious collective archetype for survival. And not even real ecological predation, which is a complex and positive relation even for prey populations, in certain respects; rather, we are seeing the anthropomorphic phantasm of predation as an *individual* struggle, without norms and without mercy, for one's own survival: eat or be eaten. Such deeply rooted unconscious schemas distort our understanding of the evolutionary forces that have produced us.

The problem, then, lies in the fact that metaphors of competition and struggle for survival, which have a certain relevance over long spans of time and for populations of variants, are applied to individual lives, as if each one were *experienced* as struggle and competition. It would be a major step forward to provide a representation of living beings in which that ideological image has been dislodged: in which each individual life is viewed neither as a struggle against variant members of the same species nor as a struggle against prey or predators.[19]

Individual competition is not completely absent, especially in certain vegetable or bacterial lineages, but competition is not a name for life itself. Evolutionary discrimination plays out on another scale entirely, more in differential reproduction over long time spans rather than in differential survival in direct conflicts. In any case, the ideological representation of survival based on competition far exceeds the eco-evolutionary reality of relations.

It is not ecological competition per se that is in question, for such competition does exist on the populational level between closely related species for the occupation of a given niche: what is in question is the idea that the individual lives of living beings are experienced as competitions between the better and the less good, as survivalist struggles, conflicts over domination, victory or defeat. It is on this point that the Victorian philosophical and political liberalism of thinkers like Spencer has inflected and taken over Darwin's theory, the thrust of which was above all descriptive and scientific.

Returning to the critique of the idea of "survival of the fittest," we need to consider another question: If it is so difficult to envision the multiplicity of ecological relations that constitute a species, how can we determine the real sense of the difference in fitness that is the basis for natural selection?

The disappearance of *Canis dirus*, the "terrible wolf," to the benefit of *Canis lupus*, a smaller and less powerful wolf, less well equipped to attack large prey, occurred in the blink of an eye about ten million years ago on the North American continent, and it offers good evidence that the survival of the fittest has nothing to do with the survival of the strongest.

Calculations made by Alfred J. Lotka and Vito Volterra show that a slight increase in the yield from predation can lead to the disappearance of the prey, and this in turn can bring about the disappearance of predators in a given space.[20] The cohort of magnificent, powerful wild animals, hunting machines, that has disappeared, ought to leave us wondering about the ideological representations of evolution. *Fitness* is still imagined as performance, or instrumental effectiveness in meeting primary needs. It is unquestionably the most effective individual that has the best local fitness, at a given moment, in an abstract comparison between two variants with respect to a *single* external parameter.

Nevertheless, the problem has to be addressed by including in fitness the totality of the *ecological relations* in which the individual is caught up. On this scale, one can hypothesize that the individuals that survive are the ones *best related* to the entire surrounding biotic community: members of the same species of all ages, partners of the opposite sex, prey, feeding companions, predators, parasites, and so on, along with the abiotic conditions—precisely because these individuals maintain a complex and metastable ecological relation with all the rest. To borrow the terms used by Blandin and Bergandi, the successful individual is the one whose multiple transactions allow the most viable coevolutions.

To this phenomenon we must add the problem of niche construction: an extraordinarily successful predator would induce a niche construction that would leave the individual's descendants a territory emptied of all their potential prey; this would be an unsustainable relation to the environment. At a given moment, and with respect to hunting, by contrast with a less effective member of the species, this individual would be the most successful; but in the long run, which requires sustainability, his or her fitness would be deplorable; this individual is not the best related. To clarify this hypothesis, let us call on the concept of creative selection.

Konrad Lorenz's concept of creative selection consists in recognizing that every variant is, through its insertion in the multifaceted biotic community, constantly subjected to a series of different and even contradictory selective pressures. As we have seen, domestic animals are good examples of the disappearance of creative selection: overdomestication implies hyperselection centered on one or two criteria pertaining to human use. In contrast, wild animals are subjected to multiple pressures, and their life forms must be understood as virtually optimal for navigating *heterogeneous* exigencies. Grasped in this way, wild animals are articulated simultaneously with all the parameters with which they are in relation: each individual being is a knot through which these relations are processed. The life form must be conceptualized as an emergent creation of the ecocomplex,[21] in the form of a viable solution to several intertwined selective pressures.

On a single criterion (predation, reproduction, care of the young), competency is a matter of performance; but as soon as life is viewed as *dependency on a multiplicity of biotic and abiotic partners*, the individual that is the best related to each partner and to all, by regular, discreet, but tenacious bonds, is the one that will manifest differential reproductive success.

The problem, then, comes down to determining what ecology does to evolution.

The philosophical comprehension of the evolutionary vector we owe to scientific ecology needs to be profoundly transformed so we can pass from the idea of the survival of the most competent in terms of performance to the idea of the survival of the *best related*.

Who has the best *inclusive fitness*? I am postulating here that the fittest is the variant that is constituted by the best relations, the best transactions, the one that is the best integrated into the network of complex ecological relations (mutualisms, commensalisms, facilitations, sustainable predations). The fittest is the one that has the most harmonious relation with the sustainability of its prey, the best understanding with its rivals, the most generous relation with its mutualists, the least toxic relation with its parasites, the least destructive relation with its hosts, the most respectful relation with its facilitators: this is the one that "survives"—that is, the one that achieves the best differential reproductive success in the long run. We need a broadened concept of the *health* of the relations involved: the healthiest relation, in each type of ecological interaction, would be the most mutually profitable, whenever the extinction of a population's prey or its parasites is not its best option. A deer variant that dominated every wolf would proliferate, thus destroying the forest that nourished it and its descendants; a wolf variant that systematically outclassed all the deer during hunts would extinguish its prey, and thereby starve its own descendants.

In her ethological analysis of interactions among wolves, Jane Packard shows that the behavior of the parent and that of the offspring has coevolved.[22] But there is coevolution among all behaviors: behaviors toward the other members of the pack (a dominant wolf that systematically injured fellow pack members to impose control would limit the hunting potential of the pack, and thus the feeding of his pups); display behaviors; hunting and flight behaviors. Thus only a wolf in whom selection has composed these contradictory injunctions in the most harmonious way will succeed in differential reproductive success over time. All behaviors coevolve in a complex creative selection in which the best related is favored. The ones that emerge from these coevolutions as the most violent, the most imperious, the best adapted to *domination* of their conspecifics or to the milieu are not necessarily favored, for the problem is really a matter of integrating the individual into the complex tissue of the group and of the surrounding biotic community. The idea of dominating the milieu is a translation of Darwinian ecology by a despotic metaphysics whose relation to nature consists in an aggressive-defensive posture nourished by an age-old hostility. What sense does it make to postulate that an animal has to *dominate* the milieu to see its *fitness* increase?

In short, domination of the milieu is anything but an evolutionary triumph: wolves that dominate deer or deer that dominate wolves kill each other and themselves as well, and they also kill their mountain, to put it in

Leopoldian terms. On local scales (for normativity in living beings can be conceived only by precisely distinguishing the scales), the best related is the one that survives: neither the most dominating nor the most autonomous, but the one freed by its mutualist ties.

Survivors are individuals with the healthiest constitutive relations—the most durable relations in periods of stability—and the capacity to reestablish healthy new relations when the milieu changes. Here is the technical sense—to be spelled out and tested—in which visible ecological harmony can come about. If the coevolution of each individual with multiple others is more important than performance in localized tasks, if coevolution dominates the form of evolution brought about by *isolated* adaptive advantages, then a variant is more likely to survive in relation to other members of its population because its constitutive relations—not just with members of its own species but also with its entire biotic community—are the healthiest, the most mutually stable and life-sustaining.

Evolution becomes the survival of the best cluster of sustainable and practical relations.[23]

Advances in the ecological sciences suggest that we need to transform our conception of living species, and of the human species in particular, as autonomous entities caught up *secondarily* in relations with the biotic community, whereas in reality the historical relations of all species with the biotic community, *Homo sapiens* included, are at the origin of the forms of life as we know them. These relations are not secondary but rather constitutive of the contemporary vegetable, animal, and human populations. Mutilating these relations that constitute us amounts to mutilating ourselves.

How the Others Constitute Us

If it is true, then, that our historical and biotic relations are what constitute us, it becomes hard to distinguish different camps, as in the classic diplomatic paradigm that opposes nations. To reconfigure the conception of experience by considering that relations are more important than the *relata*, the entities related, implies an overturning of the way we conceive of morality. For the fundamental problems of our traditional conception of morality are formulated according to a substantialist conception of the world. In what would an ethics of relations consist? My hypothesis is that the elaboration of an ethics of relations would constitute a decisive step in the invention of the practice of animal diplomacy. It would allow us to get beyond the aporias of the use of diplomacy as continuation of the war against nature by other means, and it would allow us to envision a compass for mutualist action toward the species that cohabit with us, in conflictual situations, on the planet.

A DIPLOMATIC ETHICS

An age-old problem of morality is how to distinguish what is good from what is bad in relations between *different* entities. It is necessary, for example, for the other to be intrinsically *other* for the demand that I love my neighbor as myself to be a commandment and not self-evident. It is necessary to postulate a radical *substantialist* separation between the beings in presence to establish morality as a dialectic between myself and *the other*.[24] But let us imagine for a second that this ontological framework, this infrastructural map of the world, is false: that there is no self apart from my constitutive relations to what is "other," to many, to most of the others. Under these conditions, what becomes of morality? It becomes an ethics of relations. An ethology-ethics of relations as diplomacy.

The humanist moralizers, conveyors of an ontology of separate and autonomous substances, always have the same objection with regard to the defenders of the other than human: you favor animals over humans, wolves over shepherds, whales over underpaid Japanese fishermen; in so doing, you are misanthropic. This is what can be called the sophistry of anthropocentric priorities. Its discreet flaw lies in the fact that it is based on a substantialist definition of humanity that is intrinsically distinct and separatist. This definition overlooks the fact that the very essence of humanity is fractured in its constitutive, ecological, and evolutionary relations with the rest of the life forms with which it is in contact. Thus to speak of humans as substances is to formulate the problem badly. The bearer of an ethics of constitutive relations secretly lives in another world, on a different map of the world, asking open-ended questions: If one favors the relation *between* entities, and not one entity to the detriment of another, what happens? If one works for the benefit of a constitutive relation, what happens? One can imagine a credo of an *ethic of relations* that would be formulated like this: What is good for the constitutive relation is good for the entities involved. For each of the entities. Its strong version would even say: What is best for each of the entities is necessarily what is best for the relation.[25] If you favor one to the detriment of the other, you are creating an inequality, conflict, thus an infrastructural stress among all. And this is so even if the supremacy of the one is absolute. Nothing that is good *only* for the one as a separate substance, and not for its constitutive relations with the others, is *really* good for it.[26] In authentic diplomacy, where relations are ontologically preeminent, what we call the "self," what we feel as ourselves, is only a secondary effect of the relations we maintain with the others.

Continue the War or Revitalize Relations?

We are now in a position to resolve an enigma formulated earlier in this study: In diplomacy with living beings, how can we distinguish between the point where this diplomacy is only a continuation of war by other means and the point where it amounts to effective diplomacy in the service of the relationship? We had to take a detour through the ontology and the ethics of relations to reach a solution.

Diplomacy has always been a problem of geopolitics and cohabitation. Its principal tool is understanding the foreign, accommodating and translating in order to grasp the others' customs, their manner of being, their mode of existence in its most exotic, most remote, and most intimate dimensions. But these ethosophistic and polycephalic modes of comprehension have been, along the axis of the Neolithic tradition of direct positive action, in the service of a certain conception of diplomacy. In both interhuman and interanimal geopolitics, these means have been placed at the service of diplomacy as continuation of war against nature by other means (trapping, poisoning, and extermination also require ethological competencies). This has to do with the fact that diplomacy has been deployed on a metaphysical map that granted entities a fundamental priority. Entities came ahead of relations, ontologically and chronologically, and thus the ethical problem consisted in fighting on behalf of one entity against another. Diplomacy seemed to fight for the entity that was its own nation, against other nations—and this has indeed been the daily work of most diplomats in embassies. Animal diplomacy, too, understood in this sense, has been omnipresent in the history of the heirs of the Neolithic metaphysics, as a way of continuing the war against nature by other means: comprehension via a strategy of interpreting animal behaviors, while it has allowed hunting and gathering as relations of constitutive exchanges with a giving environment, has also made it possible to put in place methods of eradication, regulation, and transcendent control. The campaign against the Four Pests in Mao's China, with its festive massacres of sparrows, was based on minimal knowledge of the specific behavioral structures of the animals in their *Umwelt*, put in the service of absolute domination.

Credit: Photograph Éditions Wild Project

Figure 19. Ernest Thompson Seton: A Diplomat Torn

A great werewolf diplomat, a prescientific ethnologist, and a specialist in wolf psychology, Ernest Thompson Seton was recruited by ranchers to capture an elusive wolf, Lobo. In the 1890s in New Mexico, Lobo was decimating livestock herds, with his pack, and the trappers had not managed to catch him. Seton put in place an effective diplomacy, betting successfully on the most subtle and intimate lines of force of the wolf and his pack. He began by capturing Lobo's less vigilant female partner, thus forcing the alpha wolf to put himself in danger to protect her. Seton put his diplomatic competencies at the service of one of the two camps; it was only in the intense remorse he expressed after the fact that his sensitivity as an animal diplomat became clear, his feeling that he had betrayed what he respected most. He never managed to reach the level of a logic of relations, however, and he constantly oscillated, in the painful schizophrenia characteristic of many people responsible for wildlife, between the interests of a human camp, with its hegemonic way of organizing society that leaves no place for nonhumans, and the camp of a wild world endangered by humans. Seton nevertheless finally became one of the first conservationists.

The case of Ernest Thompson Seton, a naturalist (in the traditional sense) and a painter, is remarkable in this connection (see figure 19).[27]

Nevertheless, the skills required for diplomacy as the continuation of war point to a way forward, for ethics is an extension of technique. Knowing how to do a thing well leads to the elaboration of standards of good conduct with respect to that thing. In any real artisan we can see the emergence of a moral distinction between doing a careless job and working with respect for the raw material. Knowledge and skill do not leave us scot-free: they call for respectful, attentive, comprehensive behaviors toward an entity whose behavior we have come to understand.

Thus, while the skills involved in diplomacy between warring parties and those required for diplomacy of relations may sometimes be hard to tell apart, as Seton showed, the former can create an ethological and ecological consciousness that points toward the latter. For evidence of this process, we can look to the cohort of hunters who became conservationists, with E. T. Seton and Aldo Leopold in the vanguard.

The path taken by diplomacy in a context of war is a philosophical and practical dead end. The problem can be made more visible if we shift to the level of metaphysical infrastructures. The relation of conflict between humans and nature implies a substantialist metaphysics in which humans believe they have succeeded in extracting themselves from biotic communities, opposing themselves to the rest of the living world the way separate, fixed substances can be opposed to one another. But this dualist conception of the relation between humans and nature is both outdated and toxic. Its toxicity is visible in the current ecological crisis.

It is a question of pitting "good" diplomatic intelligence against what we can call, simplistically, the bad kind: harmonious versus discordant cohabitation. Practitioners of the latter seek to dominate by generating powerlessness in the other party, targeting that party's weak points. A whole sector of the techno-scientific emancipation of the West set up as a model a form of cohabitation based on dominance that entails living in disharmony with nature. In the twentieth century, this was the hidden subtext of the Green Revolution, for example—hidden by the extraordinary ease it produced. It would be intellectually dishonest not to recognize the concrete advantages of using diplomacy in pursuit of victory in a relation to nature coded as conflict and extraction of resources: the effects are spectacular and reassuring. The paradigmatic case of pesticides is eloquent: they have been received as liberating, sparing a significant amount of work, worry, and attention in situations that had earlier required a constant struggle against parasitic organisms. And even committed ecologists may be tempted, when aphids keep coming back into their kitchen, scarcely thwarted by organic essential oils, to resort to a good dose of pesticide, which would make it possible to turn their attention elsewhere once and for all. This is the big problem: wanting not to have to do it all over again. Wanting to do it once and for all—a profound temptation. Eradicating wolves solves a problem of pastoralism once and for all. And from this standpoint, as with pesticides, the most ecological approaches seem to be regressive with respect to technological progress and its catalyzing power to produce comfort: it is a step backward that goes against the logic of the world itself. Looking for local and temporary solutions, refining our diplomatic arrangements over and over—this approach takes time, work, and intelligence, all things that we do not possess in infinite quantities. But pesticides have shown us the tragic consequences that can ensue when we solve the problem "once and for all": consequences for ecology, public health, and even philosophy. Wanting to get something over with once and for all is an age-old bad habit; it consists in generalizing a conception of our relation to life forms that is not relational but substantial, in which the quest is not for "good understanding" but for the technical savoir-fair, however unsystematic and short-term, that makes work easier while mutilating deeper relationships. "Good understanding" is characterized by its eco-sensitivity: a sensitivity to the vibrant interweavings of the living world, to its cosmos rife with meanings and interactions. It is a timeless ecological understanding that we left behind somewhere, as it were, as soon as we began to think of the environment as a giver, like Nature, and then began to think of Nature as matter and locked ourselves into our anthropo-narcissistic impasse, losing contact with the great life-sustaining politics of the animal and plant communities. That old understanding needs to be reinvented for today, nourished by knowledge from the sciences and by the evocatory powers of the arts, so we can cohabit in synergy with the living world around us and within us.

If it is to be fully understood, animal diplomacy has to rest on a relational conception of the human with respect to biotic communities, so that the war against wild nature can become an aberration, for our relations with the rest of the biotic community constitute what we are *as humans*, in our survival as in our lives in the noble sense.

THE WILKINSON-PICKETT PARADOX

The epidemiologists Richard G. Wilkinson and Kate Pickett have produced data that provide a decisive example of this phenomenon in interhuman diplomacy: in sum, they maintain that in a given society, the poverty *of others* reduces the quality of life *of the wealthy*.[28]

They show that, with identical average incomes, a population marked by inequality suffers decidedly more than a more egalitarian population: even the health of the dominant members (here, the richest) is more fragile in an inegalitarian society. The richest are subjected to more stress, more violence, greater distrust, and objectively poorer health when the context is more inegalitarian. The two researchers succeed in demonstrating a relation of causality between these two phenomena, by showing that a rise in inequality produces deleterious health and societal effects in just a few years in a statistically significant way. According to the authors, if inequalities have such effects, it is because they engender violence around the problem of gaps in social status, and this leads to a lack of security shared by all, even the wealthiest.

The empirical value of Wilkinson and Pickett's demonstration stems from the quantifiable character of the data they use: its numerical wealth. The dimension of quality of life is hard to quantify and thus not often addressed, but we may offer the hypothesis that it follows the pattern of this discovery. Economic equality is only the quantifiable form of a relation that, understood in its constitutive nature, deserves to be valued more highly than the individual elements in the relation (the wealth of each member). Still hypothesizing, we can propose to extend this reasoning to a broader scale, beyond the simple equality of income or patrimony: criticizing the generalized toxicity of domination amounts to valuing the relation that each maintains with all, rather than valuing certain elements to the detriment of others.

I use the term "Wilkinson-Pickett paradox" to characterize this logic that is found in the reasoning of every authentic diplomat: in a relationship, even the *dominant* party suffers from the effects of domination. The more the domination is hegemonic and toxic for the dominated individual, the more the dominant one suffers from it. A reduction in domination improves the effective quality of life on *both* sides.

This is the intuition of relational diplomats. On their map of the world, relations exist prior to the entities involved and constitute those entities. History overflows with characters whose powerful bonds have not been isolated: diplomats who have not worked to continue a war by turning their comprehension of the other to their own advantage, but who have chosen the advantage of the relation itself. Poorly understood, not very visible, they are precursors: Nelson Mandela, Gandhi, Cabeza de Vaca, John

Fire Lame Deer, millions of others; and toward the rest of the living world, the werewolf diplomats whose portraits have been sketched here.

This understanding of diplomacy does not require compromises, for it changes the entire moral field of interests. Diplomacy conceived as compromise is based on the ontological map of the parties: there is no compromising except between the interests of each camp. The relational diplomacy in question, like animal diplomacy, is without concessions: it does not make any compromises where the interests of the *relation* are concerned. The relational diplomat prioritizes the interests of the relation above everything else, at the risk of making enemies among members of both camps who do not think in these terms.

Werewolf diplomats are indeed humans, they do belong to a camp, but they do not seek to win the war for that camp by diplomatic means. Nor do they betray their own camp in favor of the other, as those who stigmatize the defenders of animal rights as misanthropes fantasize. Werewolf diplomats have understood that that original war, which claims to unify humans under the banner of domination of nature, has always been a civil war. They have understood that only mutualist negotiations achieve a lasting good for oneself.

Diplomacy is the name of the ethics of relations as opposed to the ethics of entities: diplomats focus their attention ontologically on the relations between beings, transcending the blindness of the Moderns regarding everything that cannot be discerned as well-defined entities. They take care of relations *first*. The shift to an ontology of relations that configures an ethics of relations is the technical name for werewolf diplomacy, or animal diplomacy. The practical corollary of this relational ontology is a form of perspectivism: how one views others has an *effect* on the identity of the others and thus also on the nature of the interaction and on the form of the relation that constitutes them.

THE DIPLOMATIC APPROACH TO CONFLICTS BETWEEN
HUMANS AND WILD ANIMALS

Scattered instances of the diplomatic approach have already provided us with relational success stories. The African elephants of the Lake Turkana region in Kenya, relatively protected thanks to the national parks and the 1989 ban on trade in ivory, nevertheless come into confrontation with a growing human population and intensifying agricultural practices. In the face of such conflicts between humans and animals, biologist Fritz Vollrath, and later his student Lucy King, sought a solution.[29] Their quest can be interpreted as a search for a diplomatic pact, with the goal of a cohabitation that would endure and that would *therefore* be beneficial to both parties—a pact that would nurture the human-animal relationship itself. African elephants are exceedingly powerful animals that are hard to keep under control, unless one can find—through animal diplomacy and understanding of the animals' own rationality—what frightens them: in the elephants' case this turns out to be *Apis mellifera scutellata*, the African honeybee.[30] Experience has shown that certain zones of elephants' bodies (around the eyes and trunk) are very sensitive to bee stings, and the use of recorded bee sounds near these huge animals provokes unmistakable defensive behaviors (they shake their heads, flap their ears, sprinkle themselves with dust). The researchers' project in relational conservation biology consisted in setting up enclosures around fields that integrated traditional local beehives. In comparison with a barrier of thorny bushes, the beehive barrier proved to be more effective in reducing the number of elephants trampling on the crops and thus reducing the intensity of conflicts. But the bees also supplied honey, and this gave the villagers an idea for a new food-producing and commercial activity, apiculture. This case is emblematic of what I shall call enriched or eco-ethical mutualism. It consists in multiplying the dimensions according to which relations between human and nonhuman animals can be conceived as beneficial, and in inventing new arrangements that stress, catalyze, and link together the aspects of the relation that are in fact mutually beneficial. Vincent Devictor formulates this approach in the specific field of conservation biology as follows: "Restoring an ecosystem should also mean restoring the relations of persons with that ecosystem."[31] And, conversely, if we take an ontology of ecological relations seriously, working for the real quality of life of human populations (through socioeconomic development or a certain degrowth) implies restoring its constitutive relations with the biotic community.[32]

Diplomacy seems to be the optimal attitude toward every entity about which we cannot say how its relation to us constitutes *us*, and thus what sort of treatment it requires. It is not a matter of reactivating a cult of the "balance of nature"; certain species are functionally redundant in ecosystems,[33] and no past state can constitute a "pristine" state (or a state to refer back to) in any absolute way. Ecological entities are basically processes of coevolution devoid of any stable harmony.[34] The problem lies elsewhere: we are often unaware of the constitutive relations in which we are caught up with other life forms—relations that are constitutive of our survival but also of

Credit: Photograph Éditions Wild Project

Figure 20. Lucy King: The Perspectivist Diplomat

In the field of perspectivist reasoning, the approach of Lucy King and Fritz Vollrath is as dizzying as it is elegant. Putting their transformation masks into action, they were able to see that, if a bee is only a bucolic insect from our point of view, from that of elephants—who terrify us—a bee is a terror. Rather than ruining very poor agricultural endeavors via the purchase of monumentally expensive fencing, this diplomatic approach substituted an informational obstacle, as effective as it is inexpensive: bees. This solution can even be applied on a very large scale: Lucy King's team showed that when elephants are subjected to recorded bee sounds, the vocalizations they produce seem to signify to the animals, over great distances in all directions, that they should stay far away from danger. By analogy with certain defense measures taken against wolf predation, physical fences, circumstantial and inert, have to be distinguished from the subtle, volatile cognitive barriers used on a broad scale, owing to the very intelligence of the animals targeted. Biofences work for elephants and wolves alike.

a life that is rich and intense, not amputated or mutilated. In conservation biology, we are becoming aware that a species that has been perceived as a weed or pest like any other is a "keystone species" when its disappearance results in the fall of an entire network of ecosystemic relations. It is when networks collapse that the anecdotal species show their faces as the hidden kings of an ecosystem, like, for example, the gecko *Phelsuma cepediana*, endemic to Mauritius and unique in its genus; or the Yellowstone wolf, whose return has led to major trophic cascades.[35]

We do not know what we have lost by eradicating the wolves of Western Europe, in terms of ecological relations constitutive of our ecosystems or in terms of relations constitutive of our identities by affiliation. We do not know what is being reconstituted since their return. Ecologists postulated that the predator-prey relations have significant effects through top-down regulation, but in Yellowstone, no one suspected at the time of their reintroduction in 1995 that the wolves would change the physiognomy of rivers by transforming the grazing behavior of elk even without being in the immediate vicinity.[36] "One need not doubt the unseen."[37] Trophic relations are hidden like the complex relations of the myriad species hidden in forest soil: ecological (facilitations, mutualisms, symbioses, and so on), but also psychic, cultural, social, and political. These relations are the immaterial living tissue of the biosphere, and we are still extraordinarily ill-informed about them, for they are difficult to grasp, while the entities participating in them are obvious. This is the moment when conservation biology, this fringe of scientific ecology interested in the protection of biodiversity (and, here, of wolves) becomes what it should be, according to Vincent Devictor: "an interrogation of the very meaning of our relation to the world, the place of humans vis-à-vis nonhumans."[38] As Edward O. Wilson puts it: "The truth is that we never conquered the world, never understood it; we only think we have control. We do not even know why we respond a certain way to other organisms, and need them in diverse ways, so deeply."[39] This profound ignorance is the great lesson of scientific ecology. In doubt, we would perhaps do better to be diplomats.

Mutualism: From Ecology to Environmental Ethics

Mutualism, in its strict ecological sense, is a continuous ecological interaction between two or more species, each one of which essentially benefits from the relationship. According to the ecologist Claude Combes, mutualism is distinguished from parasitism by a difference in "the social relationship between the partners . . . 1) in parasitism, it is very much in the victim's (the host's) interest to get rid of the aggressor; 2) in mutualism, owing to the fact that each one exploits the other, it is in no one's interest to get rid of anyone."[40]

But the conceptual difference between mutualism and parasitism is not that well stabilized in scientific ecology. In fact, the benefit is conceptualized only on a certain time scale, so that predation and parasitism are essentially coded as nonmutualist relations, since they induce mortality or morbidity in one of the two partners. But if we change scales, we can already inflect this first sense of mutualism, by taking into account ecological interactions over long periods of time. From this viewpoint, certain species that seem harmful for another turn out in fact to be very important in the long run, to ensure the continuation of the other's lineage, or the biodiversity on which its subsistence is based.[41] If we change scales, then relations of predation appear from the perspective of a community of interests between the antagonists. In 1887, evoking two predatory species, the Darwinian ecologist Stephen A. Forbes exposed with great prescience the strange "community of interests" that connects, for example, deer and wolves:

> The interest of both parties will . . . be best served by an adjustment of their respective rates of multiplication such that the species devoured shall furnish an excess of numbers to supply the wants of the devourer, and that the latter shall confine its appropriations to the excess thus furnished. We thus see that there is really a close *community of interest* between these two seemingly deadly foes. . . . Two ideas are thus seen to be sufficient to explain the order evolved from this seeming chaos; the first that of a general community of interests among all the classes of organic beings here assembled, and the second that of the beneficent power of natural selection which compels such adjustments of the rates of destruction and of multiplication of the various species as shall best promote this common interest.[42]

To take another example, let us note that the parasites that have affected *Homo sapiens* during the species' evolution have, through lasting interactions, played a role in the robustness of the human immune system, so that their harmfulness has become ambiguous. What constitutes parasitism in the short term can thus be construed in the long term as mutualism: it is a question of scale.

Since its plasticity makes this possible, I should like to develop here an enriched concept of mutualism that goes beyond the field of scientific ecology and plays a role in environmental ethics. More than a simple ecological interaction, mutualism becomes an arrangement of mutually beneficial relations between two different species on various levels—ecological,

Credit: Aldo Leopold seated on the edge of a cliff with a bow and arrows, Rio Gavilan, Mexico, photograph by Starker Leopold © The Aldo Leopold Foundation

Figure 21. Aldo Leopold: The Mountain Diplomat

"I now suspect that just as a deer herd lives in mortal fear of its wolves, [s]o does a mountain live in mortal fear of its deer. And perhaps with better cause, for while a buck pulled down by wolves can be replaced in two or three years, a range pulled down by too many deer may fail of replacement in as many decades.

"So also with cows. The cowman who cleans his range of wolves does not realize that he is taking over the wolf's job of trimming the herd to fit the range. He has not yet learned to think like a mountain. Hence we have dustbowls, and rivers washing the future into the sea" (Leopold, *A Sand County Almanac*, 116).

ethological, evolutionary, symbolic, economic, aesthetic—that deserve to be studied. Seeking, elaborating, and maintaining mutualism is precisely the ecological equivalent of the ethical approach that consists in taking care *of relations first and foremost*. It becomes possible to institute the spelling out of mutualisms as the point toward which the compass of relational diplomacy is pointed, even with a species as prima facie antagonistic as that of wolves.

In the strict ecological sense, to be sure, we cannot speak of mutualisms between humans and wolves, for this concept implies repeated and lasting mutually beneficial interactions. In the rigorous ecological sense, following a nuance proposed by Raphaël Larrère, what become mutually beneficial are the *limits* put in place by the diplomatic project rather than the ongoing interactions.[43] But in the enriched sense evoked earlier, which consists in looking for positive interactions on various levels, if these interactions are more intense than negative ones, then we can envision an eco-ethical mutualism with these predators that have long been labeled pests.

This conception of mutualism is not some sort of pie in the sky: it implies muscular negotiations, vigorous defenses, firm limits. As Combes says, moreover, "Defenses exist at the very heart of mutualist systems. It is just that they are not used to strike down the other, but rather to prevent the selfishness of the other from producing excessive harm to oneself."[44] Selfishness must be understood here in a metaphysical sense, but the formula remains on target: we see clearly how necessary defensive measures are to prevent wolf predation from going to excesses that are harmful to us, in order to prevent the vindictiveness of humans from going to excesses that would be harmful to them.

Mutualism appears as the solution every time cohabitation is necessary and *can* be life-affirming. But looking for mutualisms does not necessarily mean that we have to take "nature" as our moral guide. If we were to do that, nothing would prevent us from treating wolves the way wolves treat the coyotes that traverse their territories: by killing them. Thus we have to make room for a difference: our ethical specificity resides here in the fact that we can *seek, plan, and attribute value to* mutualisms—this is the ethical form maintained in relational diplomacy. Our specificity as animal diplomats lies in the power of play, the plasticity that we manifest in our relations to living beings, permitted by our skills and refined knowledge of the way beings behave. This flexibility allows us to transform competitions, predations, harmful relations into mutualisms. It is an art that, for plants, is called allelopathy.[45] A whole swath of contemporary agropastoralism can be interpreted as driven by an analogous ambition, from agroecology to permaculture. Harmfulness will not disappear for all that: nature is not an irenic place from which conflict must be banished. We are all destined to consume one another, and this is not a curse but the serene order of things. Every self-consistent practitioner of all-inclusive animal ethics focused on individual organisms as possessing absolute value is condemned to starve to death, for there is no agriculture, no matter how responsible and ecological, that does not have to defend itself, for example, against species that devour harvests. But these populations will be harmful only with regard to an *optimum of mutualist ecological relations* that have been successfully put in place by allelopathy, and not, as is the case today, solely with regard to economic productivity, or with regard to exclusively human advantages to the detriment of all others. A whole field of research, of which we are not yet capable, could be mapped out. Generalized allelopathy as relational diplomacy: look for relationships that are life-enhancing for the participants within a given biotic community, and if they do not exist, minimize the mutual damage. What relations are truly constitutive for us? Which ones do we want to maintain, inflect, or extend?

It is not a question of a morality of intrinsic value, nor is it a question of duty, but rather a question of an ethics in Spinoza's sense: a matter of organizing encounters with what is being constituted along with us in the interest of greater shared power.

In fact, the specificity of mutualist diplomacy, from an ethical standpoint, consists in not inventing values ex nihilo, and in not seeing the values we need in a heaven of principles revealed here or there. It consists in grasping a descriptive concept (mutualism) referring to a type of relations omnipresent in living beings, and asking ourselves to what extent—because this relation is valorized by living beings, and valorizable to multiple degrees—it might warrant, in certain situations, being set up as an ethical *value* in our relations to it. The fact that these relations are present in living beings means that certain values, or evaluations, surpass us and constitute us: we do not invent them arbitrarily, we choose them of our own free will, but they are not constraining. We can choose, for example, between health and illness, between food and poison. But something in us valorizes health more than illness. The problem consists, then, in seeking good and bad relations in the immanent biotic community, because the immanent biotic community is normative. Ethics becomes, as in Spinoza's philosophy, a matter of valorizing certain real relations among the possible relations: those that produce an increase in shared power, to the detriment of those that produce shared impotence.

In environmental ethics, this implies valorizing relations that are beneficial to the parties involved (mutualisms) and seeking to *steer* coevolution with nonhumans in that direction.

Steering is possible, for scientific ecology has shown that ecological interactions are highly malleable: predations can rapidly turn into mutualisms, and vice versa, as a function of transformations in the environment. A given species of ant that protects aphids even while feeding on their honeydew ends up devouring the aphids as soon as it finds a more accessible source of nutrition. Similarly, could not a relation of competition between humans and large predators be inflected toward mutualism in the enriched sense developed earlier?

We could find support in this reversibility of relations to steer our ecological interactions with biodiversity, following the course laid out by ecologist Patrick Blandin.[46] Given that the ecological biotic community is essentially a fluid process, a trajectory, we cannot pretend that we can maintain it in a static state perceived to be intrinsically satisfactory. We have to agree to steer biodiversity. But steer it in what direction, toward what destination?

In fact, the concept of steering biodiversity creates problematic biases: by postulating that ecological systems are only trajectories, and thus have no ideal reference state, the concept of steering deprives these systems of any immanent normativity, that is, of conditions that would be better or worse *for themselves*—in more technical terms, there are no immanent gradients of health or vitality for these systems, only those conventionally defined by human collectivities. In returning to the ecological idea of trajectory, Blandin runs the risk of leaving to every human community the absolute monopoly on determining the value of states of ecological dynamics, and thus on valuing any potentially destructive industrial policy, to the extent that it would be a democratic choice of steering. Injecting mutualism into this decision-making process as a criterion of environmental ethics would make it possible to limit that risk. To avoid the loss of reference points during the steering process, one could aim, every time it is possible to do so, with regard to nonhumans, and even with certain species that seem to be in direct conflict with us (via predation or competition), to inflect these interactions toward complex mutualisms.[47]

Steering biodiversity could then consist in valorizing immanent mutualisms, setting up immanent mutualisms as models, or inflecting harmful relations in the direction of mutualisms, because relations are malleable and historical. Find the bee! We are constrained by our relational essence to play a role in the evolution of other living beings. Our technological impact accentuates that necessity: we can no longer claim to be leaving nature outside, or letting evolution take its course. But unconstrained steering, oriented exclusively toward human interests, however democratic, would be a philosophical error.

Taking as a guide the idea of valorizing mutualisms with the biodiversity that constitutes us limits both the anthropocentrism of this steering and its risks: mutualisms already exist, it is not a question of inventing a nature by synthesis, but rather of taking inspiration from the existing mutualisms, deepening and refining them. It is a question of inserting ourselves within the evolutionary history of ecological relations in order to valorize certain relations more than others. This nevertheless requires a subtle and enriched conception of mutualisms. Mutualism enriched as a compass of environmental ethics for humans can be formulated as mutually beneficial cohabitation integrated with the most capacious biodiversity: the most capacious in terms of trophic levels, as well as in terms of multiplicities of niches and interspecies interactions.

Let us note, however, that the forms of cohabitation with a capacious diversity are neither given nor imposed by nature. We can always *invent* others, as we see from permaculture, which creates mutualist relations among species that have not necessarily evolved together. Humans have not finished inventing all the mutualist, potentializing, emancipating relations that they might conceive with regard to the species of their biotic communities, and from this standpoint no strictly natural canon can constitute a norm.

But the past coevolution of living beings remains a "gentle guide," as Montaigne said about Nature, for this coevolution has a sometimes invisible antiquity and subtlety of relations; it has the blind overview of evolution itself, which ecological science does not yet possess.

Chapter 14

What Mutualisms in Our Relations with Wolves?

Now that we have established the search for mutualisms (old and new) as a compass for diplomatic ecology, how can it be applied to cohabitation with wolves? The diplomatic approach is constructed to articulate a dimension of environmental ethics with a dimension of concrete and practical conservation biology. Werewolf diplomacy can thus constitute the art and manner of handling our relations with these large predators, and a middle way of cohabitation.

Objective Alliances: "Finding the Bee"

An ethics of relations seems at first glance to solve no practical problem, since it prevents any hierarchical ranking of interests, whereas ranking seems to be at the heart of every practical ecological question: Must wolves take *precedence* over shepherds, as the pastoral world complains, or must livestock farmers take precedence over wolves? But perhaps this is not really the right way to put the question. Does it not change the very formulation of the practical problems if we set what is good for the *relation* between farmers and wolves as our ultimate goal, our magnetic north?

Trying to inflect the relation to wolves away from competition toward mutualism in the enriched sense, following the example of the relation of Kenyan farmers to elephants, may seem utopian, given the intensity of the current conflict between wolves and pastoralists. Still, working in that direction seems more reasonable than either trying to eradicate wolves or maintaining the current status quo, which is toxic for sheep-raising, detrimental to wolves, and shortsighted in terms of steering biodiversity—in a word, the status quo seems unsustainable. What needs to be imagined, in addition to measures intended to limit predation on herds, are measures designed to bring benefits from the presence of wolves to populations living in close contact with them, for there is evidence that no politics of conservation can work in the long run if the animal presence is in direct opposition to human activities in the territory occupied by both groups.[1]

For Community-Based Conservation

It seems, then, that the most reasonable solution to the crisis induced by the return of wolves is also the most counterintuitive: wolf management not on the scale of national planning or national parks, but on the scale of the populations directly concerned—management in terms of *community-based conservation*. The term designates approaches to protecting nature based on biotic communities—that is, adopting policies for preserving biodiversity whose benefits accrue first of all to the local populations that actually cohabit with and constitute part of that diversity. But it also implies that human desires and reasons for cohabiting with wolves can be shared by those who live in close contact with them, precisely those who seem at present radically *opposed* to wolves, influenced by the discourse of ovine pastoralism.[2]

But the approach I am proposing may not be as radical as some might suppose: indeed, we may wonder whether the hostility of the rural world to the wolves' return is not a product of media pressure on some of its members, whose position may not be representative of the entire community. According to sociologist Maïa Martin's work in the Cévennes, it seems that the individuals featured most prominently by the media are conflated with the rural population as a whole.[3] Many rural residents appear to be favorably disposed toward wolves,[4] but this attitude is overshadowed by the media attention given to statements by shepherds and livestock farmers, and it receives little public expression owing to the imaginary culpability attributed to wolves by terms such as "surplus killing" (associated with a position of urban condescension), and owing to the lack of positive arguments.

What is needed, then, is a way to bring to light attitudes favorable to wolves within the rural world by giving wolves the means to express themselves, supplying scientific and philosophical arguments emphasizing the importance of their return, and imagining—in collaboration with the rural residents themselves—initiatives fostering social and economic development.

In the Abruzzo region of Italy, the presence of wolves and bears thus constitutes, for some, a decisive factor in the economic revitalization of rural life. A livestock farmer puts it this way: "With the milk of my animals, I make twenty kinds of cheese and I sell the meat: I welcome to my home people who are coming to see bears and wolves. *Orso* and *lupo* are my two best advertising agents for the sale of all my agricultural products (cheese, meat, hospitality, organic produce, and so on)."[5]

But plans for development must first undertake to make wolves catalysts for improving the quality of life in the regions where they have settled. The benefits for the population must not be conceived exclusively in economic terms; that would be to yield to the misleading idea of "ecosystemic services," an idea that does not recognize the pluralism and the incommensurability of nonmonetary values, a fundamental concept in ecological economics.[6] New approaches might emphasize opportunities to make pastoral activity more sustainable (by limiting extensive breeding, for example), and less dependent on subsidies, with an employment policy permitted by shepherding practices requiring a larger workforce.[7] To stop the population drain from mountain regions, finally, one might consider introducing activities of agrotourism around wolves, an approach that would bring direct benefits to the valleys involved. And many other such measures remain to be imagined.

In other words, we need to envision a situation in which pastoralism and the surrounding rural populations in wolf country ensure the existence of the Great Predator and defend its presence. This looks like the most implausible solution, and yet it is the only conceivable one, if this case of conservation biology and the political philosophy of cohabitation are not to be more deeply bogged down than ever in the current aporetic conflict: increasingly disproportionate compensations, deteriorating relations between the activities of predators and those of humans, increasing undifferentiated hatred for the predators; reinvestment of the notion of pest applied more extensively (including to wild boar), and a rhetoric of terrorism ("The Wolf Is the Saddam Hussein of the Animal World").[8]

Relational diplomacy allows us to envision a broadening of the idea of community when we speak of community-based conservation, by understanding it as the local biotic community in its entirety. If we postulate that the greatest benefits that a local population can obtain from its environment depend on invigorating its constitutive relations with that environment, then the welfare of the biotic community is identified with the welfare of the local human community. Relational diplomacy thus allows us to envision a *biotic community-based conservation*.

From this standpoint, we can think about the possible benefits of cohabitation between pastoralism and wolves.

By taking a certain distance from the intensity of the conflict, we may come up with new questions. To what extent can wolves catalyze changes in pastoral techniques and modes of production that would get the sector out of the "ovine crisis" that began well before the wolves' return? To what extent can the effects of wolves on ecosystems—as with the well-documented trophic cascades in Yellowstone—benefit the very earth that is the nourishing soil of pastoral activity, of its sheep? In what ways could a more vigorous, more enriched mountain with healthier ecological dynamics be beneficial to pastoral activity? To what extent could commitments on the part of livestock farmers to protective measures allowing cohabitation with wolves constitute arguments in favor of French meat, through the mechanism of something like a professional charter called "Land of the Wolf"?[9] Would this be capable of revalorizing French mutton, which is currently downgraded in favor of inexpensive New Zealand lamb? To what extent could the touristic effects of the wolves' return benefit local sales of local meat, relying on the argument of a pastoralism respectful of a wild biodiversity? Might "finding the bee" become the watchword of a relational diplomacy between humans and wolves?[10]

We have to hope that future generations of farmers, more familiar with the contemporary formulations of the environmental stakes, will be able to highlight the common causes of lambs and wolves.

We can also reflect on the *current benefits*, seemingly paradoxical, to be sure, of the presence of wolves for sheep farmers today. To what extent has the spotlight focused on the pastoral world owing to the wolves' return already led to an awareness of the "ovine crisis" that *preceded* the wolves' return? Has not that awareness led to the institution of socioeconomic support structures that make the profession healthier than it was before? This is a question that warrants careful examination by sociologists and economists. Finally, has the presence of wolves not played a determining role in the development of arguments about the necessity of preserving ovine pastoralism as an endangered cultural form and as a trump card for maintaining a certain biodiversity? All these elements of discourse, which weigh heavily in today's public debates, would not have come to light without the return of the wolves. They would not have taken on such argumentative acuity or such visibility, for little attention was being paid to sheep farmers' unions in comparison to the political groupings of practitioners of intensive farming in the large agricultural basins.

In fact, there have *already* been odd alliances between wolves and livestock farmers: if we look at the problem from a certain distance, without minimizing the trauma experienced by farmers who find their sheep slaughtered, the relation of co-presence has already been beneficial in certain respects to the profession as a whole.

Among these unexpected alliances, some are manifested at the most unexpected level, which is the most spiritual. The shepherd and sheep owner Thierry Geffray is eloquent on the subject. Skilled at finding nourishment in contradictions, he attests that wolf attacks on his herd have increased both his identification with his sheep and at the same time his respect for their predators. The experience that he relates resembles a spiritual accomplishment of *perspectivist animal diplomacy*: the diplomacy that consists in "thinking like a mountain," that is, in understanding the territory by *circulating* freely among the antagonistic viewpoints that populate and constitute it (that of the sheep, the wolves, the grasses, the shepherd, and so on). Geffray thus comes to think of the wolf as an "accelerator" of the emergence, in himself, of a new, resilient relation to nature. Here is how he puts it:

> There is nature, which offers you things, like wolves. Wolves: I was one of the first to say: "Wolves mustn't come here; they'd be real killjoys for us property managers." In this distanced relation you have with a little mountain, with a valley, all of a sudden a wolf attacks (we ourselves have been attacked eighteen times in just one year), you can't see the valley, the grove of trees, the forests, in the same way. All of a sudden you're in the skin of a sheep, wondering where the wolf is going to turn up, what his strategy is, his intelligence. At bottom, there's an intelligent and very crafty being who's living in the same spaces as you, and who's bringing you into a perceptual relation to the forest, to the slope, to everything around you that you didn't have before. What's really curious is that this wolf brings you up short, he's opening you up to new ways of seeing your environment. It's really quite brilliant . . . It's completely unexpected. It's responsible for the way you are with your sheep, you *are* a sheep, you're paying attention, you're recognizing the intelligence of other beings that share your space. So you somehow find yourself getting into a form of respect for that intelligence, while saying, "We can get upset, we can get riled up, he's a real pain, the fact remains that the wolf is repopulating, recolonizing, defending his rights a little,

despite all the means we have to eliminate him." And so here we've got a real initiation to nature and to the environment.[11]

TOWARD THE RIGHTS OF ECOSYSTEMS

In the inaugural lecture of the colloquium "Comment penser l'anthropocène?" (How to conceptualize the Anthropocene), Philippe Descola evoked the need to reform Western law, whose infrastructures are products of the ontological schema of modernity. By isolating our own exotic custom of recognizing only human persons (or collective entities that can be treated as persons) as subjects of property law, he brought out the necessity of devising an ecological system of laws for tomorrow, one in which biotic and abiotic groupings would be considered no longer as objects of law nor as proprietary subjects of law but as, in a sense, bearers of rights. Certain ecosystems whose dynamics are vital to several life forms would be endowed with rights, in this view, and would no longer be the property of humans.[12] Humans would be *representatives* of these rights: they would ensure the just distribution of the relevant amenities to the humans and nonhumans that cohabit the ecosystem in question. Several formal objections can be made to this hypothesis, in particular the arbitrary character of the delimitation of ecosystems (these can be isolated in fact only as frameworks for analysis in functional ecology, which can choose any scale at all for studying the flow of energy and information and the circulation of materials in trophic networks, from a leaf to a bioregion). But "rights" are wholly constructed on the basis of arbitrary conventions: one can imagine varying the scale on which this proposition can make sense (landscapes in the sense of "landscape ecology," social-ecological systems, ecological dynamics such as water retention and distribution, and so on); it suffices to agree and pass laws.

In this fictional approach to law (but our most solidly established systems of law began as fictions), ecosystems could be considered according to the model of an unappropriated and unappropriable commons, and the question becomes no longer one of ownership but rather one of shared use. We can also imagine rights of co-ownership over ecosystems (the legal apparatus is available) attributed to collectives composed of humans and nonhumans, domestic and wild.

What is interesting about this fiction is that it is already a reality, here and there. In particular forms of tacit and oral law in several different pastoral traditions in Eastern Europe (in the Carpathian Mountains, for example), we find the analogous idea that mountain pastures are an unusual form of commons in which solar energy is shared. This common law is made visible in the way shepherds (who are known in certain areas as *batsa*, independent entrepreneurs[13]) reveal their almost serene acceptance of wolf predation on livestock *as long as it does not exceed a certain threshold*: they suggest that, in the small herd *they* own, one sheep *belongs* to the wolves and two to the bears.

Variants on this phenomenon can presumably be found in the customs and proverbs of many pastoral cultures (the French expression *la part du loup*, "the wolf's share," probably comes from this tradition). It would be useful to undertake an ethnographic study of this family of representations and customs, looking for available forms that would help us imagine new legal constructions.

Should we think in terms of a property right belonging to the shepherd who *owns* the sheep and agrees to give a few of them back, or rather in terms of shared ownership?

On what is such sharing based? Is it only a matter of making a virtue of necessity, or is it rather an intuition of a duty to adopt a more equitable distribution among the cohabitants of the *same* giving environment, whose goods belong *by that very fact* to all? The environmental ethics that presides over these customs is still enigmatic: Should we think of it in the form of a principle of reciprocity in cohabitation—the shepherd returning to the ecosystem (emblematized here by wolves) their share in the energy that has allowed the sheep to grow? Or rather, in a more Leopoldian perspective, is there a share specifically owed to wolves, inasmuch as their presence is understood as necessary to the health of the ecosystem that the shepherd traverses?

The Leopoldian mountain offers a clarifying parable here: we can also imagine this arrangement as recognition by livestock farmers that the sheep *belong* to them only in an ambiguous sense, for what the farmers live on (that is, what allows sheep to grow) does not belong to anyone and remains unappropriable—it is the very supply of solar energy, in the assorted phenomenological forms of plant and animal biomasses, which we call an ecosystem, and of which a share, in all fairness, should accrue to the other inhabitants of the system.

This is already a way of recognizing animal rights over the shared energy constituted by an ecosystem. Animals are no longer written off as "natural contingencies" (like the weather, or illness), but viewed as *inhabitants of a particular biotic community* who are consequently owed a share in the primary net production of the biomass resulting from photosynthesis, that is, from the energy stocked in plants and then converted into flesh in the herbivorous animals that graze or browse in the ecosystem. This is, in a sense, a right "based on usage," where ownership of a good is justified only by the use made of it: for example, among the Inuits, a man who does not use his fox trap has to allow another individual to set it.[14] This right is distinguished from the individual right to real property, an exclusively human right, which most likely first appeared during the Neolithic period.

The question of rights becomes the question of determining what share should go to each party, and what measures should be taken to distribute the shares, so that pastoral activity does not suffer from the share allotted to wolves.

In this type of configuration, which has yet to be fully imagined, diplomats play yet another role:[15] they ensure the equitable distribution, between humans and nonhumans, of the amenities that the ecosystem has to bestow (as a biotic community with its abiotic conditions).

In any case, we would need to return to an earlier stage in our ontology of living beings, to a pre-Neolithic time before the invention of the fiction according to which the farmer *produces* domestic animals, whereas their engendering and their growth result in fact from the energy that derives, as it does elsewhere, from the sun and from evo-ecological dynamics. We would then recognize the plethora of living energy that is appropriated in the pastoral system and of which a share should legitimately accrue to its wild cohabitants.

To do this we would have to go back to a time before the founding myths of our pastoral civilization: before Abel—the first shepherd of the Old Testament—and his amnesia. It was to a God on high that Abel made his offerings in thanks for the health of his flock, and not to the actual mountain before his eyes that nourished and sustained his sheep. In a contemporary context where that God is dead, the mountain, the great forgotten being in this long historical parenthesis of inattention to the living earth here below, has not yet taken God's place. Yet if there are duties of reciprocity and gratitude toward something other than human, then Abel's were toward the mountain.

Reconciliation Diplomacy

Reflection on the possibility of changing the law, or, in the short run, of setting up *community-based conservation*, must not obscure the fact that the presence of wolves on our territories is not only, and not even primarily, the problem of livestock farmers.

By postulating that the only real relationship with wolves is theirs, and that all others (in other words, those of city-dwellers, ex-urbanites, and tourists who do not live with wolves) are illusory, the wolf-fearers have obscured the fact that we must interrogate ourselves, as a collective, on the desire for and the benefits of cohabiting with wolves, in a collective of living human and nonhuman beings on a territory that is affected and transformed by the wolves' return. What is at issue is the relation between society and the presence of wolves, and not only the relation between the pastoral world and these animals, though the latter relation tends to monopolize the debate, because the pastoral world alone feels the weight of the wolves' return.

Before the conflicts between wolves and farmers can be resolved, then, the very fact of the wolves' return compels reflection. This return has given rise to conflictual situations that reveal the deep structures in our ways of conceptualizing living beings and our relations with them. From this standpoint, it becomes equally important to detect mutualisms on a broader scale than that of the rural milieu. Wolves in Europe do not deserve to be defended merely because they belong to a natural patrimony, or out of guilt for having eradicated them, or by an awakened biocentric moral awareness, or through a Romantic valorization of the wild, but rather because wolves reestablish trophic diversity in European ecological dynamics—in other words, their presence restores a trophic level that had disappeared on a very large scale. Taken as a species, wolves are just one among others. But from the standpoint of functional ecology, their role in the trophic pyramid is such that, without them, the pyramid is decapitated. The nontruncated pyramid, better represented as networks, is what João Pedro Galhano Alves calls total biodiversity.[16] Total biodiversity is not a historically dated referential state but a functional state of the ecosystemic dynamics in which the abundant presence of large predators, like that of wild ungulates, permits a reconstitution of top-down ecological regulation. This functional state makes trophic cascades possible, and it corresponds to healthier, more resilient, and more sustainable ecological dynamics.[17]

The paradigm of conservation biology in which one can formulate the return of wolves is not that of providing sanctuaries: although wolves are charismatic animals, lavishly praised by members of the "cult of wild nature," we have seen that it is dangerous not to enter into interactions with them in order to let them know their limits. Moreover, their identification with wilderness in American culture was misguided: they are animals that can live spontaneously among us, in our interstices. Similarly, restoration is not what is called for: it is a question of a natural return, not chosen, not willed, and one that does not correspond to a natural patrimony that the French countryside spontaneously wanted to rediscover (like large deer, chamois, or certain large raptors). If we look closely, it seems that the best model is that of "reconciliation ecology."

Reconciliation ecology is defended by the ecologist Michael Rosenzweig in a book published in 2003.[18] Rosenzweig's original intuition is simple: no one can live self-sufficiently in the desert, and no one can return to the Stone Age. Destroying biodiversity or completely renouncing our human appropriation of nature are both impossible paths, in his view. He argues that the two major approaches to conservation ecology, restoring populations and creating sanctuaries, are no longer sufficient; from now on we have to reconcile human uses of the planet with those of the other species.

It is the evolutionist dimension of his project that is the best developed; it is a question of allowing the expansion of autonomous and resilient—self-supporting—wild populations on the lands we inhabit: "It will take a lot of work. But imagine the result: a vast area of diverse anthropogenic habitats that meet nature halfway instead of trampling her underfoot."[19]

Nevertheless, Rosenzweig knows that these spaces will not be ideally suited for the needs of the existing species. The challenge is not only to create sanctuaries for the species as they are now: the challenge is to create cohabitations on territories that have been seriously "anthropized" by our uses, cohabitations that would be capable of making enough room for other species to "give natural selection the time and space in which to work, and thus could save the overwhelming majority of today's species."[20] In reality, the former habitats of other species are "obsolete," in the sense that they belong to a world of wilderness that no longer exists and that will not come back. The virgin sanctuary spaces we have are microscopic. Between the lines, we understand that what is at stake is a plan not simply for safeguarding the ecosystems of the past, but also for accompanying and supporting an adaptive transition of the species around us so that they can adjust to the world as it is and as it will be—so that natural selection can develop coevolutions between biodiversity and sustainable human uses of the territories, and not hostile relations. Global warming accentuates this necessity. To create new habitats, we must take our inspiration from the old ones. This is a form of diplomacy: we must "figure out what is essential and what species can do without. Finally, we can reassemble the critical components into new habitats and landscapes of which we are also a part."[21]

The question comes down to this: How can we rearticulate, together, in harmonious complicity, the human uses of the biotic community and the revitalization of its own evolutionary potential? In a profound sense, reconciliation ecology must be based on the ambition to invent complexes of new mutualist socioeconomic relations, by setting up ecological interactions capable of reactivating or bringing into being mutually beneficial, integrated coevolutions on territories that are in every case particular.

There are nevertheless real dangers in Rosenzweig's proposals, dangers essentially tied to what could be called their immaturity in terms of *political* economy and ecology. Rosenzweig claims in effect that every time an ecological conflict regarding distribution arises between exploiters and protectors of nature, reconciliation *can* be achieved.[22] Recuperated by the dominant parties, this logic precludes any radical defensive political action on the part of a territory or a species: by allowing even the most destructive human uses, if they make room (but what room?) for other species, reconciliation ecology could become the new discourse justifying the most cynical exploiters. This is certainly not Rosenzweig's goal, but it is a possible effect, and recuperation is likely. His proposition fails to take into account a phenomenon of political psychology that is as insidious as it is simple: in a conflict between dominant and dominated parties, if you speak out in favor of a negotiation that is both reconciliatory and egalitarian, you are nevertheless always giving more to the dominators than to the dominated—you are justifying the dominators' asymmetrical position and their asymmetrical uses of the commons in question. The Unnecessary Imposed Mega Projects (UIMP) are good examples. Every approach of reconciliation ecology around the UIMP, which would imply accepting their institution if they make an effort in favor of local biodiversity, means abandoning the struggle to prevent ecological and economic aberrations: in these very asymmetrical cases, for the dominated party, reconciliation means submission.

The most worrying point is Rosenzweig's fascination with development projects that make room for biodiversity but whose spectacular dimension is ensured by success in strictly economic terms. The risk lies in what seems to be the author's belief in the myth of growth and development as the alpha and omega of human activity: the typically capitalist belief formulated by Walt W. Rostow according to which human *development* always passes *first* through an increase in wealth (Rosenzweig's examples of successful reconciliations are successes in green capitalism).

But if Rosenzweig's project requires clarification from the standpoint of philosophy and maturation from the standpoint of political economics, it is nevertheless promising from the standpoint of ecology: this author understands that the problem is fundamentally one of habitat (how to ensure that the territories in which we find shelter and that generate wealth remain habitable for the other species that share the space) and of uses (how to revitalize the uses made by the other species). These are two well-documented intuitions, which are nourished by an understanding of evolution as lacking in referential states or norms but rich in normativity. Thus, in the potential for instituting forms and norms provided that minimal conditions of revitalization are put in place, we allow for an emancipatory conception of everyday conservation, such as the Backyard Wildlife Habitat. In addition to creating sanctuaries, restoring evolutionary potentials, and becoming politically militant, we also provide for conservation, in those places where radical ecological militancy is not necessary or possible, but where we nevertheless have to live, and where living better consists in living together.

In the diplomatic perspective, reconciliation ecology must not become the slogan of a narrow policy of conservation; rather it is the name of a basic attitude toward living beings. This is an infrastructural philosophical concept and it is the name of a path: the Diplomatic Path. A path in the Asian sense of the term: a series of technical skills to incorporate, a series of successive satoris, intuitive experiences of enlightenment opening onto lives other than our own, a series of apprenticeships in harmonious arrangements, an ethologico-philosophical asceticism, and the internalization of a different political relation to beings other than humans.

The Crypto-potentiality of the Wolves' Return

What is so singular about the wolves' return? It is probable that the dispersing flow toward France, originating from the residual wolf populations in Europe, has never dried up. There may well have been wolf dispersals in France in every decade since the wolves were eradicated. But the significant phenomenon is their effective recolonization, in the sense of a *permanent reinstallation* in the French countryside. This recolonization is correlated with two interrelated phenomena that are, on different scales, profoundly meaningful. They set up the return of wolves—which might have been trivial—as a marker of a civilizational mutation and an event in political ecology.

The first phenomenon is the depopulation of rural areas. It has a sociological dimension, and it shows that the possibility for predators to recolonize stems from a human disengagement from the territories in question. We have left room. Quite precisely, we have left room for the forests, by deserting the extensive pastures and fields that limited the advance of pioneering forest fronts. It is owing to the fact that it is almost as possible today as it was in the wooded Gaul of two thousand years ago to traverse France's territory without leaving the cover of forests (apart from highways, rivers, and train lines, which animals have learned to cross) that wolves have been able to come back.

The second phenomenon, which results from the first and is perhaps the more profound, is the dimension of economic ecology associated with the abandonment of rural territories: the decrease in human appropriation of "net primary production," that is, the production of biomass through terrestrial photosynthesis, a concept developed as an index by Peter Vitousek and his collaborators.[23] The potential net primary production is a theoretical value corresponding to the energy accumulated in the vegetal biomass through photosynthesis on a hypothetical Planet Earth after the subtraction of *Homo sapiens*.

> The NPP [net primary production] is the amount of energy that the primary producers, the plants, make available to the rest of living species, the heterotrophs. It is measured in terms of dry biomass, in tons of carbon or in energy units. Of this NPP, humankind "co-opts" around 40 per cent in terrestrial ecosystems. The higher the HANPP [human appropriation of NPP], the less biomass is available for "wild" biodiversity. The proportion of NPP appropriated by humans is increasing because of population growth, and also because of increasing demands on land per person for urbanization, for growing foodstuffs, for growing timber. . . . Humans should decide whether they want HANPP to go on increasing, crowding out other non-domesticated species, or whether they want to reduce HANPP to 30 or 20 per cent in terrestrial ecosystems.[24]

It is this decrease in human appropriation of net primary production in Western Europe over the twentieth century that is the hidden cause, the underlying cause, the invisible structure, of the wolves' return. It is the infrastructural reality, in all its ambiguity, that takes away from this event its unpredictability, its characterization as a contingent accident.[25]

> In the European Union, where biomass is used very little as fuel and where intensive agriculture is based on the use of energy

from fossil fuels taking up less land, the HANPP, which had been increasing for decades, is currently decreasing. This is why wolves and bears are once again populating certain forests from which they had disappeared. Let us note here that this index signals improved sustainability, on this particular geographic scale, but it is obvious that this tendency will not be the same throughout the world.[26]

The wolves' return was predictable precisely because it was necessary: an ecological necessity. The ecological dynamics of a population rests on a dispersing proliferation: the reason for the absence of a species in an ecosystem (or a bioregion) that it had inhabited previously, except in cases of definitive extinction, is always a positive, factual, and constantly renewed obstacle related to ecofragmentation or to the occupation of the species' ecological niches by other species—by humans, for example. Darwin had already theorized that life forms tend to colonize spontaneously all the accessible "gaps" in the economy of nature, through variation, proliferation, and adaptation induced by selection; and that they are absent only in cases of defeat in the "struggle for survival" against stressful conditions (temperature, salinity, and so on) or against other species.[27]

In the Camargue region in southern France, when one learns to read the landscape, one grasps the fact that *oyat*, or *marram* grass (*Ammophilia arenaria*), owing to the singularity of its rhizomatic structure (first horizontal, then vertical, when the outer shafts are covered by sand), comes in to colonize sandy beaches where other plants cannot establish themselves, structuring dunes and preventing the wind from flattening them so that other plant species can grow right up to the water's edge. It becomes visually evident that the absence of life somewhere is never anything but a manifestation of a stubborn, relentless resistance to it by external conditions, struggling against the tireless colonization by forms of life.

This is what has happened with the wolves. Ecofragmentation, pastures, silviculture, and agriculture have driven the wolves away as surely as hunting and poisoning in the period between the wars; in any case, these phenomena kept wolves at a distance for more than fifty years, actively preventing the animals' return. As soon as all these pressures were lessened, the indefatigable process of colonization could start up again.

But this ecological colonization must not be interpreted according to the negative political connotations associated with the concept, entailing a fear of being submerged by uncontrollable wild beings. The mentality inherited from the Neolithic revolution is what leads to thinking in these terms. The colonization in question in no way challenges our presence; it suffices to think of it as cohabitation, in the terms of reconciliation ecology. We are a species that tends to colonize by totally excluding others. But there are forms of ecological competition that maintain plurality, where relations of mutualism between species and differences in ecological niches welcome all sorts of cohabitants on the same biotope. As a species, we tend to confuse the act of taking a place in a biotic community with the act of excluding other species on a massive scale, thereby risking the destruction of the biodiversity that sustains us on a daily basis, gives us the vegetal oxygen we breathe, supplies us with food, and populates our imaginations.

The decrease in HANPP is not a neutral bit of data; it is an index of increased sustainability according to ecological economics: "living in a territory in a sustainable way, that is, without harming the basis of its resources."[28]

This implies that there is an intrinsic positive value to the decrease in the appropriation of the biomass by human society, a phenomenon that forcefully induces the return of wolves, in the case that concerns us here. It is not unjustifiable to feel the wolves' return as a return of wildness, as the return of a wilder life among us, in our interstices: this is the intuitive formulation of the decrease in HANPP, which restores part of the net primary production to wild biodiversity. We can legitimately grasp this return as a revitalization of the diverse life forms around us, thus as an improvement in our relations with the ecosystems on which our own life form is based. This is the intuitive formulation of the relation between the decrease in HANPP and the improved sustainability of a social metabolism in terms of an ecological economy. Shepherds are simply bearing the weight of the collateral effect of an odd *improvement* in our constitutive relations with the biotic community—these relations are ambiguous, but they are to be celebrated, for they are rare.

The wolves' return is not taking place in a wild nature independent of our economy: it is a direct collateral effect of the decrease in human appropriation of the living production of nature, which induces both increased sustainability and rural economic mutations. In this sense, it is at least partly accurate to say that the wolves did not *come back spontaneously*. Not because anyone reintroduced them,[29] but because the sociological and economic transformations of our relations to the ecosystems are what allowed them to return—the transformations of the ways in which we exploit nature. There is no nature *outside of which* we can position ourselves. We cannot formulate the problem accurately if we accept the classic separation that has grown out of the American distinction between wilderness and cultivated or urban sites. We *have* no wilderness. We are *woven* of wilderness—and this wilderness is always historicized, anthropized.

The concept of HANPP, beyond its power as an index for managing the ecological economy, has considerable philosophical weight: it discreetly resituates humans *within* ecosystems, as heterotrophic consumers of the energy produced by photosynthesis, just like all other living animals. It discreetly encompasses all human economy, politics, and history, in the field of ecological phenomena in relation to the biotic community. It challenges the assimilation universe whose energy would be strictly physiochemical. But the energy that sustains us is not physiochemical; it is living energy. It underwrites our insertion in the biotic community, our relations to fauna and flora and the constraints that these imply.

The wolves' return is thus the symptom and the emblem of a phenomenon that has profound implications for civilization: the decrease in HANPP, an index of improved sustainability.[30] We can hypothesize that HANPP has had a *tendency* to increase at different paces, or to remain stable, since the Neolithic. As a result, nearly half of the terrestrial surface of the planet has been transformed into lands destined for agriculture or livestock grazing, and more than half of the world's forests and woodlands have been lost during the same period.

The human appropriation of net primary production was the hidden name of human progress, the "conquest of the earth," the colonization of all the earth's milieu, and later the rationalization of agriculture, technoscientific progress, and civilization. In the twentieth century, for the first time perhaps in ten thousand years, the human appropriation of net primary production in Western Europe decreased. The wolves' return is only an effect and a symptom of this change. We are at the tipping point of this slight, cryptic, foundational inversion, a phenomenon that calls out for interpretation. It is the most subtle of the major events in our ecological history—that is, of real history, the history that refuses to be limited to our confining anthropo-narcissistic tales, the history that instead weaves us together with the living whole from which we in fact have never been separated.[31]

The wolves' return reflects back to us what we have been, what we are no longer—a discreet recession, more or less involuntary, it must be said. It is a terraforming opportunity: Should we treat it with the same timeless logic of appropriation of net primary production by humans, or should we take as our guide what these animals show us by their return? In a sense they show us, unintentionally, a possible path; they make us aware of the unprecedented situation constituted by the decrease in HANPP; and they constitute a major obstacle that prevents us from returning to our habits of appropriation, for we cannot help but find in them an irreducible value. *Canis lupus* is an "umbrella species" in a profound sense: it is the entire human appropriation of nature as an incorporated attitude that the wolves are calling into question, just by returning to a place that we have left behind. What we believed to be our forest and our mountains are inhabited by large predators who call into question our sense of being the owners of these spaces.[32] There is nothing mystical in saying that they are sending us a message by their very presence, though the message is hard to read. The interpretation I am proposing here is that we must reconsider anew our genealogy as a species, in our constitutive relations to the living beings within us and apart from us.

Alongside the problems of political ecology that the wolves bring up, we discover metaphysical problems, highlighted by the return of the animals themselves, unearthed by these animals who think and who make us think. The wolf crisis constitutes a local exacerbation of the crisis of our constitutive relations with biotic communities. The wolves that have come back to France are whistleblowers drawing attention to the most architectonic ecological and ontological structures of the Moderns: they are bringing these structures out into broad daylight.

Notes

Introduction

1. Between one-fourth and one-third of the population of wolves less than two years old become dispersers. Their travels last from a week to a year. An individual can cover several hundred kilometers, seeking a partner of the opposite sex with whom to establish a new pack. See L. David Mech and Luigi Boitani, eds., *Wolves: Behavior, Ecology, and Conservation* (Chicago: University of Chicago Press, 2003), chapters 1 and 6. "Dispersers" explore beyond all boundaries: young wolves carrying pollen in their fur seek a new kingdom; migrating birds carrying seeds in their crops colonize distant islands.

2. See Jacques Gaillard, "L'année du loup," *Le Monde*, May 12, 1999: "The sacred is what is set apart, left to its terrifying purity, beyond good and evil, in a territory that humans voluntarily give up, except to place themselves in the service of a cult. The very idea of sheltering wolves from human violence, in a sanctuary in which their natural destructive capacity would be unthreatened, nourished by socially accepted sacrifices (compensation for every lamb killed), stems from an archaic form of religiosity." [All translations from the French not otherwise attributed are my own. —*Translator's note*]

3. On this point, certain animal protection associations react to initiatives meant to transform wolves' predatory behaviors toward herds by condemning them as attempts to "educate" wild creatures.

4. See John Dewey, *How We Think* (Boston: D. C. Heath, 1910).

5. See Patrick Degeorges and Antoine Nochy, "Le loup affaire d'État," *Les Cahiers du Proses* 9 (May–June 2004): 26, www.houmbaba.com: "But this 'regulation' of a species that cannot be viewed as proliferating tends, through semantic slippage, to maintain wolves in the position of 'harmful.'"

6. "The errors of central governments in this matter are amply documented by the report of the [2003 French] Parliamentary Commission of Inquiry. Preceded by an unquestioned reputation as dangerous, wolves were perceived by local populations as intruders and invaders" (Degeorges and Nochy, "Le loup affaire d'État," 26).

7. Baptiste Morizot, "Penser le concept comme carte, une pratique deleuzienne de la philosophie," in *La Géophilosophie de Gilles Deleuze: Entre esthétiques et politiques*, ed. Mauro Carbone and Paride Broggi (Paris: Mimésis, 2012), https://hal.archives-ouvertes.fr/hal-01476141.

8. Gilbert Simondon, *L'individuation à la lumière des notions de forme et d'information* (Grenoble: Millon, 2005), 212.

9. See Sergio Dalla Bernardina, *Le retour du prédateur: Mises en scène du sauvage dans la société post-rurale* (Rennes: Presses Universitaires de Rennes, 2011).

10. Maïa Martin, "Entre affection et aversion, le retour du loup en Cévennes comme problème public," *Terrains et travaux*, no. 20 (2012): 17.

11. Jürgen Rohmeder, "L'invasion des loups à travers l'Autriche avance," *Horizons et débats*, no. 7 (February 22, 2010): 8.

12. Dave Grossmann, *On Killing: The Psychological Cost of Learning to Kill in War and Society* (Boston: Little, Brown, 1995).

13. Adolf Portmann, *La forme animale* (Paris: La Bibliothèque, coll. L'ombre animale, 2013).

14. This phenomenon is described impeccably by Aldo Leopold in *A Sand County Almanac and Other Writings on Ecology and Conservation* (New York: Library of America, 2013 [1949]), 77: "One need not doubt the unseen." Nicolas Lescureux and John Linnell have documented similar phenomena in an ethnographic study: "Knowledge and Perceptions of Macedonian Hunters and Herders: The Influence of Species Specific Ecology of Bears, Wolves, and Lynx," *Human Ecology* 38, no. 3 (2010): 389–399.

15. After spending more than three years tracking wolves in France, I managed to spot one on only three occasions, each time essentially from a car, during tracking sessions in areas where their potential paths had been painstakingly triangulated; evidence of presence had been crosschecked to produce hypotheses about their habitual paths. At Yellowstone National Park, it took only a couple of weeks to observe, sometimes for hours on end, two packs of six or seven individuals.

16. Even in the current situation in which herds are sometimes not well protected and breeders not yet optimally trained and informed, 84–91 percent of wolves' nutrition in France consists in wildlife, according to the data supplied by the ONCFS (the French National Office for Hunting and Wildlife). Moreover, the situation has allowed for a significant increase in the ungulate population, especially roe deer, in recent years.

Chapter 1. The Diplomatic Model

1. It is interesting to note that, over time, the accounts of these journeys manifest a tendency to shift the focus away from the male Western explorer as protagonist and hero in favor of the indigenous female interpreter, who more often takes on the principal role in contemporary reformulations.

2. We need to envision, for wolves, the equivalent of Nathan Wachtel's approach, in his book telling the story of the *Conquista* from the vantage point of the Amerindian peoples rather than that of the conquerors: see *The Vision of the Vanquished: The Spanish Conquest of Peru through Indian Eyes, 1530–1570*, trans. Ben and Siân Reynolds (New York: Barnes and Noble Books, 1977). At stake is a way of taking literally the proverb according to which, until lions have their own storytellers, hunting tales will continue to glorify the hunters.

3. On this point, see the various ethological arrangements envisioned at the end of chapter 3, "Understanding and Influencing Behavior."

4. Philippe Descola, *Beyond Nature and Culture*, trans. Janet Lloyd (Chicago: University of Chicago Press, 2013 [2005]), 12.

5. For an initial outline of this metaphysics, see the foundational intuition of André-Georges Haudricourt on the constitutive difference between direct positive action and indirect negative action, in "Domestication des animaux, culture des plantes et traitement d'autrui," *L'Homme* 2, no. 1 (1962): 40–50.

6. Paul Shepard, *Nous n'avons qu'une seule terre*, trans. Bertrand Fillaudeau (Paris: José Corti, 2013 [1996]), preface, 18 (Shepard supplied the preface to the French translation of *The Only World We've Got: A Paul Shepard Reader* [San Francisco: Sierra Club Books, 1996]). Shepard's analysis echoes an enigmatic statement by Karl Marx: "At the same pace that mankind masters nature, man seems to become enslaved to other men or to his own infamy": see "Speech at Anniversary of the *People's Paper*," delivered in London on April 19, 1856, published in *Marx/Engels Selected Works*, vol. 1 (Moscow: Progress, 1969), 500.

7. Strictly speaking, there is no such thing as "the Neolithic." Rather, there have been processes of Neolithization that differ in nature and in length and should not be amalgamated, for amalgamation runs the risk of instituting a Manichean opposition between a Paleolithic era of the "noble savage" (Romantic nomadism and phantasmatic life in the wild) and an exclusively destructive Neolithic era of which we are the heirs. As we shall see further on, the term "Neolithic" is used here in a more local sense, to isolate in time and space (in the Middle East, between eleven thousand and six thousand years ago) the emergence of a new relation to animals and to life forms in general, that can be characterized as "direct positive action," in the context of increasingly widespread domestication and pasturing. This new relation led to a new ontological phenomenon: domesticated animals became the model for animality in general.

8. Steven H. Fritts, Robert O. Stephenson, Robert D. Hayes, and Luigi Boitani, "Wolves and Humans," in *Wolves: Behavior, Ecology, and Conservation*, ed. L. David Mech and Luigi Boitani (Chicago: University of Chicago Press, 2003), 300.

9. During the summer of 2014, trackers in the Haut-Var region in France found a complex array of wolf paths revealing at least three individual wolves who were repeatedly identified at the exit of a canyon where human presence was significant. The situation remained a mystery (proximity with humans even though wilder areas were accessible; constant back and forth traveling in mud), until an

explanatory hypothesis emerged: proximity to or distance from humans was not what mattered to the wolves; they were after crayfish, which they found in that particular spot. The discovery of freshwater crayfish and of partially eaten remains reinforced this hypothesis.

10. Erkki Pulliainen, "The Status, Structure and Behaviour of Populations of the Wolf (Canis I. Lupus L.) along the Fenno-Soviet Border," *Annales Zoologici Fennici* 17, no. 2 (1980): 107–112.

11. Luigi Boitani, "Wolf Management in Intensively Used Areas of Italy," in *Wolves of the World: Perspectives of Behavior, Ecology, and Conservation*, ed. Fred H. Harrington and Paul C. Paquet (Park Ridge, NJ: Noyes, 1982), 158–172.

12. Bruno Latour, *An Inquiry into Modes of Existence: An Anthropology of the Moderns*, trans. Catherine Porter (Cambridge, MA: Harvard University Press, 2013).

13. A whole series of recent theoretical projects aim at improving the representation of nonhumans in politics, from Sue Donaldson and Will Kymlicka's *Zoopolis: A Political Theory of Animal Rights* (Oxford: Oxford University Press, 2011) to Bruno Latour's "Make It Work 'theater of negotiation'" presentation for a Paris climate conference in spring 2015. These important projects are nevertheless paradoxical. In the face of the crisis of representation, they seem to react as a modernizing front: if modernity is in crisis, it is because we are not yet sufficiently modern. If representation is in crisis, let us produce still more representations. What distinguishes the figure of the diplomat I am presenting here is that this figure is not first and foremost a representative of nonhumans in human assemblies. I am interested, instead, in the technological and philosophical arrangements that together make it possible to *present ourselves* to nonhumans decently, as diplomats making an overture toward foreigners who live among us and with whom forms of cohabitation must be reinvented. It is not a matter of diplomacy among humans representing nonhumans, but of diplomacy carried out directly *with* nonhumans. The model is the explorer, not the deputy: diplomats here do not represent their own camp, they present it; they do not defend their own interests, they defend the interests of the *relationship itself.*

14. Paul the Deacon, *History of the Lombards*, trans. William Dudley Foulke, ed. Edward Peters (Philadelphia: University of Pennsylvania Press, 1974 [1907]), book 1, chapter 11, 20. The ninth-century theologian Ratramnus of Corbie wrote a letter asking whether cynocephalics should be viewed as men (*Epistola de Cynocephalis ad Rimbertum presbyterum scripta*, in *Patrologia Latina* 121: 1153–1156); see "Ratramnus and the Dog-Headed Humans," in *Carolingian Civilization*, 2nd ed., ed. Paul Edward Dutton (Peterborough, ON: Broadview Press, 2004), 452–455.

15. See Giorgio Agamben, *The Open: Man and Animal* (Stanford, CA: Stanford University Press, 2004).

16. The anthropologist Eduardo Kohn has played a role in this reinvestment of the therianthropic mytheme through his analysis, for other purposes, of the "runa puma" (the puma equivalent of a werewolf) in his anthropology, which extends

beyond the human. On this point, see his *How Forests Think: Toward an Anthropology beyond the Human* (Berkeley: University of California Press, 2013).

17. See Gilles Deleuze and Félix Guattari, *What Is Philosophy?*, trans. Hugh Tomlinson and Graham Burchell (New York: Columbia University Press, 1994).

18. The compound French term *loup-garou* is a pleonasm, as Henriette Walter notes, since *garou*, from the Frankish *wariwulf* or *werwulf*, already means "wolf-man"; see Henriette Walter and Pierre Avenas, *L'étonnante histoire des noms de mammifères* (Paris: Payot, 2003).

19. Bernard Charlier, "Faces of the Wolf, Faces of the Individual: Anthropological Study of Human, Non-human Relationships in West Mongolia," PhD thesis, Cambridge University, 2010.

20. Callières was a plenipotentiary diplomat under Louis XIV and signatory of the Treaty of Ryswick, which ended the war with William III of Orange and his Grand Alliance. See François de Callières, *The Art of Diplomacy*, ed. and trans. H. M. A. Keens-Sopher and Karl W. Schweizer (New York: Holmes & Meier, 1983 [1716]).

21. This point will be discussed at length in part 3.

22. On this point, see chapters 2 and 3. The formula is from Callières, *The Art of Diplomacy*, chapter 1, 65–66: "Every Christian Prince ought to lay it down as a principal maxim of his government, not to have recourse to arms for the maintenance and defence of his right, until he has once tried what he can do by the force of reason and persuasion; and it is his interest to join also therewith favours and good offices, which is the surest way of all to establish and increase his power. But it is necessary that he make choice of fit instruments, who know how to apply those means rightly, in order to gain the hearts and inclinations of the persons they have to deal with. And it is this chiefly, that the science of treating and negotiating consists."

23. In the conclusion of this book, this model for negotiation is analyzed in the light of the win-win approach proposed under the label "reconciliation ecology" by the ecologist Michael Rosenzweig in *Win-Win Ecology: How the Earth's Species Can Survive in the Midst of Human Enterprise* (New York: Oxford University Press, 2003).

24. See T. A. Newsome and W. J. Ripple, "A Continental Scale Trophic Cascade from Wolves through Coyotes to Foxes," *Journal of Animal Ecology* 84, no. 1 (2015): 49–59, and W. J. Ripple and R. L. Beschta, "Trophic Cascades in Yellowstone: The First 15 Years after Wolf Reintroduction," *Biological Conservation*, no. 145 (2012): 205–213.

25. See João Pedro Galhano Alves, "Des hommes, des grands carnivores et des grands herbivores: Une approche anthropologique et comparative internationale," *ANTROPOlógicas*, no. 7 (2003). The idea of total biodiversity will be analyzed in the final chapter.

26. Élie During and Laurent Jeanpierre, interview with Bruno Latour, "L'universel, il faut le faire," *Critique*, no. 786 (November 2012): 955.

27. During and Jeanpierre, interview with Latour.

28. See Aldo Leopold, *A Sand County Almanac and Other Writings on Ecology and Conservation* (New York: Library of America, 2013 [1949]). In the present text, my use of the term oscillates between these two meanings, depending on the problem under consideration.

29. On this point, see J. Baird Callicott's work, in which he calls for the creation of a "new image of nature," in the ecological terms of the biotic community and the evolutionist fraternity, especially in *Beyond the Land Ethic* (Albany: State University of New York Press, 1999), and *Earth's Insights: A Survey of Ecological Ethics from the Mediterranean Basin to the Australian Outback* (Berkeley: University of California Press, 1997 [1994]).

Chapter 2. Seeking King Solomon's Ring

1. This story is told in chapter 21 of *The Little Flowers of St. Francis of Assisi*. The text was originally written in Latin between 1327 and 1340, probably by Ugolino da Montegiorgio, then translated into Vulgar Latin.

2. Here is what Francis said to seal the agreement: "Brother wolf, thou hast done much evil in this land, destroying and killing the creatures of God without his permission . . . but I will make peace between them and thee, O brother wolf, if so be thou no more offend them, and they shall forgive thee all thy past offences, and neither men nor dogs shall pursue thee any more." This was the first English translation of Ugolino's *The Little Flowers of St. Francis of Assisi*, revised and emended by Dom Roger Hudleston, with an introduction by Arthur Livingston (New York: Heritage Press, n.d.); the text is in the public domain.

3. Thomas A. Sebeok founded the zoosemiotic approach, based on three classic stages of analysis: the syntactic stage, which amounts to a physical description of the signal; the semantic stage, which looks at the qualitative information transmitted by the signal; and the pragmatic stage, which considers the potential uses of the signal, the role it plays in interactions. See Thomas A. Sebeok, *Perspectives in Zoosemiotics* (The Hague: Mouton, 1972).

4. Warren Weaver, "Some Recent Contributions to the Mathematical Theory of Communication," in *The Mathematical Theory of Communication* by Claude E. Shannon and Warren Weaver (Urbana: University of Illinois Press, 1964 [1949]), 1–29.

5. Hildegard of Bingen (1098–1179), an adventurous spirit, undertook zoological research for therapeutic purposes. Taking her inspiration from the theory of the humors, she developed an analogous conception of God's creatures: "Foxes, thanks to the science of lions in which they share, know many things; because they have some aspects of panthers' behavior; they have a variable character and some familiarity with men. Lions possess something of human strength and something of the nature of beasts. Wolves have some aspects of lion behavior and it is thanks to their lion nature that they know and understand humans and sense them from afar.

Dogs have something in common with humans in their behavior, which belongs to their nature, just as donkeys appreciate humans because they touch human nature through some aspects of their own" (cited in Dominique Lestel, *Les origines animales de la culture* [Paris: Flammarion, 2009], 34; translated here from Lestel's French version). In this analogic theory, the beings of creation share elements that make mutual comprehension possible. It is a theory of specific contiguous natures, in which the nature of one "touches through some aspects" the nature of another. This text pinpoints the pre-Darwinian empirical intuition of a commonality beneath difference, an immanent commonality that is not based on the possession of a transcendental code (the Word), but rather on an infrastructural correspondence among natures, that is, Aristotelian specific essences, reintroduced into Christian cosmology by scholastics.

6. On November 29, 1979, Pope John Paul II proclaimed St. Francis the patron saint of "those who promote ecology," in the apostolic letter *Inter Sanctos Praeclara Que Viros* (available in English translation at https://francis35.org/english/papal-declaration-francis-patron-ecology/).

7. On this point, see John Dewey, "The Influence of Darwin on Philosophy," in *The Influence of Darwin on Philosophy and Other Essays* (New York: Henry Holt, 1910), 1–19.

8. Charles Darwin, *The Expression of Emotions in Man and Animals* (London: John Murray, Albemarle Street, 1872), 12.

9. A more appropriate metaphor would be that of a single coral, since coral lacks any hierarchical structure, and only the branches at the outer surface are still living.

10. Let us recall that, of the "four questions" posed by the ethologist Nikolaas Tinbergen, which have become canons in the classic ethological method, two dealt with the evolutionary dimensions of behavior. See Niko Tinbergen, "On Aims and Methods of Ethology," *Zeitschrift für Tierpsychologie* 20 (2010): 410–433.

11. Lorenz wrote this text in 1973 in conjunction with his receipt of the Nobel Prize. Konrad Lorenz—Biographical, NobelPrize.org, Nobel Media AB 2019, https://www.nobelprize.org/prizes/medicine/1973/lorenz/biographical, accessed February 20, 2019.

12. Konrad Z. Lorenz, *King Solomon's Ring: New Light on Animal Ways* (New York: Thomas Y. Crowell, 1952).

13. Gerrit François Makkink, *Het leven von onze wadvogels* (Amsterdam: L. J. Veen, 1963).

14. See Daniel R. MacNulty, L. David Mech, and Douglas W. Smith, "A Proposed Ethogram of Large-Carnivore Predatory Behavior, Exemplified by the Wolf," *Journal of Mammalogy* 88 (2007), www.digitalcommons.unl.edu.

15. It is on the horizon opened up by this idea that we must understand the analyses of convergences in modes of existence between wolves and humans carried out by Amerindians and Kyrgyz observers as well as by wolf experts: these analyses

are based not on anthropomorphism but on predatomorphism: collective hunting of large game, social and hierarchical strategies, family groups, parental loyalty, shared participation by parents in child-rearing, defense of the territory, dispersal of the young to prevent endogamy. The ontological nature of these resemblances, like the epistemological model of its conceptualization, warrants analysis in its own right.

16. On this point, see Paul Shepard, ed., *The Only World We've Got: A Paul Shepard Reader* (San Francisco: Sierra Club Books, 1996).

17. See the concept of evolutionary genetics, *gephe*, developed by Virginie Orgogozo, Arnaud Martin, and Baptiste Morizot, which encapsulates a *geno*typical variation on a locus and a difference of states that is *phe*notypic in character, and that is found in species that are very far apart on the tree of life: *gephe* modules are thus shared by animals, and even plants, without regard to their phylogenetic remoteness: "The Differential View of Genotype-Phenotype Relationships," *Frontiers in Genetics* 6, article 179 (May 2015), https://doi.org/10.3389/fgene.2015.00179.

18. Recent discoveries show that researchers have underestimated the capacity for organisms that are widely separated in genetic terms to have, on common portions of DNA, similar mutations that produce similar phenotypical effects; this development has facilitated very broad interspecies comparisons; see Arnaud Martin and Virginie Orgogozo, "The Loci of Repeated Evolution: A Catalog of Genetic Hotspots of Phenotypic Variation," *Evolution* 67, no. 5 (2013): 1235–1250. In other words, the common genetic tool kit constitutes the major portion of the genome: each life form is first and foremost a combinatoric and a combination on the basis of the same set of genetic modules. It is this common base that once again ensures the possibility of comparison.

19. William Timberlake, "Animal Behavior: A Continuing Synthesis," *Annual Review of Psychology* 44, no. 1 (February 1993): 675–706.

20. Oswald Spengler, *Man and Technics: A Contribution to a Philosophy of Life*, translated from the German (New York: A. A. Knopf, 1963 [1932]); Desmond Morris, *The Naked Ape: A Zoologist's Study of the Human Animal* (London: Cape, 1967); Shepard, *Only World*.

21. Shepard, *Only World*, 1–20.

22. Eduardo Viveiros de Castro, *Cannibal Metaphysics*, ed. and trans. Peter Skafish (Minneapolis, MN: Univocal, 2014), 87.

23. Vinciane Despret offers a lovely ethological analysis of the idea of "good translation" in terms of being tested, as a researcher, "on my language and my sphere of experience": see *What Would Animals Say If We Asked the Right Questions?*, trans. Brett Buchanan, foreword by Bruno Latour (Minneapolis: University of Minnesota Press, 2016), 172–173.

24. Shepard, *Only World*; see especially 51–53.

25. Karl Lorenz, "Der Kumpan in der Umwelt des Vogels," *Journal für Ornithologie* 83, no. 2 (April 1935): 137–213.

26. See Jean-Luc Renck and Véronique Servais, *L'éthologie: Histoire naturelle du comportement* (Paris: Seuil, 2002), 200: "The circulation of information among individuals is a vital necessity that works to regulate the formation and function of their associations, whether stable or momentary (couples, harems, families, cat groups, populations) or, conversely, their dispersals."

27. The prodigious vertical leaps made by springboks do not serve to optimize racing speed. This behavior, called stotting (rebounding) or pronking (showing off) has received several different explanations. It occurs when the animal is in the presence of threatening predators. To escape, it would be faster to run closer to the ground. Although this stereotypical behavior can be subverted by an individual animal and turned to other uses (to express joy, to signal to the herd, directly or indirectly, the presence of a predator, to play), it is very probably based on a selected hereditary matrix. It has been hypothesized that these arabesques constitute an "honest signal" for predators hunting them (lions, leopards): a display that exposes their power, their vitality, and discourages the predator from attacking those who are leaping with so much grace. To the extent that the energy cost of the hunt to the predator is a central problem, these leaps mean: "If you pursue me, you will be a loser as well, for you will be risking failure and exhaustion." This is an animal negotiation, a prey-predator negotiation in which signs are sent in such a way that, *by anticipation*, the attacker renounces the hunt. Let us note that "stotting" behavior is also manifested by domestic sheep, but as a relic present only among the young. We can hypothesize that it was present to a greater degree among their wild ancestors, the urial mouflons, and that it could have played an analogous defensive role against wolves.

28. Jean-Marc Landry, *Le Loup: Biologie, moeurs, mythologie, cohabitation, protection* (Paris: Delachaux & Niestlé, coll. La bibliothèque du naturaliste, 2006), 175.

29. To convince oneself of this, it suffices to spend some time watching a feline on a hunt, a lioness on the savanna or a cat in the garden, quivering with the desire to leap but disciplined by a controlling patience, its inner conflict echoed by the increasing trembling of its muscles as it approaches its prey.

30. Confronted with the selection of courageous behaviors in bison, wolves have acquired a strange behavior on their own part: they stare fixedly and with intensity at their potential prey. This is probably another behavior that has an evolutionary basis, but which one? Any "just-so" story would fit the case (some evoke the capacity of wolves to read the weaknesses of their prey, others evoke their pugnacity)—but evolution is often much subtler than our crude economic reasoning.

31. Renck and Servais, *Éthologie*, 215.

32. Frans de Waal, *The Bonobo and the Atheist: The Search for Humanism among the Primates* (New York: W. W. Norton, 2013).

33. See Daniel Dennett, *Darwin's Dangerous Idea: Evolution and the Meanings of Life* (New York: Simon & Schuster, 1995), 73–83.

34. See *Bulletin Réseau Loup*, no. 28, 11: "The main goal is not to count wolves, but rather to detect the presence of the year's cubs within the packs in order to assess reproduction rates and compare them from year to year. The investigations are carried out by using wolf calls to provoke responses in order to localize the 'meeting places' where wolves gather during the post-reproduction period. An array of sampling points, distributed over each zone of permanent presence (ZPP), is studied at night. From 1 to 6 repetitions are undertaken in August and September, a period during which the presence of cubs can be identified thanks to differences in their vocal timbre. The protocol is ended with the first positive cub detection. This arrangement has made it possible to detect the species on 17 ZPP and on one sector outside of the ZPP zones, and to identify reproduction on 14 of the zones."

Chapter 3. Understanding and Influencing Behavior

1. Known as Ohiyesa, "The Winner," in his early youth, Eastman was brought up by relatives and schooled in the Sioux culture after the death of his mother and the presumed death of his father. At age fifteen he was reunited with his father, who had adopted the colonizers' ways and persuaded the boy to do the same. Eastman excelled in his studies and earned a degree in medicine from Boston University after graduating from Dartmouth. His legacy includes a number of books on Native American life, starting with the autobiographical *Indian Boyhood* (New York: McClure, Phillips, 1902). For more information, see http://www.worldwisdom.com/public/authors/Charles-Eastman.aspx.

2. See Jean-Marc Landry, *Le Loup: Biologie, moeurs, mythologie, cohabitation, protection* (Paris: Delachaux & Niestlé, coll. La bibliothèque du naturaliste, 2006), 106; see also Rolf O. Peterson and Paolo Ciucci, "The Wolf as a Carnivore," in *Wolves: Behavior, Ecology, and Conservation*, ed. L. David Mech and Luigi Boitani (Chicago: University of Chicago Press, 2003), 128; and L. David Mech and Rolf O. Peterson, "Wolf-Prey Relations," in *Wolves*, 145.

3. On this point, see the hypothesis of the red queen proposed by Leigh Van Valen in "A New Evolutionary Law," *Evolutionary Theory* 1 (1973): 1–17.

4. "Programmed to kill whenever possible because it is rarely possible to kill, wolves automatically take advantage of an unusual opportunity" (Mech and Peterson, "Wolf-Prey Relations," 145). We recognize the mechanistic lexicon (programmed, automatically), which is meant to guarantee to behavioral ecology its status as an objectifying science, that is, a deterministic science from which intentions, as ultimate causes, have been expurgated.

5. Paul Shepard, ed., *The Only World We've Got: A Paul Shepard Reader* (San Francisco: Sierra Club Books, 1996), 34.

6. In *Evolution of the Brain and Intelligence* (New York: Academic Press, 1973), looking at comparative brain size in prey and predators, Harry J. Jerison documents a phase of continuous increase in which carnivores have a higher index

of cephalization than their prey; this creates selective pressure on the prey, whose brain size increases in turn, and the cycle continues.

7. André-Georges Haudricourt, "Domestication des animaux, culture des plantes et traitement d'autrui," *L'Homme* 2, no. 1 (1962): 42.

8. Catherine Larrère and Raphaël Larrère, *Penser et agir avec la nature: Une enquête philosophique* (Paris: La Découverte, 2015).

9. See Raphaël Larrère's comprehensive article "Le loup, l'agneau et l'éleveur" in *Ruralia* (1999), electronic publication January 25, 2005, http://ruralia.revues.org/114.

10. On this point there is a troubling analogy with the case of the man-eating sharks in the Indian Ocean. "Thus on the one hand we attract and starve the sharks, and on the other we persecute them because they approach and attack surfers." See the appeal to protect the sharks of Réunion from which this quote is taken: https://labavedukrapo.wordpress.com/2015/04/20/requinsdelareunion.

11. Haudricourt, "Domestication," 42.

12. See 207–208 in this volume.

13. See Carl Schmitt, *The Concept of the Political*, trans. George Schwab (Chicago: University of Chicago Press, 2007).

14. See part 5, "An Ecology of Relations," in Philippe Descola's *Beyond Nature and Culture*, trans. Janet Lloyd (Chicago: University of Chicago Press, 2013 [2005]). Descola's discussion of this topic has been neglected in favor of his spectacular analysis of ontological schemas, but it has important implications for political ecology.

15. See Lynn White Jr., "The Historical Roots of Our Ecologic Crisis," *Science* 155, no. 3767 (1967): 1203–1207, https://doi.org.10.1126/science.155.3767.1203. Callicott describes it this way: "It seems clearly the intent of God that man be master and nature slave, since not only is man given dominion over the earth, he is expressly enjoined to subdue (Hebrew: *kabas*, 'stamp down') the earth—as if nature were created unruly and were in need of breaking to become complete." *Earth's Insights: A Survey of Ecological Ethics from the Mediterranean Basin to the Australian Outback* (Berkeley: University of California Press, 1994), 15.

16. See J. Baird Callicott, "After the Industrial Paradigm, What?," in *Beyond the Land Ethic: More Essays in Environmental Philosophy* (Albany: State University of New York Press, 1999), 301–302.

17. See Catherine Perlès's work, especially "Pourquoi le néolithique? Analyse des théories, évolution des perspectives," in *L'homme, le mangeur, l'animal qui nourrit l'autre?*, ed. J.-P. Poulain (Paris: OCHA, 2007), 16–29.

18. Jocelyne Porcher, ed., *The Ethics of Animal Labor: A Collaborative Utopia*, translated from the French (Cham, Switzerland: Palgrave Macmillan, 2017 [2011]), 14–15.

19. Porcher, *Ethics of Animal Labor*, 106.

20. Porcher, *Ethics of Animal Labor*, 105.

21. It is important to avoid confusing a-Neolithic and Paleolithic. The former refers to life forms that unfolded apart from the pastoral metaphysics of direct positive action, and it does not imply any fantasies about some Paleolithic Eden. In parallel

to a critical cartography of the pastoral metaphysics, a forthcoming book designed to complete this one, *We Have Invented Animals*, will develop the concept of wildness.

22. Landry, *Le loup*, 207.

23. The Anthropocene is a concept in geological chronology developed to characterize the epoch of world history inaugurated when human activities began to produce a significant global impact on the biochemical and geochemical systems of the planet.

24. See William Tomkins, *Indian Sign Language* (San Diego, CA: Dover, 1969 [1931]).

25. Haudricourt, "Domestication."

26. See the many examples of these monsters selected through industrial breeding that Temple Grandin, a specialist in overdomestication, offers in *Animals in Translation: Using the Mysteries of Autism to Decode Animal Behavior* (New York: Scribner, 2005).

27. On this point, see Paul Shepard, ed., *The Only World We've Got: A Paul Shepard Reader* (San Francisco: Sierra Club Books, 1996), chapter 7, "The Domesticators."

28. The concept of transaction in the philosophy of ecology is developed by Donato Bergandi from the starting point of John Dewey's pragmatist epistemology; we shall analyze this concept later on. See, for example, Bergandi's "Niveaux d'organisation: Évolution, écologie, et transaction," in *Le tout et les parties dans les systèmes naturels*, ed. Thierry Martin (Paris: Vuibert, 2007), 47–55.

29. There are beings that demand, owing to the sole fact of being, something like independence, and this is not the case of Gaia alone. We can see such beings as messengers of Gaia, in Bruno Latour's sense, or as dispatchers, scattered and dispersed heralds who let us know at the same time all that is resisting us and the systemic non-unity of Gaia, the fact that Gaia is only a name for what is beyond our grasp, in the effects of our feedback loops and of reaction on the planet. See Bruno Latour, *Facing Gaia*, trans. Catherine Porter (Cambridge: Polity, 2017 [2015]).

30. Why "animal"? First, because we practice it as animals among other animals. Then because, if we look at it closely, if we pay attention, for example, to the sixth extinction, not all living beings are equal in the face of the effects of human action and climate change: animal life is on the front lines, and, according to the data, animals are suffering the greatest harm, compared to plants or bacteria or fungi. We hear a lot these days about the massive sixth extinction of species; we must make clear that it is first of all a question of the extinction of animal life, that is, of heterotrophs—organisms that depend on external sources of nutrition—and specifically of vertebrates. According to Elizabeth Kolbert, the average rate of loss of vertebrate species in the last century was 114 times higher than what it would have been without human activity. Elizabeth Kolbert, *The Sixth Extinction: An Unnatural History* (New York: Henry Holt, 2014).

31. See Kristen Nowell and Peter Jackson, *Wild Cats: Status Survey and Conservation Action Plan* (Gland, Switzerland: International Union for Conservation of Nature and Natural Resources, 1996), 57 and 195.

32. Nowell and Jackson, *Wild Cats*. Peter Jackson reported that no woodcutter wearing such a mask was attacked during a three-year period, whereas twenty-nine persons who were not wearing masks had been killed during the preceding eighteen months. It is likely that the tiger involved ended up understanding the ruse, and the measure became slightly less effective over the years.

33. The ecopolitical problem of tiger conservation, in India in particular, is nevertheless much more complex, and this ruse must not be allowed to mask the deeper stakes, which set the post-materialist cult of wild nature against popular ecologism. On this point, see Ramachandra Guha and Joan Martinez-Alier, "L'environnementalisme des riches," in *Écologie politique*, ed. Émilie Hache and Cyril Le Roy (Paris: Éditions Amsterdam, 2012), 51–65.

34. See E. Sue Savage-Rumbaugh, Shelly L. Williams, Takeshi Furuichi, and Takayoshi Kano, "Language Perceived: *Paniscus* Branches Out," in *Great Ape Societies*, ed. William C. McGraw, Linda F. Marchant, and Toshisada Nishida (Cambridge: Cambridge University Press, 1996), 173–184.

35. E. O. Wilson, *Sociobiology: The New Synthesis* (Cambridge, MA: Belknap Press of Harvard University Press, 1975), 268.

36. Dave Ausband, "Pilot Study Report for Using a Biofence to Manipulate Wolf Pack Movements in Central Idaho," *Montana Cooperative Wildlife Research Unit*, November 2010, accessed October 13, 2019, at https://idfg.idaho.gov/old-web/docs/wolves/reportAnnual11.pdf.

37. In the American West, in the frontier period, legal arrangements granted colonizers, under certain conditions, the opportunity to own lands that they could traverse on horseback in a single day. This practice was called "land grabbing." We can see here how conventional and legal logic could be grafted onto a life form and a biomorphic use of territorial marking to signal occupation of a land area.

38. I thank Antoine Nochy for this valuable nuance, offered in a personal communication.

39. This was emphasized by an esteemed eighteenth-century observer of wild behaviors, Georges Leroy, lieutenant of the royal hunt and administrator of the royal forests, in his letters on animals: "The shaking of a leaf rouses in a young wolf only a simple movement of curiosity; but an experienced wolf, who has known this fluttering to precede the appearance of a man, takes fright at it with reason, because he has perceived the connection of the two phenomena. When these judgments have been repeatedly formed, and by this repetition the actions to which they lead have become habitual, the rapidity with which the action follows the judgment gives it a mechanical character; but a little reflection enables us to recognize the steps which led to it, and refer it to its true cause." If the impression of the relation between

leaf movement and human presence becomes very vivid, "it becomes fixed in the memory as a general idea, and the wolf becomes subject to illusions and to false judgments, which are the fruit of the imagination; and if these false judgments extend to a certain number of objects, he becomes the sport of an illusory system, which will lead him into infinite mistakes, although perfectly consistent with the principles which have taken root in his mind." Georges Leroy, *The Intelligence and Perfectibility of Animals from a Philosophic Point of View*, translated from the French (London: Chapman and Hall, 1870 [1768]), 23–24.

40. See Georges Canguilhem's deconstruction of this point in *Knowledge of Life*, ed. Paola Marrati and Todd Meyers, trans. Stefanos Geroulanos and Daniela Ginsburg (New York: Fordham University Press, 2008 [1952]).

41. Letter to Stéphane Le Foll, drafted by the association Houmbaba, unpublished.

42. Cf. the letter to Stéphane Le Foll: "This is to say that it has not occurred to anyone—something that is nevertheless self-evident in wolf country—to change the behavior of these animals by characterizing the various aspects of the territory they share with humans."

43. The use of this technique in France—a technique that is the basis for wolf management at Yellowstone National Park in the United States—is being advocated by the Houmbaba Association under the direction of Antoine Nochy. Nochy brought catch-and-release technology back from Yellowstone and has adapted it to the French context, with its own philosophical dimension. The argument on catch-and-release that follows is based on Nochy's discussion.

44. Antoine Nochy, "Le loup reflète notre rapport au sauvage," *Terre sauvage*, no. 267 (January 2011): 63.

45. Jean-Marc Landry and Fabien Matter, "Projet de création d'un collier 'répulsif' agissant à distance pour protéger le bétail de la prédation du loup," accessible at http://www.protectiondestroupeaux.ch/fileadmin/doc/Berichte/Studien/Projet_collier_r%C3%A9pulsifs_Nov-Agridea.pdf.

46. On this point, see the site of the Institute for the Promotion of and Research on Protector Animals (IPRA), and the downloadable document by Jean-Marc Landry, "Étude sur les interactions loup-troupeau-chien de protection pour l'amélioration des chiens et systèmes de protection des troupeaux," 2014 activity report, December 2014, CanOvis Project 2013–2017, https://www.ipra-landry.com/en/.

47. Landry, "Étude sur les interactions," 22.
48. Landry, "Étude sur les interactions," 18.
49. Landry, "Étude sur les interactions," 18.
50. Landry, "Étude sur les interactions."
51. Landry, "Étude sur les interactions," 24.
52. Landry, *Le loup*.
53. Personal communication.

54. John A. Shivik, Adrian Treves, and Peggy Callahan, "Nonlethal Techniques for Managing Predation: Primary and Secondary Repellents," *USDA National Wildlife Research Center—Staff Publications*, paper 272, published in *Conservation Biology* 17, no. 6 (December 2003): 1531–1537.

55. Niko Tinbergen, *The Herring Gull's World: A Study of the Social Behavior of Birds* (New York: Basic Books, 1961).

56. This term characterizes arrangements that tend to prevent an animal from repeating certain behaviors. They may be primary—physically preventing access—or secondary—associating repellent stimuli with certain experiences. See Shivik et al.

57. A statement offered by Antoine Nochy in a personal communication.

Chapter 4. Animal Political Philosophy

1. Researcher Pierre Charbonnier has provided the key to this way of looking at the various approaches in terms of political philosophy, especially in his article "Prendre les animaux au sérieux: De l'animal politique à la politique des animaux," *Tracés*, special issue (2015): 167–186.

2. See Peter Singer, *Animal Liberation: A New Ethics for Our Treatment of Animals* (New York: New York Review/Random House, 1975).

3. See Tom Regan, *The Case for Animal Rights* (Berkeley: University of California Press, 2004 [1983]).

4. Sue Donaldson and Will Kymlicka, *Zoopolis: A Political Theory of Animal Rights* (Oxford: Oxford University Press, 2011).

5. Michel Foucault, "Intellectuals and Power," conversation with Gilles Deleuze, March 4, 1972, in *Language, Counter-Memory, Practice: Selected Essays and Interviews by Michel Foucault*, trans. and ed. Donald Bouchard (Ithaca, NY: Cornell University Press, 1977), 208.

6. According to Pierre Charbonnier, what justifies skepticism about a diplomatic approach toward "classical positions, is that they fall into a sort of obsession with status: they question what animals are, what type of thing." In the diplomatic approach, "it is the ethological and technical, thus practical, relation that must be privileged, and that governs reflection about duties" (personal communication).

7. It is a major philosophical challenge to show that symbolism and conventional behaviors—including communication, the sharing of information and impressions—exist outside of human language. The philosopher Gilbert Simondon proposes to extend the field of communication to the world of machines and physical interactions in *Communication et information: Cours et conférences* (Chatou: Éditions de la Transparence, 2010). The anthropologist Eduardo Kohn, for his part, proposes an "anthropology beyond the human" that brings to light the omnipresent relations of semiotic communication that are present in living beings in *How*

Forests Think: Toward an Anthropology beyond the Human (Berkeley: University of California Press, 2013).

8. Rudolph Schenkel, "Expression Studies on Wolves," 1947 (http://davemech.org/wolf-news-and-informatino/schenkels-classic-wolf-behavior-study-available-in-english/).

9. Jane Packard, "Wolf Behavior: Reproductive, Social, and Intelligent," in *Wolves: Behavior, Ecology, and Conservation*, ed. L David Mech and Luigi Boitani (Chicago: University of Chicago Press, 2003), 53.

10. L. David Mech and Luigi Boitani, "Wolf Social Ecology," in *Wolves: Behavior, Ecology, and Conservation*, ed. L. David Mech and Luigi Boitani (Chicago: University of Chicago Press, 2003), 18.

11. See Daniel Dennett, *The Intentional Stance* (Cambridge, MA: MIT Press, 1987), 258. This expository tactic has the epistemological function of making it possible to imagine the experimental protocols that would be necessary to isolate the actual degree of intentionality present in this instance of animal behavior.

12. Exaptation is a concept in evolutionary theory that characterizes unanticipated changes in function: biological features selected for an initial use deviate, in a later phase, toward a new function. For example, the feathers of dinosaurs, ancestors of our birds, were not selected initially to allow flight but for heat regulation or for display. Only in a second phase did they facilitate the appearance of flight. See Stephen Jay Gould and Elisabeth S. Vrba, "Exaptation: A Missing Term in the Science of Form," *Paleobiology* 8, no. 1 (Winter 1982): 4–15.

13. Charles Sanders Peirce, *Elements of Logic*, in *Collected Papers of Charles Sanders Peirce*, vol. 2, ed. Charles Hartshorne and Paul Weiss (Cambridge, MA: Harvard University Press, 1932), §228.

14. Charles Sanders Peirce, *The Essential Peirce: Selected Philosophical Writings*, vol. 2 (1893–1913) (Bloomington: Indiana University Press, 1998), 461.

15. Peirce, *Elements of Logic*, §249.

16. Roberte Hamayon, *La chasse à l'âme: Esquisse d'une théorie du chamanisme sibérien* (Nanterre: Société d'ethnologie, 1990), 394.

17. Edward Chace Tolman, "Cognitive Maps in Rats and Men," *Psychological Review* 55, no. 4 (1948): 189–208, https://doi.org/10.1037/h0061626.

18. During a nighttime tracking session by car, in a zone of the Var region that we knew to be traversed by a pack, we saw a wolf cross through a children's playground that was isolated between two villages. This image, which could well reactivate ancestral fears, has to be interpreted in terms of scientific ecology: when two rival species cohabit, a phenomenon of niche segregation leads them to avoid occupying the same places at the same time.

19. R. B. Wielgus and K. A. Peebles, "Effects of Wolf Mortality on Livestock Depredation," *PLoS ONE* 9, no. 12 (2014).

20. Heather M. Bryan et al., "Heavily Hunted Wolves Have Higher Stress and Reproductive Steroids than Wolves with Lower Hunting Pressure," *Functional Ecology* 29, no. 3 (2015): 347–356.

21. Dave Ausband, "Pilot Study Report for Using a Biofence to Manipulate Wolf Pack Movements in Central Idaho," *Montana Cooperative Wildlife Research Unit*, November 2010, https://idfg.idaho.gov/old-web/docs/wolves/reportAnnual11.pdf.

22. Other possibilities include *turbo fladries* (barriers consisting of flags floating in the wind, which seem to stop wolves when they are associated with electric shocks) that have been tried experimentally by the Férus Pastoraloup program in the French Alps. An article by Ed Bangs and colleagues lists the lethal and nonlethal defense measures that have been tried, indicates their advantages and disadvantages as evaluated experimentally in the field, and offers the best current synthesis on this question: "Nonlethal and Lethal Tools to Manage Wolf-Livestock Conflict in the Northwestern United States," in *United States Department of Agriculture Review* (Davis: University of California Press, 2008), 7–16. A presentation of these initiatives intended for livestock breeders is found in an excellent brochure, *Livestock and Wolves: A Guide to Nonlethal Tools and Methods to Reduce Conflicts*, available on the Defenders of Wildlife site: www.defenders.org.

23. On this point, see the excellent article by Arnaud Halloy and Véronique Servais, "Enchanting Gods and Dolphins: A Cross-Cultural Analysis of Uncanny Encounters," *Ethos* 42, no. 4 (December 2014): 479–504. Halloy and Servais isolate the ethological and ethnological arrangements of an experience of enchantment, while maintaining an intention to explain that would not be reductionist.

24. The best way not to see the intelligence and plasticity of other beings, their capacity to take in information and to modulate their collective behavior politically, boils down to deciding a priori that one is dealing with mere beasts: in other words, denying all the immaterial overtures of the creatures.

25. In a memorandum from July 2015, the French minister of ecology announced the creation of ten positions for young people to help manage the "wolf dossier." Among the competencies expected of the applicants, no ethological or ecological knowledge was required, only a hunting license and skill in the use of a rifle. This approach illustrates how far the national plan for wolf management still remains from any diplomatic grasp of the problem.

26. Kohn, *How Forests Think*, 1.

27. John Alcock, *Animal Behavior: An Evolutionary Approach*, 9th ed. (Sunderland, MA: Sinauer Associates, 2009), 281–282.

28. Alain Testart, *Avant l'histoire: L'évolution des sociétés, de Lascaux à Carnac* (Paris: Gallimard, 2012), 496; emphasis added.

29. Testart, *Avant l'histoire*, 496.

30. There is an echo here that would be worth analyzing in relation to natural law as theorized by Spinoza, in which my rights extend precisely to the limits of my power: if I can do it, I have the right to it.

31. Hamayon, *Chasse à l'âme*, 296.

32. It is in a sense a law based on usage in which property is justified only by use, and one cannot appropriate what one does not use: for example, among

the Inuits, a man who does not use his own fox trap must allow another person to place it" (Testart, *Avant l'histoire*, 409).

33. Hamayon, *Chasse à l'âme*, 311.

34. With Neolithization, the ontological status of animals was transformed: considered as *products* through the act of domestication and breeding (and no longer received or taken), they could then become *property*, following the model of land ownership rather than that of usufruct. Whereas in the symbolic system of hunter-gatherers an animal had been a particular, individual form of common good included in a system of exchange in a benevolent environment, in the system of livestock farming it became a product included in a system of property ownership on an inanimate and appropriable earth.

35. Jean de La Fontaine, *The Complete Fables of Jean de La Fontaine*, trans. Norman R. Shapiro (Urbana: University of Illinois Press, 2007), book 10, no. 4, 273–274.

Chapter 5. Orienting Wolf Pack Cultures

1. R. O. Stephenson, "Nunamiut Eskimos, Wildlife Biologists, and Wolves," in *Wolves of the World: Perspectives of Behavior, Ecology, and Conservation*, ed. Fred H. Harrington and Paul C. Pacquet (Park Ridge, NJ: Noyes, 1982), 438, 439.

2. On these epistemological points, see the excellent prospective synthesis edited by Florence Burgat, *Penser le comportement animal: Contribution à une critique du réductionnisme* (Paris: Quae, 2010).

3. Frans de Waal, *The Bonobo and the Atheist: In Search of Humanism among the Primates* (New York: W. W. Norton, 2013).

4. During a tracking session in the Haut-Var region, my companions and I spent a long time following an enigmatic set of trails: massive prints, whose form implied an adult male, probably the reproducer, were followed by small prints implying a cub. These two lines ran parallel to a claylike riverbank. Several times, the prints of the alpha dug perpendicularly into the riverbed for a meter or two and then stopped. Behind this track, the prints of the cub turned toward the river, but remained on the bank. This schema remained mysterious, until we came across scattered crayfish shells emptied of their meat. The hypothesis became clear: we had been following a fishing lesson. The cub followed its father, then stopped to watch him from the bank every time the father went into the relatively shallow water to hunt a crayfish.

5. Steven H. Fritts, Robert O. Stephenson, Robert D. Hayes, and Luigi Boitani, "Wolves and Humans," in *Wolves: Behavior, Ecology, and Conservation*, ed. L. David Mech and Luigi Boitani (Chicago: University of Chicago Press, 2003), 308.

6. On this point, see Eytan Avital and Eva Jablonka, *Animal Traditions: Behavioural Inheritance in Evolution* (Cambridge: Cambridge University Press, 2005 [2000]).

7. Heinrich Rickert, *Science and History: A Critique of Positive Epistemology*, trans. George Reisman (Princeton, NJ: Van Nostrand, 1962 [1899]).

8. *Webster's Third New International Dictionary* defines nomology as "the science of the laws of the mind" (Springfield, MA: G. R. C. Merriam, 1963).

9. William Whewell, *History of the Inductive Sciences from the Earliest to the Present Time* (New York: D. Appleton, 1858).

10. Alfred de Vigny, "La maison du berger," a 336-line poem in the collection *Les destinées* (Paris: Droz, 1947 [1864]), 54.

Chapter 6. Toward the Social Sciences of Wolves: Interiority, Variability, Sociality

1. Thelma Rowell, "A Few Peculiar Primates," in *Primate Encounter: Models of Science, Gender, and Society*, ed. Shirley C. Strum and Linda Marie Fedigan (Chicago: University of Chicago Press, 2000), cited in Vinciane Despret, "Sheep Do Have Opinions," trans. Liz Carey-Libbrecht, in *Making Things Public: Atmosphere of Democracy*, ed. Bruno Latour and Peter Weibel (Cambridge, MA: MIT Press, 2005), 361.

2. The approach I am adopting in this chapter entails looking for trails to follow rather than relying on established foundations, improvising tools rather than discovering existing structures, and envisioning methodological attitudes rather than propositions that would be demonstrably "true" from the standpoint of the prevailing epistemological regimes.

3. Jane Packard, "Wolf Behavior: Reproductive, Social, and Intelligent," in *Wolves: Behavior, Ecology, and Conservation*, ed. L. David Mech and Luigi Boitani (Chicago: University of Chicago Press, 2003), 42.

4. Packard, "Wolf Behavior," 56.

5. Packard, "Wolf Behavior," 56.

6. That animal subjectivities exist is now a commonplace in ethology. From now on, we have to ask what is meant by "animal subjectivity." We may legitimately be skeptical of what certain thinkers present as gifts offered by Moderns to animals, such as the status of subject, or personhood. Might these actually be poisoned gifts, based on a misguided anthropomorphism? A better way to put the question might be to ask what would be capable of restoring to animals the ontological dignity that belongs to them. "Personhood" was in fact originally a theological concept developed by Boethius that established moral and legal responsibility through the possession of a soul offered by God. Is this really what we mean to confer on nonhuman animals? "Subjecthood" is an ontological concept that rests on a transcendent separation from one's environment, which is reified, construed as consisting in objects; this concept underlies the mode of existence of the Moderns, which has nothing in common with the mode of existence of animals—experienced in the *bios*, in their own

environment—and indeed fails even to account for all human modes of existence. We have to be suspicious of the implications that such a concept brings along in its wake. Tom Regan's idea of a "subject-of-a-life" seems more economical, from this standpoint; see Tom Regan, *The Case for Animal Rights* (Berkeley: University of California Press, 2004 [1983]).

7. See L. David Mech, "Alpha Status, Dominance, and Division of Labor in Wolf Packs," *Canadian Journal of Zoology* 77 (1999): 1196–1203.

8. See, for example, Bruno Latour, *Politics of Nature*, trans. Catherine Porter (Cambridge, MA: Harvard University Press, 2004), and Eduardo Vivieros de Castro, *Cannibal Metaphysics*, ed. and trans. Peter Skafish (Minneapolis, MN: Univocal, 2014).

9. That of a hyper-living being, not of an extra-living being (in the sense of extraterrestrial), one might say.

10. Quoted in Packard, "Wolf Behavior," 60.

11. Erik Zimen, *The Wolf: A Species in Danger* (New York: Delacorte, 1981), 173.

Chapter 7. A Laboratory Called Yellowstone

1. Douglas W. Smith and Gary Ferguson, *Decade of the Wolf* (Guilford, CT: Lyons Press, 2005).

2. Smith and Ferguson, *Decade of the Wolf*, 63.

3. Smith and Ferguson, *Decade of the Wolf*, 91.

4. Smith and Ferguson, *Decade of the Wolf*, 71–72.

5. Why is this science taboo? Essentially for reasons proper to the sociology of science: it requires departing from the protocols of scientific discourse and from the linked quantification and mathematization of experiments, an approach that constitutes the dominant regime for delivering proof in the natural sciences. "Serious" researchers have to publish in *Science* and *Nature*—but these journals are not yet endowed with a reliable animist epistemology. On animist epistemology, see section 9 of the present volume: "A Differently Rational Shamanism."

6. Thus, in order to theorize intelligence, psychology has had to protocolize its definition by breaking it down into quantitative concepts, producing, for example, the concept of an "intelligence quotient," or IQ. Alfred Binet, the inventor of the intelligence test, grasped the limits of protocolization in an elegant paradox, and he had a way of replacing the complex, polysemic notions of common sense with stipulative concepts defined by the meaning assigned to them. A stipulative definition cannot be precise or imprecise: the concept itself defines the thing. To a critic who asked Binet: "But what is intelligence, after all?" Binet responded: "It is what my test measures."

7. This is an observation on my part; I have not managed to analyze the causes or reasons for the phenomenon.

8. We can hypothesize that the philosophically most fruitful knowledge acquired by the Yellowstone wolf specialists reverts to the heretical science encrypted in their popular works. The same thing may be true of many prominent ethologists and primatologists (for example, Jane Goodall, Thelma Rowell, Frans de Waal, or the Premacks); it suffices to compare the articles they have published in peer-reviewed journals (which are invaluable for advancing knowledge on one front, known as "scientific") with the formulas that they allow themselves to propose in the works they write for a general audience (which advance knowledge on a different front: the one that opens the door, philosophically, to alternative ways of thinking about nonhuman animals). The articles of these scientists pave the path of knowledge, while their books blaze other trails and shed new light on our relations to living beings and their mutations.

9. Smith and Ferguson, *Decade of the Wolf*, 77.
10. Smith and Ferguson, *Decade of the Wolf*, 76.
11. Smith and Ferguson, *Decade of the Wolf*, 78.
12. Smith and Ferguson, *Decade of the Wolf*, 78.
13. Smith and Ferguson, *Decade of the Wolf*, 78.
14. Smith and Ferguson, *Decade of the Wolf*.
15. Smith and Ferguson, *Decade of the Wolf*, 80–81.
16. Smith and Ferguson, *Decade of the Wolf*, 82.
17. Smith and Ferguson, *Decade of the Wolf*, 82.
18. Smith and Ferguson, *Decade of the Wolf*, 83.

19. Her story is told in the documentary film *Wolves: A Legend Returns to Yellowstone* (National Geographic, 2007).

20. Cited in Michael Gibney, "The Rise and Fall of the Druid Empire," *Bozeman Daily Chronicle*, March 20, 2010.

21. Personal communication reported by Antoine Nochy.

22. Strictly speaking, it seems that "feudalism" designates the mode of production as described by Karl Marx and Georges Duby, whereas "feudality" designates the political and territorial relations between overlords and vassals. See Karl Marx and Friedrich Engels, *The German Ideology*, translated from the German (New York: International, 1970 [1845]), and Georges Duby, *Féodalité* (Paris: Gallimard, 1996).

23. Most of today's major wolf experts have engaged in the exercise of revealing their own anthropomorphic understanding of wolves' mysterious mode of existence. Some of this work has been brought together in a book explicitly designed to give these experts the right to use "unscientific" discourse to present their findings. The result is a work of unprecedented philosophical richness about what a wolf can be, as seen by trained ethologists: Richard P. Thiel, Allison C. Thiel, and Marianne Strozewski, *Wild Wolves We Have Known* (Minneapolis, MN: International Wolf Center, 2013).

24. Thelma E. Rowell, "The Concept of Social Dominance," *Behavioral Biology* 11, no. 2 (June 1974): 131–154.

25. Finally, thanks to the circularity reconquered by biomorphism in the nexus of the animal world, these behavioral sequences become enlightening for the understanding of humans themselves. (Who receives attention before the group heads to the dinner table?)

26. In very large packs, the breeders are not always the ones who take the lead.

27. Rudolph Schenkel, "Expression Studies on Wolves," 1947 (http://davemech.org/wolf-news-and-informatino/schenkels-classic-wolf-behavior-study-available-in-english/).

28. On this point, see Peter Steinhart, *The Company of Wolves* (New York: Alfred A. Knopf, 1995).

29. The philosopher Hans Blumenberg introduced the term "metaphorology" to describe the study of metaphors of a given discourse as a way of bringing to light the intrinsic difficulties in conceptualization and thereby the underlying meaning of that discourse. Blumenberg views metaphors as "fossil conductors," "antechambers of the formation of concepts," means of surmounting the resistances that reality opposes to attempts to grasp it. The historical truth of absolute metaphors, he writes, "is *pragmatic* in a very broad sense. By providing a point of orientation, the content of absolute metaphors determines a particular attitude or conduct [*Verhalten*]; they give structure to a world, representing the nonexperienceable, nonapprehensible totality of the real." See Hans Blumenberg, *Paradigms for a Metaphorology*, trans. Robert Savage (Ithaca, NY: Cornell University Press, 2010 [1960]), 14.

30. Andrew Whiten, Jane Goodall, W. C. McGrew, et al., "Cultures in Chimpanzees," *Nature* 399 (1999): 682–685; Rick McIntyre, https://www.yellowstone.org/rick-mcintyres-notes-from-the-field/; Frans de Waal, *The Bonobo and the Atheist: In Search of Humanism among the Primates* (New York: W. W. Norton, 2013); Karl von Frisch, *The Dancing Bees: An Account of the Life and Senses of the Honey Bee*, trans. Dora Isle and Norman Walker (London: Methuen, 1966 [1927]).

31. See Rowell, "Peculiar Primates," cited in Vinciane Despret, "Sheep Do Have Opinions," trans. Liz Carey-Libbrecht, in *Making Things Public: Atmosphere of Democracy*, ed. Bruno Latour and Peter Weibel (Cambridge, MA: MIT Press, 2005), 366: "The way in which males organize themselves has proved to be far more unpredictable. Making it visible requires constant attention to repetitions. Only after a long time does the researcher notice that every time the flock is about to move, one of the males makes a gesture that is almost imperceptible to humans, consisting of lifting its head slightly and pointing its muzzle in a particular direction. Sometimes the group starts walking, sometimes not until another male produces a similar gesture and possibly leads the group in the indicated direction."

32. See Daniel Dennett's analysis in *The Intentional Stance* (Cambridge, MA: MIT Press, 1987), 250–257.

33. Some documentaries about the wolves in Yellowstone have taken a different and liberating narrative direction: see for example "The She Wolf of Yellowstone," "In the Valley of the Wolves," or "The Rise of the Black Wolf."

34. The Katmai National Park in Alaska has installed cameras that film certain key points of its wilderness continuously. In the summer, one can watch live footage on one's own screen for days on end, without commentary, without set-ups, without staging, as grizzlies fish salmon in the rapids of a rushing stream: www.explore.org/live-cams.

Chapter 8. On Intentionality: Toward an Animist Epistemology

1. Daniel Dennett, *The Intentional Stance* (Cambridge, MA: MIT Press, 1987).

2. Daniel Dennett, *Darwin's Dangerous Idea: Evolution and the Meanings of Life* (New York: Simon & Schuster, 1995), 212–220.

3. Dennett, *Intentional Stance*, 246. Cf. C. Lloyd Morgan, *An Introduction to Comparative Psychology* (London: W. Scott, 1894).

4. Dennett, *Intentional Stance*, 246–247.

5. Robert M. Seyfarth and Dorothy L. Cheney, "How Vervet Monkeys Perceive Their Grunts: Field Playback Experiments," *Animal Behavior* 30, no. 3 (August 1982): 739–751.

6. Dennett, *Intentional Stance*, 252.

7. Richard Dawkins, *The Selfish Gene* (Oxford: Oxford University Press, 2016 [1976]).

8. Dennett, *Intentional Stance*, 258.

9. Dennett, *Intentional Stance*, 258.

10. Dennett, *Intentional Stance*, 258.

11. Mark Rowlands, *The Philosopher and the Wolf: Lessons from the Wild on Love, Death and Happiness* (New York: Pegasus, 2009).

12. See Rowlands, *Philosopher*, 60.

13. Rowlands, *Philosopher*, 61.

14. Rowlands, *Philosopher*, 62.

15. Rowlands, *Philosopher*, 63.

16. Rowlands, *Philosopher*, 78.

17. Rowlands, *Philosopher*, 80.

18. In an interview, McIntyre spoke of his affection and esteem for the alpha male of the Druid Peak Pack, Number 21, whom he observed over nearly a decade.

19. Rowlands, *Philosopher*, 103, 101.

20. Konrad Lorenz spontaneously uses an analogous metaphor in *King Solomon's Ring: New Light on Animal Ways*, trans. Marjorie Kerr Wilson (New York: Thomas A. Crowell, 1952). In a situation where a wolf losing a battle offers his neck to his adversary, "the victor will definitely not close in on his less fortunate rival. You can see that he would like to, but he just cannot!" (188). "The supplicant always offers to his adversary the most vulnerable parts of his body, or, to be more exact, that

part *against which every killing attack is inevitably directed!"* (193). Lorenz goes on to evoke examples from the Homeric epics and Nordic sagas in which "an appeal for mercy does not seem to have raised an 'inner obstruction' which was entirely insurmountable. Homer's heroes were certainly not as softhearted as the wolves of Whipsnade! In any case, the poet cites numerous instances where the supplicant was slaughtered with or without compunction. . . . It was not till the era of knight-errantry that it was no longer considered 'sporting' to kill a man who begged for mercy. The Christian knight is the first who, for reasons of tradition and religious morals, is as chivalrous as is the wolf from the depth of his natural impulses and inhibitions" (196). Acknowledging that wolves' behavior is not truly analogous to human social mores, Lorenz nevertheless admits to "harbouring sentimental feelings: I think it a truly magnificent thing that one wolf finds himself unable to bite the proffered neck of the other, but still more so that the other relies upon him for this amazing restraint." He goes on to confess that he draws from this observation of the ethological arrangements for inhibiting interspecies aggression "a new and deeper understanding" of the Gospel injunction to 'turn the other cheek'" (197). A wolf has "enlightened" him: the point of this etho-theological maxim is not to invite a second blow but to inhibit the enemy's very desire to attack, the impulse to act with violence.

21. This analysis can be expanded by evoking an enigmatic parallel between the motifs of wolf and human life. First of all, there is the model of the dispersant wolf, who, as an adolescent, can leave the pack led by his father, the alpha male who monopolizes reproductive power. The young wolf's adventurous wandering, driven by inaccessible motives (the desire to reproduce? To get out from under the hierarchical yoke imposed by the pack?) leads him to look for a female companion with whom he will establish a new pack on new territory, founding a dynasty. Here we find with disconcerting precision the fundamental motif of the medieval or chivalric initiatory adventure (found in Vladimir Propp's morphology of folktales, for example): the young prince leaves the family hearth out of a desire to prove himself and escape the royal yoke; he goes off on an adventure, meets a princess, and—thanks to the matrimonial alliance—conquers a new kingdom, founding a dynasty. This motif is echoed by another intriguing one: we could posit that the omega individual in the pack, who is subject to opprobrium and onto whom all the accumulated frustrations of the pack are loaded, is systematically a physically weak individual at the low end of the hierarchy. It turns out that this wolf is often an *older* beta male or female, that is, someone just below the head of the pack, who has rebelled against the alpha wolf or has not accepted the latter's dominance gracefully enough and has been defeated in a fight. Here there is a parallel with the model of the Devil's destiny in Judeo-Christian mythology. It is as if the structures of wolf life revealed animal primordia: transcendentals of essential human structures supplying deep-seated cultural and mythological schemas. In other words, a common architectonic *form of life*, allowed by eco-etho-evolutionary convergences of the conditions of life that make this existential and mythological parallelism comprehensible.

22. Rowlands, *Philosopher*, 109. Rowlands's error in this new Nietzschean metaphorics lies in his undifferentiated assimilation of humans to apes, whereas Nietzsche's more fine-grained approach finds both ape and wolf types in human beings, and perhaps in each human being. Rowlands makes a conceptual error when he metaphorizes the status of the ape, then takes seriously its phylogenetic affiliation with the human; in so doing, he induces a latent misanthropy that is unfounded here. The moral type that he finds in wolves also exists in humans; that is why humans are drawn to it, why it is not forbidden to them. If we read Nietzsche carefully, we find that this type is even quite widespread among humans, who are not biologically, specifically, a species condemned to ressentiment.

23. Rowlands, *Philosopher*, 78.

24. On the epic, struggle and conquest, we come back to the question of animal primordia. It is intriguing that it is among wolves that we are rediscovering today the epic thrust that is often lacking in human existence. Is this attributable to the coupling of their ethological-ethical and political tonality with the presence of risk? This is possible. The fact remains that they recall passions that we have forgotten, and they sketch out animal primordia whose philosophical status still needs to be clarified.

Chapter 9. A Differently Rational Shamanism

1. Philippe Descola, *Beyond Nature and Culture*, trans. Janet Lloyd (Chicago: University of Chicago Press, 2013 [2005]).

2. See Eduardo Vivieros de Castro, *Cannibal Metaphysics*, ed. and trans. Peter Skafish (Minneapolis, MN: Univocal, 2014), and also his excellent monograph on the Araweté, *From the Enemy's Point of View: Humanity and Divinity in an Amazonian Society*, trans. Catherine V. Howard (Chicago: University of Chicago Press, 2020).

3. See Philippe Descola, *La vie des idées*: "To whom does nature belong"? www.laviedesidees.fr, and his book *L'écologie des autres: L'anthropologie et la question de la nature* (Paris: Quae, coll. Sciences en question, 2011).

4. Philippe Descola, *La composition des mondes* (Paris: Flammarion, 2014).

5. A technical objection emerges once we understand animism in Descola's rigorous sense, which postulates a "discontinuity of physicalities" that seems to be discordant with our most fundamental beliefs about organic and inorganic matter.

6. On this point, see Daniel Chamovitz, *What a Plant Knows: A Field Guide to the Senses* (New York: Scientific American, 2013).

7. See the excellent article by Sunita A. Ramesh et al., "Signalling Modulates Plant Growth by Directly Regulating the Activity of Plant-Specific Anion Transporters," *Nature Communications* 6 (2015): 10.1038/ncomms8879.

8. This example points up the fact that there is a concept capable of sketching a fringe common to the modes of existence of living beings, if we keep open a sufficiently large spectrum of meaning: *stress* is in fact a concept that, in varied but

unified senses, characterizes an existential status of single-celled organisms, plants, animals, humans, and perhaps even complex ecological entities.

9. See the introduction to Grégory Quenet, *Qu'est-ce que l'histoire environnementale?* (Paris: Champ Vallon, 2014).

10. This attitude converges on several points with the attention to the "powers to act" that Bruno Latour calls for in *Facing Gaia* (trans. Catherine Porter [Cambridge: Polity, 2017]), especially in the second lecture titled "How Not to [De]animate Nature?" The difference between the two approaches lies nevertheless in the stress placed, in ethocentrism, on a strictly ethological approach, which reconsiders the problem of the passivity of matter not in terms of powers to act but in differentiated types of *behaviors*. In the process, Latour gives a specificity to living beings, to the extent that, unlike the Mississippi River in Latour's example, living beings have behaviors in which something like their own interests are always involved. What is involved in the behavior of the Mississippi River is the biotic community of which it constitutes the a-biotic conditions.

11. See for example her key book: Val Plumwood, *Environmental Culture: The Ecological Crisis of Reason* (New York: Routledge, 2002).

12. Val Plumwood, "Nature in the Active Voice," *Australian Humanities Review* 46 (2009): 121; cited by Deborah Bird Rose in "Val Plumwood's Philosophical Animism: Attentive Interactions in the Sentient World," *Environmental Humanities* 3, no. 1 (1 May 2013): 98.

13. Plumwood, *Environmental Culture*, 175.

14. Cited in Rose, "Plumwood's Philosophical Animism," 106. Upon reflection, it seems that the tone and narrative choices in the introduction to my own book have converged coincidentally with Plumwood's project.

15. See the National Wildlife Federation site, www.nwf.org.

16. See Michael L. Rosenzweig, *Win-Win Ecology: How the Earth's Species Can Survive in the Midst of Human Enterprise* (New York: Oxford University Press, 2003), 7: "We can learn how to reconcile our own use of the land with that of many other species. Maybe even most of them. If they have access to our farm fields, our forests, our city parks, schoolyards, military bases, timberlands, yes, even to our backyards, then they have a chance. We shall thus be able to minimize their risk of extinction."

17. A solitary face-to-face encounter with a wolf can resemble a disappointing meeting with a lover. One night, after spotting a wolf in a pack on the hunt, or crossing paths with him rummaging in a rodent's hole, it struck me that I was investing this encounter with a prominent symbolic and affective dimension, whereas the wolf evinced sovereign disdain for the event and left the scene, either trotting or galloping.

18. This philosophical approach to tracking has been described by Georges Leroy, a lieutenant of royal hunts who was close to the encyclopedists Diderot and d'Alembert: "The sportsman, in his pursuit of the animal, has no object but the

discovery of its hiding-place; but the philosopher reads in its steps the history of its thoughts, detects its perplexities, its fears, its hopes; sees the grounds upon which it has moved cautiously, has quickened or suspended its course; and there is no doubt as to these grounds, unless . . . we choose the alternative of supposing effects without a cause." See Georges Leroy, *The Intelligence and Perfectibility of Animals from a Philosophic Point of View*, translated from the French (London: Chapman and Hall, 1870 [1768]), 25.

19. See the excellent field guide by James C. Halfpenny (a PhD in biology) and Tracy Furman, *Tracking Wolves: The Basics* (Gardiner, MT: A Naturalist's World, 2010).

20. Michael Soulé and Reed Noss, "Rewilding and Biodiversity: Complementary Goals for Continental Conservation," *Wild Earth* (Fall 1998): 19–28.

21. See her plea for the preservation of spaces in which the large predators can move freely: Cristina Eisenberg, *The Carnivore Way: Coexisting with and Conserving North America's Predators* (Washington, DC: Island Press, 2014).

22. Cited in Eisenberg, *Carnivore Way*, 21.

23. Eisenberg, *Carnivore Way*, 30.

24. Wilhelm Dilthey, *The Formation of the Historical World in the Human Sciences*, ed. Rudolf A. Makkree and Frithjof Rodi, translated from the German (Princeton, NJ: Princeton University Press, 2002 [1910]).

25. Castro, *Cannibal Metaphysics*, 55.

26. Castro, *Cannibal Metaphysics*, 60.

27. Eduardo Kohn, *How Forests Think: Toward an Anthropology beyond the Human* (Berkeley: University of California Press, 2013), 2.

28. From this angle, perspectivism appears as the *corollary* to an ontology of relations (as we shall see in part 3), in the field of practical philosophy.

29. Philippe Descola, "Un monde animé," in *La fabrique des images: Visions du monde et formes de la représentation*, ed. Philippe Descola (Paris: Somogy, 2010), 26.

30. Descola, "Un monde animé," 26. If the inner life of an animal is said here to be perceived as human, it is in order to depict with precision the "personality" of the animal: its ontological status as "who." We shall look more closely at this aspect of Amerindian perspectivism further on. There are theoretical controversies over the meaning of "human" in the passage cited. In the strong sense, the word refers to the idea that the human form is at the origin of all the other forms of life. In a broad sense, "human" can be understood as the most self-evident way, for us humans, to designate a "person," in the sense of a being endowed with an inner life. I am choosing to interpret the word in the broad sense here.

31. For a more detailed look at such objects, see Descola, "Un monde animé," 21–69.

32. See his website: www.sanfordwilliams.com.

33. See Denis Duclos, *The Werewolf Complex: America's Fascination with Violence*, trans. Amanda Pingree (Oxford: Berg, 1998).

34. This said, one observes with alarm that this is perhaps true of all things that have a history, that is, of everything.

35. Castro, *Cannibal Metaphysics*, 60–61.

36. Castro, *Cannibal Metaphysics*, 61n.22.

37. Castro, *Cannibal Metaphysics*, 56.

38. Boethius's canonical text, *Contra Eutychen et Nestorium, De duabus naturis*, 1337 (Turnhout, Belgium: Brepols, 2010), is presented as a critique of heresies in the mid-fourteenth century.

39. As demonstrated by Michel Foucault, for example, in *The Order of Things: An Archaeology of the Human Sciences*, translated from the French (New York: Pantheon, 1971 [1970]).

40. See, for example, Georges Canguilhem, *Knowledge of Life*, trans. Stefanos Geroulanos and Daniela Ginsburg, ed. Paola Marrati and Todd Meyers (New York: Fordham University Press, 2008 [1952]), chapter 5, "The Living and Its Milieu," 98–120; and Hans Jonas, *The Phenomenon of Life: Toward a Philosophical Biology* (New York: Harper & Row, 1966).

41. Through this perspectivist reasoning, Van Hoven rejoins the singular experience described by Aldo Leopold as "thinking like a mountain," identifying himself with the "mortal fear" that vegetation can sustain toward herbivores. Aldo Leopold, *A Sand County Almanac and Other Writings on Ecology and Conservation* (New York: Library of America, 2013 [1949]), 114–117.

42. On this discovery, made by the zoologist Wouter Van Hoven from the University of Pretoria, see, for example, Sylvia Hughes, "Antelope Activate the Acacia's Alarm System," *New Scientist*, no. 1736 (September 29, 1990).

43. This local discovery had profound implications: among other things, it led to the deduction of an elegant explanation for a timeless mystery concerning the large African herbivores in the savanna, namely, why they tended to feed by following tree lines *against the wind*.

44. On this point, see Bernd Heinrich, *Mind of the Raven: Investigations and Adventures with Wolf-Birds* (New York: Harper Perennial, 2007). Heinrich, a corvid specialist, only discovered the strict ethological meaning of the interactions between wolves and crows by accrediting, as a hypothesis, the Inuit belief that crows *deliberately guide* human hunters or wolves, with their thrice-repeated feeding call, toward reindeer, so as to feed, later, on the carcasses of prey that they cannot kill themselves.

45. Daniel Dennett, *Kinds of Minds: Toward an Understanding of Consciousness* (New York: Basic Books, 1996).

46. Archie Fire Lame Deer and Richard Erdoes, *Gift of Power: The Life and Teachings of a Lakota Medicine Man* (Santa Fe, NM: Bear, 1992), 88.

47. Lame Deer and Erdoes, *Gift of Power*, 88.

48. Of course, "the language of animals" has a richer and broader range of meanings in animism or shamanism, from the song that charms prey to the interpretation of dream dialogues. On this point, see, for example, Philippe Descola, *The*

Spears of Twilight: Life and Death in the Amazon Jungle, trans. Janet Lloyd (New York: New Press, 1996 [1994]). It is important to distinguish between the various meanings of animism and the various meanings of shamanism. By animism, I refer here to an ontological scheme that recognizes interiority among nonhumans, following the lead of Castro and Descola. By shamanism, I refer to a mode of managing human experience rooted in hunting cultures, in the wake of Hamayon's work.

49. On the specificity of influence as a mode of action, see the proposals of Tobie Nathan, especially in *L'influence qui guérit* (Paris: Odile Jacob, 2009).

50. See Roberte Hamayon, *La chasse à l'âme: Esquisse d'une théorie du chamanisme sibérien* (Paris: Société d'ethnologie, 1990), 741: "It is as though shamanic action were aimed precisely at governing the random aspects of life, by bending them to desire or by denying them; isn't tossing a dissymmetrical object into the air again and again until it lands on the 'right' side a way of betting on the future?" Hamayon characterizes Siberian shamanism as follows: "It involves a rudimentary, all-purpose mediation procedure that presupposes a specific conception of human beings, the world, and society, as well as their interrelationships. The notion of exchange is at the heart of shamanic thought" (740). Above all, there is a fundamental connection between hunting, alliances, and shamanism: thus Hamayon posits that shamanism in itself is rooted in the hunting life, by virtue of a relation of necessity based on what seems to characterize shamanism on the most general level: management of what is random, unpredictable.

51. Permaculture claims to offer models for action of this order: "Traditional agriculture was labour intensive, industrial agriculture is energy intensive, and permaculture-designed systems are information and design intensive." David Holmgren, *Permaculture: Principles and Pathways beyond Sustainability* (Hepburn, Australia: Holmgren Design Services, 2002), 13.

Chapter 10. On Tracking

1. Patrick Blandin and Maxime Lamotte, "Recherche d'une entité écologique correspondant à l'étude des paysages: La notion d'écocomplexe," *Bulletin d'écologie* 19, no. 4 (1988): 547–555; Patrick Blandin and Maxime Lamotte, "L'organisation hiérarchique des systèmes écologiques," *Atti del 3° Congresso Nazionale della Societa Italiana di Ecologia*, Siena, October 21–24, 1987 (Siena: ATTI 7, 1989), 35–48.

2. See Louis Liebenberg, *The Art of Tracking: The Origin of Science* (Claremont, South Africa: David Philip, 1990), and *The Origin of Science: The Evolutionary Roots of Scientific Reasoning and Its Implications for Citizen* Science (Cape Town, South Africa: Cyber Tracker, 2013).

3. See John Joseph Shea, "The Origins of Lithic Projectile Technology: Evidence from Africa, the Levant, and Europe," *Journal of Archaeological Science* 33, no. 5 (2006): 823–846.

4. The human animal is too slow to catch an antelope by sprinting, not agile enough to leap on it like a panther, not strong enough to kill it with a bite like a lion's, not able to sustain running speed long enough to tire the animal out and finish it off as wolves do. Hence the general conclusion that humans need to be "intelligent," since their physical attributes are insufficient for success in the natural hunting process. Yet it seems that our specificity is based on our athletic attributes, which are as effective as those of other animals: our distinctive attributes as primates who have become naked runners (prodigious athletes in endurance races, athletes gifted in eye-hand coordination, athletes excelling at hurling projectiles). So intelligence has not developed owing to some vague physical weakness, but rather from a certain athleticism combined with mental exigencies. To get beyond our archaic myths about the origins of our intelligence, we need a hypothesis that is far more precise and more rigorously evolutionist.

5. See the extraordinary sequence in the BBC's *The Life of Mammals* (2002–2003), with commentary by David Attenborough, available on YouTube.

6. "The art of tracking involves each and every sign of animal presence that can be found in nature: scent, feeding signs, urine, feces, saliva, pellets, territorial signs, paths, shelters, vocal and other auditory signs, visual signs, incidental signs, circumstantial signs, and skeletal signs. Spoor are not left by living creatures alone. Leaves and twigs rolling in the wind, long grass sweeping the ground, and dislodged stones rolling down a steep slope each leave their distinctive signs." Louis Liebenberg, Adriaan Louw, and Mark Elbroch, *Practical Tracking: A Guide to Following Footprints and Finding Animals* (Mechanicsburg, PA: Stackpole Books, 2010), 89.

7. Liebenberg, *Art of Tracking*, 18.

8. Liebenberg et al., *Practical Tracking*, 118–119.

9. Louis Liebenberg, *A Field Guide to the Animal Tracks of Southern Africa* (Cape Town, South Africa: David Philip, 1990), 33.

10. Liebenberg et al., *Practical Tracking*, 83.

11. We should also note the existence of *random prediction*, an alternative to giving up when there are no visible clues. It is not a stretch to suppose that the recourse to shamanism can be attributed in part to this practice: the need to master the unpredictable, to trace paths despite absolute uncertainty. The Kalahari Bushmen traditionally used divination with leather discs for this purpose, consulting the discs before a hunt to determine what direction to take, in the absence of any information whatsoever. Liebenberg offers two hypotheses: either the discs were interpreted in the light of what was already known about the movements of the game animals, or else they were used to diversify the search routes in a random fashion, in recognition of the animals' ability to change their habits in response to the known habits of the hunters, and thus to introduce a compensatory unpredictability into the hunt. Liebenberg et al., *Practical Tracking*, 120.

12. Liebenberg et al., *Practical Tracking*, 121–122.

13. During a tracking session in the spring of 2015, I followed the trail of a female wolf, track by track, on a clay path, when I came across a very long, wide, flat stone. No traces of claws on the rock or the moss. I raised my head and saw, in the distance beyond the stone, a hole in the brush, between juniper bushes, which could have caught the attention of the wolf and spurred her desire to go straight ahead. By following the imaginary route, I quickly found her traces on the muddy surface of this path; and there was the same claw mark with a crack at the right front; and there was urine behind the back feet: I had found my female. I lost her again at the next flat rock, but the limestone formed gullies that channeled displacements, so by choosing the one that went in the basic direction of her movement, I found her tracks again in one of the valleys.

14. For Peirce, "induction designates, rather, the testing of hypotheses, whether the test ends up in a confirmation or a refutation": Claudine Tiercelin offers this clarification in her discussion of Peirce's three-phase method, *C. S. Peirce et le pragmatisme* (Paris: Presses Universitaires de France, 1993), 95–98.

15. Ian Hacking, "'Vrai'—les valeurs et les sciences," *Actes de la recherche en sciences sociales*, no. 141 (2002): 13–20, DOI: 10.3917/arss.141.0013, https://www.cairn.info/revue-actes-de-la-recherche-en-sciences-sociales-2002-1-page-13.htm.

16. Liebenberg et al., *Practical Tracking*, 87.

17. Liebenberg, *Origin of Science*, 37.

18. Liebenberg, *Origin of Science*, 38–39.

19. The paradox is that, quite late in the history of humanity, this original and matricial act we know as tracking was delegated to wolves domesticated as dogs (this is Estelle Zhong Mengual's idea, shared with me in a personal communication). For perhaps some thirty-five thousand years (but this dating will surely change as archaeological studies advance), dogs have maintained an activity that underlies our humanity. This enigmatic phenomenon can be interpreted in terms of a master-slave dialectic, or in terms of reducing the selective pressure on the function (tracking) of a trait (cognitive capabilities) that is a condition of exaptation. The trait became available for fulfilling other functions: abstract thought, inquiries into weather, plants, stars, seas, death, childbearing, good and evil. This would give an additional dimension to the temporal coincidence between the symbolic explosion of humanity some forty-five thousand years go and the domestication of dogs more than thirty-five thousand years ago.

20. On this point, see Carlo Ginzburg's genealogy of research skills in history viewed as functional exaptations on the basis of cognitive capacities selected for hunting during the process of evolution, in "Clues: Roots of an Evidential Paradigm," *Clues, Myths, and the Historical Method*, trans. John Tedeschi and Anne C. Tedeschi (Baltimore, MD: Johns Hopkins University Press, 1994), 96–125.

21. Stephen Jay Gould and Elisabeth S. Vrba, "Exaptation: A Missing Term in the Science of Form," *Paleobiology* 8, no. 1 (Winter 1982): 13.

22. For the historian Carlo Ginzburg, reading tracks is also at the origin of the cognitive capacity that consists in going back from apparently insignificant experimental facts to a complex reality that is not directly subject to experimentation. According to Ginzburg, the gesture of the prehistoric tracker is the oldest gesture in the intellectual history of the human genus. For millennia, humans, through their hunting activity, have learned to reconstruct the forms and movements of invisible prey on the basis of prints preserved in mud, traces left behind. Man "learned to execute complex mental operations with lightning speed, in the depth of a forest or in a prairie full of ambushes" (*Clues*, 102). From this perspective, tracking can be seen as the source of semiotics: behavior oriented toward the analysis of individual cases that can only be reconstructed on the basis of traces, symptoms, clues. It can also be seen as the basis for the evidential paradigm that characterizes a whole swath of modern science, according to Ginzburg: medicine, jurisprudence, history, and paleontology.

23. Paul Shepard, ed., *The Only World We've Got: A Paul Shepard Reader* (San Francisco: Sierra Club Books, 1996), 37.

24. The word "giss" characterizes the mobile essence of a species: it is what allows us, in the field, to distinguish the species from others at a single glance. It is the species' distinctive allure, or its incomparable way of flying or moving, which allows us to pin down its identity even before our analytic consciousness has been able to break down its attributes in detail in order to identify it formally.

25. "The combined biases are what we call human nature. . . . Although the evidence is far from all in, the brain appears to have kept its old capacities, its channeled quickness" (Edward O. Wilson, *Biophilia* [Cambridge, MA: Harvard University Press, 1984], 101). For Wilson, it is in the biophilia of the naturalists (in the traditional sense) that we find the cognitive and affective legacy of the original hunters: biological field work becomes the sublimated form of hunting, as tracking down knowledge about life forms.

26. Temple Grandin and Catherine Johnson, *Animals in Translation: Using the Mysteries of Autism to Decode Animal Behavior* (New York: Scribner, 2005), 94.

27. Grandin and Johnson, *Animals in Translation*, 95.

28. Grandin and Johnson, *Animals in Translation*, 96.

29. It is noteworthy that, during the hunt and then the killing, the neuronal circuits of rage (activated in intraspecies aggression or in self-defense) are not aroused: "the killer is always quiet" (Grandin and Johnson, *Animals in Translation*, 138). We can see how far the reality of predation is from the moral interpretation that attributes sadism or cruelty to wolves, accusing them of killing for pleasure. Thus the tracking and hunting process, long construed as testosterone-fueled bellicosity centered on killing, can be seen instead as a quest, a search, an awakening of the senses and the animal brain.

30. Grandin and Johnson, *Animals in Translation*, 98.

31. Grandin and Johnson, *Animals in Translation*.

32. Here we find again, grounded in biomorphy, a conceptual nuance proposed by Gilles Deleuze: the distinction in value between pleasure and desire. It is a mistake to link pleasure to an intensification of existence: pleasure is circumstantial, it fulfills and lulls us. Dopamine is rather the chemical index of desire: it is what procures the vivifying joys and the intensification of existence that hedonism believes it is seeking in pleasure but—owing to this confusion—fails to find.

33. Wilson, *Biophilia*, 101.

34. This is also what gives me both the strength to write these lines and the joy I take in doing so, as perhaps it plays a role in the tenacious energy with which the reader concentrates on reading them.

35. Here, nonreductionism means not downgrading these affects, not reducing them to crude, instrumental, or mechanical determinants. In its instinctual rather than its epistemological sense, reductionism is built on the negative joy of lowering, degrading—what Deleuze calls the joy of ressentiment. It is manifested in attempts to explain complex, delicate things by unidirectional models of causality: balls that bump into each other, mechanisms triggered by levers.

36. Liebenberg, *Origin of Science*, 82–83.

Chapter 11. The Power That Is Diplomacy

1. See Dominique Lestel, *Les origines animales de la culture* (Paris: Flammarion, 2009), 208: What distinguishes human intelligence is that it "solves problems that are not essential to human survival as a species." In this formula, which picks up the outdated formula "survival of the species," Lestel is actually targeting the paradox named after Alfred Russel Wallace: Why does the human species possess certain cognitive capacities that seem to confer no direct adaptive advantage on which natural selection might have weighed?

2. Pat Shipman, *The Animal Connection: A New Perspective on What Makes Us Human* (New York: Norton, 2011).

3. On this point, see Paul Shepard, *Thinking Animals: Animals and the Development of Human Intelligence* (New York: Viking Press, 1978).

4. See Temple Grandin and Catherine Johnson, *Animals in Translation: Using the Mysteries of Autism to Decode Animal Behavior* (New York: Scribner, 2005).

5. We can nevertheless hypothesize that all predators have a certain capacity to understand how their prey behave, that is, to transport themselves into their prey the better to understand them.

6. On this point, see Marc Azéma, *L'art des cavernes en action* (Paris: Errance, 2009). Azéma allows us to see, in ornate wall frescoes, the ethological subtleties that are invisible to the untutored eye: information about an animal's sex and age, its relation to others, and even an individual's *state of mind*.

7. As we have seen, the ninth-century theologian Ratramnus of Corbie wrote a letter, *Epistola de Cynocephalis*, asking whether the cynocephalics should be viewed as men. This picturesque anecdote conceals a question that is worth reconfiguring. When an animal comes to be understood as something other than the primal basis of humankind from which the latter must raise itself up, the theological question can be reversed, from that of the humanity of the hybrid to that of the constitutive hybridity of humanity. The therianthrope, recognized in its constitutive and ennobling humanity by virtue of its ancestral animality as well as by its ecological relations to the animals that are the basis of its form of existence, would then be, paradoxically, a definitive figure of the human.

8. The formula is borrowed from Nurit Bird-David, "The Giving Environment," *Current Anthropology* 31, no. 2 (April 1990): 189–196.

9. Paul Shepard, *Nous n'avons qu'une seule terre*, trans. Bertrand Fillaudeau (Paris: José Corti, 2013 [1996]), preface, 18.

10. In scientific ecology, we know that ecological interactions manifest great plasticity: mutual relations can shift very quickly into relations of predator and prey, and vice versa, as a function of transformations in the environment. In a diplomatic approach to living beings, with respect to certain species that seem to be in direct conflict with us (whether through predation or ecological competition), we can set the goal of inflecting our interactions toward complex relations of mutuality. We shall look further into this point in the concluding chapter.

Chapter 12. We Have Invented the Wolf

1. On this point, see the analyses of Hans Kruuk, a zoologist who specializes in carnivores, in *Chasseurs et chassés* (Paris: Delachaux & Niestlé, 2003).

2. As for the precise data, the researchers making the second set of claims merit the greatest confidence, not owing to their status but because they have submitted their assertions to the norms of verification governed by their academic field, which takes the form of intense critique and skeptical examination, by peers, of the work of others. This process provides more guarantees of the reliability of a proposition than can be supplied by any genius or any individual of undisputed probity. The reliability of data attested in this way is further manifested by the use of a method of data capture and disclosure that is made public in the claims themselves. On this point, see the admirable method of the historian Jean-Marc Moriceau, in *Histoire du méchant loup: 3 000 attaques sur l'homme en France (15e–20e siècles)* (Paris: Fayard, 2007).

3. There have, however, been some documented attacks; see Steven H. Fritts, Robert O. Stephenson, Robert D. Hayes, and Luigi Boitani, "Wolves and Humans," in *Wolves: Behavior, Ecology, and Conservation*, ed. L. David Mech and Luigi Boitani (Chicago: University of Chicago Press, 2003), 302.

4. Moriceau, *Histoire*.

5. L. David Mech, *The Wolf: The Ecology and Behavior of an Endangered Species* (New York: Doubleday, 1970); John D. C. Linnell et al., *The Fear of Wolves: A Review of Wolf Attacks on Humans* (Trondheim: Norwegian Institute for Nature Research, 2002).

6. Cornelius Osgood, "Contributions to the Ethology of the Kutchin," *Yale University Publications in Anthropology*, no. 7 (New Haven, CT: Yale University Press, 1936).

7. Luigi Boitani, "Ecological and Cultural Diversities in the Evolution of Wolf-Human Relationships," in *Ecology and Conservation of Wolves in a Changing World*, ed. Ludwig N. Carbyn, Stephen H. Fritts, and Dale R. Seip (Edmonton: Canadian Circumpolar Institute, 1995), 6.

8. Fritts et al., "Wolves and Humans," 293.

9. Nicolas Lescureux has done admirable work on the representation of lynx and bears in Macedonia, showing that the cultural representations of these animals are not determined but structured and also constrained by ecological and ethological data. See Nicolas Lescureux, "The Good, the Bad, and the Ghost: The Influence of Interaction Experience on Macedonian Hunters and Livestock Breeders' Perceptions of Bears, Wolves, and Lynx," *Annales de la Fondation Fyssen*, no. 24 (2009): 248–253.

10. See Fritts et al., "Wolves and Humans," 305.

11. Man-eating wolves have to be distinguished from other documented types of wolves that also attack humans. Rabid wolves account for the majority of attacks on humans. Moriceau attributes half of all attacks between the fifteenth and twentieth centuries in France to rabid wolves, and the census taken by the Norwegian Ministry of the Environment shows that such attacks have been by far the most numerous on a planetary scale since the nineteenth century (Linnell et al., *Fear of Wolves*, 2). Other wolves attack in reaction to intrusions or aggressions, or when they are cornered by humans. Given the particular factors that have to be taken into account in the behavior of rabid wolves and cornered wolves who act in self-defense, it seems necessary to distinguish these wolves from the properly man-eating wolves that we shall be considering here. However, the widespread presence of rabies and of attacks by rabid wolves on humans has probably helped to develop or reinforce, in Europe, the imaginary figure of the devil-wolf.

12. Moriceau, *Histoire*, chart, 511.

13. Moriceau, *Histoire*, 17.

14. Jean-Marc Moriceau, "La dangerosité du loup sur l'homme: Une enquête à l'échelle de la France (16e–20e siècles)," in *Repenser le sauvage grâce au retour du loup: Les sciences humaines interpellées*, ed. Jean-Marc Moriceau and Philippe Madeline (Caen: Presses Universitaires de Caen, 2010), 66.

15. An analogous phenomenon takes place with respect to predation on domesticated animals. It has been shown that burning animal carcasses reduces wolf

predation, for the possibility of feeding on carcasses facilitates later attacks on the herd (Fritts et al., "Wolves and Humans," 309).

16. Ernst Haeckel, *Generelle Morphologie der Organismen* (Berlin: G. Reimer, 1866).

17. From June 1764 to June 1767, the Gévaudan, a region to the north of the Cévennes mountains in France, experienced an intense series of wolf attacks on humans. These attacks gave rise to a great many fantastic speculations about the nature of the man-eating animal, who was christened "the Beast of the Gévaudan."

18. Moriceau, *Histoire*, 287.

19. Analogous phenomena have appeared when other human populations have been caught up in similar ecological relations with wolves. From the eastern Uttar Pradesh in India there is a documented report about a man-eating wolf that attacked seventy-six times in seven months, with deaths every five days of children ranging from four months to nine years of age. See Y. V. Jhala and D. K. Sharma, "Child-Lifting by Wolves in Eastern Uttar Pradesh, India," *Journal of Wildlife Research* 2 (1997): 94–101. This region in northern India is very poor. Children work and travel alone. The environment has been devastated: it has no wild fauna and only emaciated herds. Very high government compensations for the loss of children may have worsened the situation, according to some sources (Fritts et al., "Wolves and Humans," 303).

20. Fritts et al., "Wolves and Humans," 308.

21. Farid Benhammou, "Crier au loup pour avoir la peau de l'ours: Une géopolitique locale de l'environnement à travers la gestion et la conservation des grands prédateurs en France," PhD thesis, École normale supérieure, Lyon, 2007, 380. Available at http://geoconfluences.ens-lyon.fr/doc/breves/2006/popup/These-Benham.pdf.

22. Benhammou, "Crier au loup," 355.

23. Laurent Rieutort, *L'élevage ovin en France: espaces fragiles et dynamique des systèmes agricoles* (Clermont-Ferrand: CERAMAC, Université Blaise Pascal, 1995).

24. Benhammou, "Crier au loup," 455.

25. Benhammou, "Crier au loup," 359.

26. Benhammou, "Crier au loup," 381.

27. David W. Stephens and John R. Krebs, *Foraging Theory* (Princeton, NJ: Princeton University Press, 1986).

28. Fritts et al., *Wolves and Humans*, 305.

29. In landscape ecology, the landscape is defined as a heterogeneous portion of territory composed of interacting sets of ecosystems. Thus we are looking at the level of organization of ecological systems, higher than that of a single ecosystem. The spatial and functional structure of a landscape is made up of three types of entities: habitat spots, themselves made up of an interior milieu and an ecotone or border zone; corridors that are the linear landscape elements allowing displacements

of species between habitat spots; and the matrix, which is the dominant type of occupation of the space by humans and whose role in the ecological functioning of the landscape depends on its degree of hospitality to the species concerned. There is fragmentation when there are portions of the space viewed as matrices. See Françoise Burel and Jacques Baudry, *Écologie du paysage: Concepts, méthodes et applications* (Paris: TEC & DOC, 1999).

30. See *Fragmentation de l'habitat due aux infrastructures de transport*, a report issued by the French Ministère de l'Équipement, des Transports et du Logement (Ministry of Infrastructure, Transportation, and Housing) in 2000.

Chapter 13. Constitutive Relations

1. The creatures of the depths have had few constitutive relations with us, unless we consider their cascading effects on other organisms or on the abiotic conditions of the earth's atmosphere. But in the last analysis, even the seemingly most remote aspects of the biotic community in our current form of life are effects of relationship. The fossil energies that are the basis for industrial civilization—coal, oil, natural gas—are in fact only products of the methanization of living beings that have lain dead and buried in the ground for several dozens of millions of years, often ancient forests.

2. Gilbert Simondon, *L'individuation à la lumière des notions de forme et d'information* (Grenoble: Millon, 2005 [1964]).

3. Arne Naess, "The Shallow and the Deep, Long-Range Ecology Movement: A Summary," *Inquiry*, no. 16 (1973): 95–100; J. Baird Callicott, *Earth's Insights: A Survey of Ecological Ethics from the Mediterranean Basin to the Australian Outback* (Berkeley: University of California Press, 1994); Paul Shepard, ed., *The Only World We've Got: A Paul Shepard Reader* (San Francisco: Sierra Club Books, 1996).

4. Ernst Haeckel, *Generelle Morphologie der Organismen* (Berlin: G. Reimer, 1866), cited from "Ernst Haeckel: Pioneer of Modern Science," News Release, Friedrich-Schiller-Universität Jena, May 17, 2019, https://www.eurekalert.org/pub_releases/2019-05/fj-ehp051719.php.

5. Simondon, *L'individuation*, 63.

6. See, for example, James Ladyman, Don Ross, David Spurret, and John G. Collier, *Every Thing Must Go: Metaphysics Naturalized* (Oxford: Oxford University Press, 2007), and Callicott, *Earth's Insights*.

7. Simondon, *L'individuation*, 32.

8. Shepard, *Only World*, 32.

9. Callicott, *Earth's Insights*, 206–207.

10. These notions are presented, for example, in a pair of excellent articles: Donato Bergandi, "Niveaux d'organisation: Évolution, écologie, transaction," in

Le tout et les parties dans les systèmes naturels, ed. Thierry Martin (Paris: Vuibert, 2007), 47–55, and Patrick Blandin, "L'écosystème existe-t-il? Le tout et la partie en écologie," in *Le tout et les parties*, 21–46.

11. Blandin, "L'ecosystème," 44.

12. Alfred Lord Tennyson, "Ulysses," https://www.poetryfoundation.org/poems/45392/ulysses.

13. We find an analogous theoretical stance in another philosopher of ecology, under the formula of internal or intrinsic relations. Probably inherited from the idealism of Johann Gottlieb Fichte and Francis Herbert Bradley, in the work of Arne Naess the first point of deep ecology implies "the relational, total-field image. Organisms as knots in the biospherical net or field of intrinsic relations. An intrinsic relation between two things A and B is such that the relation belongs to the definitions or basic constitutions of A and B, so that without the relation, A and B are no longer the same things" (Naess, "The Shallow and the Deep," 95).

14. See Georges Guille-Escuret, *L'écologie biologique* (Paris: Presses Universitaires de France, 2014).

15. However, the choice of the term "competition" to qualify ecological relations between species that occupy the same niche, along with the idea of an "evolutionarily stable strategy" in John Maynard Smith, probably bring in epistemological obstacles similar to those induced by the metaphors listed here.

16. Georges Canguilhem, *Knowledge of Life*, trans. Stefanos Geroulanos and Daniela Ginsburg, ed. Paola Marrati and Todd Meyers (New York: Fordham University Press, 2008 [1952]).

17. Georgy F. Gause, "Experimental Studies on the Struggle for Existence," *Journal of Experimental Biology* 9 (1932): 389–402.

18. Charles Darwin, *The Origin of Species by Means of Natural Selection* (London: John Murray, Albemarle Street, 1910 [1859]), 46.

19. Long hours of observation during interactions among wolves, bison, elk, grizzly bears, crows, and coyotes in the Lamar Valley have shown prey and predators intermingling nonchalantly for prolonged periods, with rivals jostling now and again over a carcass; it seems as though, apart from the rare moments when active, mortal combat breaks out, the tonality of life can be described as a form of collective détente, or what might be described as "chill" in contemporary jargon.

20. Alfred J. Lotka, *Elements of Physical Biology* (Baltimore: Williams & Wilkins, 1925); Vito Volterra, "Fluctuations in the Abundance of a Species Considered Mathematically," *Nature* 118 (1926): 558–560.

21. Patrick Blandin and Maxime Lamotte, "Recherche d'une entité écologique correspondant à l'étude des paysages: La notion d'écocomplexe," *Bulletin d'écologie* 19, no. 4 (1988): 547–555.

22. Jane Packard, "Wolf Behavior: Reproductive, Social, and Intelligent," in *Wolves: Behavior, Ecology, and Conservation*, ed. L. David Mech and Luigi Boitani (Chicago: University of Chicago Press, 2003), 35–65.

23. In crude representations of evolution, the notion of competition has been expanded from differential reproduction between two variants to the population scale over a long time period (which, as we have seen, is not experienced as direct competition), and ultimately to total competition, a war of all against all in the biotic community. Actual instances of interspecies competition have compounded this misunderstanding: in cases of multiple occupations of a given niche, there have in fact been situations of interspecies competition that ended up with the elimination of one to the benefit of the other. Confirmed by the ideology of Progress as emancipation with respect to a cruel nature, war against the milieu, victory against environmental constraints, this was all it took to distort intrinsically our understanding of our relations to the biotic community and of the relations that prevail within it. It is not *performance in conflict* that is the criterion that leads a variant to be selected: it is the quality of the variant's relations with the biotic community and the biotope (nonexhaustion of resources, catalysis of the variant's vitality, effects of trophic cascades, facilitating factors, durable positive interactions).

24. By contrast, the hospitality of nomad cultures is not a moral commandment but an ethical intent, for the stranger who arrives exhausted and thirsty at the entrance to my tent is none other than myself, yesterday or tomorrow.

25. In a roundabout way, Émilie Hache usefully evokes the analogous idea of "making room": "One of [the] common features [of collective practices] is that they do not require the persons involved to *choose* between what is good for them individually and what is good collectively. . . . What is good for the consumers—or coproducers—would be good for the producers as for the lands, the animals, or the plants concerned." Émilie Hache, *Ce à quoi nous tenons* (Paris: La Découverte, 2011), 205.

26. Can we extend this argument by postulating that what is bad for the relation is bad for the entities? This is a task for the most penetrating meta-ethicists; here, it suffices to use the formula as a compass.

27. See the autobiographical story of the hunt for the wolf named Lobo related by Ernest Thompson Seton in *Wild Animals I Have Known* (New York: C. Scribner's Sons, 1898).

28. Richard G. Wilkinson and Kate Pickett, *The Spirit Level: Why Equality Is Better for Everyone* (London: Penguin, 2010).

29. Lucy E. King, Joseph Soltis, Iain Douglas-Hamilton, Ann Savage, and Fritz Vollrath, "Bee Threat Elicits Alarm Call in African Elephants," *PLoS ONE* 5, no. 4 (April 26, 2010), https://doi.org/10.1371/journal.pone.0010346.

30. See the excellent article by Bruno Corbara, "Des abeilles pour éloigner des éléphants," *Espèces: Revue d'histoire naturelle*, no. 6 (December 2012): 74–75.

31. Vincent Devictor, *Nature en crise: Penser la biodiversité* (Paris: Seuil, 2015), 322.

32. Other projects that might be decoded in terms of animal diplomacy are presented in David Western and Michael Wright, eds., *Natural Connections: Per-*

spectives in Community-Based Conservation (Washington, DC: Island Press, 1994). Similarly, initiatives for cohabiting with baboons observed by Shirley Strum and local populations have been brilliantly analyzed by Vinciane Despret in *Quand le loup habitera avec l'agneau* (Paris: Les empêcheurs de penser en rond, 2002).

33. On the question of constitutive relations and the difficult problem of substitution and redundant species, see Dieter Birnbacher, "Limits to Sustainability in Nature Conservation," in *Philosophy and Biodiversity*, ed. Markku Oksanen and Juhani Pietarinen (Cambridge: Cambridge University Press, 2004), 180–195.

34. On this point, see Patrick Blandin, *De la protection de la nature au pilotage de la biodiversité* (Paris: Quae, 2009).

35. See I. A. Newsome and W. J. Ripple, "A Continental Scale Trophic Cascade from Wolves through Coyotes to Foxes," *Journal of Animal Ecology* 84, no. 1 (2015): 49–59, and also W. J. Ripple and R. L. Beschta, "Trophic Cascades in Yellowstone: The First 15 Years after Wolf Reintroduction," *Biological Conservation*, no. 145 (2012): 205–213.

36. See the recent synthesis by R. O. Peterson, J. A. Vucetich, J. M. Bump, and D. W. Smith, "Trophic Cascades in a Multicausal World: Isle Royale and Yellowstone," *Annual Review of Ecology, Evolution, and Systematics* 45 (November 2014): 325–345.

37. Aldo Leopold in *A Sand County Almanac and Other Writings on Ecology and Conservation* (New York: Library of America, 2013 [1949]), 77.

38. Devictor, *Nature en crise*, 208.

39. Edward O. Wilson, *Biophilia* (Cambridge, MA: Harvard University Press, 1984), 139–140.

40. Claude Combes, *Interactions doubles: Écologie et évolution du parasitisme* (Paris: Dunod, 2001), 213.

41. On this point, see the enlightening book by Claude Combes, *Interactions doubles*.

42. Stephen A. Forbes, "The Lake as a Microcosm," *Illinois Natural History Survey* 15 (1925 [1887]): 549–550. Aldo Leopold's remarks on the interaction between wolves and deer are enlightening in this connection (see, for example, *Sand County Almanac*, 427 or 526). Predation by wolves is not positive for deer in the short run; in terms of durable relations, it could be a different story. For the absence of predators leads to the proliferation of prey, in proportions that destroy the resources on which the animals' subsistence depends and that multiply epidemics. In this sense, the relation of predation between wolves and deer leads to mortality for deer in the near term but constitutes a mutualism in the enriched sense in the long term.

43. "In the case of wolves, what must be sought is a coexistence that will never be entirely peaceful, but that will hold up within limits thanks to diplomatic efforts, and these limits are what will be mutually beneficial" (personal communication).

44. Combes, *Interactions doubles*, 215.

45. Hans Molisch, an Austrian specialist in plant physiology, analyzed the molecules that plants send into the soil through their roots, and the complex chemical relations they engage in. With his publication of *Der Einfluss einer Pflanze auf die Andere-allelopathie* (Jena: Fischer, 1937), Molisch opened the door to a new discipline that he called allelopathy, combining two Greek words: *allelon* (reciprocal) and *pathos* (suffering). Some molecules enter into competition and some help one another, as happens in permaculture, for example, between leeks and strawberries, or tomatoes and carrots, where one plant drives off the other's parasites.

46. Blandin, *De la protection*.

47. In the idea of steering biodiversity, Blandin is making an ethical gesture of great humility that consists in taking away the ecological expert's right to determine what a policy of conservation should look like. We must not conclude from this that the expert must be absent or marginalized during the steering processes themselves; in the model proposed here, the expert must first formulate the negative constraints, and at the same time bring his or her knowledge to bear on the mutualisms that can be imagined. The expert takes on the second sense of diplomacy with the biotic community. Local communities, through their knowledge of the prevailing relations, are in a position to identify mutualisms that observers from the outside would not have seen.

Chapter 14. What Mutualisms in Our Relations with Wolves?

1. David Western and Michael Wright, eds., *Natural Connections: Perspectives in Community-Based Conservation* (Washington, DC: Island Press, 1994).

2. This position is stressed complacently by conservative mayors who seize on the symbolics of the predator to win the aura of upholders of justice struggling against savagery. In a municipal decree dated May 18, 2015, mayor Christian Hubaud of Pelleautier (Hautes-Alpes) gave the order that wolves "or any other predator" were to be shot by "any adult citizen equipped with a weapon and the ability to use it." Moreover, the use of the term "predation" in a metaphoric sense—for example, to characterize the looting of natural resources by neoliberalism—maintains this ecologically destitute misunderstanding: condemning predation as immoral stems from a Christian pastoralism that is proving difficult to escape.

3. Personal communication; see also Maïa Martin, "Entre affection et aversion, le retour du loup en Cévennes comme problème public," *Terrains et travaux*, no. 20 (2012): 15–33.

4. This attitude was expressed in particular during a survey of public opinion carried out in France by the Ministry of Sustainable Development; the survey noted widespread disapproval of the increase in the number of wolves to be killed in 2015–2016; see www.consultations-publiques-developpement-durable.gouv.fr.

5. Quoted in "Dialogues avec des habitants du parc national des Abruzzes," *La Gazette des Grands Prédateurs*, no. 56 (May 2015): 14.

6. On the question of an economics that asserts the incommensurability of values with the monetary dimension alone, see Joan Martínez Alier, *The Environmentalism of the Poor: A Study of Ecological Conflicts and Valuation* (Cheltenham, UK: Edward Elgar, 2002). [Translator's note: An updated version exists in a French translation of the third Spanish edition: *L'écologisme des pauvres: Une étude des conflits environnementaux dans le monde*, trans. André Verkaeren (Paris: les Petits Matins, 2014). Where the passage cited does not appear in the English original, I translate from the 2014 French edition.]

7. A certain number of shepherds and farmers in the Pyrenees defend the presence of bears in the mountains. What seems to be a paradox on their part is in fact a deep sense of relational diplomacy: they maintain that the bears, by transforming sheep-pasturing techniques so that herds are smaller and shepherds more numerous, "ensure full employment in the mountains." If predators are reconceived in terms of mutualist relations, they can become unexpected socioeconomic allies. In Poland, wolves have become allies of the forest industry, for they control the number of ungulates.

8. Hank Fischer, *Wolf Wars: The Remarkable Inside Story of the Restoration of Wolves to Yellowstone* (Helena, MT: Falcon Press, 1995), 147. All these extreme declarations are moreover capable of inducing dangerous poaching activity, even to the extent of poisoning with strychnine or its derivatives, elements that are toxic to the entire mammalian community.

9. This idea has been proposed by the Houmbaba association. On the model of the "Land of the Bears" charter (see www.paysdelours.com), it would entail building a cooperative network of professionals who would commit to defending the "quality of the environment" and the presence of wolves; the network would function as a label attesting to the quality of the territory and its products.

10. My thanks to Donato Bergandi, who encapsulated in this laconic formula the project I am defending here.

11. This text was transcribed from a videotaped interview titled "Les accélérateurs de métamorphose," accessible at www.eco-psychologie.com. I am grateful to Denis Chartier for bringing these remarks to my attention.

12. For example, in the form of the law of the commons. On this point, see the important work of Elinor Ostrom, who maintains that the idea of "a commons" refers to a type of entity that is neither a private good nor a public good (fishing zones, open pastures, irrigation systems, and so on), and that is at once nonexclusive and competitive. These are goods to which it is difficult to forbid or restrict access, except by establishing rules for their use. In the classic approach, their collective management consists in constant renegotiation of the distribution of their usage among humans. The originality of Ostrom's proposal lies in viewing their management as a distribution of rights of use among humans and nonhumans.

See especially Elinor Ostrom, *Governing the Commons: The Evolution of Institutions for Collective Action* (Cambridge: Cambridge University Press, 1990) and *Future of the Commons: Beyond Market Failure and Government Regulation* (London: Institute of Economic Affairs, 2012).

13. On the social and economic structure of this form of pastoralism, see Anna Kowalska-Lewicka, *L'élevage et la vie pastorale dans les montagnes de l'Europe au Moyen Âge et à l'époque moderne* (Clermont-Ferrand: Presses Universitaires Blaise Pascal,1984).

14. Alain Testart, *Avant l'histoire: L'évolution des sociétés, de Lascaux à Carnac* (Paris: Gallimard, 2012), 409.

15. My thanks to Pierre Charbonnier, who had the *intuition* of this connection.

16. João Pedro Galhano Alves, *Vivre en biodiversité totale: Des hommes, des grands carnivores et des grands herbivores sauvages—Deux études de cas* (Lille: ANRT, 2000).

17. Not to mention the biological unconscious that they make it possible to revitalize, enriching our inner lives.

18. Michael Rosenzweig, *Win-Win Ecology: How the Earth's Species Can Survive in the Midst of Human Enterprise* (New York: Oxford University Press, 2003).

19. Rosenzweig, *Win-Win Ecology*, 8.

20. Rosenzweig, *Win-Win Ecology*, 8.

21. Rosenzweig, *Win-Win Ecology*, 8.

22. He writes, for example: "Georgia-Pacific and Weyerhaeuser corporations are not about to sell their tree farms for the restoration of the primary forest, and reconciliation ecology says they need not" (Rosenzweig, *Win-Win Ecology*, 9).

23. Peter M. Vitousek, Paul R. Ehrlich, Anne H. Ehrlich, and Pamela A. Matson, "Human Appropriation of the Products of Photosynthesis," *BioScience* 36, no. 6 (1986): 368–373.

24. Martínez Alier, *Environmentalism of the Poor*, 39. Martínez Alier's figures have been strongly contested, essentially in view of the difficulty involved in calculating the virtual data in the constitution of the index. One article from 2013 estimates, for example, that the global HANPP has risen by 116 percent in scarcely one hundred years, culminating in 14.8 billion tons of carbon in 2005, or 25 percent of the primary production as opposed to 13 percent in 1910: see Fridolin Kraussmann et al., "Global Human Appropriation of Net Primary Production Doubled in the 20th Century," *Proceedings of the National Academy of Sciences of the United States of America* 110, no. 31 (July 31, 2007): 12942–12947. See also Helmut Haberl et al., "Quantifying and Mapping the Human Appropriation of Net Primary Production in Earth's Terrestrial Ecosystems," *Proceedings of the National Academy of Sciences of the United States of America* 104, no. 3 (June 18, 2013): 10324–10329. It is important to note that while HANPP is still rising worldwide, it began to decrease in Western Europe during the twentieth century. Still, we must use this index with caution: to make it relevant, we have to compare it to the consumption of biomass per inhabitant and to the efficiency with which the biomass is used.

25. We must also note that this decrease is possible only thanks to the "phantom acres" induced by hydrocarbons, and the massive importation of agroalimentary products, whose synthesis *increases* the HANPP of developing countries. On "phantom acres," see Pierre Charbonnier, "Le rendement et le butin: Regard écologique sur l'histoire du capitalisme," *Actuel Marx*, no. 23 (2013): 92–105.

26. Martínez Alier, *Écologisme des pauvres*, 108.

27. In his work on fertilization, Darwin proposed a thought experiment in which a single orchid, *if all its seeds germinated*, would cover the entire surface of the Earth with its descendants in four generations. See Charles Darwin, *On the Various Contrivances by Which British and Foreign Orchids are Fertilised by Insects, and on the Good Effects of Intercrossing* (London: John Murray, 1862), 276–278.

28. Martínez Alier, *Écologisme des pauvres*, 124.

29. The debate over whether the wolves had returned on their own or had been reintroduced was settled years ago when a commission of the French parliament, seeking to prove the hypothesis of reintroduction, was forced by the data to acknowledge the contrary; astonishingly, the debate continues to flourish among the wolf-phobic. If the latter were to prove that the wolves had actually been reintroduced, the animals would no longer be protected by the Bern convention and would lose their legal sanctuary status. This fact is certainly not insignificant. See Raphaël Larrère, "Rumeurs de loup," *Revue semestrielle de droit animalier*, no. 1 (2014): 257–260.

30. On this point, see Martínez Alier, *Écologisme des pauvres*, 110.

31. On environmental history, see John Robert McNeill, *Something New under the Sun: An Environmental History of the Twentieth-Century World* (New York: W. W. Norton, 2000), and Grégory Quenet, *Qu'est-ce que l'histoire environnementale?* (Paris: Champ Vallon, 2014).

32. The first time I saw a wolf trail in the snow, above the hamlet of Boréon, I was seeing the massive tracks of a male who was moving around as if he were at home. This encounter induced the intense—and rare—feeling that I had arrived *in someone's home*. My attitude, my behaviors in the place, became more respectful and courteous. I had the same feeling before the den of a boreal female lynx in Savoie. We probably experience this feeling less often when we encounter our natural prey, such as deer, wild boar, or hares (and we should learn to see these differently). Perhaps wolves trigger this reaction because they are apex predators like ourselves, familial, territorial, socially organized, training their offspring collectively: their tracks in the snow are like an etho-ecological mirror. They can generate anxiety in us about our sovereignty over the world, opening up a space for dizzying questions.

Bibliography

Agamben, Giorgio. *The Open: Man and Animal.* Stanford, CA: Stanford University Press, 2004.

Alcock, John. *Animal Behavior: An Evolutionary Approach*, 9th ed. Sunderland, MA: Sinauer Associates, 2009.

Andersen, Reidar, John D. C. Linnell, Håkon Hustad, and Scott M. Brainerd. *Large Predators and Human Communities in Norway: A Guide to Coexistence for the 21st Century.* Trondheim: Norwegian Institute for Nature Research, 2003.

Ausband, Dave. "Pilot Study Report for Using a Biofence to Manipulate Wolf Pack Movements in Central Idaho." *Montana Cooperative Wildlife Research Unit*, November 2010, https://idfg.idaho.gov/old-web/docs/wolves/reportAnnual11.pdf, 10/31/19.

Avital, Eytan, and Eva Jablonka. *Animal Traditions: Behavioural Inheritance in Evolution.* Cambridge: Cambridge University Press, 2005 (2000).

Azéma, Marc. *L'art des cavernes en action.* Paris: Errance, 2009.

Bangs, Ed, Mike Jimenez, Carter Niemeyer, and Joe Fontaine. "Nonlethal and Lethal Tools to Manage Wolf-Livestock Conflict in the Northwestern United States." In *United States Department of Agriculture Review*, 7–16. Davis: University of California Press, 2008.

Benhammou, Farid. "Crier au loup pour avoir la peau de l'ours: Une géopolitique locale de l'environnement à travers la gestion et la conservation des grands prédateurs en France." PhD thesis, École normale supérieure de Lyon, 2007, http://geoconfluences.ens.lyon.fr/doc/breves/2006/popup/TheseBenham.pdf.

Bergandi, Donato. "Niveaux d'organisation: Évolution, écologie, transaction." In *Le tout et les parties dans les systèmes naturels*, edited by Thierry Martin, 47–55. Paris: Vuibert, 2007.

Bingen, Hildegard von. *De animalibus.* In *Liber simplicis medicinae*, book 7.

Bird-David, Nurit. "The Giving Environment." *Current Anthropology* 31, no. 2 (April 1990): 189–196.

Birnbacher, Dieter. "Limits to Sustainability in Nature Conservation." In *Philosophy and Biodiversity*, edited by Markku Oksanen and Juhani Pietarinen, 180–195. Cambridge: Cambridge University Press, 2004.

Blandin, Patrick. *De la protection de la nature au pilotage de la biodiversité.* Paris: Quae, 2009.
Blandin, Patrick. "L'écosystème existe-t-il? Le tout et la partie en écologie." In *Le tout et les parties dans les systèmes naturels*, edited by Thierry Martin, 21–46. Paris: Vuibert, 2007.
Blandin, Patrick, and Maxime Lamotte. "L'organisation hiérarchique des systèmes écologiques." *Atti del 3° Congresso Nazionale della Societa Italiana di Ecologia.* Siena, October 21–24, 1987 (Siena: ATTI 7, 1989), 35–48.
Blandin, Patrick, and Maxime Lamotte. "Recherche d'une entité écologique correspondant à l'étude des paysages: La notion d'écocomplexe." *Bulletin d'écologie* 19, no. 4 (1988): 547–555.
Blumenberg, Hans. *Paradigms for a Metaphorology.* Translated by Robert Savage. Ithaca, NY: Cornell University Press, 2010 (1960).
Boethius. *Contra Eutychen et Nestorium, De duabus naturis.* Turnhout, Belgium: Brepols, 2010 (1337).
Boitani, Luigi. "Ecological and Cultural Diversities in the Evolution of Wolf-Human Relationships." In *Ecology and Conservation of Wolves in a Changing World*, edited by Ludwig N. Carbyn, Stephen H. Fritts, and Dale R. Seip, 3–12. Edmonton: Canadian Circumpolar Institute, 1995.
Boitani, Luigi. "Wolf Management in Intensively Used Areas of Italy." In *Wolves of the World: Perspectives of Behavior, Ecology, and Conservation*, edited by Fred. H. Harrington and Paul C. Paquet, 158–172. Park Ridge, NJ: Noyes, 1982.
Bryan, Heather M., Judit E. G. Smits, Lee Koren, Paul C. Paquet, Katherine E. Wynne-Edwards, and Marco Musiani. "Heavily Hunted Wolves Have Higher Stress and Reproductive Steroids than Wolves with Lower Hunting Pressure." *Functional Ecology* 29, no. 3 (2015): 347–356.
Bulletin Réseau Loup, no. 28: 11.
Burel, Françoise, and Jacques Baudry. *Écologie du paysage: Concepts, méthodes et applications.* Paris: TEC & DOC, 1999.
Burgat, Florence, ed. *Penser le comportement animal: Contribution à une critique du réductionnisme.* Paris: Quae, 2010.
Callicott, J. Baird. "After the Industrial Paradigm, What?" In *Beyond the Land Ethic: More Essays in Environmental Philosophy*, 269–291. Albany: State University of New York Press, 1999.
Callicott, J. Baird. *Beyond the Land Ethic: More Essays in Environmental Philosophy.* Albany: State University of New York Press, 1999.
Callicott, J. Baird. *Earth's Insights: A Survey of Ecological Ethics from the Mediterranean Basin to the Australian Outback.* Berkeley: University of California Press, 1997 (1994).
Callicott, J. Baird. "Genesis and John Muir." In *Beyond the Land Ethic: More Essays in Environmental Philosophy*, 187–219. Albany: State University of New York Press, 1999.

Callières, François de. *The Art of Diplomacy.* Edited and translated by H. M. A. Keens-Soper and Karl W. Schweizer. New York: Holmes & Meier, 1983 (1716).

Canguilhem, Georges. *Knowledge of Life.* Translated by Stefanos Geroulanos and Daniela Ginsburg. Edited by Paola Marrati and Todd Meyers. New York: Fordham University Press, 2008 (1952).

Castro, Eduardo Vivieros de. *Cannibal Metaphysics.* Edited and translated by Peter Skafish. Minneapolis, MN: Univocal, 2014.

Castro, Eduardo Vivieros de. *From the Enemy's Point of View: Humanity and Divinity in an Amazonian Society.* Translated by Catherine V. Howard. Chicago: University of Chicago Press, 2020.

Chamovitz, Daniel. *What a Plant Knows: A Field Guide to the Senses.* New York: Scientific American, 2013.

Charbonnier, Pierre. "Prendre les animaux au sérieux: De l'animal politique à la politique des animaux." *Tracés,* special issue (2015): 167–186.

Charbonnier, Pierre. "Le rendement et le butin: Regard écologique sur l'histoire du capitalisme." *Actuel Marx,* no. 23 (2013): 92–105.

Charlier, Bernard. "Faces of the Wolf, Faces of the Individual: Anthropological Study of Human, Non-human Relationships in West Mongolia." PhD thesis, Cambridge University, 2010.

Combes, Claude. *Interactions doubles: Écologie et évolution du parasitisme.* Paris: Dunod, 2001.

Corbara, Bruno. "Des abeilles pour éloigner des éléphants." *Espèces: Revue d'histoire naturelle,* no. 6 (December 2012): 74–75.

Dalla Bernardina, Sergio. *Le retour du prédateur: Mises en scène du sauvage dans la société post-rurale.* Rennes: Presses Universitaires de Rennes, 2011.

Darwin, Charles. *The Expression of the Emotions in Man and Animals.* London: John Murray, Albemarle Street, 1872.

Darwin, Charles. *On the Various Contrivances by Which British and Foreign Orchids Are Fertilised by Insects, and on the Good Effects of Intercrossing.* London: John Murray, 1862.

Darwin, Charles. *The Origin of Species by Means of Natural Selection.* London: John Murray, Albemarle Street, 1910 (1859).

Dawkins, Richard. *The Selfish Gene.* Oxford: Oxford University Press, 2016 (1976).

Defenders of Wildlife. *Livestock and Wolves: A Guide to Nonlethal Tools and Methods to Reduce Conflicts.* www.defenders.org.

Degeorges, Patrick, and Antoine Nochy. "Le loup affaire d'État." *Les Cahiers du Proses* 9 (May–June 2004): www.houmbaba.com.

Deleuze, Gilles, and Félix Guattari. *What Is Philosophy?* Translated by Hugh Tomlinson and Graham Burchell. New York: Columbia University Press, 1994.

Dennett, Daniel. *Darwin's Dangerous Idea: Evolution and the Meanings of Life.* New York: Simon & Schuster, 1995.

Dennett, Daniel. *The Intentional Stance*. Cambridge, MA: MIT Press, 1987.
Dennett, Daniel. *Kinds of Minds: Toward an Understanding of Consciousness*. New York: Basic Books, 1996.
Descola, Philippe. *Beyond Nature and Culture*. Translated by Janet Lloyd. Chicago: University of Chicago Press, 2013 (2005).
Descola, Philippe. *La composition des mondes*. Paris: Flammarion, 2014.
Descola, Philippe. *L'écologie des autres: L'anthropologie et la question de la nature*. Paris: Quae, coll. Sciences en question, 2011.
Descola, Philippe, ed. "Un monde animé." In *La fabrique des images: Visions du monde et formes de la representation*, edited by Philippe Descola, 21–69. Paris: Somogy, 2010.
Descola, Philippe, *The Spears of Twilight: Life and Death in the Amazon Jungle*. Translated by Janet Lloyd. New York: New Press, 1996 (1994).
Descola, Philippe. *La vie des idées*: "To whom does nature belong?" www.laviedesidees.fr.
Despret, Vinciane. *Quand le loup habitera avec l'agneau*. Paris: Les empêcheurs de penser en rond, 2002.
Despret, Vinciane. "Sheep Do Have Opinions." Translated by Liz Carey-Libbrecht. In *Making Things Public: Atmosphere of Democracy*, edited by Bruno Latour and Peter Weibel, 360–370. Cambridge, MA: MIT Press, 2005.
Despret, Vinciane. *What Would Animals Say If We Asked the Right Questions?* Translated by Brett Buchanan. Foreword by Bruno Latour. Minneapolis: University of Minnesota Press, 2016.
Devictor, Vincent. *Nature en crise: Penser la biodiversité*. Paris: Seuil, 2015.
de Waal, Frans. *The Bonobo and the Atheist: The Search for Humanism among the Primates*. New York: W. W. Norton, 2013.
Dewey, John. *How We Think*. Boston: D. C. Heath, 1910.
Dewey, John. "The Influence of Darwin on Philosophy." In *The Influence of Darwin on Philosophy and Other Essays*, 1–19. New York: Henry Holt, 1910.
"Dialogues avec des habitants du parc national des Abruzzes." *La Gazette des Grands Prédateurs*, no. 56 (May 2015).
Dilthey, Wilhelm. *The Formation of the Historical World in the Human Sciences*. Translated from the German. Edited by Rudolf A. Makkree and Frithjof Rodi. Princeton, NJ: Princeton University Press, 2002 (1910).
Donaldson, Sue, and Will Kymlicka. *Zoopolis: A Political Theory of Animal Rights*. Oxford: Oxford University Press, 2011.
Duby, Georges. *Féodalité*. Paris: Gallimard, 1996.
Duclos, Denis. *The Werewolf Complex: America's Fascination with Violence*. Translated by Amanda Pingree. Oxford: Berg, 1998 (1994).
During, Élie, and Laurent Jeanpierre. "L'universel, il faut le faire." Interview with Bruno Latour. *Critique*, no. 786 (November 2012): 949–963.
Eastman, Charles A. *Indian Boyhood*. New York: McClure, Phillips, 1902.

Eisenberg, Cristina. *The Carnivore Way: Coexisting with and Conserving North America's Predators.* Washington, DC: Island Press, 2014.

Fischer, Hank. *Wolf Wars: The Remarkable Inside Story of the Restoration of Wolves to Yellowstone.* Helena, MT: Falcon Press, 1995.

Forbes, Stephen A. "The Lake as a Microcosm." *Illinois Natural History Survey* 15 (1925 [1887]): 537–550.

Foucault, Michel. "Intellectuals and Power." In *Language, Counter-Memory, Practice: Selected Essays and Interviews by Michel Foucault,* translated and edited by Donald Bouchard, 205–217. Ithaca, NY: Cornell University Press, 1977.

Foucault, Michel. *The Order of Things: An Archaeology of the Human Sciences.* Translated from the French. New York: Pantheon, 1971 (1970).

Frisch, Karl von. *The Dancing Bees: An Account of the Life and Senses of the Honey Bee.* Translated by Dora Isle and Norman Walker. London: Methuen, 1966 (1927).

Fritts, Steven H., and L. David Mech. *Dynamics, Movements, and Feeding Ecology of a Newly Protected Wolf Population in Northwestern Minnesota.* Wildlife Monographs no. 80. October 1981.

Fritts, Steven H., Robert O. Stephenson, Robert D. Hayes, and Luigi Boitani. "Wolves and Humans." In *Wolves: Behavior, Ecology, and Conservation,* edited by L. David Mech and Luigi Boitani, 289–316. Chicago: University of Chicago Press, 2003.

Gaillard, Jacques. "L'année du loup." *Le Monde,* May 12, 1999.

Galhano Alves, João Pedro. "Des hommes, des grands carnivores et des grands herbivores: Une approche anthropologique et comparative internationale." *ANTROPOlógicas,* no. 7 (2003).

Galhano Alves, João Pedro. *Vivre en biodiversité totale: Des hommes, des grands carnivores et des grands herbivores sauvages—Deux études de cas.* Lille: ANRT, 2000.

Gause, Georgy F. "Experimental Studies on the Struggle for Existence." *Journal of Experimental Biology* 9 (1932): 389–402.

Ginzburg, Carlo. *Clues, Myths, and the Historical Method.* Translated by John Tedeschi and Anne C. Tedeschi. Baltimore, MD: Johns Hopkins University Press, 1994.

Gould, Stephen Jay. *The Structure of Evolutionary Theory.* Cambridge, MA: Belknap Press of Harvard University Press, 2002.

Gould, Stephen Jay, and Elisabeth S. Vrba. "Exaptation: A Missing Term in the Science of Form." *Paleobiology* 8, no. 1 (Winter 1982): 4–15.

Grandin, Temple, and Catherine Johnson. *Animals in Translation: Using the Mysteries of Autism to Decode Animal Behavior.* New York: Scribner, 2005.

Grossmann, Dave. *On Killing: The Psychological Cost of Learning to Kill in War and Society.* Boston: Little, Brown, 1995.

Guha, Ramachandra, and Joan Martinez-Alier. "L'environnementalisme des riches." In Émilie Hache and Cyril Le Roy, eds., *Écologie politique,* 51–65. Paris: Éditions Amsterdam, 2012.

Guille-Escuret, Georges. *L'écologie biologique.* Paris: Presses Universitaires de France, 2014.

Haberl, Helmut, Karl-Heinz Erb, Fridolin Krausmann, et al. "Quantifying and Mapping the Human Appropriation of Net Primary Production in Earth's Terrestrial Ecosystems." *Proceedings of the National Academy of Sciences of the United States of America* 104, no. 3 (June 18, 2013): 10324–10329.

Hache, Émilie. *Ce à quoi nous tenons*. Paris: La Découverte, 2011.

Hacking, Ian. "'Vrai'—les valeurs et les sciences." *Actes de la recherche en sciences sociales*, no. 141 (2002): 13–20. DOI: 10.3917/arss.141.0013. https://www.cairn.info/revue-actes-de-la-recherche-en-sciences-sociales-2002-1-page-13.htm.

Haeckel, Ernst. *Generelle Morphologie der Organismen*. Berlin: G. Reimer, 1866.

Halfpenny, James C., and Tracy Furman. *Tracking Wolves: The Basics*. Gardiner, MT: A Naturalist's World, 2010.

Halloy, Arnaud, and Véronique Servais. "Enchanting Gods and Dolphins: A Cross-Cultural Analysis of Uncanny Encounters." *Ethos* 42, no. 4 (December 2014): 479–504.

Hamayon, Roberte. *La chasse à l'âme: Esquisse d'une théorie du chamanisme sibérien*. Nanterre: Société d'ethnologie, 1990.

Haudricourt, André-Georges. "Domestication des animaux, culture des plantes et traitement d'autrui." *L'Homme* 2, no. 1 (1962): 40–50.

Heinrich, Bernd. *Mind of the Raven: Investigations and Adventures with Wolf-Birds*. New York: Harper Perennial, 2007.

Holmgren, David. *Permaculture: Principles and Pathways beyond Sustainability*. Hepburn, Australia: Holmgren Design Services, 2002.

Hughes, Sylvia. "Antelope Activate the Acacia's Alarm System." *New Scientist*, no. 1736 (September 29, 1990): https://www.newscientist.com/article/mg12717361-200-antelope-activate-the-acacias-alarm-system/.

Huxley, Thomas Henry. "On the Relations of Man to the Lower Animals." In *Man's Place in Nature and Other Anthropological Essays*, 77–156. New York: D. Appleton, 1896.

Huxley, Thomas Henry. Preface. *De la place de l'homme dans la nature* [French translation of *Man's Place in Nature*]. Translated by E. Dally. Paris: J. B. Baillière et fils, 1868.

Jackson, Peter. *Wild Cats: Status Survey and Conservation Action Plan*. Gland, Switzerland: IUCN, 1996.

Jerison, Harry J. *Evolution of the Brain and Intelligence*. New York: Academic Press, 1973.

Jhala, Y. V., and D. K. Sharma. "Child-Lifting by Wolves in Eastern Uttar Pradesh, India." *Journal of Wildlife Research* 2 (1997): 94–101.

John Paul II. "Papal Declaration of Francis as Patron of Ecology." Translation of *Inter Sanctos Praeclara Que Viros*. https://francis35.org/english/papal-declaration-francis-patron-ecology/.

Jonas, Hans. *The Phenomenon of Life: Toward a Philosophical Biology*. New York: Harper & Row, 1966.

King, Lucy E., Joseph Soltis, Iain Douglas-Hamilton, Ann Savage, and Fritz Vollrath. "Bee Threat Elicits Alarm Call in African Elephants." *PLoS ONE* 5, no. 4 (April 26, 2010): https://doi.org/10.1371/journal.pone.0010346.

Kissinger, Henry. *Years of Renewal.* New York: Simon & Schuster, 1999.

Kohn, Eduardo. *How Forests Think: Toward an Anthropology beyond the Human.* Berkeley: University of California Press, 2013.

Kolbert, Elizabeth. *The Sixth Extinction: An Unnatural History.* New York: Henry Holt, 2014.

Kowalska-Lewicka, Anna. *L'élevage et la vie pastorale dans les montagnes de l'Europe au Moyen Âge et à l'époque moderne.* Clermont-Ferrand: Presses Universitaires Blaise Pascal, 1984.

Krausmann, Fridolin, Karl-Heinz Erb, Simone Gingrich, Helmut Haberl, Alberte Bondeau, Veronika Gaube, Christian Lauk, Chrisoph Plutzar, and Timothy D. Searchinger. "Global Human Appropriation of Net Primary Production Doubled in the 20th Century." *Proceedings of the National Academy of Sciences of the United States of America* 110, no. 31 (July 31, 2007): 12942–12947.

Kruuk, Hans. *Chasseurs et chassés.* Paris: Delachaux & Niestlé, 2003.

La Fontaine, Jean de. *The Complete Fables of Jean de La Fontaine.* Translated by Norman R. Shapiro. Urbana: University of Illinois Press, 2007.

Ladyman, James, Don Ross, David Spurret, and John G. Collier. *Every Thing Must Go: Metaphysics Naturalized.* Oxford: Oxford University Press, 2007.

Lame Deer, Archie Fire, and Richard Erdoes. *Gift of Power: The Life and Teachings of a Lakota Medicine Man.* Santa Fe, NM: Bear, 1992.

Landry, Jean-Marc. "Étude sur les interactions loup-troupeau-chien de protection pour l'amélioration des chiens et systèmes de protection des troupeaux." IPRA 2014 activity report, December 2014, CanOvis Project 2013–2017, https://www.ipra-landry.com/en/.

Landry, Jean-Marc. *Le loup: Biologie, moeurs, mythologie, cohabitation, protection.* Paris: Delachaux & Niestlé, coll. La bibliothèque du naturaliste, 2006.

Landry, Jean-Marc, and Fabien Matter. "Projet de création d'un collier répulsif agissant à distance pour protéger le bétail de la prédation du loup." http://www.protectiondestroupeaux.ch/fileadmin/doc/Berichte/Studien/Projet_collier_r%C3%A9pulsifs_Nov-Agridea.pdf.

Larrère, Catherine, and Raphaël Larrère. *Penser et agir avec la nature: Une enquête philosophique.* Paris: La Découverte, 2015.

Larrère, Raphaël. "Le loup, l'agneau et l'éleveur." *Ruralia* (January 25, 2005 [1999]): http://ruralia.revues.org/114.

Larrère, Raphaël. "Rumeurs de loup." *Revue semestrielle de droit animalier*, no. 1 (2014): 257–260.

Latour, Bruno. *An Inquiry into Modes of Existence: An Anthropology of the Moderns.* Translated by Catherine Porter. Cambridge, MA: Harvard University Press, 2013.

Latour, Bruno. *Facing Gaia*. Translated by Catherine Porter. Cambridge: Polity, 2017 (2015).
Latour, Bruno. "Make It Work 'theater of negotiations.'" PowerPoint presentation, Paris Climate 2015, posted February 1, 2015, http://www.bruno-latour.fr/node/621.html.
Latour, Bruno. *Politics of Nature*. Translated by Catherine Porter. Cambridge, MA: Harvard University Press, 2004.
Lecacheur, Marc. *Transhumance: 14 000 km à vélo à la rencontre des bergers d'Europe*. Coudray-Macouard: Éditions Cheminements, 2006.
Leopold, Aldo. *A Sand County Almanac and Other Writings on Ecology and Conservation*. New York: Library of America, 2013 (1949).
Leroy, Georges. *The Intelligence and Perfectibility of Animals from a Philosophic Point of View*. Translated from the French. London: Chapman and Hall, 1870 (1768).
Lescureux, Nicolas. "The Good, the Bad, and the Ghost: The Influence of Interaction Experience on Macedonian Hunters and Livestock Breeders' Perceptions of Bears, Wolves, and Lynx." *Annales de la Fondation Fyssen*, no. 24 (2009): 248–253.
Lescureux, Nicolas, and John Linnell. "Knowledge and Perceptions of Macedonian Hunters and Herders: The Influence of Species Specific Ecology of Bears, Wolves, and Lynx." *Human Ecology* 38, no. 3 (2010): 389–399.
Lestel, Dominique. *Les origines animales de la culture*. Paris: Flammarion, 2009.
Liebenberg, Louis. *The Art of Tracking: The Origin of Science*. Claremont, South Africa: David Philip, 1990.
Liebenberg, Louis. *A Field Guide to the Animal Tracks of South Africa*. Claremont, South Africa: David Philip, 1990.
Liebenberg, Louis. *The Origin of Science: The Evolutionary Roots of Scientific Reasoning and Its Implications for Citizen Science*. Cape Town, South Africa: Cyber Tracker, 2013.
Liebenberg, Louis, Adriaan Louw, and Mark Elbroch. *Practical Tracking: A Guide to Following Footprints and Finding Animals*. Mechanicsburg, PA: Stackpole Books, 2010.
Linnell, John D. C., Reidar Andersen, Zanete Andersone, et al. *The Fear of Wolves: A Review of Wolf Attacks on Humans*. Trondheim: Norwegian Institute for Nature Research, 2002.
Lorenz, Konrad. "Der Kumpan in der Umwelt des Vogels" [The companion in the bird's environment]. *Journal für Ornithologie* 83, no. 2 (April 1935): 137–213.
Lorenz, Konrad. *King Solomon's Ring: New Light on Animal Ways*. New York: Thomas Y. Crowell, 1952 (1949).
Lotka, Alfred J. *Elements of Physical Biology*. Baltimore: Williams & Wilkins, 1925.
MacNulty, Daniel R., L. David Mech, and Douglas W. Smith. "A Proposed Ethogram of Large-Carnivore Predatory Behavior, Exemplified by the Wolf." *Journal of Mammalogy* 88 (2007): www.digitalcommons.unl.edu.

Makkink, Gerrit François. *Het leven van onze wadvogels.* Amsterdam: L. J. Veen, 1963.
Martin, Arnaud, and Virginie Orgogozo. "The Loci of Repeated Evolution: A Catalog of Genetic Hotspots of Phenotypic Variation." *Evolution* 67, no. 5 (2013): 1235–1250.
Martin, Maïa. "Entre affection et aversion, le retour du loup en Cévennes comme problème public." *Terrains et travaux*, no. 20 (2012): 15–33.
Martínez Alier, Joan. *The Environmentalism of the Poor: A Study of Ecological Conflicts and Valuation.* Cheltenham, UK: Edward Elgar, 2002.
Martínez Alier, Joan. *L'écologisme des pauvres: Une étude des conflits environnementaux dans le monde.* Translation of the third Spanish edition by André Verkaeren. Paris: les Petits Matins, 2014.
Marx, Karl. "Speech at Anniversary of the *People's Paper*." April 19, 1856. In *Marx/Engels Selected Works*, vol. 1, 500. Moscow: Progress, 1969 [1856].
Marx, Karl, and Friedrich Engels. *The German Ideology.* Translated from the German. New York: International, 1970 (1845).
McIntyre, Rick. https://www.yellowstone.org/rick-mcintyres-notes-from-the-field/.
McNeill, John Robert. *Something New under the Sun: An Environmental History of the Twentieth-Century World.* New York: W. W. Norton, 2000.
Mech, L. David. "Alpha Status, Dominance, and Division of Labor in Wolf Packs." *Canadian Journal of Zoology* 77 (1999): 1196–1203.
Mech, L. David. *The Wolf: The Ecology and Behavior of an Endangered Species.* New York: Doubleday, 1970.
Mech, L. David, and Luigi Boitani. "Wolf Social Ecology." In *Wolves: Behavior, Ecology, and Conservation*, edited by L. David Mech and Luigi Boitani, 1–34. Chicago: University of Chicago Press, 2003.
Mech, L. David, and Luigi Boitani, eds. *Wolves: Behavior, Ecology, and Conservation.* Chicago: University of Chicago Press, 2003.
Mech, L. David, and Rolf O. Peterson. "Wolf-Prey Relations." In *Wolves: Behavior, Ecology, and Conservation*, edited by L. David Mech and Luigi Boitani, 131–160. Chicago: University of Chicago Press, 2003.
Ministère de l'Équipement, des Transports et du Logement. *Fragmentation de l'habitat due aux infrastructures de transport*, 2000.
Molisch, Hans. *Der Einfluss einer Pflanze auf die Andere-allelopathie.* Jena: Fischer, 1937.
Morgan, C. Lloyd. *An Introduction to Comparative Psychology.* London: W. Scott, 1894.
Moriceau, Jean-Marc. "La dangerosité du loup sur l'homme: Une enquête à l'échelle de la France (16ᵉ–20ᵉ siècles)." In *Repenser le sauvage grâce au retour du loup: Les sciences humaines interpellées*, edited by Jean-Marc Moriceau and Philippe Madeline, 41–74. Caen: Presses Universitaires de Caen, 2010.
Moriceau, Jean-Marc. *Histoire du méchant loup: 3 000 attaques sur l'homme en France (15ᵉ–20ᵉ siècles).* Paris: Fayard, 2007.

Morizot, Baptiste. "Penser le concept comme carte, une pratique deleuzienne de la philosophie." In *La Géophilosophie de Gilles Deleuze: Entre esthétiques et politiques*, edited by Mauro Carbone and Paride Broggi. Paris: Mimésis, 2012. https://hal.archives-ouvertes.fr/hal-01476141.

Morris, Desmond. *The Naked Ape: A Zoologist's Study of the Human Animal*. London: Cape, 1967.

Naess, Arne. "The Shallow and the Deep, Long-Range Ecology Movement: A Summary." *Inquiry*, no. 16 (1973): 95–100.

Nathan, Tobie. *L'influence qui guérit*. Paris: Odile Jacob, 2009.

Newsome, T. A., and W. J. Ripple. "A Continental Scale Trophic Cascade from Wolves through Coyotes to Foxes." *Journal of Animal Ecology* 84, no. 1 (January 2015): 49–59.

Nochy, Antoine. "Le loup reflète notre rapport au sauvage." *Terre sauvage*, no. 267 (January 2011): 62–65.

Nowell, Kristen, and Peter Jackson. *Wild Cats: Status Survey and Conservation Action Plan*. Gland, Switzerland: International Union for Conservation of Nature and Natural Resources, 1996.

Orgogozo, Virginie, Arnaud Martin, and Baptiste Morizot. "The Differential View of Genotype-Phenotype Relationships." *Frontiers in Genetics* 6, article 179 (May 2015): https://doi.org/10.3389/fgene.2015.00179.

Osgood, Cornelius. "Contributions to the Ethology of the Kutchin." *Yale University Publications in Anthropology*, no. 7. New Haven, CT: Yale University Press, 1936.

Ostrom, Elinor. *Future of the Commons: Beyond Market Failure and Government Regulation*. London: Institute of Economic Affairs, 2012.

Ostrom, Elinor. *Governing the Commons: The Evolution of Institutions for Collective Action*. Cambridge: Cambridge University Press, 1990.

Packard, Jane. "Wolf Behavior: Reproductive, Social, and Intelligent." In *Wolves: Behavior, Ecology, and Conservation*, edited by L. David Mech and Luigi Boitani, 35–65. Chicago: University of Chicago Press, 2003.

Paul the Deacon. *History of the Lombards*. Translated by William Dudley Foulke. Edited by Edward Peters. Philadelphia: University of Pennsylvania Press, 1974 (1907).

Peirce, Charles Sanders. *Elements of Logic*. In *Collected Papers of Charles Sanders Peirce*, vol. 2, edited by Charles Hartshorne and Paul Weiss. Cambridge, MA: Harvard University Press, 1932.

Peirce, Charles Sanders. *The Essential Peirce: Selected Philosophical Writings*, vol. 2 (1893–1913). Bloomington: Indiana University Press, 1998.

Perlès, Catherine. "Pourquoi le néolithique? Analyse des théories, évolution des perspectives." In *L'homme, le mangeur, l'animal qui nourrit l'autre?*, edited by J.-P. Poulain, 16–29. Paris: OCHA, 2007.

Peters, R. P., and L. David Mech. "Scent-Marking in Wolves." *American Scientist* 63, no. 6 (1975): 628–637.

Peterson, Rolf O., and Paolo Ciucci. "The Wolf as a Carnivore." In *Wolves: Behavior, Ecology, and Conservation*, edited by L. David Mech and Luigi Boitani, 104–130. Chicago: University of Chicago Press, 2003.
Peterson, R. O., J. A. Vucetich, J. M. Bump, and D. W. Smith. "Trophic Cascades in a Multicausal World: Isle Royale and Yellowstone." *Annual Review of Ecology, Evolution, and Systematics* 45 (November 2014): 325–345.
Plumwood, Val. *Environmental Culture: The Ecological Crisis of Reason*. London: Routledge, 2002.
Plumwood, Val. "Nature in the Active Voice." *Australian Humanities Review* 46 (2009): 113–129.
Porcher, Jocelyne. *The Ethics of Animal Labor: A Collaborative Utopia*. Translated from the French. Cham, Switzerland: Palgrave Macmillan 2017 (2011).
Portmann, Adolf. *La forme animale*. Paris: La Bibliothèque, coll. L'ombre animale, 2013.
Pulliainen, Erkki. "The Status, Structure and Behaviour of Populations of the Wolf (Canis I. Lupus L.) along the Fenno-Soviet Border." *Annales Zoologici Fennici* 17, no. 2 (1980): 107–112.
Quenet, Grégory. *Qu'est-ce que l'histoire environnementale?* Paris: Champ Vallon, 2014.
Ramesh, Sunita A., Stephen D. Tyermn, Bo Xu, et al. "Signalling Modulates Plant Growth by Directly Regulating the Activity of Plant-Specific Anion Transporters." *Nature Communications* 6 (July 29, 2015): 10.1038/ncomms8879.
Ratramnus of Corbie. "Epistola de Cynocephalis." *Patrologia Latina* 121, 1153–1156, in *Patrologia Latina* database. Alexandria, VA: Chadwick-Healy, 1995– ; English translaton: "Ratramnus and the Dog-Headed Humans." In *Carolingian Civilization*, 2nd ed., edited by Paul Edward Dutton, 452–455. Peterborough, Ontario: Broadview Press, 2004.
Regan, Tom. *The Case for Animal Rights*. Berkeley: University of California Press, 2004 (1983).
Renck, Jean-Luc, and Véronique Servais. *L'éthologie: Histoire naturelle du comportement*. Paris: Seuil, 2002.
Rickert, Heinrich. *Science and History: A Critique of Positive Epistemology*. Translated by George Reisman. Princeton, NJ: Van Nostrand, 1962 (1899).
Rieutort, Laurent. *L'élevage ovin en France: Espaces fragiles et dynamiques des systèmes agricoles*. Clermont-Ferrand: CERAMAC, Université Blaise Pascal, 1995.
Ripple, W. J., and R. L. Beschta. "Trophic Cascades in Yellowstone: The First 15 Years after Wolf Reintroduction." *Biological Conservation*, no. 145 (2012): 205–213.
Rohmeder, Jürgen. "L'invasion des loups à travers l'Autriche avance." *Horizons et débats*, no. 7 (February 22, 2010): 8, http://horizons.myhostpoint.ch/indexd876.html?id=2050.
Rose, Deborah Bird. "Val Plumwood's Philosophical Animism: Attentive Interactions in the Sentient World." *Environmental Humanities* 3, no. 1 (May 1, 2013): 93–109.

Rosenzweig, Michael L. *Win-Win Ecology: How the Earth's Species Can Survive in the Midst of Human Enterprise.* New York: Oxford University Press, 2003.
Rowell, Thelma. "A Few Peculiar Primates." In *Primate Encounter: Models of Science, Gender, and Society*, edited by Shirley C. Strum and Linda Marie Fedigan, 57–70. Chicago: University of Chicago Press, 2000.
Rowell, Thelma E. "The Concept of Social Dominance." *Behavioral Biology* 11, no. 2 (June 1974): 131–154.
Rowlands, Mark. *Animal Rights: A Philosophic Defence.* Houndsmills: Macmillan, 1998.
Rowlands, Mark. *The Philosopher and the Wolf: Lessons from the Wild on Love, Death and Happiness.* New York: Pegasus, 2009.
Savage-Rumbaugh, E. Sue, Shelly L. Williams, Takeshi Furuichi, and Takayoshi Kano. "Language Perceived: *Paniscus* Branches Out." In *Great Ape Societies*, edited by William C. McGraw, Linda F. Marchant, and Toshisada Nishida, 173–184. Cambridge: Cambridge University Press, 1996.
Schenkel, Rudolph. "Expression Studies on Wolves." 1947. http://davemech.org/wolf-news-and-informatino/schenkels-classic-wolf-behavior-study-available-in-english/.
Schmitt, Carl. *The Concept of the Political.* Translated by George Schwab. Chicago: University of Chicago Press, 2007.
Sebeok, Thomas A. *Perspectives in Zoosemiotics.* The Hague: Mouton, 1972.
Seton, Ernest Thompson. *Wild Animals I Have Known.* New York: C. Scribner's Sons, 1898.
Seyfarth, Robert M., and Dorothy L. Cheney. "How Vervet Monkeys Perceive Their Grunts: Field Playback Experiments." *Animal Behavior* 30, no. 3 (August 1982): 739–751.
Shea, John Joseph. "The Origins of Lithic Projectile Technology: Evidence from Africa, the Levant, and Europe." *Journal of Archaeological Science* 33, no. 5 (2006): 823–846.
Shepard, Paul. *Nous n'avons qu'une seule terre.* Translated by Bertrand Fillaudeau. Paris: José Corti, 2013 (1996).
Shepard, Paul, ed. *The Only World We've Got: A Paul Shepard Reader.* San Francisco: Sierra Club Books, 1996.
Shepard, Paul. *Thinking Animals: Animals and the Development of Human Intelligence.* New York: Viking Press, 1978.
Shipman, Pat. *The Animal Connection: A New Perspective on What Makes Us Human.* New York: Norton, 2011.
Shivik, John A., Adrian Treves, and Peggy Callahan. "Nonlethal Techniques for Managing Predation: Primary and Secondary Repellents." *USDA National Wildlife Research Center—Staff Publications*, paper 272. *Conservation Biology* 17, no. 6 (December 2003): 1531–1537.
Simondon, Gilbert. *Communication et information: Cours et conférences.* Chatou: Éditions de la Transparence, 2010.

Simondon, Gilbert. *L'individuation à la lumière des notions de forme et d'information.* 1964. Grenoble: Millon, 2005.
Singer, Peter. *Animal Liberation: A New Ethics for Our Treatment of Animals.* New York: New York Review/Random House, 1975.
Smith, Douglas W., and Gary Ferguson. *Decade of the Wolf.* Guilford, CT: Lyons Press, 2005.
Soulé, Michael, and Reed Noss. "Rewilding and Biodiversity: Complementary Goals for Continental Conservation." *Wild Earth* 8, no. 3 (Fall 1998): 19–28.
Spengler, Oswald. *Man and Technics: A Contribution to a Philosophy of Life.* Translated from the German. New York: A. A. Knopf, 1963 (1932).
Steinhart, Peter. *The Company of Wolves.* New York: Alfred A. Knopf, 1995.
Stephens, David W., and John R. Krebs. *Foraging Theory.* Princeton, NJ: Princeton University Press, 1986.
Stephenson, R. O. "Nunamiut Eskimos, Wildlife Biologists, and Wolves." In *Wolves of the World: Perspectives of Behavior, Ecology, and Conservation,* edited by F. H. Harrington and P. C. Pacquet, 434–440. Park Ridge, NJ: Noyes, 1982.
Tennyson, Alfred, Lord. "Ulysses." https://www.poetryfoundation.org/poems/45392/ulysses.
Testart, Alain. *Avant l'histoire: L'évolution des sociétés, de Lascaux à Carnac.* Paris: Gallimard, 2012.
Thiel, Richard P., Allison C. Thiel, and Marianne Strozewski. *Wild Wolves We Have Known.* Minneapolis, MN: International Wolf Center, 2013.
Tiercelin, Claudine. *C. S. Peirce et le pragmatism.* Paris: Presses Universitaires de France, 1993.
Timberlake, William. "Animal Behavior: A Continuing Synthesis." *Annual Review of Psychology* 44, no. 1 (February 1993): 675–706.
Tinbergen, Niko. *The Herring Gull's World: A Study of the Social Behavior of Birds.* New York: Basic Books, 1961.
Tinbergen, Niko. "On Aims and Methods of Ethology." *Zeitschrift für Tierpsychologie* 20: 410–433.
Tolman, Edward Chace. "Cognitive Maps in Rats and Men." *Psychological Review* 55, no. 4 (1948): 189–208, https://doi.org/10.1037/h0061626.
Tomkins, William. *Indian Sign Language.* San Diego: Dover, 1969 (1931).
Ugolino da Montegiorgio (?). *The Little Flowers of St. Francis of Assisi.* Edited and translated by Dom Roger Hudleston. Introduction by Arthur Livingston. New York: Heritage Press, n.d.
Valen, Leigh Van. "A New Evolutionary Law." *Evolutionary Theory* 1 (1973): 1–49.
Vigny, Alfred de. "La maison du berger." In *Les destinées,* 42–55. Paris: Droz, 1947 (1864).
Vitousek, Peter M., Paul R. Ehrlich, Anne H. Ehrlich, and Pamela A. Matson. "Human Appropriation of the Products of Photosynthesis." *BioScience* 36, no. 6 (1986): 368–373.

Volterra, Vito. "Fluctuations in the Abundance of a Species Considered Mathematically." *Nature* 118 (1926): 558–560.
Wachtel, Nathan. *The Vision of the Vanquished: The Spanish Conquest of Peru through Indian Eyes, 1530–1570.* Translated by Ben and Siân Reynolds. New York: Barnes and Noble Books, 1977.
Walter, Henriette, and Pierre Avenas. *L'étonnante histoire des noms de mammifères.* Paris: Payot, 2003.
Weaver, Warren. "Some Recent Contributions to the Mathematical Theory of Communication." In *The Mathematical Theory of Communication*, by Claude E. Shannon and Warren Weaver, 1–29. Urbana: University of Illinois Press, 1964.
Western, David, and Michael Wright, eds. *Natural Connections: Perspectives in Community-Based Conservation.* Washington, DC: Island Press, 1994.
Whewell, William. *History of the Inductive Sciences from the Earliest to the Present Time.* New York: D. Appleton, 1858.
White, Lynn, Jr. "The Historical Roots of Our Ecologic Crisis." *Science* 155, no. 3767 (1967): 1203–1207.
Whiten, Andrew, Jane Goodall, W. C. McGrew, et al. "Cultures in Chimpanzees." *Nature* 399 (1999): 682–685.
Wielgus, Robert B., and Kaylie A. Peebles. "Effects of Wolf Mortality on Livestock Depredations." *PLoS ONE* 9, no. 12 (2014): 1–16.
Wilkinson, Richard G., and Kate Pickett. *The Spirit Level: Why Equality Is Better for Everyone.* London: Penguin, 2010.
Wilson, Edward O. *Biophilia.* Cambridge, MA: Harvard University Press, 1984.
Wilson, Edward O. *Sociobiology: The New Synthesis.* Cambridge, MA: Belknap Press of Harvard University Press, 1975.
Zimen, Erik. *The Wolf: A Species in Danger.* New York: Delacorte, 1981.